Communications in Computer and Information Science 876

Commenced Publication in 2007
Founding and Former Series Editors:
Phoebe Chen, Alfredo Cuzzocrea, Xiaoyong Du, Orhun Kara, Ting Liu,
Dominik Ślęzak, and Xiaokang Yang

Editorial Board

More information about this series at http://www.springer.com/series/7899

A. V. Deshpande · Aynur Unal
Kalpdrum Passi · Dharm Singh
Malaya Nayak · Bharat Patel
Shafi Pathan (Eds.)

Smart Trends in Information Technology and Computer Communications

Second International Conference, SmartCom 2017
Pune, India, August 18–19, 2017
Revised Selected Papers

 Springer

Editors
A. V. Deshpande
SKNCOE
Pune, Maharashtra
India

Aynur Unal
Department of Mechanical Engineering
Indian Institute of Technology Guwahati
Guwahati, Assam
India

Kalpdrum Passi
Department of Mathematics
  and Computer Science
Laurentian University
Sudbury, ON
Canada

Dharm Singh
Namibia University of Science
  and Technology
Windhoek
Namibia

Malaya Nayak
IT Buzz Limited
Dagenham
UK

Bharat Patel
Yudiz Solutions
Ahmedabad
India

Shafi Pathan
Sinhgad Group of Institutions
Pune
India

ISSN 1865-0929   ISSN 1865-0937   (electronic)
Communications in Computer and Information Science
ISBN 978-981-13-1422-3   ISBN 978-981-13-1423-0   (eBook)
https://doi.org/10.1007/978-981-13-1423-0

Library of Congress Control Number: 2018950844

This Springer imprint is published by the registered company Springer Nature Singapore Pte Ltd.
The registered company address is: 152 Beach Road, #21-01/04 Gateway East, Singapore 189721, Singapore

Preface

The Second International Conference on Smart Trends for Information Technology and Computer Communications (SmartCom 2017) targeted state-of-the-art as well as emerging topics pertaining to Information, Computer Communications, and effective strategies for its implementation for engineering and managerial applications.

The conference attracted a large number of high quality submissions and stimulated the cutting-edge research discussions among many pioneering academic researchers, scientists, industrial engineers, and students from all around the world and provided a forum to researchers to propose new technologies, share their experiences, and discuss future solutions for the design infrastructure for ICT. It also provided a common platform for pioneering academic researchers, scientists, engineers, and students to share their views and achievements and enriched technocrats and academicians by presenting their innovative and constructive ideas. Finally, SmartCom 2017 focused on innovative issues at international level by bringing together the experts from different countries.

The conference was held during August 18–19, 2017, at Hotel Four Points by Sheraton, Pune, India, and organized and supported by the College of Engineering, Pune, Computer Society of India, Division IV, Singhad Group of Institutions, and Global Knowledge Research Foundation.

Research submissions in various advanced technology fields were received and, after a rigorous peer-review process, the Program Committee members and 56 external reviewers accepted 37 out of 400 papers (acceptance ratio of 0.13) from authors of 8 different countries, including Algeria, Australia, Canada, France, India, Iran, Sri Lanka, and Turkey.

To make this event possible, we received a lot of support and help from many people and organizations. We would like to express our sincere thanks to the authors for their remarkable contributions, all the Technical Program Committee members for their time and expertise in reviewing the papers within a very tight schedule, and Springer for their professional help. This is the second conference of the series SmartCom in which proceedings were published as a CCIS volume by Springer. We greatly appreciate our two distinguished scholars for accepting our invitation to deliver keynote speeches to the conference and the six technical session chairs for analyzing the research work presented by the researchers. Last but not least, we are indebted to the local support from local chairs and their hard work for the conference. This series has already been made a continuous series which will be hosted at a different location every year.

May 2018

A. V. Deshpande
Kalpdrum Passi
Aynur Unal
Malaya Nayak
Dharm Singh
Bharat Patel
Shafi Pathan

Organization

Honor-General Chair

B. B. Ahuja   College of Engineering, India

General Chairs

A. V. Deshpande   Sinhgad Institutes and SKNCOE, India
Dharm Singh   Namibia University of Science and Technology, Namibia
Bharat Patel   COO Youdiz Solutions, India

Organising Chairs

Durgesh Kumar Mishra (Chairman)   Division IV, Computer Society of India, India
Sunil B. Mane   College of Engineering, India
Parikshit N. Mahalle   Sinhgad Group of Institutions, Pune, India

Program Chairs

Malaya Kumar Nayak   IT and Research Group, UK
Kalpdrum Passi   Laurentian University, Canada
Shafi Pathan   Sinhgad Group of Institutions, India

Technical Committee Members

Ting-Peng Liang   University of Taipei, Taiwan
Nedia Smairi   CNAM Laboratory, France
Subhadip Basu   University of Iowa, USA
Abrar A. Qureshi   University of Virginia, USA
Louis M. Rose   University of New York, USA
Ricardo M. Checchi   University of Massachusetts, USA
Brent Waters   University of Texas at Austin, USA
Prasun Sinha   University Columbus, USA
N. M. van Straalen   University Amsterdam, The Netherlands
Rashid Ansari   University of Illunios, USA
Russell Beale   University of Birmingham, UK
Dan Boneh   Stanford University, USA
Alexander Christea   University of Warwick, UK
Mustafizur Rahman   Endeavour Research Fellow, Australia
Hoang Pham   Rutgers University, USA

Harshal Arolkar	CSI Ahmedabad Chapter, India
Bhavesh Joshi	Advent College, India
K. C. Roy	Kautaliya, India
Mukesh Shrimali	Pacific University, India
Sanjay M. Shah	GEC, India
Salam Shuleenda Devi	NIT Silchar, India
Amira Ashour	Tantra University, Egypt
S. Mishra	CSI, KEC Dwarahat, India
Chirag S. Thaker	GEC, Bhavnagar, India
Nisarg Pathak	SSC, CSI, India
Meenakshi Tripathi	MNIT, India
S. N. Tazi	Engineering College, India
Shuhong Gao	Clemson University, USA
Sanjam Garg	University of California, Los Angeles, USA
Faiez Gargouri	University Tunisia, Tunisia
A. Garrett	Jacksonville State University, USA
Leszek Antoni Gasieniec	University of Liverpool, UK
Ning Ge	Tsinghua University, China
Garani Georgia	University of North London, UK
Hazhir Ghasemnezhad	University of Technology, Iran
Andrea Goldsmith	Stanford University, USA
Saeed Golmohammadi	University of Tabriz, Iran
K. Gong	Chongqing Jiaotong University, China
Crina Gosnan	Babes-Bolyai University, Cluj-Napoca, Romania
Mohamed Gouda	The University of Texas at Austin, USA
Mihai Grigore	Information Systems Zürich, Switzerland
Cheng Guang	Southeast University, China
Venkat N. Gudivada	Marshall University Huntington, USA
Sankhadeep Chatterjee	UEM Kolkata, India
Ambika Annavarapu	GRIET, India
Wang Guojun	Zhong Nan University, China
Nguyen Ha	University of Saskatchewan, Canada
Z. J. Haas	Cornell University, New York
Mohand Said Hacid	Lyon University, France
Haffaf Hafid	University of Oran, Algeria
M. Tarafdar Hagh	Islamic Azad University, Iran
Ridha Hamdi	University of Sfax, Tunisia
Dae Man Han	Kongju National University, South Korea
Xiangjian He	University of Technology, Sydney, Australia
Richard Heeks	University of Manchester, UK
Walid khaled hidouci	Ecole Nationale Supérieure d'Informatique, Algeria
Sayan Chakraborty	BCET, India
Simona Moldovanu	Universitatea Dunarea de Jos Galati, Romania
Achim Hoffmann	University of New South Wales, Australia
Ma Hong	University of Science and Technology, China
Hyehyun Hong	Chung-Ang University, South Korea

Qinghua Hu	Harbin Institute of Technology, China
Honggang Hu	University of Science and Technology of China, China
Fengjun Hu	Zhejiang University, China
Qinghua Huang	University of Technology, China
Chiang Hung-Lung	Taichung University, Taiwan
Kyeong Hur	University of Education, South Korea
Wen-Jyi Hwang	National Taiwan Normal University, Taiwan
Gabriel Sebastian Ioan Ilie	University of Connecticut, USA
Sudath Indrasinghe	John Moores University, UK
Ushio Inoue	Engineering Tokyo Denki University, Japan
Stephen Intille	Boston University, USA
Soumen Banerjee	UEM Kolkata, India
Prasenjit Chatterjee	MCKV, India
Nileshsingh V. Thakur	College of Engineering and Management, India
M. T. Islam	Universiti Kebangsaan Malaysia, Malaysia
Lillykutty Jacob	NIT Calicut, India
Anil K. Jain	Michigan State University, East Lansing, USA
Dagmar Janacova	Czech Republic
Kairat Jaroenrat	Bangkok University, Thailand
Don Jyh-Fu Jeng	National Cheng Kung University, Taiwan
Minseok Jeon	Yonsei University, South Korea
Guangrong Ji	Ocean University of China, China
Yoon Ji-Hyeun	Yonsei University, South Korea
Zhiping Jia	Shandong University, China
Syeda Erfana Zohora	Taif University, KSA
Amartya Mukherjee	IEM Kolkata, India
Samarjeet Borah	Sikkim Manipal University, India
Sarwar Kamal	East West University, Bangladesh
Liangxiao Jiang	University of Geosciences, China
David B. Johnson	Carnegie Mellon University, USA
Chen Junning	Anhui University, China
Seok Kang	University of Texas at San Antonio, USA
Ghader Karimian	University of Tabriz, Iran
S. Karthikeyan	College of Applied Science, Oman
Michael Kasper	Institute for Secure Information Technology, Germany
L. Kasprzyczak	Institute of Innovative Technologies EMAG, Poland
Zahid Khan	University of Edinburgh, Scotland
Jin-Woo Kim	Korea University, South Korea
Muzafar Khan	COMSATS University, Pakistan
Jamal Akhtar Khan	Salman bin Abdulaziz University, Saudi Arabia
Kholaddi Kheir Eddine	University of Constantine, Algeria
Fouad Khelifi	Northumbria University, UK
Shubhalaxmi Kher	College of Engineering, Jonesboro, USA
Sally Kift	James Cook University, Australia
Sunkyum Kim	Yonsei University, South Korea
Leonard Kleinrock	University of California, Los Angeles, USA

Dirk Koch	University of Manchester, UK
Zbigniew Kotulski	Warsaw University of Technology, Poland
Ray Kresman	Bowling Green State University, USA
Ajay Kshemkalyani,	University of Illinois, USA
Madhu Kumar	Nanyang Technological University, Singapore
Anup Kumar	University of Louisville, USA
Md Obaiduallh Sk	Aliah University, India
Kaiser J. Giri	Islamic University, India
Sirshendu Hore	HETC, India
Hemanta Dey	TICT, India
James Tin-Yau Kwok	University of Science and Technology, Hong Kong, SAR China
Zhiling Lan	Illinois Institute of Technology, USA
Hayden Kwok-Hay So	University of Hong Kong, Hong Kong, SAR China
Zhiling Lan	Illinois Institute of Technology, USA
K. G Langendoen	Delft University of Technology, The Netherlands
Michele Lanza	University of Lugano, Switzerland
Shalini Batra	Thapar University, India
Shajulin Benedict	St. Xavier's College of Engineering, India
Rajendra Kumar Bharti	Bipin Chandra Tripathi Kumaon Engineering College, India
Murali Bhaskaran	College of Technology, Salem, India
Komal Bhatia	YMCA University, India
S. R. Biradar	SDM College of Engineering and Technology, India
Prayag Tiwari	National University of Science and Technology MISIS, Russia
Surekha B.	K. S. Institute of Technology, India
A. K. Chaturvedi	IIT Kanpur, India
Jitender Kumar Chhabra	NIT Kurukshetra, India
Pradeep Chouksey	TIT College, India
Chhaya Dalela	JSSATE, Noida, India
Jayanti Dansana	KIIT University, India
Soura Dasgupta	SRM University, India
Apurva A. Desai	South Gujarat University, India
V. Susheela Devi	Indian Institute of Science, India
Bikash Kumar Dey	IIT Bombay, India
Vijay Pal Dhaka	National University, India
K. Bhattachary Dhruba	Tezpur University, India
Mohammad Doja	Jamia Millia Islamia, India
Sagayaraj Francis	Pondicherry Engineering College, India
K. Ganesh	Private Limited McKinsey & Company, Gurgaon, India
Vinit Grewal	Guru Nanak Dev University, India
P. S. Grover	University of Delhi, India
S. Hemalatha	College of Engineering and Technology, Dindigul, India

Contents

Smart Data and IT Innovations

Smart and Service Computing

Smart and Secure Systems

Network Intrusion Detection System Using Ensemble of Binary Deep Learning Classifiers

Aniruddha Parvat, Souradeep Dev, Siddhesh Kadam[✉], and Jai Chavan

Sinhgad Institute of Technology, Lonavala, India
aniruddhaparvat@gmail.com, souradeep15@gmail.com, sid.kadam19@gmail.com,
jaipmohite@gmail.com
http://www.sinhgad.edu

Abstract. An Intrusion Detection System (IDS) is a software or a device that monitors a network or system to detect malicious activities. A Network Intrusion Detection System (NIDS) helps to detect security breaches in a network. There are many challenges while developing an efficient and flexible NIDS. In this work, we propose an NIDS using an ensemble of multiple binary classifiers. Each binary classifier is deep learning model. Deep learning is a model of machine learning loosely based on the structure and functioning of biological neural networks. We test our system on a benchmark network intrusion dataset: NSL-KDD. We present the performance of the proposed system and compare it with previous works. We evaluate the system performance by checking the accuracy, precision, recall and f1-score values for both binary as well as five class classifier.

Keywords: Network intrusion detection system
Deep learning · Machine learning · NSL-KDD

1 Introduction

With the rapid improvements in network technologies, the number of network intrusions also increases. An NIDS is placed at a strategic point in the network where it monitors all the traffic. It analyses the traffic to detect possible attacks. Based on the method of intrusion detection NIDS can be categorised into two classes:

- Signature based NIDS (SNIDS): SNIDSs have a predefined database of attack signatures. The system matches the incoming data with the dataset. SNIDS can easily detect known attacks but fail for new attacks.

- Anomaly based NIDS (ANIDS): ANIDS are better at detection of new attacks than SNIDS. A machine learning model is trained to differentiate between normal and malicious activity. The major drawback of these systems is the high false positive rate.

© Springer Nature Singapore Pte Ltd. 2018
A. V. Deshpande et al. (Eds.): SmartCom 2017, CCIS 876, pp. 3–10, 2018.
https://doi.org/10.1007/978-981-13-1423-0_1

There are many challenges in creating an ANIDS for new and unknown attacks. First, unavailability of labelled dataset representing a real network data. Although there are datasets like KDD CUP 98/99 dataset, they have received some criticism [2] and are a bit outdated. NSL-KDD [3] is an improvement over this dataset. Second, as machine learning is used when new data about a new attack is available, the model needs to be trained again. The model should accommodate new data without any decrease in detection rate of the previous set of attacks. Normally the model will need to be trained again on the whole data which can be time-consuming. Many machine learning models have been used to differentiate between normal and anomalous traffic like artificial neural networks (AAN), decision trees, logistic regression, etc [4].

Deep learning is the study of artificial neural networks that contain more than one hidden layer [1]. Recently deep neural networks have been very successful in image recognition, language translation, etc. Deep learning models are very successful when the training data is abundant. With this motivation, we use an ensemble of binary deep neural networks to develop a NIDS.

2   Related Work

In this section, we discuss work which uses the NSL-KDD dataset with more focus on works the use artificial neural networks. This allows more accurate comparison of the work presented in this paper with other found in the literature.

Chae et al. [5] proposed a feature selection technique using feature average of total and each class. This paper proposed feature selection methods using AR and compared it with correlation based feature selection, gain ratio and information gain. They evaluated their work by measuring accuracy. A J48 (an implementation of ID3 by WEKA team) decision tree classifier was trained with 10-fold cross validation. The highest accuracy was 99.794% using 22 features on the NSL-KDD training data [5].

Niyaz et al. [6] have proposed a deep learning based multi-vector DDoS detection system in a software-defined network (SDN) environment. SDN provides flexibility to program network devices for different objectives and eliminates the need for third-party vendor-specific hardware. The detection system consists of three modules: (i) Traffic Collector and Flow installer (TCFI), (ii) Feature Extractor (FE), and (iii) Traffic Classifier (TC). The proposed system was able to identify individual DDoS attack class with an accuracy of 95.65%. It classified the traffic in normal and attack classes with an accuracy of 99.82%.

Subba et al. [7] have proposed a simple feedforward Artificial Neural Network (ANN) based IDS model. The proposed IDS model uses the back propagation algorithms along with various other optimisation techniques [7] to train the neural network. Their model is a simple three-layered neural network i.e. only one hidden layer. The results show that the model has comparable performance to other machine learning algorithms like decision tree, while it outperforms some like Naive Bayes. The IDS had average accuracy of 95.05% using 36 features. The IDS can be trained faster compared to other model as it only has one hidden layer [7].

Tang et al. [8] have proposed a deep learning approach for flow-based anomaly detection in an SDN environment [8]. A deep learning model was trained on NSLKDD dataset. The model has 3 hidden layers. The structure is [6, 12, 6, 3, 2]. In this work, six basic features (protocol_type, count, duration, srv_count, dst_bytes and src_bytes) out of the 41 features of NSL-KDD dataset were used to train the model. The authors got an accuracy of about 91.7% on the training dataset and 75.75% on the testing dataset [8].

Ingre et al. [9] have implemented an Intrusion detection system using ANN on the benchmark NSL-KDD dataset. The model was trained and tested for both binary, as well as five class classifier. The IDS system that has been proposed by the authors uses Levenberg-Marquardt (LM) and BFGS quasi-Newton Backpropagation algorithm for learning [9]. Here analysis was done on training and testing dataset with full features and also reduced features. Result evaluation was done on basis of accuracy, detection rate and false positive rate. It was observed that the proposed technique gave a training accuracy of 99.3% for binary class and 98.9% for five class. On testing dataset, an accuracy of 81.2% for binary class and 79.9% for five class was achieved.

Sadek et al. [10] focused on the effect of feature reduction using attribute selection on building an IDS with high accuracy. They have proposed a new hybrid algorithm, neural networks with indicator variable using rough set theory for feature reduction [10]. Experiments showed that the proposed algorithm reduced the features upto 8 which led to improvement in detection accuracy to 96.7% on training dataset.

3   Dataset

As discussed earlier, we use the NSL-KDD dataset for evaluation of our work. There are many publicly available datasets like the DARPA datasets (1998,1999, 2000), the KDD-98, KDD-99, etc. NSL-KDD is a dataset created to solve some of the problems of the KDD'99 dataset. Although, this new version of the KDD data set still suffers from some of the problems discussed by McHugh [2]. Although the NSL-KDD has received some criticism recently saying that is it not a proper representation of real modern networks, it still can be used for testing NIDS models. It still is one of the most used datasets, because of lack of other public NIDS datasets. Advantages of NSL-KDD:

- The number of records in NSL-KDD is reasonable; this makes experimentation on the complete dataset possible.
- To make the classifiers unbiased towards frequent records, redundant data were removed.

Each record in the dataset has 43 attributes: 41 features, one label column and the last column represents the difficulty level of detection. The 42 attribute contains data about the various classes and are categorised as one normal class and four attack class. The four attack classes are Probe, R2L, DoS, U2R. Out of 41 features, four are binary, three are nominal, and remaining 34 features are continuous. The training data contains 23 classes. The test data contains 38 classes that include 21 attacks from training data, 16 novel attacks and 1 normal class. This makes the dataset more realistic. Table 1 shows the major attacks in both testing and training datasets (Table 2).

Table 1. Major attacks on both testing and training datasets

Attacks in dataset	Attack type
DoS	Apache2, Worm, Pod, Mailbomb, Udpstorm, Land, Neptune, Teardrop, BackSmurf, Processtable
Probe	IPsweep, Portsweep, Saint, Mscan, Satan,Nmap
U2R	Guess_password, Imap, Multihop, Xlock, Snmpguess, Sendmail, Ftp_write, Phf, Warezmaster, Xsnoop, Snmpgetattack, Httptunnel, Named
R2L	Sqlattack, Buffer_overflow, Perl, Xterm, Loadmodule, Rootkit, Ps

Table 2. Traffic record distribution for testing and training datasets.

Traffic	Training	Test
Normal	67343	9711
DoS	45927	7458
U2R	52	67
R2L	995	2887
Probe	11656	2421

4   Proposed Method

We propose a 2 phase NIDS. The basic idea is to undertake multiclass classification using binary classifiers with a divide and conquer strategy. We use One-vs-All (OVA) decomposition strategy. OVA decomposition divided n class problem into n classification problem. Each classifier is responsible for distinguishing/detecting one of the classes from all other classes. In our case we need five classifiers for DoS, Probe, u2r, r2l and normal detection. While training each classifier, the subset of training data belonging to one class is marked as positive and rest all are marked as negative. For example, for DoSDetector all sample in dos category are marked as "1" and rest all marked as "0". Note, not only normal data was encoded as "0" but data for other classes too.

Each classifier in phase 1 is a deep neural network. Each network has 3 hidden layers. The number input neurons, hidden units vary for each classifier, output layer has only one neuron. The number of input neurons differs because each classifier is trained on different features. Domain knowledge is used to select

Table 3. Features used for each classifier

Class	Features
DoS (9)	Duration,protocol_type,flag,src_byte, count, dst_host_same_srv_rate, dst_host_srv_serror_rate, dst_host_rerror_rate, dst_host_serror_rate
Probe (5)	flag, duration, protocol_type, service, src_bytes
U2R (8)	Hot, num_compromised, root_shell, num_root, num_file_creation, num_shells, num_access_files, is_host_login
R2L (14)	duration, is_host_login, is_guest_login, service, flag, src_byte, hot, logged_in, num_compromised, num_file_creation, num_shell, num_access_files, protocol_type, num_failed_logins
Normal (21)	Duration, is_host_login ,protocol_type, flag, src_byte, count, dst_host_serror_rate, flag, src_bytes, hot, num_compromised, dst_host_rerror_rate, root_shell, num_root, num_file_creation, num_shells, num_access_files, dst_host_srv_serror_rate, dst_host_same_srv_rate, is_guest_login, service

the features similar to Guleria et al. [11]. All the neurons except output have ReLU shown in Eq. 2 activation, the output layer/unit has sigmoid shown in Eq. 3 activation. Sigmoid was because it has output range from 0 to 1. Each classifier outputs probability. Table 3 shows features used for each class. The features for NormalDetector is all the features from other classifiers. Figure 2 shows the structure of neural network used to detect Probe attack in Phase 1.

Sigmoid activation function:

$$f(x) = \frac{1}{1 + e^{-x}} \tag{1}$$

ReLU activation function:

$$f(x) = max(0, x) \tag{2}$$

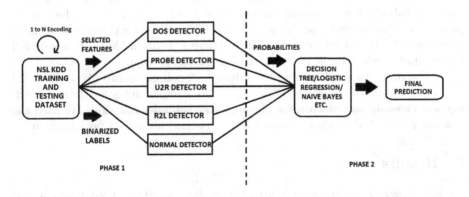

Fig. 1. System architecture.

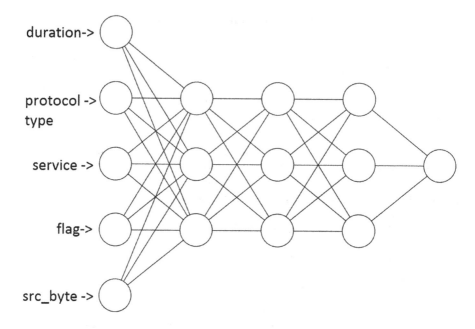

Fig. 2. DNN model to detect probe attacks in Phase 1.

Phase 2 is the aggregation phase. The output of all classifiers needs to be combined to get the final result. Voting is the most used aggregation technique for this type of problem but was not used in this system as it resulted in a decrease in performance and restricted the flexibility of the whole system. As mentioned earlier each classifier outputs probability for each class so in voting strategy the output may be unstable in case of equal probabilities by two or more classifiers. Phase 2 has other classifiers which treat the probabilities as features and produce the final label. This provides flexibility to the system. When new type of attack data is available, the system can adapt by training a new classifier in phase one without disturbing other classifiers and retraining the classifier in phase 2. Table 4 shows the structure and results of each individual classifier in phase 1. Figure 1 shows system architecture. Figure 2 shows the neural network responsible for detecting Probe attacks in phase 1. It has 3 hidden layers with 3 hidden units each, 5 input neurons and one output neuron.

The system was implemented in python 3.5.2 using libraries like Keras 1.2.2 [12] for neural network implementation, NumPy and Pandas for dataset reading and cleaning and Sklearn for phase 2 models implementation. We used the efficient gradient algorithm proposed in [13] (adam) for weight optimization.

5   Results

Table 4 shows accuracy of each attack classifiers in phase 1 on training and testing data with their structure.

Table 4. Structure and results of each individual classifier in phase 1

Classifier	Training accuracy	Testing accuracy
Dos [9,7,7,7,1]	98.578%	90.831%
Probe [5,3,3,3,1]	96.448%	88.884%
R2L [14,10,10,10,1]	99.223%	85.903%
U2R [8,6,6,6,1]	99.995%	98.900%

Table 5 show the final accuracy of 2 class and 5 class classifiers on training and testing dataset. The system is flexible for the classifier used in phase 2 as evident from Table 5 (Table 6).

Table 5. Final accuracy

Algorithm	2 class training	2 class testing	5 class training	5 class testing
GausianNB	99.02%	81.37%	96.59%	72.36%
Logistic regression	99.18%	81.18%	98.14%	72.57%
Decision tree	99.99%	79.28%	99.89%	74.90%

Table 6. Classification report

	Training dataset			Testing dataset		
	Precision	Recall	F1-score	Precision	Recall	F1-score
Normal	1	0.99	0.99	0.72	0.91	0.81
Anomaly	0.99	1	0.99	0.91	0.74	0.82
Average	0.99	0.99	0.99	0.83	0.81	0.82

6   Conclusion and Future Work

We proposed a flexible and efficient NIDS using ensemble of deep neural networks. We tested the system on the NSL-KDD dataset. The system is flexible in phase 2 as it works with different classifiers. Highest accuracy observed on training data is 99.99% for binary and 99.89% for five class, both using decision tree for aggregation in phase 2. Highest accuracy observed on testing data is 81.27% using Gaussian naive bayes classifier for binary and 74.90% for five class using decision tree. We observed that the system performed very well compared to other NIDS implementations found in literature. In future, we plan to test the system using more and different classifiers in phase 1 and 2. Additionally, testing the system on live data.

References

1. LeCun, Y., Bengio, Y., Hinton, G.: Deep learning. Nature **521**, 436–444 (2015)
2. Tavallaee, M., Bagheri, E., Lu, W., Ghorbani, A.: A detailed analysis of the KDD CUP 99 data set. In: 2009 IEEE Symposium on Computational Intelligence for Security and Defense Applications (2009)
3. http://www.unb.ca/cic/research/datasets/nsl.html
4. Haq, N.F., Onik, A.R., Hridoy, M.A.K., Rafni, M., Shah, F.M., Farid, D.M.: Application of machine learning approaches in intrusion detection system: a survey. Int. J. Adv. Res. Artif. Intell. **4**, 9–18 (2015)
5. Chae, H., Jo, B., Choi, S., Park, T.: Feature selection for intrusion detection using NSL-KDD. In: Recent Advances in Computer Science, pp. 184–187 (2013)
6. Niyaz, Q., Sun, W., Javaid, A.: A deep learning based DDoS detection system in software-defined networking (SDN). arXiv preprint arXiv:1611.07400 (2016)
7. Subba, B., Biswas, S., Karmakar, S.: A neural network based system for intrusion detection and attack classification. In: 2016 Twenty Second National Conference on Communication (NCC) (2016)
8. Tang, T.A., Mhamdi, L., McLernon, D., Zaidi, S.A.R., Ghogho, M.: Deep learning approach for network intrusion detection in software defined networking. In: 2016 International Conference on Wireless Networks and Mobile Communications (WINCOM), pp. 258–263. IEEE, October 2016
9. Ingre, B., Yadav, A.: Performance analysis of NSL-KDD dataset using ANN. In: 2015 International Conference on Signal Processing and Communication Engineering Systems (2015)
10. Sadek, R., Soliman, M., Elsayed, H.: Effective anomaly intrusion detection system based on neural network with indicator variable and rough set reduction. Int. J. Comput. Sci. Issues (IJCSI) **10**, 227–233 (2013)
11. Guleria, D., Chavan, M.: Intrusion detection system based on conditional random fields. Int. J. Comput. Sci. Netw. Secur. (IJCSNS) **13**, 80 (2013)
12. https://github.com/fchollet/keras
13. Kingma, D., Ba, J.: Adam: a method for stochastic optimization. arXiv preprint arXiv:1412.6980 (2014)

Benchmarks for Evaluation of Wireless Sensor Network Clustering

Nishi Gupta[1](✉), Pranav M. Pawar[2], and Satbir Jain[1]

[1] Netaji Subhas Institute of Technology, Dwarka, New Delhi, India
nishigupta99@gmail.com, jain_satbir@yahoo.com
[2] STES'sSmt. Kashibai Navale College of Engineering, Pune, India
pmpawar@sinhgad.edu

Abstract. Wireless Sensor Networks (WSNs) require sensor nodes to collect, aggregate and transmit data to the sink when they sense an event. Clustering has been proven to be an effective technique to do this job with increased efficiency. In clustering, the network is divided into smaller regions, namely clusters, and each cluster has a Cluster Head (CH). Data from all the member nodes in a cluster is collected by CH and then forwarded to the sink after aggregation and processing. Different clustering techniques have different advantages and disadvantages, trade-offs among desired properties and have been assessed using different parameters and metrics. This paper studies various clustering techniques and draws comparisons among them based on their basic working and properties. It also signifies the importance of benchmarking in WSNs and aims to identify benchmarks for the evaluation of the clustering techniques in wireless sensor networks.

Keywords: Wireless Sensor Networks · Clustering · Benchmarking
Load balancing · Energy balancing

1 Introduction

Wireless Sensor Networks (WSNs) comprise of special light weight nodes which are used to sense and record events. The data is collected by the sensor nodes and information is transferred to an infrastructural node, called the sink. Energy is major constraint in any WSN because the sensor nodes have low energy back-up and low computational power. Increasing the transmission range has high energy requirements. In many of the networks, it is highly probable that nodes cannot be replaced or charged. Thus there is a need for the algorithms and procedures to be designed in such a manner that minimum energy is utilized and also that energy usage is balanced among nodes, otherwise some nodes may die earlier and cause network to partition.

Clustering is a solution to energy and load balancing. The network is divided into smaller areas called the clusters and each has a Cluster Head (CH). The CH acts as communication link between nodes of its cluster, called the member nodes, and any other cluster or sink. The nodes send collected data to their respective CHs, which aggregate it and transmits to the sink in single-hop or multi-hop via other CHs with

© Springer Nature Singapore Pte Ltd. 2018
A. V. Deshpande et al. (Eds.): SmartCom 2017, CCIS 876, pp. 11–20, 2018.
https://doi.org/10.1007/978-981-13-1423-0_2

sink as the final destination. This leads to higher energy consumption at the CH so role of CH is alternated among nodes periodically or statistically.

Different algorithms have their own advantages and disadvantages. Some are faster, some are more energy efficient, some work for longer time, and some allow the network to focus on quality of service. Algorithms have to make a trade-off among various desirable properties of the network as it is quite challenging to attain all the advantages in a single algorithm.

Benchmarking for evaluation of WSN clustering mechanism allows the researchers to study and assess different algorithms. It also aids in choosing appropriate procedure to be applied in the required application. The main objective of this paper is to study and compare existing clustering techniques to identify benchmarks for the evaluation of clustering mechanism for WSNs. Physical parameters, implementation tools, testing scenarios, metrics used and variables used for measuring performance of the algorithms act as the benchmarks.

The remainder of the paper is organised as follows: Sect. 2 deals with the details and comparison of clustering techniques in WSNs. In Sect. 3, various evaluation benchmarking parameters for clustering have been identified. Section 4 concludes the paper.

2 Literature Review

In 2000, Heinzelman et al. [1] proposed Low-energy Adaptive Clustering Hierarchy (LEACH), the first clustering protocol for WSNs. Virtual Area Partition Algorithm (VAP-E) [2] clusters or partitions the network virtually after calculating optimal number of CHs which are then evenly distributed in the network. It results in efficient communication in the network. Authors in [3] proposed partition based LEACH (pLEACH). Sink calculates optimal number of CHs, divides the network into clusters and disseminate CH information in the network. Virtual Area Partition Clustering protocol with Assistant Cluster Head (VAPC-ACH) was introduced in [4] where load balancing is done with the help of an Assistant Cluster head (ACH) which is appointed if the residual energy of CH is low. In [5], authors proposed a clustering mechanism for non-uniformly distributed nodes in a circular WSN. The network is partitioned into concentric rings with different density of sensor nodes and CH is computationally elected for each of the rings. A distributed self-organizing balanced clustering mechanism was proposed in [6]. Cluster creation uses residual energy, connectivity density and distance from sink as parameters. Authors in [7] explore the fact that sink is abundant in resources and energy. It scans the area and divides nodes into different rings and zones. This reduces load on the sensor nodes which have less resources. Energy Delay Index for Trade-off (EDIT) [8] selects next hop and CH on basis of residual energy and delay. Both hop count and Euclidian distance are kept into consideration to decide path between CH and member node. DEAD message is used by node to declare itself dead if it has energy less than threshold value. In fan-shaped clustering [9, 10] the network is divided into rings and then rings are further divided into regions of equal area for load balancing. CH is selected in each area based on its residual energy and central location in its cluster. Re-clustering is done if CH needs to be changed. A separate relay node is selected to forward aggregated data to the sink. In [11] TDMA schedule and node replacement are added to LEACH. CSMA/CD is used by the nodes to send data to the CH and to the sink according to a TDMA schedule. A self-configurable clustering scheme was presented in [12] to maintain the clusters. Type 2 Fuzzy Logic System (FLS) is used to select CH and backup CH (BCH) by applying fuzzy logic on energy, distance from neighbours and centrality in the cluster. Node with maximum FLS-output is chosen as CH. FLS-output list is periodically updated to choose CH and handle any failure. A solution to balanced sized clusters was proposed in [13] as nodes join a cluster based on threshold distance from CH. Also there is a threshold on number of nodes that can join one cluster. Unclustered nodes, if any, join a cluster in the rescue phase. Two level tree structure is used in [14] for clustering. CHs are chosen for each cluster and a super leader for entire network. Periodic CH selection is done for clusters whose sizes lie between lower and upper threshold. The states of cohesion, strong cohesion and absolute cohesion determine if communication between CH and sink will be multi hop or single hop. In Regional Energy Aware Clustering with Isolated Nodes (REAC-IN) [15] CH is selected based on weight i.e. residual energy and average regional energy. Regional energy and distance from sink are used to determine who the isolated nodes will send data to, i.e. CH or sink. In [16], Enhanced-Optimized Energy Efficient Routing Protocol (E-OEERP) uses Particle Swarm Optimization (PSO) technique to cluster the network. Each CH has an assistant node to share the overhead. Gravitational Search Algorithm (GSA) is used for routing where force (position, velocity, energy) between CH and nodes is used to decide next hop. [17] introduces a multi-layer clustering approach ROI is to divide network into concentric circles with sink at the centre. CHs are chosen on basis of residual energy, degree and volunteer parents within a radius. Leader node collects and aggregates data. It sends data to CH and CH forwards it to the sink. Clustering Hierarchy Protocol using improved PSO was proposed in [18] which uses relay nodes and improved PSO to periodically select CH. CH is selected on the basis of residual energy and distance from sink. Relay acts as the next hop to CHs. CH collects data, aggregates it and sends to relay to forward to sink. Dynamic Cluster Head Selection Method [19] exploits redundancy in the network. Nodes with death priority and which don't affect the coverage are chosen as CH. Next set of CHs is selected on residual energy and average network energy.

Table 1 shows the comparative analysis of the studied clustering techniques. The techniques have been compared on the basis of their basic working, advantages and disadvantages, performance metrics, most efficient scenario for an algorithm. It reflects the trade-off that is to be done to attain a certain advantage over another mechanism. It also helps in choosing most appropriate mechanism of clustering in a given environment and for a certain application. The comparison criteria provide benchmarks for any new mechanism developed to be checked and compared against the existing ones.

Table 1. Comparative analysis of clustering techniques in wireless sensor networks

Reference no.	Advantages	Disadvantages	Physical parameters & testing scenario	Tool used	Metrics	Performance variable	Equal sized clusters	Optimal no. of clusters	Presence of ACH	Sink assistance
[2]	Load balancing Low energy dissipation Prolonged stability Increased lifetime Efficient communication	Non-uniform clusters CH not central	Heterogeneous WSN Uniform distribution Optimal channel	NS2	Number of live nodes Number of packets received at sink	Lifetime PDR Throughput	No	Yes	No	No
[3]	Low energy dissipation Increased lifetime	Non-uniform clusters CH not central	Adjustable transmission range Random distribution	NS2	Residual energy Number of live nodes	Energy consumption Lifetime	Yes	Yes	No	Yes
[4]	Low energy dissipation Load balancing Increased lifetime Improved performance	Non-uniform clusters CH not central	Heterogeneous WSN Random distribution Different ranges Location information.	NS2	Number of live nodes Number of packets received at sink	Lifetime Throughput PDR	No	Yes	Yes	Yes
[5]	Efficient in non-uniform scenario	Non-uniform clusters CH not central	Random deployment Circular sensor field	NS2	Balanced clusters	Throughput PDR	No	Yes	No	No
[6]	Balanced clusters Increased lifetime Low energy dissipation Scalable	CH not central	Residual energy is randomly distributed function Random distribution	NS2	Number of live nodes	Lifetime	Yes (in same layer)	No	No	No
[7]	Load balancing Low message overhead Increased lifetime	Non-uniform clusters CH not central	Edge based network Adjustable transmission range Random distribution	NS2	Balanced clusters Number of live nodes Number of packets received at sink	Energy consumption PDR Lifetime Throughput	No	No	No	Yes
[8]	Energy balancing Load balancing Delay balancing	Non-uniform clusters CH not central	Delay constraint application Random distribution	Castalia	Number of packets received at sink Residual energy Number of live nodes	Energy consumption Lifetime	No	No	No	Yes
[9, 10]	Low overhead of re-clustering Easy re-clustering Minimize intra-cluster communication cost Minimize partition cost	No QoS	Large scale WSN Random distribution Circular sensor field Sink in centre	MATLAB	Number of live nodes Residual energy	Energy consumption Lifetime	Yes	No	No	Yes

(continued)

Table 1. (*continued*)

Reference no.	Advantages	Disadvantages	Physical parameters & testing scenario	Tool used	Metrics	Performance variable	Equal sized clusters	Optimal no. of clusters	Presence of ACH	Sink assistance
[11]	Energy balancing Reduced delay No collision	Non-uniform clusters CH not central	Random distribution	NS2	Delay Number of packets received at sink	Throughput PDR	No	No	No	No
[12]	Increased lifetime Reduced traffic Identifies dead CH and replaces them	No QoS Non-uniform clusters	Large scale WSN Random distribution Sink in the centre Uniform initial energy	MATLAB	Data loss ratio Message overhead	Energy consumption PDR	No	No	Yes	No
[13]	Formation of even clusters	CH not central	Homogenous WSN Fixed nodes No GPS	MATLAB	Number of live nodes	Lifetime	Yes	Yes	No	No
[14]	Low energy dissipation Formation of even clusters Balance between multi & single hop packet delivery	CH not central	Stable network Knowledge of neighbours.	NS2	Number of clusters Balanced clusters	Cohesion Running time of algorithm	Yes	No	Yes	No
[15]	Increased lifetime Prolonged stability Communication for an isolated node is decided	Non-uniform clusters CH not central	Large scale WSN Sink in centre	NS2	Residual energy Number of live nodes Number of packets received at sink	PDR Lifetime Energy consumption	No	No	No	No
[16]	Removes isolated nodes Increased lifetime	Non-uniform clusters CH not central	Random distribution	NS2	Number of isolated nodes Load balancing	Throughput PDR Lifetime	Yes	Yes	Yes	No
[17]	Low energy dissipation Increased lifetime Efficient intra-cluster communication	Non-uniform clusters	Homogenous WSN Random distribution Sink in the centre Circular sensor field Stationary nodes	NS2	Number of live nodes Residual energy Number of packets received at sink	Lifetime PDR Throughput Energy consumption	No	No	No	No
[18]	Increased lifetime Low energy dissipation Load balancing Minimize transmission distance	Non-uniform clusters CH not central	Homogenous WSN Stationary nodes Symmetric channel Adjustable transmission range	MATLAB	Number of live nodes	Lifetime Energy consumption	No	No	Yes	No
[19]	Increased coverage Increased lifetime Low energy dissipation	Non-uniform clusters CH not central	Heterogeneous WSN Different transmission range	MATLAB	Coverage hole appearance Number of live nodes Residual energy	Cohesion Energy consumption Lifetime	No	No	No	Yes

3 Evaluation Benchmarks

3.1 Physical Parameters

Location of Sink: Sink can be centrally placed in the sensed region or can be randomly placed. It is an important in the aspect where the communication and network is monitored by the sink. Also, sink is the ultimate destination of each data packet in a WSN. Central location will make the transmission easier and fast.

Distribution of Nodes: Uniform or random distribution of nodes decide if the load on each CH is balanced or not. Uniform distribution will result in more balanced clusters but it is less practical in real environments.

Circular Sensor Field: If the sensor field is circular, it is easier to monitor and re-cluster the network. Also the central position of sink is more convenient.

Edge Based Network: Computation when done by the node which originally senses data, results in less data movement in the network. This situation, though will lead to more energy consumption at the nodes.

Large Scale WSNs: Large scale networks can easily exploit the redundancy. Events can be recorded by more than one sensor node. Identification of critical nodes becomes important whose death will result in network partition.

GPS: Presence of GPS makes it easier for the sink to locate and track the nodes but it also leads to high computational overhead on the nodes.

3.2 Clustering Parameters

Size of Clusters: Clusters formed could be evenly sized or evenly dense. Equal sized clusters may have varying number of nodes affecting the energy usage of the CH. Clusters with equal density may result in unequal clusters and CHs may have to communicate with member nodes far away and thus resulting in uneven energy usage.

Number of Clusters: Optimal number of CH dictate the number of clusters in the system. Large number of clusters eliminates the advantage of clustering and less number of clusters lead to high energy consumption at CHs.

Location of CH: Central location of CH is advantageous for the nodes to reach CH and also for communication among CHs.

Number of Rounds: Optimal number of rounds taken for the selection of CH and cluster setup is an important factor to keep the network connected.

Aggregation Function at CH: CH aggregates the data received from its member nodes. The function used decides the energy consumed at CH and lifetime of network.

3.3 Implementation Tool

Network Simulators: Several network simulators are available to test the proposed mechanism. Simulators like NS2, Qualnet and Castalia have been used by different authors. Several metrics are plotted which help in the evaluation of the algorithm performance and the advantages it may have over other mechanisms.

MATLAB: Several researchers support their mechanism with a mathematical model which can be effectively simulated in MATLAB. It helps in assessing and comparing different mathematical models.

3.4 Testing Scenario

Homogeneity: The WSN can be homogeneous or heterogeneous on the basis of mobility, initial energy, computational power and role in the network. Homogeneous system is easy to study but is far from real networks.

Transmission Range: Nodes may be able to dynamically adjust their transmission range depending upon the distance of next hop or initially they may have different transmission powers.

Network Information: Nodes may have the information of their neighbors or this duty may be given to CH to keep track of its cluster though it will increase the overhead on the CH. Sink might also be responsible to keep network information though it will increase the flow of traffic in network and consume energy.

Mobility: The nodes may be stationary, mobile or have limited mobility which can be controlled. Presence of mobility increases computational and monitoring overhead.

Transmission Channel: Optimal channel encounters no collision and retransmission but it may introduce delay in the packet transmissions.

3.5 Metrics Used

Number of Live Nodes: Variation in time taken for the first node to die, half nodes in the network to die, and all nodes to die in different networks suggest the number of live nodes in the network and is used to indicate the lifetime of the network.

Number of Packets Delivered at Sink: Packet delivery at sink against time, events recorded, number of packets generated and number of nodes is an indicator of Packet Delivery Ratio (PDR) and throughput of the network.

Residual Energy: The energy of each node at a given point of time constitutes the residual energy and is the general criteria of choosing next CHs for the clusters. Uniform residual energy of the nodes implies load and energy balanced system. It is an indication of energy consumption in the system.

Balanced Clusters: Standard deviation in size of clusters with number of nodes is an indication whether the cluster formation is balanced or not. Balanced clusters are desirable and lead to more balanced load distribution.

Number of Isolated Nodes: Number of isolated nodes with simulation rounds and number of nodes in the network is an indication of cohesion and connectivity of the network. Less number of isolated nodes indicates better cohesion and throughput.

Coverage Hole Appearance: Appearance of coverage holes in the network with time is an indication of connectivity and lifetime of the network.

3.6 Variables for Measuring Performance

Packet Delivery Ratio (PDR): Number of packets received at the sink per packet generated is PDR. More the value of PDR, better the performance of the network.

Energy Consumption: Residual energy and energy exhausted in computation are used to indicate the energy consumption of the network. Less the energy consumption, better the life and connectivity of the network, better the performance.

Message Overhead: Synchronizing messages, other than the data create message overhead which consume more energy and increase chances of network partitioning.

Running Time of Algorithm: Each run of the algorithm consists of creating clusters, choosing CH and deciding the communication path from member nodes to CH and CH to sink. Time is a critical concern in real time applications networks.

Cohesion: The state of connectivity among the nodes is called cohesion. Stronger the cohesion, better the connectivity and better the performance of system.

Lifetime: Time for which the network is successfully able to sense events, collect data, aggregate it and transmit to sink is its lifetime. Longer lifetime is desirable.

Throughput: It is the delivery of collected data of all the events recorded to the sink. It is achieved by high PDR, connectivity and energy and load balancing.

4 Conclusion

Clustering has resulted in more efficient working of a Wireless Sensor Network where the data collected by sensor nodes is transmitted to the sink via Cluster Head nodes. Different proposed algorithms have different advantages and disadvantages which results from the fact that trade-off has to be done among properties to make the mechanism more suitable and efficient for a particular application. This paper has studied various techniques for clustering in WSNs and compared them on the basis of certain parameters which allow trade-off to be done. This has enabled us to identify the benchmarking parameters. Physical parameters like placement of nodes and sink, type of area to be sensed, distribution of nodes lay the foundation of the implementation scenario for which we have to design the algorithm. Homogeneity, transmission channel and ranges information flow can either be simulated on a simulator or mathematically derived. The metrics used like number of live nodes, residual energy, coverage hole appearance, balanced clusters are an indication of the network performance in terms of energy consumption, load balancing, lifetime, cohesion and throughput.

References

1. Heinzelman, W.R., Chandrakasan, A., Balakrishnan, H.: Energy-efficient communication protocol for wireless microsensor networks. In: Proceedings of the 33rd Annual Hawaii International Conference on System Sciences 2000. IEEE (2000)
2. Wang, R., Liu, G., Zheng, C.: A clustering algorithm based on virtual area partition for heterogeneous wireless sensor networks. In: International Conference on Mechatronics and Automation 2007, ICMA 2007. IEEE (2007)
3. Gou, H., Yoo, Y., Zeng, H.: A partition-based LEACH algorithm for wireless sensor networks. In: Ninth IEEE International Conference on Computer and Information Technology 2009, CIT 2009, vol. 2. IEEE (2009)
4. Ma, D., et al.: A virtual area partition clustering protocol with assistant cluster heads for wireless sensor networks. In: 2013 10th IEEE International Conference on Control and Automation (ICCA). IEEE (2013)
5. Tripathi, R.K., Singh, Y.N., Verma, N.K.: Clustering algorithm for non-uniformly distributed nodes in wireless sensor network. Electron. Lett. **49**(4), 299–300 (2013)
6. Liao, Y., Qi, H., Li, W.: Load-balanced clustering algorithm with distributed self-organization for wireless sensor networks. IEEE Sens. J. **13**(5), 1498–1506 (2013)
7. Muni, V.K., Kandasamy, A., Chandrasekaran, K.: Energy-efficient edge-based network partitioning scheme for wireless sensor networks. In: 2013 International Conference on Advances in Computing, Communications and Informatics (ICACCI). IEEE (2013)
8. Thakkar, A., Kotecha, K.: Cluster head election for energy and delay constraint applications of wireless sensor network. IEEE Sens. J. **14**(8), 2658–2664 (2014)
9. Lin, H., Chen, P., Wang, L.: Fan-shaped clustering for large-scale sensor networks. In: 2014 International Conference on Cyber-Enabled Distributed Computing and Knowledge Discovery (CyberC). IEEE (2014)
10. Lin, H., Wang, L., Kong, R.: Energy efficient clustering protocol for large-scale sensor networks. IEEE Sens. J. **15**(12), 7150–7160 (2015)
11. Ansari, N., Paul, R.K.: Modified leach in wireless sensor network. IOSR J. Comput. Eng. (IOSR-JCE) **16**(6), 71–78 (2014). www.iosrjournals.org
12. Izadi, D., Abawajy, J., Ghanavati, S.: An alternative clustering scheme in WSN. IEEE Sens. J. **15**(7), 4148–4155 (2015)
13. Pal, V., Singh, G., Yadav, R.P.: Balanced cluster size solution to extend lifetime of wireless sensor networks. IEEE Internet Things J. **2**(5), 399–401 (2015)
14. Benaouda, N., Mostefai, M.: A new two-level clustering scheme for partitioning in distributed wireless sensor networks. Int. J. Distrib. Sens. Netw. **11**(5), 435048 (2015)
15. Leu, J.-S., et al.: Energy efficient clustering scheme for prolonging the lifetime of wireless sensor network with isolated nodes. IEEE Commun. Lett. **19**(2), 259–262 (2015)
16. RejinaParvin, J., Vasanthanayaki, C.: Particle swarm optimization-based clustering by preventing residual nodes in wireless sensor networks. IEEE Sens. J. **15**(8), 4264–4274 (2015)

17. Siavoshi, S., Kavian, Y.S., Sharif, H.: Load-balanced energy efficient clustering protocol for wireless sensor networks. IET Wirel. Sens. Syst. **6**(3), 67–73 (2016)
18. Zhou, Y., Wang, N., Xiang, W.: Clustering hierarchy protocol in wireless sensor networks using an improved PSO algorithm. IEEE Access **5**, 2241–2253 (2017)
19. Jia, D., et al.: Dynamic cluster head selection method for wireless sensor network. IEEE Sens. J. **16**(8), 2746–2754 (2016)

Internet Traffic Intrusion Detection System Using Adaptive Neuro-Fuzzy Inference System

Mrudul Dixit and Rajashwini Ukarande[(✉)]

Department of Electronics and Telecommunication,
MKSSS's Cummins College of Engineering for Women, Pune, India
dixitma@yahoo.com, rajashwiniub@gmail.com

Abstract. Network security has become an important aspect in terms of confidentiality and integrity. To protect our system from these internet attacks, without any compromise on the security constraints, we have developed a system using the combination of two soft computing techniques, namely fuzzy and neural network. The designed system for intrusion detection is the Adaptive Neuro-Fuzzy Inference System (ANFIS), which detects whether the incoming data is normal or an attack. To train the system, we have used KDD dataset and to evaluate the performance parameters based on the confusion matrix generated. For the system to work with high accuracy, the True Negative Rate and True Positive Rate must be maximum. This paper compares the fuzzy and neural network techniques (developed previously) using the same dataset with that of neuro fuzzy. The paper mainly focuses on ANFIS and the concepts of fuzzy and neural network used to develop this system.

Keywords: Adaptive Neuro-Fuzzy Inference System · KDD cup 99
Denial of service · Probe · Fuzzy logic · Artificial neural network

1 Introduction

To monitor these suspicious activities in the network environment, we have designed a system which will be trained for both normal and attack datasets to identify the incoming data traffic by comparing it with the trained system. Here, KDD Cup 99 dataset is used which consists of training and testing data. Both these datasets hold normal as well as attack data. Out of the four attacks: Denial of Service (DoS), Remote to Local (R2L), User to Root (U2R) and Probe, we have used DoS (attribute: Neptune) and Probe (attribute: Satan). This Neuro-Fuzzy technique overcomes the weaknesses of Neural Network and Fuzzy Logic. Since, Neural Networks can recognize patterns very well but the way they reach their decisions is not clearly mentioned. Whereas, Fuzzy logic are very good at explaining their outcomes, but cannot automatically acquire the rules. Therefore, the main aim of hybridization is to design a learning mechanism that utilizes the training and learning algorithm from neural networks to find parameters of a fuzzy system [1].

A. V. Deshpande et al. (Eds.): SmartCom 2017, CCIS 876, pp. 21–28, 2018.
https://doi.org/10.1007/978-981-13-1423-0_3

2 Related Works

There have been many researches and studies on Neuro-Fuzzy technique to eliminate the attack data in network traffic by detecting and preventing them from entering into the system. One such research is the use of SOM (Self-Organizing Map) in identifying the network traffic process [2]. Support Vector Machine (SVM) or Ant Colony (ACO) algorithms to detect network intrusion [3]. The Approximate Reasoning-based Intelligent Control (ARIC) model implements a fuzzy control system by using specialized feed forward neural networks which was introduced by Berenji in 1992 [4]. The ARIC model was extended to Generalize ARIC (GARIC) [5]. It has an Action Selection Network (ASN) and an Action state Evaluation Network (AEN). This research detects the malicious (attack) and legitimate (normal) data activity making it more accurate compared to other systems. The structure of the paper is as follows: Sect. 3 is the Proposed Work, in that the utilization of KDD dataset is described. The system design and the work flow in detail. Section 3.2 is the results and performance parameters. Section 4 concludes the paper with the result analysis.

3 Proposed Work

Intrusion Detection System is designed which will train the system using the data from the KDD dataset. The information source and analysis part is done in this project. The objective is to detect maximum number of attacks with low false rates [6].

3.1 KDD Cup 99 Dataset

The KDD Cup 99 [7] was originated from DARPA'98 dataset containing 7 week training and 2 week testing data. Total, there are 4 attacks in training and testing data. KDD training dataset consists of 4,900,000 single connection vectors having 41 attributes. Attacks are categorized as: 1. Probe: For scanning the information of connected devices to find their vulnerabilities. 2. Denial of Service (DoS): For preventing the usage of network resources to its legitimate users. 3. Compromise attacks: (a) Remote to Local (R2L) attacks - To have local access to network resource. (b) User to Root (U2R) attacks - To have administrative privileges to a computer or system. Out of these, we have used Probe and the DoS attacks. Only 10% of the KDD data is applied to the system. The repeated connection vectors are eliminated, hence the total no. of training data used is 8558 and testing data is 13221. Out of the 41 attributes, we have used 4 attributes given in Table 1 (Tables 2 and 3).

For training and testing data set, the % of normal data is 65% and attack data is 35%. The same % ratio is maintained in fuzzy and neural network algorithms, so that comparison between all the 3 techniques will be fairly based on the input dataset, even if the no. of connection vectors varies for the above methods.

Table 1. Selected attributes

Attribute Index	Attributes
1	Count
2	Srv_count
3	Dest_host_same_srv_rate
4	Dest_host_diff_srv_rate

Table 2. Training dataset

Class	No. of samples	Sample %
Normal	5563	65.0035
Probe	2049	23.9425
DoS	946	11.0539
Total	8558	100

Table 3. Testing dataset

Class	No. of samples	Sample %
Normal	8594	65.0026
Probe	3682	27.8496
DoS	945	7.1499
Total	13221	100

3.2 System Design

There are 3 ANFIS modules trained to identify the intrusive activity. One is for normal and two for attack data (DoS and Probe). The system consists of 4 input attributes for each of normal, DoS and Probe data type. We have added a 5th label to the input dataset i.e. the amplitude. The normal data is given a label 0 and attack data is given a label 10. This defines that whenever the intrusion level is high, the data is attack and when it is low, data is normal. These inputs are then grouped into clusters using neuro-fuzzy sub-clustering. Figure 1 describes the system architecture for proposed method.

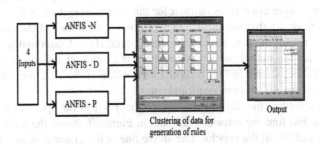

Fig. 1. System architecture block diagram.

We do not use the KDD dataset as it is, we need to sort the excel sheet as per their attack type and save the required attributes. This excel file is then converted to .mat file i.e. Matlab data file as the neuro fuzzy editor takes input in the form of .mat data file. The training data is loaded into the ANFIS editor from the workspace and new FIS is generated using sub clustering for 10 epochs. This trained .fis file is then saved and testing data is loaded from the workspace. This saved FIS file is then used for testing the testing dataset and a neuro FIS is ready to calculate the accuracy and other performance parameters.

3.3 Work Flow

There are 3 ANFIS Fig. 2 represents an FIS Editor with four inputs, one output and Sugeno model. This window is generated when we load training data and generate FIS using clustering. We can add and delete the input elements based on the application.

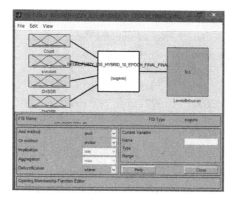

Fig. 2. Fuzzy inference system editor.

Figure 3 depicts the third input with its 4 Gaussian Membership Functions. The range of the input is from 0 to 1. Similarly other MF is designed with their respective ranges. Count – 0 to 511, Srv count – 0 to 105, DHSSR – 0 to 1 and DHDSR – 0 to 1.

The rules are designed by the NF editor when clustering of input samples is performed. Here, there are 4 rules defined for the intrusion system as shown in Fig. 4.

From Fig. 5 we see that the surface viewer gives a clear idea of the contribution of the input attributes for the detection of the attack data. Here, Count and Srv count play important role for the output to vary when there is a small change in the input.

The Rule Viewer shown in Fig. 6 signifies the value of the intrusion when the input value is changed for no. of combinational rules.

Further, to calculate the Root Mean Square Error wrt to the epochs we use the FIS file as .mat file and find the error at each epoch. Figure 7 shows the error for training and testing dataset for all the epochs. The above line is for Training data and lower line is for Testing data. When we train the data, we can see the error reduction in the testing phase.

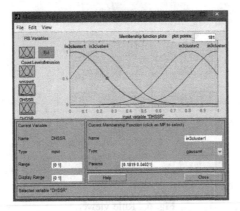

Fig. 3. Input 3 with Gaussian MF.

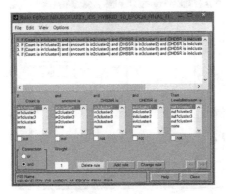

Fig. 4. Rules defined for the proposed system.

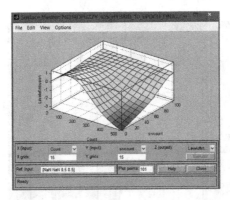

Fig. 5. Surface viewer displaying the level of intrusion wrt to inputs.

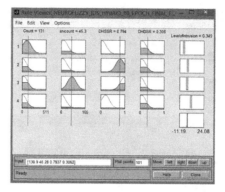

Fig. 6. Rule viewer.

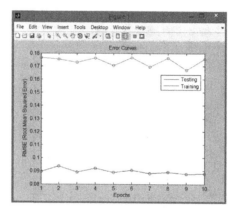

Fig. 7. Error plot for training and testing dataset.

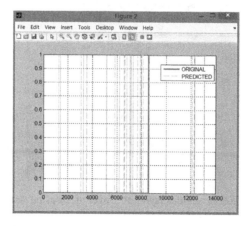

Fig. 8. Comparison of testing data with predicted output. (Color figure online)

In Fig. 8 the red line (thick line) defines the 5th attribute that is the label which is given to the testing dataset. The connection vectors from 1 to 8594 are normal hence has value 0, and from 8594 to 13321 the data is attack, hence has label 1. The yellow lines (dotted lines) represent the predicted values in normal and attack zones. Ideally the yellow lines should match the red line, but as no system can be designed with 100% accuracy, these yellow lines will be used to calculate the error in the system.

Thus, Table 4 shows a system comparison for all the 3 techniques using the same dataset. Fuzzy and Neural Network were developed previously and published in journals and this paper explains the Neuro - Fuzzy technique which uses the strength of Fuzzy and NN to detect intrusion.

Table 4. Comparison of Fuzzy Technique, Neural Network and Neuro - Fuzzy method for all the performance parameters

Parameters	Fuzzy logic	Neural network	Neuro-fuzzy
Precision	100%	74.25%	97.24%
Recall	83.33%	99.98%	99.71%
F-measure	90.91%	85.22%	98.46%
Overall accuracy	90%	74.26%	98.03%
True positive rate	83.33%	99.98%	99.71%
True negative rate	100%	99.74%	95.10%
False positive rate	0%	0.26%	4.90%
False negative rate	16.66%	0.02%	0.29%

4 Conclusion

An anomaly intrusion detection system is developed to detect the intrusion in internet traffic. Neuro - Fuzzy Inference System is designed using the fuzzy rule and neural network approach to classify the test data as normal. By analyzing the results, the neuro fuzzy system achieves 98.03% accuracy for the DoS and Probe type of attack compared to fuzzy and neural system which achieves 90% and 74.26% accuracy respectively. True Positive Rate should be as high as possible which is approximately same in Neural Network and Neuro Fuzzy Model - 99.98%. The highest True Negative Rate is achieved in Neural Network Model – 99.74%. The Precision for data security is achieved in Neuro Fuzzy. In some parameters, NN and NF go hand in hand but otherwise Neuro Fuzzy is proved to be the best system for Intrusion Detection. To achieve more accuracy in the future, number of attributes can be increased. Different Big datasets can be used.

References

1. Sivanandam, S.N., Deepa, S.N.: Principles of Soft Computing, 2nd edn. Wiley India Pvt. Ltd., New Delhi (2014)
2. Midzic, A., Avdagic, Z., Omanovic, S.: Intrusion detection system modeling based on neural networks and fuzzy logic. In: 20th Jubilee IEEE International Conference on Intelligent Engineering Systems, Budapest, Hungary (2016)

3. Dhanabal, L., Shantharajah, S.P.: Intrusion detection and classification using hybrid support vector machine and dynamic ant colony algorithm. Aust. J. Basic Appl. Sci. **9**, 328–335 (2015)
4. White, D.A., Sofge, D.A. (eds.): Handbook of Intelligent Control, Neural, Fuzzy, and Adaptive Approaches. Van Nostrand Reinhold, New York (1992)
5. Berenji, H.R., Khedkar, P.: Fuzzy rules for guiding reinforcement learning. In: International Conference on Information Processing and Management of Uncertainty in Knowledge-Based Systems (IPMU 1992), Mallorca, pp. 511–514 (1992)
6. Herringshaw, C.: Detecting attacks on networks. IEEE Comput. **30**(12), 16–17 (1997)
7. Shanmugavadivu, R., Nagarajan, N.: Network intrusion detection system using fuzzy logic. Indian J. Comput. Sci. Eng. (IJCSE) **2**(1), 101–111 (2011)

Forecasting Student's Internet Utilization Through Artificial Neural Networks

Aniket Muley[1(✉)], Parag Bhalchandra[2(✉)], and Pawan Wasnik[1(✉)]

[1] School of Mathematical Sciences, Swami Ramanand Teerth Marathwada University, Dnyan Teerth, Vishnupuri, Nanded 431606, MS, India
aniket.muley@gmail.com, pawan_wasnik@yahoo.com
[2] School of Computational Sciences, Swami Ramanand Teerth Marathwada University, Dnyan Teerth, Vishnupuri, Nanded 431606, MS, India
srtmun.parag@gmail.com

Abstract. Internet has become vital part of everyone's life. This is very true with students as they must be susceptible to the internet usage for effective learning. Our study focuses on use of the internet by students according to academic perspective. The objective is to predict most affecting variables which deal with the causes and reasons of possible restriction on usage of the internet by students. The study has deployed artificial neural network (ANN) model for taking anticipatory measures for predicting use of the internet. The Levenberg - Marquardt Back Propagation method was performed for training data with three layers with five algorithms of NN are simulated and compared the results. Optimal artificial neural network model is proposed as a final outcome. Experimentation was carried out in R software.

Keywords: Data mining · Internet susceptibility · Artificial neural network Analysis

1 Introduction

Artificial Neural Network (ANN) is widely used artificial intelligence technique which can learn, adapt, classify, and predict parameters for machine learning applications and these are foundation of biological structure of brains. Its basic terminology is borrowed from neurosciences [3, 4, 10]. The ability of ANN for prediction of parameters is significant in accuracy as compared to conventional statistical methods for prediction. ANN looks like directed graphs and have neurons, interconnections as main components in lieu of nodes and edges. ANN can have many layers and a layer can consist of many processing elements with their interconnections. They behave similar to parallel computing systems. Every neuron has interconnection strengths with former and next layers. This strength is called as weights. ANNs are adaptable to diverse learning methods. They have activation function, hidden layer, and neuron numbers to determine prediction of parameters [4, 10]. ANNs needs to be trained using experimental data. Then words, they help for prediction. This is done by writing algorithms/using programming, known as machine learning. Applications of ANNs are suitable generally to solve a variety of engineering prophecy and optimization tribulations [5–9, 22, 23].

© Springer Nature Singapore Pte Ltd. 2018
A. V. Deshpande et al. (Eds.): SmartCom 2017, CCIS 876, pp. 29–36, 2018.
https://doi.org/10.1007/978-981-13-1423-0_4

Here, the performance of artificial neural networks was estimated with five different algorithms for determining which one would have more efficient in forecasting student's internet use for academic purpose. This paper demonstrates use of ANN for prediction applicability of ANN. The main objective is to discover internet usage and affecting variables. In order to construct an ANN, we need input and output variables along with mapping weights. To find out exact input and output variables, we have analyzed some prior studies for actual experimentations, including the Özcan and Buzlu [18], Odell et al. [20], Joiner et al. [15], Frangos et al. [12], Colley [10] and Ceyhan [3]. Keeping in mind these prior studies, we have enacted our dataset for experimentations which consisted of social, personal, financial variables associated with student's data. The next subsequent sections are organized as: second section dealt with experimental study and used method. Designing of an ANN model for forecasting of the internet usage are also considered in same section. In the third section results of the modelling and simulation experiments are addressed. Finally, in the fourth section conclusion is discussed in detailed.

2   Methodology

There is no exact way for selection of proper ANNs structure and training algorithm. The finest solution can be obtained by trial and error. Therefore a neural network, which has multilayer feed forward structure with two hidden layers, was designed first. This ANN was trained by using multilayer perceptron (MLP) networks [1, 4, 10, 23]. The MLP neural networks configuration is prepared by input layer, output layer and at least one hidden layer consisting of hidden neurons as shown in Fig. 2. The precise appearance for an output value of a three layered MLP is given by Nourani et al. [19]. The related terminology regarding input selection, weight and other details are as defined in [1, 13, 14, 16, 17, 19, 23].

$$y_k = f \circ \left[\sum_{i=1}^{M_N} W_{kj} \bullet f_h \bullet \left(\sum_{i=1}^{N_N} W_{ji} \bullet X_i + W_{j0} \right) + W_{k0} \right] \qquad (1)$$

For actual experimentations, a structured type questionnaire was tailored for data collection. The questionnaire contained questions reflecting performance, habitual, social and economical background of students. The study defined in benchmark work by Bhalchandra et al. [2] and it is considered as main drive for questionnaire. The questionnaire was made up of 46 questions whose narration was revised multiple times to smooth the understanding of students in the School of Computational Sciences. The data is stored in MS Excel 2007 sheet. The descriptive, or Yes/No type questions were transformed into numeric value viz. 1 or 0. The descriptive code formation for all variables materializes in Table 1.

Correlation analysis for the specified parameter is represented in Fig. 1. For choice of ANN inputs, initially, tried to pick some variables which are associated to student's use of internet. The test significance of the parameters performed through Chi square test (p-value less than 0.05) through SPSS 22.0v software and the significant factors are used for further study.

Table 1. List of the parameters under study

Variable	Code
Course code	M.Sc. (5), M.C.A. (6)
Gender	Male (1), Female (2)
Region	Urban (1), Rural (2), Foreign (3)
Fathers annual income	0–1 lakh (1), 1.1–2 lakh (2), 2.1–5 lakh (3), 5 lakh-above (4)
Mothers annual income	0–1 lakh (1), 1.1–2 lakh (2), 2.1–5 lakh(3), 5 lakh-above (4)
Family size	As reported
D you have part time job	Yes (1), No (0)
Do you have own PC at home	Yes (1), No (0)
Free time spare for study	Excellent (1), Good (2), Satisfactory (3), Bad (4), Very bad (5)
Free time spare with friends	Excellent (1), Good (2), Satisfactory (3), Bad (4), Very bad (5)
Do you use internet	Yes (1), No (0)

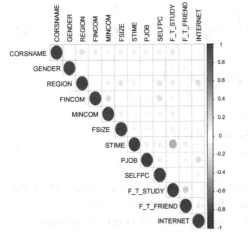

Fig. 1. Correlation matrix   **Fig. 2.** Optimal ANN model (11-10-1)

In this study, our questionnaire consists of some of the aspects viz. social, economical, personal, performance related question variables. Among these, the variables like course name, gender, region, father's income, mother's income, study time, part time job, self personal computer availability, free time to study and free time spending with friends were treated as input layers. The main concern of the study, that is, use of internet, is selected as an output to develop the model. The given information is processed as Rojas [21]. The normalization of input and output data was done before actual training vary from 0 to 1 by Eq. (2) [1, 23]:

$$\hat{X} = \frac{X - X_{min}}{X_{max} - X_{min}} \tag{2}$$

When the ANN training accomplished, the output value of the network is normalized and further, it desires denormalization in the form actual value by equation Eq. (3) [1, 23]:

$$X = \hat{X} \times (X_{max} - X_{min}) + X_{min} \tag{3}$$

Where, X is original value, X_{min} is minimum and X_{max} is maximum value in the series, respectively, and $\hat{X}$ is the normalized data.

The cross validation procedure [4, 8] was performed to split the data. The data split in terms of training and testing sessions, has an observable impact on the outcome. Based on this approach, training and testing sets were created by dividing 359 data points into them i.e. 70% (252) and 30% (107) respectively.

The coefficient of determination (R^2), root mean squared error (RMSE) and mean absolute relative error (MARE) (Eqs. 4–6) were used for evaluation of goodness of fit respectively, during the performance analysis of simulating data. The R^2 articulate the degree of the relation when two variables are linearly related. If R^2 is close up to 1, there is good correlation between variables.

$$R^2 = \left[\sum_{i=1}^{N} (P_i - \bar{P})(O_i - \bar{O}) \right]^2 \left[\sum_{i=1}^{N} (P_i - \bar{P})^2 (O_i - \bar{O})^2 \right]^{-1} \tag{4}$$

$$RMSE = \left[N^{-1} \sum_{i=1}^{N} (P_i - O_i)^2 \right]^{0.5} \tag{5}$$

$$MARE = \frac{1}{N} \sum_{i=1}^{N} \frac{|O_i - P_i|}{O_i} \times 100 \tag{6}$$

Where, N is the number of observations, P_i is the predicted values, O_i is the observed data, $\bar{P}$ and $\bar{O}$ are the mean values for P_i and O_i, respectively.

The R^2, RMSE and MARE values helped us to come with a measure for sensitivity of coefficients as well as their efficiency. If these values are larger than one, then it shows a hefty impact in defining the dependent variable. For proper demonstrations, we have created different topologies of ANN and then used them to evaluate. To predict the use of internet by students, we have created an ANN of three layers and is called a Multilayer Perceptron Network (MLP) with Levenberg-Marquardt algorithm [11, 16]. These MLP's are approximations to Newton's method [11] for correcting the weights. Trial and error method was used to come with an optimized ANN model. The first layer has eleven input variables and 10 hidden layer neurons. The output layer has one neuron included i.e. use of internet as the target. The value of the function expressed in terms of input, hidden and output layer is represented in plot (Fig. 2). The traditional, resilient back propagation with weight and without-weight backtracking; smallest learning rate and smallest absolute derivative algorithms with cross entropy method is measured and logistic function is treated as an activation function with the statement that logically output is non-linear.

We have extensively used R programming platform for deployment of the neuralnet and Metrics functions. The obtained result reveals that, the ten neurons show the optimum R^2, RMSE and MARE for all the algorithms.

3 Result and Discussion

In this study, the NN with fewer neurons is applied with five algorithms to simulate the results. The results stretch values in a representative network are useful in achieving the majority precise replication. The following Tables 2, 3, 4, 5 and 6 shows the detailed summary of sensitivity analysis performed for five algorithms through R software of our ANN model.

Table 2. Summary of sensitivity analysis of ANN performance model (traditional algorithm)

No. of hidden neurons	Error	Steps	Time	RMSE	MARE	MAPE
1	62.24	10	0.06	0.33	0.17	17.23
2	55.19	479	0.19	0.33	0.16	16.32
3	44.00	1332	0.58	0.33	0.15	15.64
4	36.88	8274	03.84	0.36	0.16	16.41
5	24.11	22280	10.78	0.36	0.15	15.97
6	38.44	1633	0.84	0.33	0.15	15.25
7	62.24	8	0	0.33	0.17	17.27
8	5.6	70527	42.12	0.40	0.16	16.92
9	5.57	18503	11.95	0.42	0.18	18.69
10	5.62	3063	2.09	0.37	0.15	15.56

Table 3. Summary of sensitivity analysis of ANN performance model (resilient back-propagation with weight backtracking)

No. of hidden neurons	Error	Steps	Time	RMSE	MARE	MAPE
1	62.24	27	0.02	0.33	0.17	17.24
2	50.89	543	0.19	0.34	0.16	16.49
3	62.24	14	0	0.33	0.17	17.27
4	34.29	7551	3.42	0.38	0.19	19.14
5	17.69	28582	13.64	0.39	0.17	17.33
6	38.41	1671	0.86	0.32	0.16	16.13
7	12.47	24073	1.34	0.35	0.13	13.87
8	5.62	20600	12.5	0.34	0.12	12.93
9	5.87	4850	3.19	0.32	0.11	11.74
10	5.61	37934	26	0.30	0.09	9.78

Table 4. Summary of sensitivity analysis of ANN performance model (resilient back-propagation without weight backtracking)

No. of hidden neurons	Error	Steps	Time	RMSE	MARE	MAPE
1	62.24	19	0.02	0.33	0.17	17.24
2	43.35	1303	0.45	0.35	0.16	16.68
3	33.42	2614	1.02	0.32	0.14	14.44
4	49.09	1462	0.61	0.33	0.15	15.95
5	31.19	2676	1.22	0.35	0.16	16.74
6	62.24	9	0	0.33	0.17	17.27
7	12.70	86491	45.58	0.37	0.16	16.07
8	5.63	20138	11.38	0.38	0.15	15.91
9	5.64	11938	7.48	0.34	0.12	12.39
10	5.56	8866	5.69	0.35	0.13	13.42

Table 5. Summary of sensitivity analysis of ANN performance model (smallest learning rate)

No. of hidden neurons	Error	Steps	Time	RMSE	MARE	MAPE
1	62.25	4	0	0.33	0.17	17.27
2	48.24	3449	1.25	0.33	0.17	17.04
3	40.47	9203	3.69	0.35	0.16	16.99
4	29.27	5201	2.33	0.34	0.14	14.54
5	23.50	6099	2.94	0.32	0.12	12.97
6	–	–	–	0.32	0.12	12.97
7	18.07	14508	8.19	0.38	0.16	16.28
8	5.76	39373	24.23	0.34	0.13	13.34
9	–	–	–	0.34	0.13	13.34
10	5.81	13890	9.56	0.36	0.13	13.91

Table 6. Summary of sensitivity analysis of ANN performance model (smallest absolute derivative)

No. of hidden neurons	Error	Steps	Time	R^2	RMSE	MARE	MAPE
1	47.89	5171	1.64	0.32	0.33	0.16	16.90
2	62.23	12	0.02	0.32	0.33	0.17	17.29
3	48.16	4553	1.81	0.32	0.33	0.16	16.94
4	32.13	6628	2.92	0.32	0.36	0.17	17.18
5	–	–	–	0.32	0.36	0.17	17.18
6	16.67	9346	4.94	0.32	0.35	0.15	15.24
7	13.30	24223	13.77	0.32	0.26	0.08	8
8	5.61	15078	8.97	0.32	0.36	0.14	14.03
9	5.57	40484	25.59	0.32	0.41	0.17	17.99
10	5.72	19924	13.45	0.32	0.37	0.14	14.85

The accuracy of MLP model is shown (Tables 2, 3, 4, 5 and 6) for the developed model. The R^2 is observed constant as 0.32 in all the cases. The RMSE, MARE and MAPE values were 0.35, 0.13 and 13.42% respectively with minimum error 5.56. The performances of MLP sculpt is precise and consistent represented (Tables 2, 3, 4, 5 and 6). The efficiency owes high degree of correlation between inputs and output variables of the model. Further, processes also have a count on the reliability of MLP model through sensitivity study to ensure the optimum results with minimum error. Tables 2, 3, 4, 5 and 6, clearly shows the model adequacy through the sensitivity analysis of the study and on the 10th hidden neuron it found to be optimum. In this study, 11-10-1 is found worth ANN model. In Table 5, hidden neurons 6 and 9, and in Table 6, the hidden neuron 5 unable to construct networks which simply shows the incompatibility with our data sets regarding to obtain optimal target.

4 Conclusion

The study highlights effective use of ANN for forecasting/prediction of the behavioral patterns of students in terms of internet usage. The prediction criteria were mainly based on socio-economic aspects of students. Experimentations, activation and training of ANN were done using R software on a personally devised dataset. Five types of neural networks algorithms were tested for prediction of students internet use for academic purpose. Through sensitivity analysis, it was observed that, our ANN model gave 11-10-1 structure as optimal one. Further, the hidden neuron numbers 6, 9 and 5 hidden layers showed inappropriateness for smallest learning rate and smallest absolute derivative algorithms. The forecasting capability of the ANN is superior in Resilient Back-propagation without weight backtracking than rest of the algorithms and it had a marginally better performance.

References

1. Barzegar, R., Moghaddam, A.A.: Combining the advantages of neural networks using the concept of committee machine in the groundwater salinity prediction. Model. Earth Syst. Environ. **2**(1), 26 (2016)
2. Bhalchandra, P., et al.: Prognostication of student's performance: an hierarchical clustering strategy for educational dataset. In: Behera, H.S., Mohapatra, D.P. (eds.) Computational Intelligence in Data Mining—Volume 1. AISC, vol. 410, pp. 149–157. Springer, New Delhi (2016). https://doi.org/10.1007/978-81-322-2734-2_16
3. Ceyhan, A.A.: Predictors of problematic internet use on Turkish university students. Cyber Psychol. Behav. **11**(3), 363–366 (2008)
4. Chang, F.J., Tsai, W.P., Chen, H.K., Yam, R.S.W., Herricks, E.E.: A self-organizing radial basis network for estimating riverine fish diversity. J. Hydrol. **476**, 280–289 (2013)
5. Chatterjee, S., Chakraborty, R., Dey, N., Hore, S.: A quality prediction method for weight lifting activity (2015)
6. Chatterjee, S., Sarkar, S., Hore, S., Dey, N., Ashour, A.S., Balas, V.E.: Particle swarm optimization trained neural network for structural failure prediction of multistoried RC buildings. Neural Comput. Appl. **28**(8), 1–12 (2016)

7. Chatterjee, S., Ghosh, S., Dawn, S., Hore, S., Dey, N.: Forest type classification: a hybrid NN-GA model based approach. In: Satapathy, S.C., Mandal, J.K., Udgata, S.K., Bhateja, V. (eds.) Information Systems Design and Intelligent Applications. AISC, vol. 435, pp. 227–236. Springer, New Delhi (2016). https://doi.org/10.1007/978-81-322-2757-1_23

8. Chatterjee, S., Hore, S., Dey, N., Chakraborty, S., Ashour, A.S.: Dengue fever classification using gene expression data: a PSO based artificial neural network approach. In: Satapathy, S.C., Bhateja, V., Udgata, S.K., Pattnaik, P.K. (eds.) Proceedings of the 5th International Conference on Frontiers in Intelligent Computing: Theory and Applications. AISC, vol. 516, pp. 331–341. Springer, Singapore (2017). https://doi.org/10.1007/978-981-10-3156-4_34

9. Chatterjee, S., et al.: Hybrid modified Cuckoo Search-Neural Network in chronic kidney disease classification. In: 2017 14th International Conference on Engineering of Modern Electric Systems, EMES, pp. 164–167. IEEE, June 2017

10. Colley, A.: Gender differences in adolescents' perceptions of the best and worst aspects of computing at school. Comput. Hum. Behav. **19**(6), 673–682 (2003)

11. Dunham, M.H.: Data Mining: Introductory and Advanced Topics. Pearson Education, India (2006)

12. Frangos, C.C., Frangos, C.C., Sotiropoulos, I.: Problematic internet use among Greek university students: an ordinal logistic regression with risk factors of negative psychological beliefs, pornographic sites, and online games. Cyberpsychol. Behav. Soc. Netw. **14**(1–2), 51–58 (2011)

13. Fijani, E., Nadiri, A.A., Moghaddam, A.A., Tsai, F.T.C., Dixon, B.: Optimization of DRASTIC method by supervised committee machine artificial intelligence to assess groundwater vulnerability for Maragheh-Bonab plain aquifer, Iran. J. Hydrol. **503**, 89–100 (2013)

14. Ghavidel, S.Z.Z., Montaseri, M.: Application of different data-driven methods for the prediction of total dissolved solids in the Zarinehroud basin. Stoch. Environ. Res. Risk Assess. **28**(8), 2101–2118 (2014)

15. Joiner, R., et al.: Gender, Internet identification, and Internet anxiety: correlates of Internet use. CyberPsychol. Behav. **8**(4), 371–378 (2005)

16. Kisi, O., Tombul, M., Kermani, M.Z.: Modeling soil temperatures at different depths by using three different neural computing techniques. Theoret. Appl. Climatol. **121**(1–2), 377–387 (2015)

17. Maqsood, I., Khan, M.R., Huang, G.H., Abdalla, R.: Application of soft computing models to hourly weather analysis in southern Saskatchewan, Canada. Eng. Appl. Artif. Intell. **18**(1), 115–125 (2005)

18. Özcan, N.K., Buzlu, S.: Internet use and its relation with the psychosocial situation for a sample of university students. Cyberpsychol. Behav. **10**(6), 767–772 (2007)

19. Nourani, V., Baghanam, A.H., Adamowski, J., Gebremichael, M.: Using self-organizing maps and wavelet transforms for space–time pre-processing of satellite precipitation and runoff data in neural network based rainfall–runoff modeling. J. Hydrol. **476**, 228–243 (2013)

20. Odell, P.M., Korgen, K.O., Schumacher, P., Delucchi, M.: Internet use among female and male college students. CyberPsychol. Behav. **3**(5), 855–862 (2000)

21. Rojas, R.: A short proof of the posterior probability property of classifier neural networks. Neural Comput. **8**(1), 41–43 (1996)

22. Sreekanth, P.D., Geethanjali, N., Sreedevi, P.D., Ahmed, S., Kumar, N.R., Jayanthi, P.K.: Forecasting groundwater level using artificial neural networks. Curr. Sci. **96**(7), 933–939 (2009)

23. Wagh, V.M., Panaskar, D.B., Muley, A.A., Mukate, S.V., Lolage, Y.P., Aamalawar, M.L.: Prediction of groundwater suitability for irrigation using artificial neural network model: a case study of Nanded tehsil, Maharashtra, India. Model. Earth Syst. Environ. **2**(4), 196 (2016)

Conversational Bots with Workflow Services Architecture for Smart Travel Systems

Hari Bhaskar Sankaranarayanan[(✉)] and Jayprakash Lalchandani

International Institute of Information Technology, Bangalore, India
s.haribhaskar@iiitb.org, jtl@iiitb.ac.in

Abstract. In this paper, we will propose and discuss an architecture with workflow services that are managed by conversational bots that enable seamless and smart travel experience for travelers. Conversational bots are modern chat messengers where the computer is trained to learn and respond to human queries using Natural Language Processing (NLP) for various languages and advanced machine learning algorithms. We propose an architecture that integrates various services using conversational bots into the travel workflow that consists of search, booking, travel documents processing like visa, immigration, checking in, onboarding and helping to provide destination services like cab booking, hotels, and events. Workflow typically maintains state, context, performers, and tasks. Conversational bots can easily integrate the input and output to such workflows through an orchestration layer that manages the business logic, context variables and enable activities for both human and conversation bot to complete a goal or task. We also built a prototype using IBM Watson platform to provide an illustration of the architecture services.

Keywords: Bots · Travel · NLP · Machine learning · Architecture

1 Introduction

The travel life cycle consists of pre-booking or search phase, booking phase, on travel phase and post trip phase. Conversational bots are disrupting various facets of business right from inspiring the traveler to pick the place to service the traveler request along with the travel life cycle. They decrease the cost for answering basic queries as it is trained to handle interactions using past user queries. They also act as round the clock support agent for traveler queries without having a travel agent or service desk to be physically available or on phone to answer the queries [1, 2]. They can automate routine jobs which don't require much manual intervention in an intelligent manner. The advent of Machine Learning (ML) algorithms and NLP techniques makes such disruption as a new world order of human-computer interaction (HCI). While bots are invented recently, it is important to appreciate the underlying complexity of travel enterprise. The travel enterprise is connected with various actors and systems in form of workflows to accomplish the phases of travel life cycle. The bots need to have a strong capability to seamlessly connect with travel enterprise workflow layer and current architectures need to support them with minimal development efforts and costs. In this research, we discuss an architecture that can help achieve the interactions between the

© Springer Nature Singapore Pte Ltd. 2018
A. V. Deshpande et al. (Eds.): SmartCom 2017, CCIS 876, pp. 37–43, 2018.
https://doi.org/10.1007/978-981-13-1423-0_5

bot and workflow services. The paper is organized into following sections, Sect. 2 discusses the motivation behind this research, Sect. 3 proposes the architecture, Sect. 4 discusses the prototype developed using IBM Watson platform for passport and visa processing, Sect. 5 highlights the limitations and future work, Sect. 6 provides related work in this area and Sect. 7 provides the conclusion.

2 Motivation for Connecting Conversational Bots and Workflow Services

The motivation for architecting the conversational bots with workflow services is discussed in the following parts:

Why are conversational bots important for present and future?

In a typical enterprise, the service desk that manages service requests uses a good amount of manpower for even answering basic queries. The existing web pages vary across different travel providers that make the learning curve high for the end traveler. Also, the traveler might expect a natural way of interactions through conversational queries. For instance searching for a travel destination based on personal preferences may be a simple natural query like "I would like to go for a weekend trip now". There are voice interfaces built on top of the conversational interfaces that is powered by voice recognition technologies like Amazon Alexa and Google Home. Conversational bots solve this problem by understanding the natural intents of the user and provide relevant results. They are meant to be simple, intuitive and stateless. They might have access to some context variables like geolocation and user profile that can even help tailor the results. They pass the user query to a conversational layer which identifies the right intent and responds with a dialog or as a set of results.

Why are workflow services important?

Most of the enterprise systems consist of a set of business processes that are connected with a set of tasks, activities that need to be performed in certain order of steps defined by the enterprise procedures and actors within a certain time which are driven by Service Level Agreements (SLA) and to accomplish the overall business objectives like resolving customer issues on time. In the case of travel systems, there are multiple systems behind the scenes that work together to accomplish a task like getting the traveler experience the right destination of weekend travel. Workflow allows the further steps like booking and managing the trip in case the user is interested in travel options. Workflow manages the end-to-end activities and it is important that layers underneath manage the human-computer interaction for a seamless travel experience. Workflow also provides additional context like hold, wait and track for user actions like booking ticket, refunds and cancellation processing respectively.

The motivation of this research is to evolve an architecture that combines the workflow capabilities along with the conversational capabilities that can solve the travel problem of managing multiple systems in an end to end fashion. Smart travel systems refer to hassle free and more seamless interaction across travelers without providing information repetitively and also add contextual interactions like geo location, session, and work flow state. The architecture layers must be capable of holding the state and context with respect to users and activities that can be managed by different stakeholders. While most of the travel booking applications provide hotel and car options while booking air travel, the bot can be configured with an under-the-hood workflow including sending messages and tracking them that uses a combination of push notifications and the traveler can act upon the notification to re-engage in a natural conversation based on the response from the bot.

3 Proposed Architecture

The proposed architecture is depicted in Fig. 1. The architecture consists of the following layers:

1. User layer – the user query the bot with natural text interface by typing in the chat window in multiple languages.
2. Bot layer – the bot consists of the bot framework client and server. The client consists of passing the queries through payload as JSON format usually to the rest service over HTTP protocol.
3. Conversational platform layer – this layer interprets the queries to entities and uses NLP, machine learning to map to the right dialog response to be returned to the user. The platform provides components that can connect with orchestration layer for complex business logic processing like workflow and connect to external systems.
4. Orchestration layer – This consists of business logic that can connect and orchestrate workflow and other functionalities like aggregation, routing and manage context on user sessions.

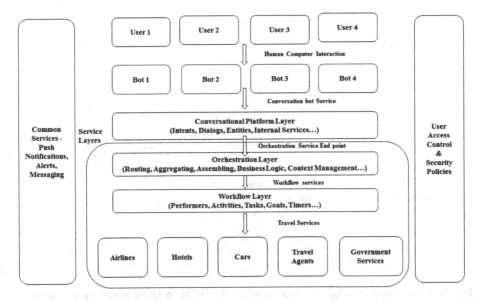

Fig. 1. Conversational bots workflow services architecture

5. Workflow layer – This is the workflow engine layer where the activities can be started, stopped, paused or resumed. The layer connects with underlying travel services layer to achieve the required business process steps.
6. Travel services layer – This layer consists of various underlying systems and end points for connecting to the airline, hotels travel agents, cars, and government services like visa processing.
7. The common services layer include user access control, security policies, alerts, push notifications and messaging that can be managed across various layers.

4   Prototype for Passport and Visa Workflow Services

To illustrate and instantiate the above architecture we have used IBM Watson [3] Conversation services and developer cloud to host the various layers. The workflow services are managed in JBoss Business Process Management Suite (jBPM) [4]. For the calendar services that can be used for booking appointments, we had used Google calendar. The objective is to demonstrate the capabilities of the architecture by integrating various layers. In this prototype, we have taken the use case of booking and tracking visa appointments. The following activity diagrams are illustrated below:

1. User queries the bot with "Get the best slot for a visa appointment". Figure 2[*] shows that orchestrator matches the appointments available with use calendar and provides calendar instances as an output to the bot.

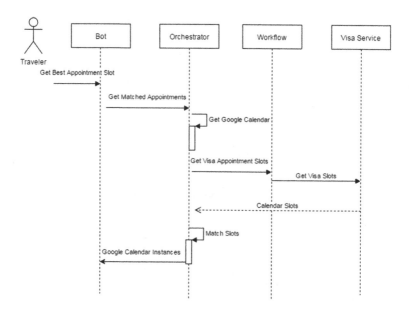

Fig. 2. Appointment booking use case activity flow ([*]UML notation used here is from free online tool draw.io)

2. User downloads, edits, and uploads the visa application form through the bot. Figure 3 shows that workflow is resumed back once the application form is edited and uploaded to the visa service.
3. User queries the bot for "Get the status of my visa application". Figure 4 highlights the courier status retrieved by the workflow and displayed to the traveler on the status of visa dispatched.

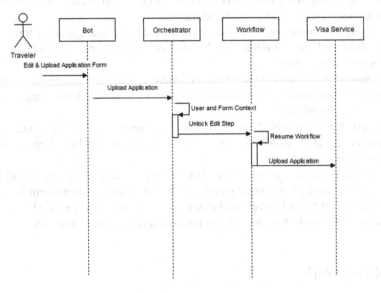

Fig. 3. Edit application form use case activity flow

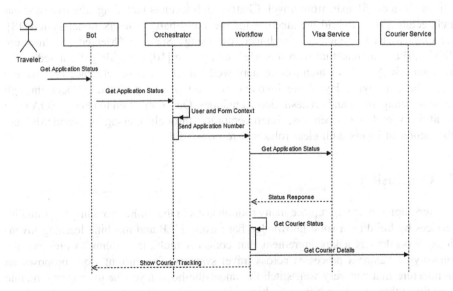

Fig. 4. Get application status use case activity flow

5 Limitations and Future Work

The current research work has certain limitations and can be extended further in scope:

- The architecture for bots is fairly nascent since the conversational message based systems based on artificial intelligence and tools are evolving over a period of time.
- The tooling and aligning multiple technologies will be a challenge for the implementation architectures since some of them are open sourced and many commercial tools expose interfaces in a restricted manner.
- Messaging platforms and bots were existent for quite some time in form of help desk chats and the adoption will be critical since natural language processing technologies are maturing.
- Workflow systems can upgrade towards a more channel-driven approach where bot framework extensions can be provided as a set of channel related components like bot service end points.
- The work can be extended for a reference architecture for future messaging platforms for travel by modeling more work flows that can be addressed through conversational interfaces.
- In this paper, we have covered very basic flow of visa services. The travel flow is vast with various phases highlighted earlier and more prototypes can be built by integrating end to end travel workflows that can touch upon multiple underlying systems. This would help to validate the architecture evolution better.

6 Related Work

Chatbots are making its way in many industries including software development [5], citizen services [6] apart from travel. Chatbot architectures including adaptive modular architecture [7], a hybrid architecture for the multi-party conversational system [8], personal assistant reference architectures using Service Oriented Architecture (SOA) [9] and architecture with serverless computing [10] are widely discussed in the literature. SOA style of architecture may well suit for chatbot reference architecture since the underlying layers are invoked by a set of encapsulated services through session management and orchestration techniques. Our motivation to choose SOA style is also to embrace openness, interoperability through messaging standards and abstraction of layers with clear roles and responsibilities.

7 Conclusion

Conversational bots will replace many routine tasks in the future providing high-quality services by building a solid knowledge base using NLP and machine learning inventions. Workflow is a key ingredient that connects multiple systems to preserve the integrity of business processes across travel systems. The current work proposes an architecture that can very well stitch the under-the-hood layer for managing dynamic workflows that can meet business objectives and expose them through simple queries for travelers. Smart travel systems need smarter architectures and combining the power of chatbots with workflows will lead to the next generation of bots which are intuitive to address the end to end travel life cycle.

References

1. Amadeus website. http://www.amadeus.com/blog/22/04/chat-bots-impact-travel-industry/
2. DirectPay website. http://blog.directpay.online/travel-businesses-benefit-chatbots
3. IBM Watson Developer Cloud. https://www.ibm.com/watson/developercloud/
4. JBPM. https://www.jbpm.org/
5. Storey, M.-A., Zagalsky, A.: Disrupting developer productivity one bot at a time. In: Proceedings of the 2016 24th ACM SIGSOFT International Symposium on Foundations of Software Engineering. ACM (2016)
6. Boden, C., Fischer, J., Herbig, K., Spierling, U.: CitizenTalk: application of chatbot infotainment to e-democracy. In: Göbel, S., Malkewitz, R., Iurgel, I. (eds.) TIDSE 2006. LNCS, vol. 4326, pp. 370–381. Springer, Heidelberg (2006). https://doi.org/10.1007/11944577_37
7. Pilato, G., Augello, A., Gagli, S.: A modular architecture for adaptive chatbots. In: 2011 Fifth IEEE International Conference on Semantic Computing, ICSC. IEEE (2011)
8. de Bayser, M.G., et al.: A hybrid architecture for multi-party conversational systems. arXiv preprint arXiv:1705.01214 (2017)
9. Zambiasi, S.P., Rabelo, R.J.: Proposal for reference architecture for personal assistant software based on SOA. IEEE Lat. Am. Trans. **10**(1), 1227–1234 (2012)
10. Yan, M., et al.: Building a chatbot with serverless computing. In: Proceedings of the 1st International Workshop on Mashups of Things and APIs. ACM (2016)

Power Mitigation in High-Performance 32-Bit MIPS-Based CPU on Xilinx FPGAs

Neha Dwivedi$^{(\boxtimes)}$ and Pradeep Chhawcharia

Department of ECE, Techno India NJR Institute of Technology, Udaipur, India
nehadwivedi18@gmail.com

Abstract. The aim of this paper is, to introduce design of a 32-bit MIPS (Microprocessor Interlocked Pipeline Stages) based processor containing five stages of pipeline, to incorporate power optimization techniques for FPGAs. The functionality of this design has been verified by writing Verilog Modules on Xilinx 14.5 selecting the target FPGA device. The design helps to improve the speed and increase the whole throughput of the processor. Synthesis and simulation results have been taken from ModelSim 6.2c. Analysis the design floorplan of 32-bit CPU and study of the detailed netlist has been performed on PlanAhead tool, which was giving accurate results. From the performance viewpoint, FPGA-based implementation of processor is totally centered on the designing of processor architectures in Verilog HDL and increasing the overall speedup with power mitigation at Spartan class (45 nm and 90 nm) FPGAs. The significant features of this work are; increased number of instructions, enhanced performance and low power consumption with HDL modification techniques. The design has 5 levels of logic and delay of 14.202 ns with the maximum frequency of operation at 70.413 MHz for Spartan-6. Optimized power observed was about 22.72% after applying power reduction techniques, which make this work useful for low power FPGAs.

Keywords: MIPS · CPU · ISA · FPGA · Verilog · RISC · ModelSim
HDL · Power reduction

1 Introduction

High-performance electronic devices releasing a large amount of heat inflict practical limitation on how far can we enhance the performance of the system. Field Programmable Gate Arrays gives time to market quickly and the re-programmability feature usually makes them the important part of the system. It can be used to implement an entire System-On-Chip (SOC). To implement a complex design like CPU system using top-down approach, the design has divided into small sub-functions which has been implemented using one logic block. Programming interconnects are the reason behind the connected sub-functions in logic blocks [23].

In 1980's, a research development on the MIPS architecture was introduced at Stanford University. The corporation was originated in 1984 to industrialize this research. Though, various companies create processor chips following MIPS-based architecture, with taking LSI logic, Philips, Toshiba NEC and NKK Switches.

© Springer Nature Singapore Pte Ltd. 2018
A. V. Deshpande et al. (Eds.): SmartCom 2017, CCIS 876, pp. 44–55, 2018.
https://doi.org/10.1007/978-981-13-1423-0_6

This MIPS design is a quarter of a century old, its chips are generally used in present systems such as CISCO Routers, other embedded applications including set-top boxes for digital TV, cable modems and DVD recorders. Because of its clean and simple architecture, it is very convenient for designers. A series of evolution has been evolved for this architecture branded as; MIPS-I, II, III and IV. Each Instruction Set Architecture (ISA) is an advanced version of the former one. Earlier MIPS i.e. I and II instruction set architectures were 32-bit architectures, 64-bit capabilities were added in MIPS-III with a subset of core 32-bit and architecture IV expanded this [21].

Today, the increased complexities in real-time application have high power requirements. That computational power can accomplish by high performance components as RISC or CISC microprocessors and non-programmable chips like Application Specific Integrated Circuits (ASICs) and FPGAs. Mostly, to upgrade the speed and performance of the system, algorithms are needed which can compute at low running time complexity. Secondary way to increase the performance is designing a high speed VLSI chip for such systems. Yet, current processor designs are more concerned with exhibiting multi-stage pipeline power for quick execution.

RISC 32-bit processor is a simple Von-Neumann computer system. RISC processor performs simple operations and it supports very few addressing modes which mostly are register based. Most of the instruction operates on data available in internal registers. Only Lw and Sw can access data in external memory. Pipelined architecture saves time in the execution of instruction because in the pipeline there is an overlapping of instruction that takes place. The minimum clock cycle time is needed to execute one instruction in pipelined architecture. Instead of that, single-cycle architecture takes more number of clock cycles for execution.

Nowadays, FPGA and other electronic devices need to be realized with power optimization methods because of power consumption and area. An integrated flow provided by Xilinx ISE with the Model Technology, ModelSim Simulator, allows the user to run simulation from the Xilinx Project Navigator. Obtaining dynamic power reduction goals in Spartan-6 and Spartan-3 using Hardware Description Language (HDL) modification was a challenging task. Static power increases with transistor size shrink; it is ruled by transistor leakage current. Dynamic power was the matter of interest at 45 nm and 90 nm CMOS technologies [20].

2 Overview

This section discusses the previous related work done on RISC processors. Low power techniques have been used related to RISC processor design including Clock gating, Power gating, Multi-Voltage gating, etc. Soumya Murthy, Usha Verma has introduced a low power reduction technique to design DLX based CPU using HDL modification [1]. In this method, Verilog HDL coding styles were used to minimize power for Xilinx FPGA. Although the dynamic power was optimized up to 13.33% but it has increased the overall path delay. Ritupurkar, Thakare, Korde presented the RISC CPU based on MIPS using VHDL [2]. It described the instruction set, architecture and timing diagram of processor and achieved reduced delay at 1.35 GHz at the cost of high power consumption. Joseph, Sabarinath has proposed a method of clock gating to reduce power. The major disadvantage for this technique is, the control logic for the clock gating increases the design area requirements [3]. Kelgaonkar, Prof. Kodgire [4] has designed 32-bit Pipelined RISC on Spartan-6 including five stage pipelined RISC CPU and implemented ALU block on Spartan-6 using Xilinx.

According to the literature survey, dynamic power has been reduced at different levels of design. In this paper, we have optimized the dynamic power on MIPS architecture by taking different FPGAs using HDL modification technique and comparing it with previous work analysis of the same technique used which is giving better results.

3   RISC Processor Specifications

This 32-bit RISC processor with five stage pipeline has the following key concepts:

1. MIPS 32-bit processor instruction set architecture, which has R-type, I-type and J-type instruction formats.
2. It consists of 32-bit wide program counter and a bank of 32 general purpose registers of 32-bit.
3. It has 32-bit address and data lines to execute any ALU operation.
4. Five stage pipeline registers: fetch, decode, execute, memory-access and write back. Better performance and throughput due to pipelined MIPS architecture designed using Verilog HDL.
5. Synthesizable code designed in Xilinx ISE for all compatible FPGA devices like Spartan-3E, Spartan-3A, Spartan-6, Virtex-5, Virtex-6, etc.
6. Power optimization at architecture and design level resulting in low power consumption.
7. Simulation results are clearly showing the proper execution of instructions.

3.1   Instruction Set Architecture

The majority of microprocessor designs start with specifying what the microprocessor is expected to be able to do, which is translated into its ISA. Instruction Set Architecture (ISA) defines the microprocessor from a machine-language programming perspective, including the following:

• Instruction set
• Structure of the register file
• Addressing modes
• Data types and data representation
• Run-time operations (exceptions for instance).

A top-down approach has been followed to illustrate the system and CPU architectures highlighting their sub-components. A CPU instruction format is a single 32-bit aligned word that are Immediate, Jump and Register.

Immediate Instructions; it is also possible to alert a constant as one of the two operands. The constant is coded into the instruction as a 16-bit integer; hence, it must remain in the range of $-32678 \leq$ constant ≤ 32767 for addi, addiu, slti or $0 \leq$ constant ≤ 65535 for andi, ori, xori. The constant is converted into a 32-bit value either by filling the upper 16 bits with a copy of the sign bit i.e. addi, addiu, slti, sltiu or with 0's i.e. andi, ori, xori [8]. The branch instructions; They have 16 bits for encoding a target address, comparative to the current instruction, making most of memory from any given location. Though, There are times, when it is necessary to transfer control to an arbitrary location [8]. R-type instructions involve arithmetic, logical, and shift operations on MIPS, which encode the operation to be executed and three general registers- Rs, Rt and Rd. It is predictable, in MIPS documentation, to refer to the two source registers as Rs and Rt, and one destination register as rd. Each of them is actually encoded in the instruction as a 5-bit integer that specifies one of the 32 general registers [8].

4   32-Bit RISC Pipelined Architecture

Pipeline improves instruction throughput instead of individual instruction execution time. The processor which has been designed is divided into five pipeline stages. The five pipelined stages are fetch, decode, execute, memory and write-back. Since, each stage has only one-fifth of the whole logic, the clock frequency is nearly five times faster. Speedup can be calculated as

$$\textbf{Speedup} = \textbf{CT}_{\textbf{old}}/\textbf{CT}_{\textbf{new}} \tag{1}$$

Therefore, the latency of each instruction is ideally unmovable; however the throughput is ideally five times better. Overall CPU time for the processor can be calculated as

$$\textbf{CPU Time} = \textbf{No. of Clock Cycles} * \textbf{Clock Cycle Time} \tag{2}$$

Steps of Pipelined MIPS are as follows:

1. Instruction Fetch Unit-	IR: Memory [PC]; PC := PC+4
2. Instruction Decode Unit-	A := Reg [IR[25:21]], B := Reg [IR[20:16]] ALUout := PC+ Sign_extend[IR[15:0]]
3. Execute| Memory Address| Branch Unit-	Memory: ALUout:= A+ IR[15:0] R-Type : ALUout:= A op B Branch: if A = B then PC := ALUout
4. Memory access| R-Type Unit-	Lw: MDR := Memory[ALUout] Sw: Memory[ALUout] := B R-Type: Reg [IR[15:11]] := ALUout
5. Write back unit-	Lw: Reg [[20:16]] := MDR

Instruction Fetch is the first stage in MIPS pipelined structure. Instruction code fetched from this stage which is obtained from the Instruction memory and then goes to

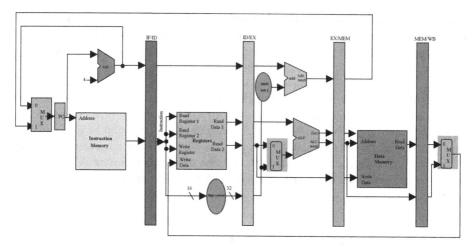

Fig. 1. MIPS datapath with five stage pipeline [8].

next stage of pipeline. Instruction Decode is the second stage in this architecture. It has dual-port memory, Register file contains register data which read and write the register data according to the opcode operation, branch targets are also calculated in this stage. This stage is having control unit who decides what values must be set to, which depends upon the given instruction. Next stage is the execution unit having the executions performing in ALU block determined by ALUop signal coming from the previous stage. Branch address is calculated by adding the PC+4 to sign extend immediate field and shift left with 2 bits using adder. The next stage of pipeline is memory access, where Lw and Sw instructions access from the data memory block [8].

During the write-back stage, mutually instructions write back their results into the register file situated in the second stage of pipeline. This pipeline architecture has been shown in Fig. 1; Where the MIPS five stage pipelined datapath is containing all the architectural blocks. This datapath has control line which is controlling all the operations and instruction executions in the datapath.

5   Power Mitigation Techniques in Xilinx FPGAs

Power consumption of any electronic design can be divided into two principal categories that is, Static power and Dynamic power. Dynamic power in overall falls as transistors minimize, small transistors have low parasitic capacitances with shorter interconnects. By using different static and dynamic power reduction techniques, for instance, Triple Oxide Method, Transistor Distribution Optimization, Integrated Blocks, Clock Gating Enhancements, LUT4 vs LUT6 and I/O Power Reduction in Spartan-6. If we compare the two Spartan class FPGAs Spartan-6 with Spartan-3A, Then the result comes as, the normal static power in Spartan-6 devices is 50% lower and dynamic power is 40% lower. Xilinx has secured power reductions in Spartan-6 FPGAs by transforming on different levels of the FPGA design [20].

Low power methodology needs dynamic power reduction at all the design abstraction layers such as Architecture Level - Parallelism, Pipelining, Redundancy, Data Encoding; Circuit Logic Level - Energy Recovery, Logic Styles and Transistor Sizing; System Level- Partitioning and Power down; Algorithm Level - Complexity, Concurrency and Regularity; Technology Level - Threshold Reduction and Multi-threshold devices. Pipelining in DSP applications reduces the dynamic power by inserting the inputs regularly and decreases net-lengths and reduces glitches [23].

Static power is developed due to quiescent current inside the transistors composed of FPGA and switching of the transistors results in generation of dynamic power.

$$P(dynamic) = C.V^2.f \qquad (3)$$

$$f = P_{dt}.f_{clk} \qquad (4)$$

Where, f = frequency at which the data transition happen and
P_{dt} = the probability of data transition.

In HDL Modification Techniques, a well-organized and high quality HDL code can lowers the unwanted data toggling of design which results the ample amount of dynamic power saving. Likewise, logic optimization, removal of redundant logic and proper resource sharing in the RTL design helps to shrink on-chip power. The IOs power consumes maximum dynamic power. Power reduction can be attained at the IOs level [1]. Multiple Verilog HDL coding options are available to optimize the dynamic power for Xilinx FPGA such as: Synchronous reset design, Minimize local resets, Controlling the use of clock enables, Low power designing for Block RAM arrays, designing small memory buildings with LUTs (<4 k bits) [22].

5.1 Data Transitions Minimizing

The data bus continues transitioning in extreme cases. Meanwhile, there is no default condition for allocating constant. There may be particular handshaking signal that shows the data is applicable so this may not affect the device functionally. But the data bus consumes power because of transitions.

5.2 Resource Sharing

There should be no redundant logic elements in RTL coding style. Any logic element has a capacitance attached to it that will contribute to power consumption. Data transitioning via the logic will again increase the power dissipation throughout the design.

5.3 Avoiding Unnecessary Transition

Few signals toggle in many designs when they are not required, but, functional verification cannot discover those unnecessary transitions because they fulfill the logical requirements. After proper checking, if that logic is twisted to overpower those pointless transitions, it can help to avoid power dissipation.

5.4 Controlling Counters

The aim of counter designing is that, they can start and stop as per the constraint. The counter may unnecessarily keep on counting due to improper coding and the unwanted counting of data can cause high amount of power dissipation through the design.

5.5 Synthesis Optimization

Specific limits and RTL coding in front end level can decrease the logic optimization. That is due to additional logic will attach the extra capacitance and that will utilize extra power. Similarly, by analyzing the code coverage reports, one can check redundant hardware generation.

5.6 Pipelined Design for DSP Implementation

Power can be reduced through pipelining by registering the inputs at regular intervals. Thus, it will reduce the total net-lengths and minimize the glitches. We can choose these techniques depending upon the latency and hardware requirements.

5.7 Register Retiming

The concept of register timing is widely used to improve timing and to reorder the combinational and sequential logics of certain datapath. In special cases, it is the saving of logic for the design, and so can help with the power consumption.

6 Functional Simulation and Results

The pin diagram of proposed five stage pipelined architecture of RISC containing RTL schematic view has been shown in Fig. 2. Synthesized design has been created successfully on FPGA using Xilinx ISE 14.5.

Above is the RTL (Register transfer level) representation of 32-bit RISC processor design. This representation (.ngr file created in XST) is generated using the Xilinx ISE. The intention of this level is to be as near as to the original HDL code. In the RTL design, the top entity is characterized in terms of blocks such as adders, multiplexers and look up tables. To check the module functionality of designed architecture with five stage pipeline, a set of instructions were executed perfectly on ModelSim 6.2c and simulation results are showing in Fig. 3.

The design was synthesized and analyzed for two different Xilinx Spartan class FPGAs. Spartan-3 and Spartan-6 (90 nm and 45 nm) FPGA chips operates at different operating frequencies and voltages. To calculate on-chip power of FPGAs, Xilinx Power Estimator tool and Xilinx Power Analyzer tool are available for power estimation and power calculation. Floorplans shown in Figs. 4 and 5 are implemented in

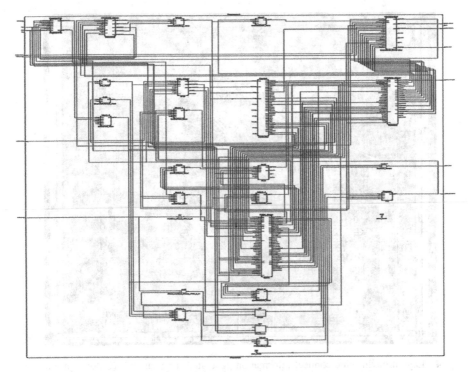

Fig. 2. RTL schematic for 32-bit RISC top entity

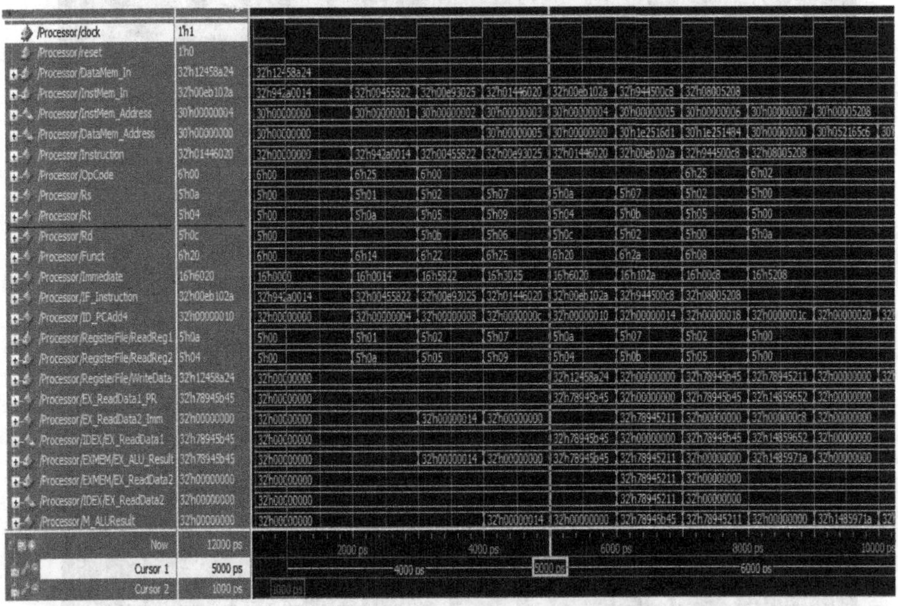

Fig. 3. Simulated results of 32-bit pipelined CPU using ModelSim 6.2c

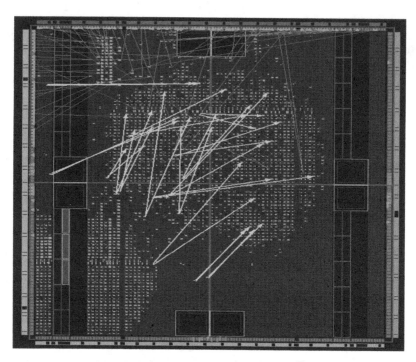

Fig. 4. Layout having interconnect information generated for Spartan-3 (Color figure online)

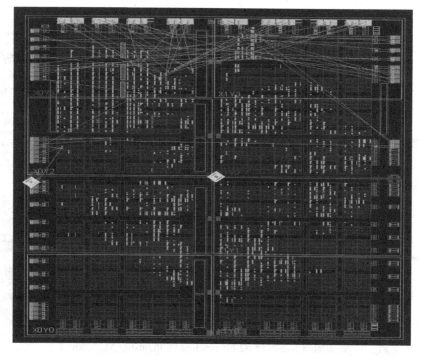

Fig. 5. Layout containing interconnects generated for Spartan-6 (Color figure online)

PlanAhead software. The floorplan is giving layout representation containing information of the utilized number of LUTs, DSPs, Slices and IOBs.

Table 1. Timing summary for Xilinx Spartan FPGAs

Timing constraints	Spartan-6	Spartan-3
Speed grade	−3	−4
Minimum period	14.202 ns (maximum frequency 70.312 MHz)	15.391 ns (maximum frequency 64.973 MHz)
Minimum input arrival time (before clock)	3.939 ns	5.691 ns
Maximum output required time (after clock)	6.722 ns	8.628 ns

In Fig. 4, is the representation of Spartan-3 FPGA where lines highlighted in yellow colour containing the information of 32-bit ALU_result interconnects and Fig. 5 is the representation of Spartan-6 having marked points in yellow are indicating the clock information. Netlist for the RTL design has been generated and interconnects have been shown clearly. Light blue and violet highlights are giving the information of number of utilized LUTs and IOBs (Table 1).

On-chip power consumption has been calculated using Xpower analyzer and estimated Xilinx power estimator tool, which has been shown using graph in Fig. 6.

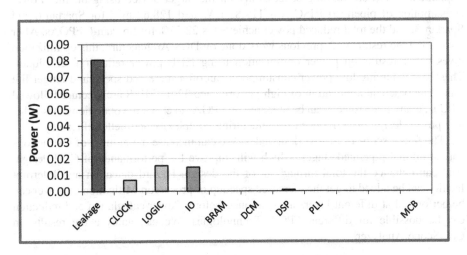

Fig. 6. On-chip power by function (Vccint = 1.23 V) for Spartan-6

To get the accurate results of total power consumption, .ncd, .xpa and physical constraint file (.pcf file) need to be loaded into XPA which is generated while implementation. Obtained power analysis and produced results have been mentioned in Table 2.

Table 2. Summary of power optimization on FPGAs

On-chip power consumption parameters	Normal power of RISC (mW)	Power optimized using DLX architecture [1] (%)	Power optimized designed using MIPS on SPARTAN-3 (%)	Power optimized designed using MIPS on SPARTAN-6 (%)
Clock	5.80	19.32	31.04	−1.55
Logic	3.39	2.07	8.56	−1.76
Signals	7.99	9.39	37.43	−1.12
IOs (dynamic)	37.74	48.79	54.96	60.26
MULTs	0.82	0	0	0
Quiescent	99.28	0.32	0.59	19.42
Total	155.03	13.33	17.04% Vccin = 1.23 V	22.72% Vccin = 1.23 V

7 Conclusion and Future Work

The high performance 5 stage pipelined MIPS- based 32-bit processor has been designed using Verilog HDL. Synthesis report for the target FPGA device shows that the proposed design has 5 levels of logic and delay of 14.202 ns and maximum operating frequency of 70.413 MHz for Spartan-6. Some blocks of the design have been implemented and are running successfully on the target device using bit file. Power consumption of pipelined RISC was 119.82 mW and 128.62 mW for Spartan-6 and Spartan-3, and the total reduced power achieved is 22.72% for Spartan-6 FPGAs. After comparing the results with previous work done on DLX Architecture, this optimization gives better results on power optimization using HDL power reduction techniques. These CPUs having low power consumption can offer increased speed and longer life time. The practical application of high performance 32-bit MIPS architecture followed CPU is, many live projects can be prepared on FPGAs to check the operations. Also, this low power design gives reduced manufacturing complexity and better efficiency.

The future scope of this work includes: We can increase the number of instructions and additional pipelined stages, which will improve the performance of CPU design. And can enhance the total throughput of the design. Hazard detection and Interrupt facility can be added to get the increased speedup of processor. Mitigation of power can be performed at different layers as mentioned before. Power calculation and reduction can be possible for different FPGA Technologies. We can analyze the results on ChipScope Analyzer.

References

1. Murthy, S., Verma, U.: Designed 32-bit RISC CPU based on DLX architecture. In: ICCUBEA, Pune, India. IEEE (2015)
2. Ritupurkar, S.P., Thakare, M.N., Korde, G.D.: RISC CPU based on MIPS using VHDL. In: ICACCS, Coimbatore, India. IEEE (2015)

3. Joseph, N., Sabarinath S.: FPGA based implementation of high performance architectural level low power 32-bit RISC core. IEEE (2009)
4. Kelgaonkar, P.S., Kodgire, S.: Designed 32-bit pipelined RISC on Spartan-6. IEEE (2016)
5. Ajith Kumar, P., Vijaya Lakshmi, M.: Design of a pipelined 32-bit MIPS processor with floating point unit. Int. J. Innov. Res. Sci. Eng. Technol. 5(7) (2016). ISSN 2319-8753
6. Topiwala, M.N., Saraswati, N.: Implementation of a 32-bit MIPS based RISC processor using Cadence. In: 2014 IEEE International Conference on Advanced Communication Control and Computing Technologies (ICACCCT) (2014)
7. Eissa, A.S., Elmohr, M.A., Saleh, M.A., Ahmed, K.E., Farag, M.M.: Advanced SHA-3 instruction set extension for a 32-bit RISC processor architecture. IEEE (2016)
8. Patterson, D.A., Hennessy, J.L.: Computer organization and design, the software hardware interface. ISBN 1-55860-604-1
9. Katke, S.P., Jain, G.P.: Design and implementation of 5 stages pipelined architecture in 32 bit RISC processor. Int. J. Emerg. Technol. Adv. Eng. 2(4), (2012). ISSN 2250-2459
10. Takahashi, Y., Sekine, T., Yokoyama, M.: Design of a 16-bit non-pipelined RISC CPU in a two phase drive adiabatic dynamic CMOS logic. Int. J. Comput. Electr. Eng. 1(1), 1793–8198 (2009)
11. Valadimas, S., Tsiatouhas, Y., Arapoyanni, A.: Cost and power efficient timing error tolerance in flip-flop based microprocessor cores. IEEE (2012)
12. Ao, Q., Jin, G., Su, W., Cai, S., Chen. S.: Optimizing memory access with fast address computation on a MIPS architecture. IEEE (2014)
13. Kumar, M.K., Shabeena Begum, M.D.: FPGA based implementation Of 32 bit RISC processor. Int. J. Eng. Res. Appl. (IJERA) 1(3), 1148–1151 (2011)
14. Xiang, Y.Z., Ding, Y.H.: Instruction decoder module design of 32-bit RISC CPU based on MIPS. IEEE (2008)
15. Lee, I., Lee, D., Choi, K.: ODALRISC: a small, low power and configurable 32-bit RISC processor. IEEE (2008)
16. Gschwind, M.: FPGA prototyping of a RISC processor core for embedded applications. VLSI 9, 241–250 (2001)
17. Kumar, M.K., Shabeena Begum, M.D.: FPGA based implementation of 32-bit RISC processor. Int. J. Eng. Res. 1(3), 1148–1151. ISSN 2248-9622
18. Plachno, R.S.: A true single cycle RISC processor without pipelining. ESS Design White Paper
19. Xilinx: Spartan-6 FPGA Datasheet: DC and Switching Characteristics, January 2015
20. Klein, M.: Power consumption at 45 nm. Xilinx, White Paper, August 2016
21. Handouts from math-cs, MIPS ISA: Computer organization, a brief introduction to the MIPS architecture (2015)
22. Xilinx: Optimizing FPGA power with ISE design tools, Xcell J. (60), 16–19 (2007)
23. Xilinx: Power methodology guide for ISE tools, April 2013
24. Dwivedi, N., et al.: Design and implementation of 32-bit RISC processor with five stage pipeline. In: International Conference on Recent Innovations in Engineering and Technology (ICRIET) (2017)
25. Naidu, R.P.: FPGA design flow, October 2013
26. Yeap, G.: Practical Low Power Digital VLSI Design. Kluwer Academic Publishers, Alphen aan den Rijn (1998)

Challenges in the Field of Aspect Level Sentiment Analysis

Neha Nandal[1(✉)], Jyoti Pruthi[1], and Amit Choudhary[2]

[1] Manav Rachna University, Faridabad, India
neha28nandal@gmail.com
[2] Maharaja Surajmal Institute, New Delhi, India

Abstract. In the field of technology, organizations come up with their brand-lines and it is becoming a trend where organizations wisely launch their on-series of their respective sources and then put it offline. The field of sentiment analysis has been playing a great role for organizations. It is becoming possible now to get to know about the opinions of customers about various sources produced by organizations in terms of positive, negative and neutral polarities. The field of aspect-level sentiment analysis comprises a goal to find and aggregate sentiment on entities mentioned within documents. This paper presents the various challenges occurred in field of sentiment analysis and Aspect level sentiment analysis. The objective is also to present the methods and tools used by various researchers to get the effective results in field of machine learning.

Keywords: Sentiment analysis · Aspect level sentiment analysis
Machine learning · Classification

1 Introduction

Sentiment Analysis is catching researcher's attention which is one of the field of NLP i.e. Natural Language Processing. It determines the polarity of various articles, blogs etc. and presents them in the form of positive, negative or neutral. This technique is useful to get to know what are the different views of individuals.

There are mainly two phases involved in the technique that is Sentiment Identification and Sentiment Aggregation and scoring. The first phase helps to find out entities in the data to be processed and perform association of different opinions with related entities. The second Phase then performs scoring of each entity related to other entities of the same class. The processing of text data can be done using Lexican based method. The other methods like POS tagging, Wordnet etc. can also be helpful in performing Sentiment analysis on various text data.

The area of Sentiment Analysis has various challenges which includes spam and fake statements, NLP overheads, summarization of opinions, bipolar words which have two meanings in the text etc. Various other issues that can be focused on are redundancy of data, extraction of features, grouping of same words, classification of opinions and if they all take together that makes a good challenge in the area.

© Springer Nature Singapore Pte Ltd. 2018
A. V. Deshpande et al. (Eds.): SmartCom 2017, CCIS 876, pp. 56–62, 2018.
https://doi.org/10.1007/978-981-13-1423-0_7

1.1   Aspect Level Sentiment Analysis

The basic model of Aspect Level Sentiment Analysis is shown in Fig. 1. The given flow of the approach shows how opinions or sentiments are extracted. The first step is to collect the data to be analysed that can be reviews, documented text, comments on social networking sites etc. The data then preprocessed where tasks like POS tagging, Spell correction are performed. This phase can also be called as Classification of aspects where the motive is to find out that opinions are positive, negative or neutral. This phase comprises of Aspect tagging of sentences. After final classification of opinions, the evaluation has been done. The challenging part in methods of learning is to find out whether the data contains the features relevant to the individuals work.

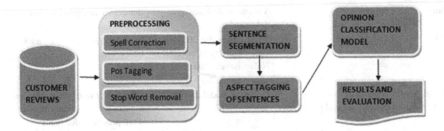

Fig. 1. Model of aspect level sentiment analysis

1.2   Sentence-Level Aspect Sentiment Analysis

The goal here is to identify the opinions with the information like Feature Detection, and Sentiment Polarity for a given opinionated document of a target entity like a gadget, a restaurant or and organization.

At the sentence-level, the annotations should be assigned taking also into account the reviews context, since there is requirement to examine the whole review for correctly identifying the pairs of a sentence and their polarities.

Sentence Level Aspect Sentiment analysis can be categorized in two parts as

- Document level Sentiment Analysis checks the polarity of the document by considering it as on box.
- Aspect Based Sentiment Analysis Checks for each aspect or feature of the text and then analyze.

Aspect based Sentiment Analysis performs better when it comes about in depth analysis of text as it concentrated on each feature while document level Sentiment Analysis give overall score.

The challenge in Aspect Based Sentiment Analysis is to find out aspect and polarity of opinions which combines the opinions of different set of reviews of individuals for entities.

In different reviews, the aspects with different sentiment are considered to find out the winning feature in the targeted document to be processed. The conflict label should be assigned in case where dominant sentiment is not clear.

2 Empirical Study

The research work presented here is based on comparing work of 18 researchers to find out which area of Aspect level sentiment analysis is challenging to work on. The review of research is presented in Table 1.

Table 1. Research review

Ref. No.	Domain	Algorithm used	Conclusion
Popescu et al. [1]	Customer reviews	**Opine**, an unsupervised opinion extraction system introduced	22% higher precision in results
Pang et al. [2]	Survey	Various techniques discussed	Sentiment analysis problem areas
Pak et al. [3]	Tweets	SVM (Alpaydin 2004), CRF (Lafferty et al. 2001), Naïve Bayes classifier (Anthony 2007)	Naïve Bayes classifier yielded best results
Tchalakova et al. [4]	Maximally occurring phrases in product reviews	Unigram model, bigram model, SVM	Different phrases were used as aspects and promising results were presented for same
Yu et al. [5]	Customer reviews (11 popular products in 4 DOMAINS)	Sentiwordnet, SVM, Maximum Entropy	SVM came up with better results
Bross et al. [6]	Customer reviews	Corpus based approach	The results presented were strongly accurate and showed that the sentiment classification performance has been improved
Virmani et al. [20]	Remarks by teachers about students	SAS, SPSS techniques	Results in tabular form as very high, high, moderate and low polarities
Mohan et al. [21]	Customer reviews on restaurant domains	KNN, Naïve Bayes	KNN performs better with increased number of instances
Mesnil et al. [7]	IMDB movie reviews	Hybrid approach used	Strong results presented as positive and negative sentiments
Saif et al. [8]	9 Twitter datasets	Entity level sentiment analysis	The amazingly great results were presented in the paper using tweets and average F-measure metric
Klenner et al. [9]	French, German, English phrases	The appraisal theory, polarity lexicon	Bipolar phrase detection using fine-grained polarity lexicon
Dong, Wei et al. [10]	Sentence level classification in documents	Adaptive multi-compositionality (AdaMC) layer	85.4% to 88.5%. Accuracy achieved
Li et al. [11]	Text data by users	Probabilistic matrix factorization (PMF)	A novel SUIT model is developed for sentiment analysis
West et al. [12]	Social network user opinions	Markov randaom field	Concluded the proposed work as NP-hard problem

(continued)

Table 1. (*continued*)

Ref. No.	Domain	Algorithm used	Conclusion
Gryc et al. [13]	2.8 million blog posts by 16,741 bloggers crawled between April 2008 and May 2009	logic-based framework and hybrid approach	The results presented to show that the classification task's complexity has been highly minimized
Shefrin et al. [15]	Corpus data	size, B/M, and the market premium factors	A fama-french three factor model is developed
Fang et al. [16]	Product reviews from Amazon	Sentiment polarity categorization	Experiments for both sentence-level categorization and review-level categorization were performed with promising outcomes
Feldman et al. [17]	Discussed various reviews used by researchers	SAS, SPSS techniques	A novel algorithm developed
Poria, Cambria, Hazarika, Vij, [18]	3 datasets used and results compared	Sentiment and emotion clues both in the framework included. CNN-SVM, CNN	Sarcasm detection using emotion and personality models. Promising results presented
María del Pilar Salas-Zárate et al. [19]	Corpus data of Twitter	N-gram method	Evaluation using precision, recall and F-measure

Popescu and Etzioni [1] projected a work on solving a problem by victimizing an automated approach to mine polarity of reviews. It is tough for a customer to read and analyze sizable amount of reviews and type a product reviews opinion. Feature based sentiment analysis specialize in completely different aspects or opinions of a product.

Pak, Paroubek et al. [3] In this paper, the focus is on using Twitter, the most popular micro blogging platform for the task of sentiment analysis. Tchalakova, Gerdemann, and Meurers [4] In this paper, Researchers identified the phrases which are used largely and developed a dataset for the same. The aim was to perform classification task on product reviews. Yu, Zha, Wang, Chua [5] In this paper, topic of aspect ranking is discussed. The online reviews of customers are used as dataset. The goal was to identify important aspects of products automatically. Bross, Ehrig [6] This Paper Projected a piece of work where mechanically analyzing the opinions expressed in customer reviews is of high connexion in several application situations. The challenging area was of context dependant phrases or text. The presented work shows a newly developed approach which helps in extending automatically the existing text to specific domain. Mesnil, Mikolov et al. [7] In this paper, Researchers compared several machine learning approaches to binary classification problem, and combine them to develop a novel approach. They showed how to use the standard generative language models for this task. Saif, He et al. [8] In this paper, Researchers used tweets fo STS-Gold dataset. They proposed a newly developed approach that catches automatically the similar context in the data and estimated the conditional probability of an entity. Klenner, Tron et al. [9] presented Bipolar phrase detection and analysis using Fine grained polarity and the appraisal theory. Dong, Wei et al. [10] Researchers presented a general framework to develop the composition of each semantic. The results presented showed the better results that presents AdaMC performs better than the other sentiment methods of classification. Li, Wang et al. [11] In this paper, Researchers presented a new topic model which can be considered as an integration between sLDA and PMF. This model can develop the topics of text and latent factors of user-items in parallel manner. West, Paskov et al. [12] In this paper, Researches proposed a model which identifies opinion of one person about the other person. The dataset used was of social networking site where both persons are signed in. They proved that this problem is NP-hard but the problem can be slightly handled with Markov random field. Gryc, and Moilanen et al. [13] In this paper, Researchers used the initial dataset of posts (nearly 700) regarding Obama. The goal was to model a blogosphere sentiment focused on Barack Obama during election in 2008. Schouten and Frasinca [14] Researchers presented a survey on Aspect Based Sentiment Analysis. The survey presented various techniques used to analyze the sentiments based on various entities. The techniques presented can be helpful in various domains. Shefrin et al. [15] In this paper, Using data from 1999–2014, Researcher presented evidence suggesting that perception of most investors are showing negative reactions towards size and positive reactions towards (B/M) book-to market equity and to market beta. This evidence supported size, B/M, and the market premium as being the basis for the Fama-French factor. Fang and Zhan [16] Researchers focused on the area of sentiment Polarity categorization. The results presented in the paper showed effective results which shows effective improvements in the focused technique. Poria, Cambria, Hazarika, Vij [18] Researchesrs, in this paper discussed about detection of Sarcasm as one of the key areas in the field of Sentiment Analysis. del Pilar Salas-Zárate et al. [19] Researchers, in this paper considered the domain of health and specifically diabetes for Aspect level sentiment analysis. The major challenge area in the field of Sentiment Analysis is shown in Table 2 below.

Table 2. Problem areas in sentiment analysis

Challenges
• The text to be analyzed can include Bi-polar phrases, NLP overheads, or SPAM and FAKE phrases which are very critical to be handled in Sentiment Analysis.
• The same word, having different meanings in different domains is very hard to analyze by standard techniques.
• The aspects of any product or resource are very challenging to be mapped to rating.
• On-time temporal behavior of any resource is hard to manage.
• Detection of Sarcasm on big corpus data.
• Use of health domains for Sentiment Analysis like stress, depression etc.
• Analysis of Behavior on the basis of surfing activities of User.

3 Conclusions and Future Plan

Sentiment Analysis helps to identify sentiments on entities in documents. There are several areas of Sentiment Analysis on which much work has been done. Various researchers worked on sentiment polarity categorization, many statistical packages available such as SAS and SPSS which has sentiment analysis modules; work on Sentiment pattern extraction also caught attention in research area. Aspect level sentiment analysis can be helpful for applications in various domains. Amazingly good results provided in finding entity or its aspect and their Sentiments. But it is still an infantry area and much more work can be done in this field. The work on health domains for Sentiment Analysis is catching much attention of Researchers. The areas like Sarcasm detection, Bipolar words, Spam and Fake words have much scope to be worked on.

The future work is to focus on the features of the domains in the area of Aspect level Sentiment Analysis. Machine Learning Approaches to get effective results will be focused on.

References

1. Popescu, A.-M., Etzioni, O.: Extracting product features and opinions from reviews. In: Kao, A., Poteet, S.R. (eds.) Natural Language Processing and Text Mining, pp. 9–28. Springer, London (2007). https://doi.org/10.1007/978-1-84628-754-1_2
2. Pang, B., Lee, L.: Opinion mining and sentiment analysis. Found. Trends Inf. Retr. 2(1–2), 1–135 (2008)
3. Pak, A., Paroubek, P.: Twitter as a corpus for sentiment analysis and opinion mining. In: LREc, vol. 10, pp. 1320–1326 (2010)
4. Tchalakova, M., Gerdemann, D., Meurers, D.: Automatic sentiment classification of product reviews using maximal phrases based analysis. In: Proceedings of the 2nd Workshop on Computational Approaches to Subjectivity and Sentiment Analysis, ACL-HLT 2011, 24, June 2011, pp. 111–117 (2011)
5. Yu, J., Zha, Z.-J., Wang, M., Chua, T.-S.: Aspect ranking: identifying important product aspects from online consumer reviews. In: Proceedings of the 49th Annual Meeting of the Association for Computational Linguistics, Portland, Oregon, 19–24 June 2011, pp. 1496–1505 (2011)
6. Bross, J., Ehrig, H.: Automatic construction of domain and aspect specific sentiment lexicons for customer review mining. In: CIKM 2013. ACM, 13/10, 27 October–1 November 2013. ISBN 978-1-4503-2263-8
7. Mesnil, G., Mikolov, T., Ranzato, M.A., Bengio, Y.: Ensemble of generative and discriminative techniques for sentiment analysis of movie reviews. arXiv organization, arXiv preprint arXiv:1412.5335 (2014)
8. Saif, H., He, Y., Fernandez, M., Alani, H.: Semantic patterns for sentiment analysis of Twitter. In: Mika, P., et al. (eds.) ISWC 2014. LNCS, vol. 8797, pp. 324–340. Springer, Cham (2014). https://doi.org/10.1007/978-3-319-11915-1_21
9. Klenner, M., Tron, S., Amsler, M., Hollenatein, N.: The detection and analysis of bi-polar phrases and polarity conflicts. In: Proceedings of 11th International Workshop on Natural Language Processing and Cognitive Science, Venice, Italy (2014)

10. Dong, L., Wei, F., Zhou, M., Xu, K.: Adaptive multi-compositionality for recursive neural models with applications to sentiment analysis. In: Twenty-Eighth AAAI Conference on Artificial Intelligence (2014)
11. Li, F., Wang, S., Liu, S., Zhang, M.: SUIT: a supervised user item based topic model for sentiment analysis. In: Twenty-Eighth AAAI Conference on Artificial Intelligence (2014)
12. West, R., Paskov, H.S., Leskovec, J., Potts, C.: Exploiting social network structure for person-to-person sentiment analysis. arXiv preprint arXiv:1409.2450 (2014)
13. Gryc, W., Moilanen, K.: Leveraging textual sentiment analysis with social network modelling. From Text Polit. Pos. Text Anal. Across Discip. **55**, 47 (2014)
14. Schouten, K., Frasincar, F.: Survey on aspect-level sentiment analysis. IEEE Trans. Knowl. Data Eng. **28**(3), 813–830 (2015)
15. Shefrin, H.: Investors' judgments, asset pricing factors and sentiment. Eur. Fin. Manage. **21**(2), 205–227 (2015)
16. Fang, X., Zhan, J.: Sentiment analysis using product review data. J. Big Data (2015). https://doi.org/10.1186/s40537-015-0015-2
17. Feldman, R.: Techniques and applications for sentiment analysis. Commun. ACM **56**(4), 82–89 (2016)
18. Poria, S., Cambria, E., Hazarika, D., Vij, P.: A deeper look into sarcastic Tweets using deep convolutional neural networks. In: COLING 2016 arXiv:1610.08815[cs.CL] (2016)
19. del Pilar Salas-Zárate, M., et. al: Sentiment analysis on Tweets about diabetes: an aspect-level approach. In: Computational and Mathematical Methods in Medicine, vol. 2017, Article ID 5140631 (2017)
20. Virmani, D., Malhotra, V., Tyagi, R.: Sentiment analysis using collaborated opinion mining. Int. J. Adv. Res. Comput. Sci. Softw. Eng. **3**(7), July 2013
21. Mohan, A., Manisha, R., Vijayaa, B., Naren, J.: An approach to perform aspect level sentiment analysis on customer reviews using sentiscore algorithm and priority based classification. (IJCSIT) Int. J. Comput. Sci. Inf. Technol.

Feature Extraction Using DCT Based Traffic Sign Recognition

Surbhi Jha[✉] and Ajay Khunteta

Rajasthan Technical University, Kota, India
surbhijha24x7@gmail.com

Abstract. Traffic sign recognition (TSR) is a complex system to recognize many traffic sign, but sometimes it does not gives the correct result. To solve the problem of this system introduced self-organization Feature map (SOFM) neural network to classify traffic sign and feature extracted by Discrete Cosine Transform (DCT) of sign images. The proposed scheme is tested under manual database and shows the effectiveness by recognition rate is high and extraction time is less as compared to literature works.

Keywords: Discrete cosine transform (DCT)
Self-organizing feature map (SOFM) · Traffic sign recognition (TSR)

1 Introduction

Traffic sign recognition is aimed to minimize the number of accidents, which can be faced during the vehicle drive in urban areas. In literate many techniques presented to detect and recognize the traffic sign [1]. SFC-tree detector is used for multiclass traffic sign detection, catch different traffic signs. This method is time saving and it directly classifying these detection categories [2]. Hough transforms have been used to Identifying the position of arbitrary shapes, most commonly circle or ellipse commonly [3, 4]. The Hough Transform is used for used extract the feature of an image. Support vector machine (SVM) has been used in traffic sign recognition method [5, 6]. Support vector machines are combined attainment process with allied learning algorithms which describe the data used for classification or regression analysis. This method is not robust at classing rate. Edge and shape are an important part of traffic sign detection process [7]. Sparse Representation Classification (SRC)-based traffic sign recognition methods used for classification purpose [8, 9]. SRC based method is robust to processing but it does not give an accurate result. There are many TSR neural network methods have been explained in the previous section for classification of different traffic sign image such as MS-CNNs, C-CNNs, M-NNs [10–12]. Generally NN based system is too slow, it takes more time to processing. Better result can be obtain by a new technic "Self- organized feature map neural network" (SOFM-NN). SOFM is multidimensional map. It take less extraction and processing time, 1000 epoch used to processing.

Color detection and image segmentation is a valuable part of the traffic sign detection process, in color detection, it gives information between objects based on

A. V. Deshpande et al. (Eds.): SmartCom 2017, CCIS 876, pp. 63–70, 2018.
https://doi.org/10.1007/978-981-13-1423-0_8

their color and Image segmentation convert the digital image into super pixels [13, 14]. High Contrast Region Extraction (HCRE), is an additional method of ROI. It is non-integral region. HCRE recommended by cascaded detection methods [15].

Feature extraction is a measuring part of a particular image data or it examines the architecture unoriginal value which mean features. It is non-redundant gives the information of the learning and universality. Feature extraction is the accomplice [16]. Discrete cosine transform (DCT) has been used for traffic sign recognition [17], it has many important parts. DCT is independent of the data point, in DCT high frequency parameters are rejected. DCT algorithm works faster than other [18, 19]. DCT is mostly used in "JPEG". In two-dimension and multi-dimension - DCT use $N \times N$ parts are computed and result in the entropy coded, in this part N is 8 normally and DCT is applied to all row and column of the container. DCT is used for Image Corporation. The reminder of this paper is organized as follow: In Sect. 2 show the Self organized feature map (SOFM). In Sect. 3 Proposed methodology of Traffic sign recognition (TSR) introduced. Section 4 show experimental result and simulation and Sect. 5 show the conclusion of the present work.

2 Self-organizing Feature Map (SOFM)

SOFM is unsupervised learning to a produce multidimensional maps. This method used for method dimensionality. There are n number input images connected according to the number of aspects to be used in the classification [18, 19]. SOFM uses neural network without hidden layer and neurons in the output layer competing with each other, so that only one neuron (the winner) can fire at a time (Fig. 1).

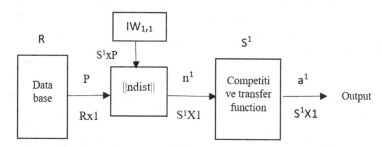

Fig. 1. Architecture of a simple SOFM neural network [19]

Figure 2 show input vector p of the above image. Input vector's value P is input for the $\| \text{ndist} \|$. The input weight matrix $IW_{1,1}$ introduced a vector, this vector produces an S^1 feature. Distances between the input image vector and vectors $jIW_{1,1}$ are negative vector. This describes the input row of the weight matrix. The $\| \text{dist} \|$ container calculates the input n^1 of a competitive layer by recommendation the Euclidean distance between input image vector p and the weight vectors. Now competitive transfer function C receives an N input image vector for a zone and again it retreat neuron output 0 for all the neurons other than the winner, the neuron afflicted with the absolute element of net input image n^1 I. The winner's output is 1. The neuron whose value is nearest to the input vector has the smallest negative net input and now for winners the competition to output is a1. Therefore, the competitive transfer function (C) produces a1 for output element a_j^1 it is equivalent to I*, the "winner". All component in a 1 or 0.

$$||X - W|| = \sqrt{\sum_{i=1}^{n} (x_i - w_i)^2} \tag{1}$$

Where Input patterns $X = (x_1, x_2, \ldots, x_n)$ is compared with the weight vector $W = (w_1, w_2, \ldots, w_n)$ of neuron in the output layer. The winner is the neuron whose weight w_l is closest to the input x in terms of Euclidean distance.

3 Proposed Methodology

Traffic signal recognition is categorized into multilevel section as illustrated in Fig. 2, show the two important part of traffic sign Recognition, feature extraction and traffic sign recognition are identified. These sections are divided into sub section.

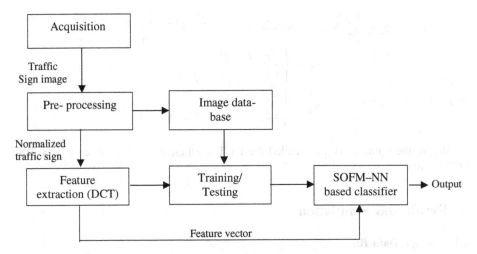

Fig. 2. Flowchart of the proposed method

3.1 Pre-processing

In the pre-processing section of the TSR, detected traffic sign is cropped from an input sign image and converted RGB image into gray scale image. The access region is now reshaped into 64 × 1 and resized into 8 × 8 bit to create the traffic sign recognition system scale invariant. Now histogram equalization is used for brightening of the sign image.

3.2   Feature Extraction Method

There are numerous technic available for feature extraction method. We are dealing with DCT for extracting the features. Feature of every image is stored in over data base, firstly extract the image than image is stored in the feature vector. Feature vector is create the unique data base consist all the feature vector. Now feature vector stored in storage device. To recover the all the images those are similar to target image than compare it with the feature vector of image. Now DCT is applied to all the traffic sign image and some of the feature is selected to generate feature vector. This feature vector gives the value of each vector.

3.3   Discrete Cosine Transform

In TSR method after feature extraction method we computed 2D-DCT of an image. Where D is an image of DCT matrix. 2D-DCT initially used to image compression of small blocks (8×8 pixel in our case). Then upper and lower (N − 2) diagonal is extracted after and before flipping D, further we computed standard deviation value. Its coefficient matrix is divided into (4N) part and each part (N) of standard deviation of each part is examine. As a result feature is formed of feature vector.

$$B_{pq} = \alpha_p \alpha_q \sum_{m=0}^{M-1} \sum_{n=0}^{N-1} A_{mn} \cos \frac{\pi(2m+1)p}{2M} \cos \frac{\pi(2n+1)q}{2N}, \quad \begin{array}{l} 0 \leq p \leq M - 1 \\ 0 \leq q \leq N - 1 \end{array}$$

$$\alpha_p = \begin{cases} \frac{1}{\sqrt{M}}, & P = 0 \\ \frac{\sqrt{2}}{M}, & 1 \leq p \leq M - 1 \end{cases}$$

$$\alpha_q = \begin{cases} \frac{1}{\sqrt{N}}, & q = 0 \\ \frac{\sqrt{2}}{N}, & 1 \leq q \leq N - 1 \end{cases} \tag{2}$$

Where the value of B_{pq} are called the DCT coefficients of A. A is an 8×8 2D-DCT matrix.

4   Result and Simulation

4.1   Image Data Base

Traffic sign images were benchmarks to the traffic sign classification. For training and testing, purpose image is sub divided into two section. During the processing of SOFM, we have used 30 images, 6 subject image and each image with a different traffic sign. Figure 3 show the image data base.

Fig. 3. Image data base

4.2   Training/Testing Image

The detected sign image is re-sized into 8 × 8 bit and then converted into gray-scale image. Now this image is reshaped into 64 × 1 array, where 64 rows and 1 column for every image. 5 test image have been used in the technique which are in turn used in the data base. This approach is performed on all traffic sign, test images to form the input data for testing the recognition system.

Accordingly, input data use 30 image of a matrix of a 64 × 30 with 64 rows and 30 columns. Each row and columns value demonstrate the singular vector value which is used in processing of DCT (8 × 8). Further, the input vectors for the expound SOFM are distributed over a 2D-input space varying over [0 255], this explains the gray scale pixels. Now SOFM neural network is used to train dimensions [64 2], Here pixel value

Fig. 4. Traffic sign recognition using SOFM-NNs output

Table 1. Comparison of different TSR methods

Different methods	Classification rate (%)			Program execution time (ms)
	Speed sign	Danger sign	Prohibitory sign	
SOFM-NN (Proposed work)	100	100	99.89	25
SVM+ESRC [2]	97.84	97.21	99.07	33
C-NN [10]	99.47	99.07	99.93	690
MS-CNN [11]	98.61	99.87	98.03	476
SRGE [8]	98.06	99.22	97.35	95

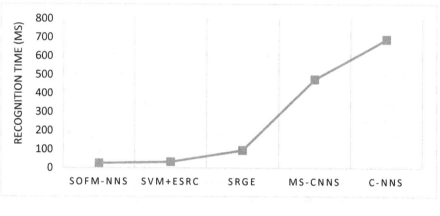

(a)

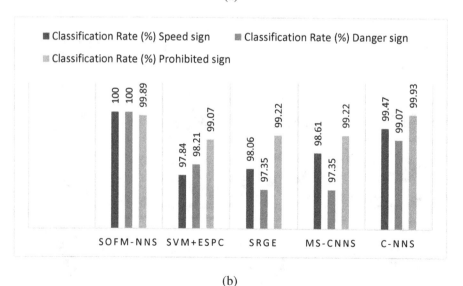

(b)

Fig. 5. TSR recognition result (a) show the classification time (b) show the classification rate (recognition rate) (%)

is 64, which is minimum and maximum value, this accent have been represented a sample of a traffic sign image. Till the end SOFM fabricated with the single-layer feed forward SOFM map, this map value is 128 weights and a competitive transfer function.

Now Euclidean distance calculate the distance between input patterns and the weight vector of neuron in the output layer and neurons in the output layer competing with each other, so that only one neuron (the winner) can fire at a time. The winner is the neuron whose weight is closest to the input pattern.

Many sign images have been used for image database for performing the experiment. Here experiment result is accomplished. As compare to other SOFM-NN gives better experiment results (Fig. 4).

5 Conclusion

Feature extraction is an important part in traffic sign recognition system, and for many other recognition problem. This paper described discrete cosine transform (2D-DCT) based feature extraction of traffic sign and classification of sign using self-organized feature map neural networks. Results shows the effectiveness of proposed scheme as shown in Table 1 and Fig. 5. The recognition rate is high and feature extraction time is less as compared to literature works. Proposed TSR system is designed on MATLAB 2015 and image processing toolbox.

References

1. Liu, C., Chang, F., Chen, Z.: Rapid multiclass traffic sign detection in high resolution image. IEEE Trans. Intell. Transp. Syst. **15**(6), 2394–2403 (2014)
2. Trivedi, M.M., Moeslund, T.B.: Fast traffic sign recognition via high-contrast region extraction and extended spare representation. IEEE Trans. Intell. Transp. Syst. **13**(4), 1484–1497 (2016)
3. Wang, G., Ren, G., Wu, Z., Zhao, Y., Jiang, L.: A robust, coarse-to-fine traffic sign detection method. In: Proceedings of the International Joint Conference on Neural Network, Dallas, TX, USA, pp. 754–758 (2013)
4. Zaklouta, F., Stanciulescu, B.: Segmentation masks for real-time traffic sign recognition using weighted HOG-based tree. In: Proceedings of the International Conference on Intelligent Transportation Systems, Washington, DC, USA, pp. 1959–1975, December 2011
5. Greenhalgh, J., Mirmehdi, M.: Real-time traffic sign detection and recognition of road traffic sign. IEEE Trans. Intell. Transp. Syst. **13**(4), 1498–1506 (2012)
6. Yuan, X., Hao, X., Chen, H., Wei, X.: Robust traffic sign recognition based on color global and local oriented edge magnitude patterns. IEEE Trans. Syst. **13**(4), 1466–1477 (2014)
7. Chandrasekhar, B.M., Babu, V.S., Medasani, S.S.: Traffic sign representation using spare-representation. In: Proceedings of the International Conference on Intelligent Systems and Signal Processing, Anand, India, pp. 369–372 (2013)
8. Lu, K., Ding, Z., Ge, S.: Spare-representation-based graph embedding for traffic sign recognition. IEEE Trans. Intell. Transp. Syst. **13**(4), 1515–1524 (2012)
9. Zhang, K., Sheng, Y., Li, J.: Automatic detection of road traffic signs from natural scene image based on pixel vector and central projected shape feature. IET Intell. Transp. Syst. **16** (3), 282–291 (2012)

10. Wu, Y., Liu, Y., Li, J., Liu, H., Hu, X.: Traffic sign detection based on convolution neural network. In: Proceedings of the International Conference on Intelligent Systems and Neural Network, Dallas, TX, USA, pp. 747–753 (2012)
11. Sermanent, P., Lecun, Y.: Traffic sign detection with multi scale convolution network. In: Proceedings of the International Conference on Intelligent Systems and Neural Network, San Jose, CA, TX, USA, pp. 2809–2813 (2011)
12. Ciresan, D., Masci, U., Schmidhuber, J.: Multi-column deep neural network for traffic sign classification. Neural Netw. **32**, 333–338 (2011)
13. Mgelmose, A., Trivedi, M.M., Moeslund, T.B.: Vision-based traffic sign detection analysis for intelligent driver assistance system: perspectives and survey. IEEE Intell. Transp. Syst. **13**(4), 1484–1497 (2012)
14. Benallal, M., Meunier, J.: Real-time color segmentation of rod sign. In: Proceedings of the International Conference on Electronics and Computer Engineering, pp. 1823–1826 (2003)
15. Baro, X., Escalera, S., Vitri, J., Pujol, O., Redeva, P.: Traffic sign recognition using evolutionary adaboost detection forest-ECOC classification. IEEE Intell. Transp. Syst. **10**(1), 113–126 (2009)
16. Koller, D., Sahami, M.: Towards optimal feature selection. In: ICML 1996, Bari, Italy, pp. 87–95, March 1996
17. Tan, K.H., Ghanbari, M.: Layered image coding using the DCT pyramid. IEEE Trans. Image Process. **4**(4), 512–516 (1995)
18. Jadon, S., Kumar, M., Rathi, Y.: Face recognition using SOM neural network with DDCT facial feature extraction technique. In: IEEE ICCSP, vol. 3, no. 4, pp. 416–442, May 2015
19. Abdallah, A., EI-Nasr, M.A., Abbott, A.L.: A new face detection technique using 2D DCT and self-organizing feature map. In: Proceedings of World Academy of Science, Engineering and Technology, vol. 21, pp. 15–19, May 2007

Exploring Cooperative Multi-agent Reinforcement Learning Algorithm (CMRLA) for Intelligent Traffic Signal Control

Deepak A. Vidhate[1](✉) and Parag Kulkarni[2]

[1] Department of Computer Engineering, College of Engineering, Pune, Pune, Maharashtra, India
dvidhate@yahoo.com
[2] iKnowlation Research Lab. Pvt. Ltd., Pune, Maharashtra, India
parag.india@gmail.com

Abstract. Traffic crisis frequently happen because of traffic burden by the large number automobiles are on the path. Increasing transportation move and decreasing the average waiting time of each vehicle are the objectives of cooperative intelligent traffic control system. Each signal wishes to catch better travel move. During the course, signals form a strategy of cooperation in addition to restriction for neighboring signals to exploit their individual benefit. A superior traffic signal scheduling strategy is useful to resolve the difficulty. The several parameters may influence the traffic control model. So it is hard to learn the best possible result. Traffic light controllers are not expert to study from previous results. Due to this they are unable to include uncertain transformation of traffic flow. Reinforcement learning algorithm based traffic control model can be used to obtain fine timing rules by properly defining real time parameters of the real traffic scenario. The projected real-time traffic control optimization prototype is able to continue with the traffic signal scheduling rules successfully. The model expands traffic value of the vehicle, which consists of delay time, the number of vehicles stopped at signal, and the newly arriving vehicles to learn and establish the optimal actions. The experimentation outcome illustrates a major enhancement in traffic control, demonstrating the projected model is competent of making possible real-time dynamic traffic control.

Keywords: Cooperation schemes · Intelligent traffic control
Reinforcement learning

1 Introduction

Large number of vehicles dispersed in a large and board urban area. This makes a difficult and complicated work to successfully take care of such a large scale, dynamic, and distributed system with a high degree of uncertainty [1]. Though the number of vehicles are getting more and more in major cities, most of the current traffic control methods have not taken benefit of a intelligent control of traffic light [2]. It is observed that sensible traffic control and enhancing the deployment effectiveness of roads is an efficient and cost effective technique to resolve the urban traffic crisis in majority urban

© Springer Nature Singapore Pte Ltd. 2018
A. V. Deshpande et al. (Eds.): SmartCom 2017, CCIS 876, pp. 71–81, 2018.
https://doi.org/10.1007/978-981-13-1423-0_9

areas [3]. Major vital part of intelligent transportation system is traffic signal lights control strategy becomes necessary [4]. There are so various parameters that have an effect on the traffic lights control. Static control method is not feasible for rapid and irregular traffic flow. The paper suggests a dynamic traffic control framework which is based on reinforcement learning [5]. The reinforcement learning can present a very crucial move to resolve the above cited problems. It is effectively deployed in resolving various problems [6]. The framework defines different traffic signal control types as action selections; the number of vehicles arriving and density of vehicle at a junction are observed as environment condition. Signal management parameters, like delay time, the number of stopped vehicles, and the total vehicle density are described as received rewards.

The article is described in four parts. Section 2 describes about the traffic estimation parameters. Cooperative multi-agent reinforcement learning algorithm (CMRLA) is proposed in Sect. 3. Section 4 discuss about the system model, including definitions pertaining the state, action, and reward function. Section 5 discuss about experiment and analysis of the results followed by concluding remark.

2 Traffic Estimation Parameters

In traffic management a very crucial responsibility is handled by signal lights control. A practical time allotment method ensures that in usual conditions the traffic moves seamlessly. Normally applied traffic estimation parameters [7] comprises of delay time, the number of automobiles stopped at intersection, and number of newly arriving automobiles.

2.1 Delay Time

The delay between the real time and theoretically calculated time for a vehicle to leave a signal is defined as delay time. In practice, we can get total delay time during a certain period of time and average delay time of a cross to evaluate the time difference. The more delay time indicates the slower average speed of a vehicle to leave a signal.

2.2 Number of Vehicles Stopped

How many vehicles are waiting behind stop line to leave the road signal gives the number of vehicles stopped. The indicator [8] is used to measure the smooth degree of road as well as the road traffic flow. It is defined as

$$stop = stopG + stopR \qquad (1)$$

where stopR is the number of automobiles stopped before the red light and stopG is the number of automobiles stopped before the green light.

2.3 Number of Vehicles Newly Arrived

The ratio of the actual traffic flow to the maximum available traffic flow gives the signal saturation. Newly arrived vehicle is calculated as

$$S = \frac{traffic\ flow}{(dr * sf)} \tag{2}$$

where s_f is traffic flow of the signal and d_r is the ratio of red light duration to green light duration.

2.4 Traffic Flow Capacity

Highest number of vehicles crossing through the signal is shown by traffic flow capacity. The result of signal control strategy is given by the indicator. Traffic signal duration and traffic flow capacity are associated with each other. Generally more signal crossing capability is a result of more crossing period.

3 Cooperative Multi-agent Reinforcement Learning Algorithm (CMRMA)

Synchronization in multi-agent reinforcement generates a complex set of presentations achieved from the different agents' actions. Portion of good performing agent group (i.e. an general form) is shared amongst the different agents via a specific form(Q_i) [9]. Such specific forms embrace the limited details about the environment. Such strategies are incorporated to improve the sum of the partial rewards received using satisfactory cooperation prototype. The action plans or forms are created by the way of multi-agent Q-learning algorithm by constructing the agents to travel for the most excellent form Q* and accumulating the rewards. When forms Q1, ..., Qx are incorporated, it is possible to construct new forms that is General Form (GF = {GF$_1$, ..., GF$_x$}), in which GF$_i$ denotes the outstanding reinforcement received by agent i all through the knowledge mode [10]. Algorithm 1 expresses get_form algorithm that splits the agents' knowledge. The forms are designed by the Q-learning used for all prototypes. Outstanding reinforcements are liable for GF which compiles all outstanding rewards. It will be shared by the way of the added agents [11, 12]. Transforming incomplete rewards as GF is considered for outstanding reinforcements to achieve the cooperation between the agents. A status utility gives the outstanding form amongst the opening states and closing state for a known form which approximates GF with the outstanding reinforcements. The status utility is calculated by summation of steps the agent needed to get to destination at the closing state and the sum of the received status in the forms amongst each opening and the closing state [13].

Algorithm1: Cooperative Multi-agent Reinforcement Learning Model
```
Algorithm get_form
1. Initialization Qᵢ(s, a) and GFᵢ(s, a)
2. for each agents i e I;
3. agents collaborate till the closing state is estab-
lish;
period ← period +1
4.   Determine the rewards by equation;
 Q(s, a)← Q(s, a) +α (r + γ Q(s', a') - Q(s, a))
5. Fcooperate (period, tech, s, a, i);
6.  Qᵢ←GF that is Qᵢ of agent i e I is customized by means
of GFᵢ.
```

The Fcooperate utility selects a coordination method. period, tech, s, a, I are the factors, in which period is current iteration, cooperation tech is {grp, dyna, gol}, s and a is state and action chosen likewise;

3.1   Cooperation Models

Various cooperation methods for cooperative reinforcement learning are proposed:

(i) *Grp model* – reinforcements are disseminated in a series of periods.
(ii) *Dyna model* – reinforcements are distributed in each action.

```
Algorithm 2 Cooperation model
Fcooperate (period, tech,s,a,i) /*cooperation among
agents as four cases*/
q : count of period
1. Switch between cases
2. In case of Grp method
        if period mod q = 0 then
        get_Policy(Qᵢ, Q*,GFᵢ);
3. In case of Dyna method
            r ← Σⱼ₌₁ˣ Qj(s,a);
            Qᵢ(s,a)← r;
            get_Policy(Qᵢ, Q*,GFᵢ);
```

Algorithm 3 get_Policy

```
Function get_Policy(Q_i,Q*,GF_i) /*find out universal agent
policy */
1. for loop for each agent i e I
2. for loop for each state s e S
3.  if status(Q_i, s) ≤ status(Q*,s) then
        GF_i(s,a) ← Q_i(s,a);
 4. end for loop
```

Grp Model: During the learning period each agents collect expertise depend rewards received from their actions. At the end of the period (step q), every agent gives cost of Qj to GF. The usefulness of another agents for given state is enhanced when reward value is appropriate. And these expertise base reinforcements will afterward supplied to the agents. Agent will carry on to make use of its rewards with the objective is for congregating latest values [11–13].

Dyna Model: The coordination in the dyna method is gained as: each act perceived by agent produces a reinforcement value (+ or −), that is summation of all together expertise depends rewards to all agents to action a achieved in state s. Each agent collaborate to achieve more the rewards sum fulfill its own policy [14].

4 Model Design

In practical environment, traffic flows of four signals with eight flow directions are considered for the development. The control coordination between the intersections can be viewed as a Markov process, denoted by $\langle S, R \rangle$ where S represents the state of the intersection, A stands for the action for traffic control and R indicates the return attained by the control agent [15].

4.1 States of System

Instantaneous traffic states are received by each agent. To present state of the road, it returns traffic control decision. Essential data such as number of vehicles newly arriving and number of vehicles currently stopped at signal are used to reflect the state of road traffic [14, 15].

Number of vehicles newly arriving = X_{max} = x_1, x_2, x_3, x_4 = 10
Number of vehicles currently stopped at junction J = I_{max} = i_1, i_2, i_3, i_4 = 20
State of the system become **Input** as (x_i, i_i).

Here, it can get together 200 possible states by combining maximum 10 arriving vehicle and maximum 20 vehicles stopped at signal (10 * 20 = 200).

4.2 Actions of System

Each policy denotes the learning agent activities at a given time in case of reinforcement learning framework. Rewards are obtained by mapping the scene to the action in reinforcement learning. It affects not only to the next scene but also to direct rewards due to which all successive rewards will be affected [15, 16]. In the study, traffic lights control actions can be categorized to 3 types: no change in signal duration, increasing signal duration, reducing signal duration.

Value	Action
1	No change in signal duration
2	Increase in signal duration
3	Reduce the signal duration

Action set for signal agent 1 is $A1 = \{1, 2, 3\}$, action set for signal agent 2 is $A2 = \{1, 2, 3\}$ and action set for signal agent 3 is $A3 = \{1, 2, 3\}$.

Each of them is for one of the following actual traffic scenarios.

The strategy of no change in signal duration is used in the case of the normal traffic flow when the lights control rules do not change [16–18]. The strategy increasing the signal duration is mostly used in the case that in one route is regular and the other route traffic flow is stopped. Two cases are possible i.e. to increase the signal duration to extend the traffic flow and to decrease signal duration when traffic flow on one route is less as compared to other route. Waiting time of other route is reduced as decreased in signal light so that vehicles pass the junction faster.

4.3 Definitions of Reward and Return

Reward function in reinforcement learning describes the target of the problem. The apparent state of the environment is mapped to a value, reinforcement, defining internal needs of the state [18].

In the work, agent makes signal control decisions under diverse traffic circumstances and returns an action sequence, so that by the actions the road traffic jamming display is the least amount. To be additional, the model provides a best traffic synchronization mode in a particular traffic state. Here, we use traffic value display to estimate the traffic flows as

Reward is calculated in the system as given below:

Assume current state $i = (x_i, i_i)$ and next state $j = (x_j, i_j)$. i.e. current state $i \rightarrow$ next state j

Case 1: $[x_i, i_i] \rightarrow [x_i, i_{i-1}]$ i.e. $[X_{max} = 10, I_{max} = 20] \rightarrow [X_{max} = 10, I_{max} = 19]$
That means: one vehicle from currently stopped vehicle is passing the junction

Case 2: $[x_i, i_i] \rightarrow [x_{i+1}, i_{i-1}]$ i.e. $[X_{max} = 9, I_{max} = 20] \rightarrow [X_{max} = 10, I_{max} = 19]$
That means: one newly arrived vehicle at junction & one vehicle is passing junction

Case 3: $[x_i, i_i] \rightarrow [x_i, i_{i-3}]$ i.e. $[X_{max} = 10, I_{max} = 20] \rightarrow [X_{max} = 10, I_{max} = 17]$
That means: More than one stopped vehicles are passing the junction

Case 4: $[x_i, 0] \rightarrow [x_{i+1}, 0]$ i.e. $[X_{max} = 2, I_{max} = 0] \rightarrow [X_{max} = 3, I_{max} = 0]$

That means: new one new vehicle is arriving and no stopped vehicle at the junction. Depending on above state transitions from current state to next state, reward is calculated as

$$
\begin{aligned}
\text{Reward is } r_p(i,\, p,\, j) &= 1 && \text{if } x_1' = x_1 + 1\ldots\ldots\ldots\text{Case 4}\\
&= 2 && \text{if } i_1' = i_1 - 1\ldots\ldots\ldots\text{Case 1}\\
&= 3 && \text{if } i_1' = i_1 - 3\ldots\ldots\ldots\text{Case 2 \& 3}\\
&= 0 && \text{otherwise}
\end{aligned}
$$

5 Experimental Results

The study learn a controller with learning rate = 0.5, discount rate = 0.9, and $\lambda = 0.6$. During learning process, cost was updated 1000 with 6000 episodes.

The grp method appears to be extremely strong converging very fast to an optimal action form Q*. Rewards obtained by the agents are produced in series of pre identified stages. They gather reasonable reward values that cause a good convergence. In the grp method the global policy converges to a best action strategy as there is an intermission of series necessary to gather good reinforcements. The general form of the dyna method is capable to assemble good reward values in small knowledge series. It is observed that after some series, the performance of global strategy reduces. This takes place since the states neighboring to the final state begin in the direction of more superior reward values giving to a restricted maximum. It will no more stay at the other states so it punishes the agent. In the dyna method as the reinforcement learning algorithm renews learning values, actions with higher gathered reinforcements are chosen through top likelihood than acts with small gathered reinforcements.

Figures 1 and 2 respectively shows that delay time vs number of state given by simple Q learning (without cooperation) and grp and dyna methods (with cooperation). Delay time obtained by cooperative methods i.e. grp and dyn methods is much less than that of without cooperation method i.e. simple Q learning for agent 1 in multi-agent scenario.

Figures 3 and 4 respectively shows that delay time vs number of state given by simple Q learning (without cooperation) and grp and dyna methods (with cooperation). Delay time obtained by cooperative methods i.e. grp and dyna methods is much less than that of without cooperation method i.e. simple Q learning for agent 2 in multi-agent scenario.

Figures 5 and 6 respectively shows that delay time vs number of state given by simple Q learning (without cooperation) and grp and dyna methods (with cooperation). Delay time duration obtained by cooperative methods i.e. grp and dyna methods is much less than that of without cooperation method i.e. simple Q learning for agent 2 in multi-agent scenario.

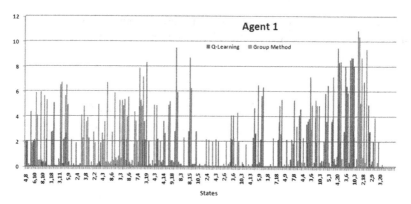

Fig. 1. States vs delay time for agent 1 by Q-learning & grp method

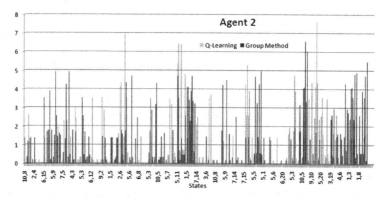

Fig. 2. States vs delay time for agent 1 by Q-learning & dyna method

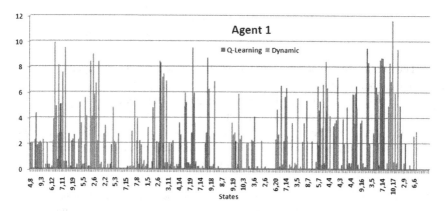

Fig. 3. States vs delay time for agent 2 by Q-learning & grp method

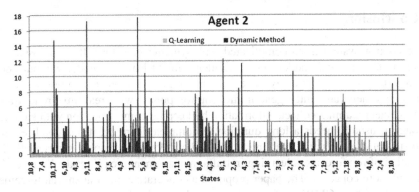

Fig. 4. States vs delay time for agent 2 by Q-learning & dyna method

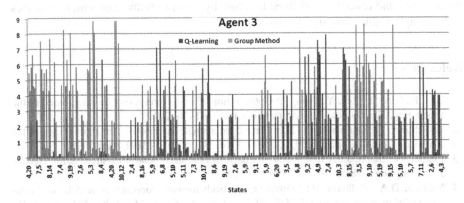

Fig. 5. States vs delay time for agent 3 by Q-learning & grp method

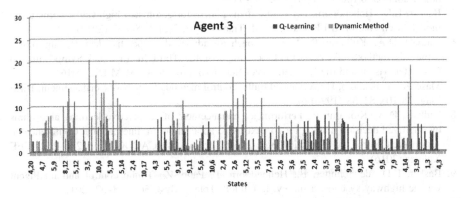

Fig. 6. States vs profit for agent 3 by Q-learning & dyna method

6 Conclusion

Traffic control system is so complicated and dynamic in nature. It is impossible to manage traffic jam and sudden traffic accidents for Q learning model without cooperation with predefined strategy. The demand is getting more and more urgent for combining timely and intelligent traffic control policy with real-time road traffic. Reinforcement learning collects information by keeping communication with situation. Although it usually needs a long duration to complete learning, it has good learning ability to complex system, enabling it to handle unknown complex states well. The application of reinforcement learning in traffic management area is gradually receiving more and more concerns. The paper proposed a cooperative multi-agent reinforcement learning algorithm (CMRLA) for traffic control optimization. The actual continuous traffic states are discretized for the purpose of simplification. Actions for traffic control are designed and rewards are defined to return by mean of traffic cost which combines with multiple traffic capacity indicators.

References

1. Zhu, F., Ning, J., Ren, Y., Peng, J.: Optimization of image processing in video-based traffic monitoring. Elektronika ir Elektrotechnika **18**(8), 91–96 (2012)
2. de Schutter, B.: Optimal traffic light control for a single intersection. In: Proceedings of the American Control Conference (ACC 1999), vol. 3, pp. 2195–2199, June 1999
3. Findler, N., Stapp, J.: A distributed approach to optimized control of street traffic signals. J. Transp. Eng. **118**(1), 99–110 (1992)
4. Vidhate, D.A., Kulkarni, P.: Innovative approach towards cooperation models for multi-agent reinforcement learning (CMMARL). In: Unal, A., Nayak, M., Mishra, D.K., Singh, D., Joshi, A. (eds.) SmartCom 2016. CCIS, vol. 628, pp. 468–478. Springer, Singapore (2016). https://doi.org/10.1007/978-981-10-3433-6_56
5. Baskar, L.D., Hellendoorn, H.: Traffic management for automated highway systems using model-based control. IEEE Trans. Intell. Transp. Syst. **3**(2), 838–847 (2012)
6. Vidhate, D.A., Kulkarni, P.: New approach for advanced cooperative learning algorithms using RL methods (ACLA). In: Proceedings of the Third International Symposium on Computer Vision and the Internet, VisionNet 2016, pp. 12–20. ACM DL (2016)
7. Mase, K., Yamamoto, H.: Advanced traffic control methods for network management. IEEE Mag. **28**(10), 82–88 (1990)
8. Vidhate, D.A., Kulkarni, P.: Performance enhancement of cooperative learning algorithms by improved decision making for context based application. In: International Conference on Automatic Control and Dynamic Optimization Techniques (ICACDOT), pp. 246–252. IEEE Xplorer (2016)
9. Baskar, L.D., de Schutter, B., Hellendoorn, J., Papp, Z.: Traffic control and intelligent vehicle highway systems: a survey. IET Intell. Transp. Syst. **5**(1), 38–52 (2011)
10. Choi, W., Yoon, H., Kim, K., Chung, I., Lee, S.: A traffic light controlling FLC considering the traffic congestion. In: Pal, N.R., Sugeno, M. (eds.) AFSS 2002. LNCS (LNAI), vol. 2275, pp. 69–75. Springer, Heidelberg (2002). https://doi.org/10.1007/3-540-45631-7_10
11. Vidhate, D.A., Kulkarni, P.: Enhancement in decision making with improved performance by multiagent learning algorithms. IOSR J. Comput. Eng. **1**(18), 18–25 (2016)

12. Wiering, M.A.: Multi-agent reinforcement learning for traffic light control. In: 17th International Conference on Machine Learning (ICML 2000), pp. 1151–1158 (2000)
13. Vidhate, D.A., Kulkarni, P.: Multilevel relationship algorithm for association rule mining used for cooperative learning. Int. J. Comput. Appl. **86**(4), 20–27 (2014)
14. Zegeye, S., de Schutter, B., Hellendoorn, J., Breunesse, E.A., Hegyi, A.: A predictive traffic controller for sustainable mobility using parameterized control policies. IEEE Trans. Intell. Transp. Syst. **13**(3), 1420–1429 (2012)
15. Vidhate, D.A., Kulkarni, P.: A novel approach to association rule mining using multilevel relationship algorithm for cooperative learning. In: 4th International Conference on Advanced Computing and Communication Technologies, pp. 230–236 (2014)
16. Chin, Y.K., Wei, Y.K., Teo, K.T.K.: Q-learning traffic signal optimization within multiple intersections traffic network. In: Proceedings of the 6th UKSim/AMSS European Symposium on Computer Modeling and Simulation (EMS 2012), pp. 343–348, November 2012
17. Vidhate, D.A., Kulkarni, P.: To improve association rule mining using new technique: multilevel relationship algorithm towards cooperative learning. In: International Conference on Circuits, Systems, Communication and Information Technology Applications (CSCITA), pp. 241–246. IEEE (2014)
18. Chin, Y.K., Lee, L.K., Bolong, N., Yang, S.S., Teo, K.T.K.: Exploring Q-learning optimization in traffic signal timing plan management. In: Proceedings of the 3rd International Conference on Computational Intelligence, Communication Systems and Networks (CICSyN 2011), pp. 269–274, July 2011

TMV: Trust-Matrix-Value Based Neighbor Peer Selection for Secure Query Forwarding in P2P Networks

R. Venkadeshan[1]([✉]) [iD] and M. Jegatha[2] [iD]

[1] Department of Computer Science and Engineering,
Amrita School of Engineering, Coimbatore, Amrita Vishwa Vidyapeetham,
Amrita University, Coimbatore, India
r_venkadeshan@ch.amrita.edu
[2] Department of Computer Science and Engineering,
Trichy Engineering College, Tiruchirappalli, Tamilnadu, India
vpragatha@gmail.com

Abstract. Today's internet exploits the P2P network for its unique and special characteristics such as resource sharing, query routing, dynamic topology construction, self-healing in communications and easy and efficient network setup. Moreover, P2P network has undergone many challenges which enable malicious nodes to launch denial of service attacks, allows the adversary peer nodes to deny the query request and even not utilizing its energy for query routing process in the network. These challenges resultant in performance degradation and reduce the query success ratio. In this paper, the authors elaborate the robust trust-based peer communication model that utilizes the scalable topology by building an overlay network with trusted neighbor peers. By having the trustworthiness among the neighbor peer nodes, the privacy, security protection in query searching and success ratio has been increased simultaneously. The main contribution of this paper is to compute Trust-Matrix-Value (TMV) for each peer node, based on the parameters such as query response (QR), resource sharing (RS), information quality (QI) and success ratio (SR). The peer nodes with higher values are considered for further query forwarding and others traffic has been blocked. A comprehensive analysis has been performed and their simulation results proved that the proposed scheme achieves efficient searching with minimal delay, discards by penalizing the malicious peer nodes from the topology, and maximizes the query success ratio in P2P networks.

Keywords: TMV · Trust-Matrix · DoS attack · Security services
Malicious peers · Attacks in P2P · Trust measures

1 Introduction

Peer-to-Peer systems comprise of several distributed applications in which each peer can allow to share their resources with other peers by simple message exchange. The primary goalmouth of the P2P system is to cooperatively sharing the resources among the peers and to aggregates the resources efficiently in order to make available at the

© Springer Nature Singapore Pte Ltd. 2018
A. V. Deshpande et al. (Eds.): SmartCom 2017, CCIS 876, pp. 82–91, 2018.
https://doi.org/10.1007/978-981-13-1423-0_10

Internet edge. In specific, Gnutella and KaZaA based file sharing of P2P system becomes a most popular model for the interchange of resources among the huge number of internet consumers. The lack of a central controller and non-hierarchical organization of peers make the P2P applications more vulnerable. Without performing the peer authentication, adversary peers can enable various security attacks such as IP spoofing, falsify messages, man-in-the-middle and denial of services (DOS) in the network. A distributed peer-to-peer system [11] should influence resources of all peers such as memory space, bandwidth, and processors to perform query searching and provides better scalability in the network. Besides, in P2P system data has been replicated in multiple peer nodes which provide fault tolerant and there is no single point of failure [13, 14]. Decentralized distributed P2P systems are highly susceptible to Sybil attacks [6], where malicious peer node obtains multiple identities of other peer nodes in the same network (called Sybil node).

To guard against this Sybil attack [4], just monitoring each peer's behavior is not adequate because all the Sybil peers can act smoothly initially, and later unveiling an attack. To overwhelm the above-discussed issues, the work focuses on the functionalities of trustworthiness among the peer nodes and ensures the node privacy while communication. The trust management scheme separates trust peers from the malicious peer nodes, based on the past communication history between them. The formation of trust communities enables each peer node to practice neighborhood of trust for query forwarding which is to defend peer confidentiality in the network.

2 Related Works

In this section, the authors have performed a literature survey based on two primary characteristics: Query searching and secure peer selection mechanisms. In a peer-to-peer network, the resource searching algorithms are hardly divided into two categories: broadcasting method and state knowledge-based searching. By broadcasting approaches like Flooding and Random-walk, the search queries can directly forward to more number of neighbor peers without any constraints. It results in huge overhead in network traffic and does not scale well which incurs variances in performance with minimum success rate and query hits [8]. In flooding based searching technique, querying peer node sends a search query to all its neighbor peers. There is another technique for improving the search efficiency stated in the algorithm [2] is based on query forwarding. Further, in [1, 5], the neighbor peers flood the search query to all of its logical neighbors, excluding the inward bound peers, until the Time-to-Live (TTL) value reaches to zero or the response of the query receives [9].

Another approach called Random-k-walker [7], which sends search queries to its k-neighbors named "k-walkers", of the querying peer. Every walker selects the next k-neighbor peers randomly then forwards the search query to that walker. This random walker selection mechanism executes until the TTL value expires or receiving the query response. The scope of the search gets an increase as the search mechanism delivered the query request to large peer count, which improves the success ratio [3, 12]. Moreover, the above-stated search mechanism selects the neighbor peer nodes without any selection strategies, so there may be a chance of performance level dissatisfaction. In [16], authors have proposed a searching technique called Query Routing Tree (QRT) in P2P networks. This technique controls the query forwarding hops without loops and reduces the query traffic significantly. Here, the authors have taken the environment as unstructured P2P networks. It is very difficult to compute the cost of the link between communicating peer nodes every time in a dynamic model [2]. In unstructured P2P networks, the peer nodes are highly mobile in nature. So, the cost of the link changes frequently as the topology change. This technique decreases the overall network performance. In [10], authors have proposed a probabilistic prototype to handle trust measures in P2P networks. It performs a local query computation and propagation of trust values of each peer node into modules of other peer nodes. It is well suited for the dynamic P2P networks where each peer has different perspectives towards the other peers with whom it interacts.

Venkadeshan and Chandrasekar [15] have proposed a technique called Peer-ID based authentication scheme in a peer-to-peer network. They have described a mechanism known as Identity-based peer authentication, which authenticates the peer node at the time of entry level into the network. By observing all the above discussion, this paper proposes the Trust-Matrix-Value (TMV) based query routing mechanism which combines the advantages of trusted peer selection and searches performance efficiency in the P2P network.

3   Constructing Trust-Based Topology

In this section, the current work focuses with the construction of a trustworthy environment for communicating peer nodes. In the topology, all the peer nodes perform self-organization of network without any central controller and express their resources with other peers in an autonomous manner. Here, the authors propose a peer selection algorithm called Trust-Matrix-Value (TMV) which constructs trustworthiness among the communicating peers in P2P networks. Each peer node computes trust value of their neighbor peers which used for further query forwarding process. In practical, computing peer's trustworthiness and collecting these trust values in the P2P network is not an easy task. For that, calculate the following characteristics for each peer node: (1) Query Response (QR) frequency, (2) Resource Sharing (RS), (3) Quality of Information (QI), (4) the query Success Ratio (SR), and (5) the transmission peer distance (PD).

Based on these characteristics, neighbor peers with higher TMV value can be targeted for further query forwarding, by this means the network traffic has been routed to trusted zone, the query success ratio is increased and reducing the network traffic overhead significantly. The key factors of this work are, peer selection and query forwarding, each peer should validate the trust value of its neighbor peer nodes before sending or receiving the traffic. The accumulated trust value of the peer nodes is considered and whose value is put down the threshold value is assumed as distrusted and the network traffic through that peer node is blocked. The trust measures are used to evaluate the query traffic from the peer nodes and based on the traffic each peer is updating the trust values of its neighbor peer nodes. In order to increase the efficiency of query search by exploiting the trustworthiness among the peer nodes intelligently,

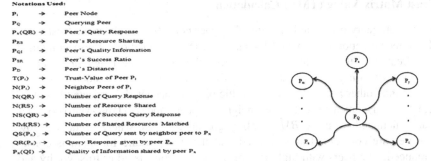

Notations Used:

P_i	→	Peer Node
P_Q	→	Querying Peer
$P_x(QR)$	→	Peer's Query Response
P_{RS}	→	Peer's Resource Sharing
P_{QI}	→	Peer's Quality Information
P_{SR}	→	Peer's Success Ratio
P_D	→	Peer's Distance
$T(P_i)$	→	Trust-Value of Peer P_i
$N(P_i)$	→	Neighbor Peers of P_i
$N(QR)$	→	Number of Query Response
$N(RS)$	→	Number of Resource Shared
$NS(QR)$	→	Number of Success Query Response
$NM(RS)$	→	Number of Shared Resources Matched
$QS(P_x)$	→	Number of Query sent by neighbor peer to P_x
$QR(P_x)$	→	Query Response given by peer P_x
$P_x(QI)$	→	Quality of Information shared by peer P_x

Fig. 1. Notations used

Fig. 2. TMV matrix and topology of querying peer P_Q

the TMV mechanism delivers the high level of security protection for the peer communication. Figure 1 illustrates the different notations used in this trust matrix model.

3.1 TMV Based Query Routing

In Trust-Matrix-Value (TMV) based query routing mechanism, the querying peer node P_Q is handling two different matrixes: Left side-Matrix and Right side-Matrix. The Left side-Matrix called as Bound-Matrix (*BM*), is a $n \times 4$ matrix, where n represents the number of neighbor peer nodes of P_Q and 4 stands for representing the four columns *QR, RS, QI,* and *SR* scores of n neighbor peers of P_Q. The four computed scores are placed in the first, second, third and fourth columns of *BM* matrix respectively. The Right side-Matrix called as Distance Matrix (*DM*), is a $n \times 1$ matrix in where n stands for the number of neighbor peers and 1 stands for the entry of neighbor peer nodes distance $D(P_x)$. By having these two *BM* and *DM* matrix, the querying peer P_Q computes the Trust-Matrix-Values (TMV), which results in $n \times 1$ matrix.

Each neighbor peer should assign the computed trust value. The querying peer P_Q uses the T_x resulted in trust value of peer from TMV matrix to choose the neighbors with the top-k scores and forward the search query. Figure 1 listed out the set of notation used and Fig. 2 illustrates the TMV matrix computation process and topology of querying peer P_Q. As depicted in Fig. 2, the neighbor peers of P_Q peer are $\{P_x, P_y, P_z, P_m$ and $P_n\}$.

$$TM(P_Q) = \begin{bmatrix} \overset{BM}{} \\ P_x(QR) \ P_x(RS) \ P_x(QI) \ P_x(SR) \\ P_y(QR) \ P_y(RS) \ P_y(QI) \ P_y(SR) \\ P_z(QR) \ P_z(RS) \ P_z(QI) \ P_z(SR) \\ P_m(QR) \ P_m(RS) \ P_m(QI) \ P_m(SR) \\ \vdots \end{bmatrix} \begin{bmatrix} DM \\ D(P_x) \\ D(P_y) \\ D(P_z) \\ D(P_m) \\ \vdots \end{bmatrix} = \begin{bmatrix} TMV \\ T_x \\ T_y \\ T_z \\ T_m \\ \vdots \end{bmatrix} \quad (1)$$

3.2   Trust-Matrix-Value (TMV) Calculation

When the search query originated, the querying peer node P_Q calculates the trust value for each of its neighbor peer nodes by using TMV computation. These computed values are treated as the parameter for selecting the appropriate neighbor peers for further query forwarding. The peers with high trust measures are considered as trustworthy peers than other peers. The peer's traffic is either accepted or rejected based on its calculated trust measures by its neighbor peer nodes. Trust-Matrix-Values (TMV) are calculated from the $BM \times DM$ aggregated values, where peers with low trust measures are considered as distrusted and the query traffic for them is consequently reduced. The peers with high trust measures are considered as trustworthy and thereafter the traffic to that peer is fully loaded. This TMV-based query routing mechanism allows the peers to dynamically update the trust values at periodic intervals. Here, the authors use the mean and standard deviation techniques to attain the trustworthiness in a P2P network. Let us consider the data set as $\{x1, x2, x3 \ldots xn\}$. Assume that, the mean value M of each column in BM is computed before calculating the standard deviation of each column of BM. It is state   •

$$\bar{M} = \frac{1}{n} * \sum_{r=1}^{n} BM(r, c). \tag{2}$$

where n is the number of neighbor peers of querying peer P_Q, $BM(r, c)$ is the rth row and c^{th} column entry of the BM matrix. The standard deviation S_D computation as follows:

$$S_D = \int \sqrt{\begin{array}{ll} \frac{1}{n-1} * \sum_{r=1}^{n} (BM(r, c) - \bar{M})^2 & \text{if } n \geq 2 \\ 0 & \text{if } n = 1 \end{array}} \tag{3}$$

At last, define the DM matrix $n \times 1$ as

$$DM(c, 1) = \frac{S_D}{\sum_{r=1}^{n} S_r} \tag{4}$$

where $DM(c, 1)$ is the weight of the cth column $(c, 1)$-entry.

3.3   Calculation of TMV Parameters

Query Response (QR). In unstructured peer-to-peer networks, several freeloaders are available who utilize the network resources without sharing any of their own resources. This freeloader has been affecting the search performance of P2P network communities. In order to thwart free loaders, QR is utilized to make difference among the peer nodes as leech peers and fervent peers. The score of QR is computed by each peer node by considering the query response frequency of its neighbor peers. The querying peer

P_Q computes $N(QR)$, the number of query responses for all its neighbor peer nodes. Formally, $P_x(QR)$ is the query response frequency of peer P_x.

$$P_x(OR) = \sum_x^{N(P_x)} N(QR) \tag{5}$$

where $N(P_x)$ is the neighbor peers of a querying peer P_Q; that is, $N(P_x)$ are one hop away peers from P_Q. Additionally, querying peer P_Q should compute $QS(P_x)$, is the number of queries sent (QS) to the peer nodes that are one step away from P_Q. The number of query response $N(QR)$ of the peer P_x is given as,

$$N(QR) = QS(P_x) - QR(P_x) \tag{6}$$

where $QR\ (P_x)$ is the query responses of peer P_x. When $N(QR)$ of peer P_x increases, the chance of trust value measures also increases.

Resource Sharing (RS). In P2P networks, an observation has been taken on the aspect of sharing network resources, in which the resource sharing among peer nodes are extremely unbalanced. It has been proven that only limited number of peer nodes is effectively sharing their resources to all other peer nodes and very few percent of peers are properly responding to requested queries. To provide a better success ratio all peers should honestly involve in query forwarding process, but only a small count of volunteer peers are involving which increases the delay in query processing. Besides, each peers' query response abilities vary because of their heterogeneity in resource sharing. In trace analysis has been taken by the authors, shows that only limited peers are sharing their resources effectively. For the reason that, query response involves matching patterns with the searching keywords of all shared resources. Here, the authors improvise the concept as increasing the number of shared files will automatically increase the query success probability. From the above observations, the authors come up with the notion of effective resource sharing (RS), which help us to govern the number of shared resources among the peer nodes in the P2P network. Every peer node should compute $P_x(RS)$ of its neighbor peers, means the number of resources shared by the peers that are one step away from querying peer P_Q.

$$P_x(RS) = \sum_x^{N(P_x)} N(RS) \tag{7}$$

It is practical that, when a peer shares its maximum resources to other peers, then it is having higher probabilities of query matching than a peer that shares limited resources.

Quality of Information (QI). In P2P network, another observation stated that not all the shared files are used for answering request queries [4]. By considering the number of shared resources with querying peers and the number of resources used to query response has a solid relationship with the responding peers. Having this in mind, exploit the feature, the "Quality of Information" that distinguishes the useful and useless resources. Consider $NM(RS)$ be the number of shared information that match with the requested queries. Each querying peer P_Q computes $P_x(QI)$ for all of its neighbor peers. It is stated as,

$$P_x(QI) = \sum_x^{N(P_x)} NM(RS) \tag{8}$$

Success Ratio (SR). The next parameter taken for analyses is the query success ratio *SR* of the neighbor peer nodes. Though the possibility of query success ratio may be influenced by the quality and quantity of resource contents, which have been taken the number of success hits provided by the neighbor peer nodes are considered for analyzes the quality of services. Each querying peer P_Q computes $NS(QR)$, is the total amount of success query response of neighbor peers that are one step away from P_Q. It is defined as,

$$P_x(SR) = \sum_x^{N(P_x)} NS(QR) \tag{9}$$

The time is taken for the query success and its efficiency in query forwarding has been improved gradually. Therefore, the queries exchanged between the peers and its traffic is minimized.

4   Experimental Setup and Performance Evaluation

This section, deals with the performance evaluation of proposed TMV-based query routing mechanism with the support of simulator and analysis the results outcome with the existing famous search mechanisms. In the simulation environment, build the topology with peers range from 100–3,000 peer nodes and Table 1 listed the different parameters used in the simulation. By considering the high mobility nature of peers in an unstructured P2P network, the topology design that allows the peer nodes can join (leave) a network at any point.

Table 1. Simulation parameters

Parameters	Values
Nodes	100–3000
Node degree	5
Max TTL	20
Query request per second	1000
Topology area	1000 m * 800 m
Simulation time	600 s

Each peer node can generate the queries with equivalent probability. Here, the comparison among the searching mechanisms like Flooding (FL), *K*-Random-Walk (*k*-RW) and Query Routing Tree (QRT) with the proposed Trust-Matrix-Value (TMV) for the parameters Response Time, Query Success Rate, Searching Hop in Query Hit were

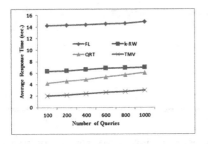

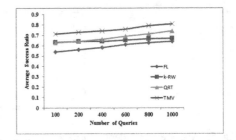

Fig. 3. Average response time of search queries

Fig. 4. Average query success ratios for 1000 peers

considered. During simulation, peers in the topology can randomly generate the query message and perform forwarding it to neighbor peers. Figure 3 illustrates the average response time taken to hit the target peer. The outcome of the experiment shows that the proposed TMV achieves the minimum response time than another searching mechanism. In practical, TMV utilizes a minimum amount of network resources to find query matches, it attains the best response time than k-RW and QRT. On the other hand, it also acquires low network traffic. Even though the number of query generation increases, TMV performs effectively because it selects trusted neighbor peers each time for further query forwarding. Following it, perform the simulation against the computation of average success rate of searching queries as stated in Fig. 4.

It shows that TMV achieves 70–80% of query responses for the request, whereas FL achieves only 50–60% of query responses due to its high traffic overhead and RW produces only 42–49% of responses because of non-deterministic neighbor selection whereas QRT achieves 61–70%. As an outcome, the proposed TMV reduces the network traffic cost with higher success rate. Figure 5 shows the result of an average number of search nodes with the number of queries. As discussed, TMV has been choosing the neighbor peer nodes based on its trust measures, it uses only a minimum number of hops to obtain the query response. Whereas FL, k-RW and QRT searching algorithms consider most of the peer nodes in the process of query searching, the network resources have not been utilized properly. As shown in the result, TMV achieves query response with minimum peer utilization. In the second simulation setup, compare the trusted and distrusted peer-to-peer network by evaluating the following parameters: Success Ratio, and Delay. In Fig. 6, it has been proven that the trusted P2P network achieves high success rate with increasing search query counts than the distrusted environment. In a distrusted network, some of the peer nodes are selfish in nature; it should not use its own resources for query searching and forwarding process.

Figure 7 shows the comparison between query response delay and a number of query nodes. From the outcome, it has been proven that the query delay increases when the number of querying peer increases. The time delay taken for query response is minimal in trusted network compared to distrust network even the querying peer nodes increases.

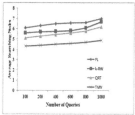

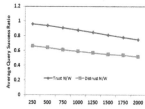

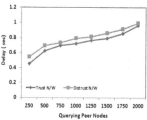

Fig. 5. Average search depths of query for 1000 peers

Fig. 6. Average success rate comparisons between trust and distrust netword

Fig. 7. Average query response delays for 2000 peers

5   Conclusion

In this work, the authors have proposed a Trust-Matrix-Value (TMV) based query searching mechanism for peer-to-peer networks, which is built on the trust management scheme. The key idea of this work is to establish the trustworthiness among the communicating peer nodes before sending or accepting query traffic. Each peer should examine the trust of the neighbor peers before query forwarding. The simulation has been executed to analysis the performance level of TMV algorithm with FL, k-RW and QRT. The results exhibit that TMV increases the network performance gradually even under dynamic circumstances. Through the simulation results, TMV is an effective query searching mechanism and optimized algorithm to enhance the query hits in peer-to-peer networks.

References

1. Chavez, E., Graff, M., Navarro, G., Tellez, E.S.: Near neighbor searching with K-nearest references. J. Inf. Syst. **51**, 43–61 (2015). https://doi.org/10.1016/j.is.2015.02.001
2. Chen, K., Shen, H., Zhang, H.: Leveraging social networks for P2P content-based file sharing in disconnected MANETs. IEEE Trans. Mob. Comput. **13**, 235–249 (2015). https://doi.org/10.1109/TMC.2012.239
3. Chiu, Y.M., Eun, D.Y.: On the performance of content delivery under competition in a stochastic unstructured peer-to-peer network. IEEE Trans. Parallel Distrib. Syst. **21**(10), 1487–1500 (2010). https://doi.org/10.1109/TPDS.2010.15
4. An, D., Ha, B., Cho, G.: A robust trust management scheme against the malicious nodes in distributed P2P network. Int. J. Secur. Appl. **7**(3), 317–326 (2013)
5. Gaeta, R., Sereno, M.: Generalized probabilistic flooding in unstructured peer-to-peer networks. IEEE Trans. Parallel Distrib. Syst. **22**(12), 2055–2062 (2011). https://doi.org/10.1109/TPDS.2011.82
6. Gheorghe, G., Lo Cigno, R., Montresor, A.: Security and privacy issues in P2P streaming systems: a survey. Peer-to-Peer Netw. Appl. **4**, 75–91 (2011). https://doi.org/10.1007/s12083-010
7. Hieungmany, P., Souma, T., Shioda, S.: Directional-random-walk - based contents search for unstructured P2P systems. IEICE Trans. Commun. **J98-B**(2), 132–140 (2015)

8. Hsiao, H.-C., Su, H.: On optimizing overlay topologies for search in unstructured peer-to-peer networks. IEEE Trans. Parallel Distrib. Syst. **23**(5), 924–935 (2012). https://doi.org/10.1109/tpds.2011.241

9. Filali, I., Huet, F.: Dynamic TTL-based search in unstructured peer-to-peer networks. Published by IEEE in CCGrid, pp. 438–447 (2010). https://doi.org/10.1109/ccgrid.2010.66

10. Chen, K., Hwang, K., Chen, G.: Heuristic discovery of role-based trust chains in peer-to-peer networks. IEEE Trans. Parallel Distrib. Syst. **20**, 83–96 (2009). https://doi.org/10.1109/tpds.2008.60

11. Lee, H., Nakao, A.: A feasibility study of P2P traffic localization through network delay insertion. IEICE Trans. Commun. **E95-B**(11), 3464–3471 (2012). https://doi.org/10.1587/transxom.e95.b.3464

12. Ghorbani, M.: An adaptive k-random walks method for peer-to-peer networks. Adv. Comput. Sci.: Int. J. **2**(3) (2013)

13. Radhika, N., Thejiya, V.: Trust-based solution for mobile ad-hoc networks. Int. J. Adv. Res. Comput. Sci. Soft. Eng. **4**(5), 73–82 (2014)

14. Shyamala, C.K., Padmanabhan, T.R.: A trust-reputation model offering data retrievability and correctness in distributed storages. Int. J. Comput. Appl. **36**, 56–63 (2015)

15. Venkadeshan, R., Chandrasekar, M.: Effective communication in P2P network by introducing GOSIP-PHE algorithms. Wirel. Pers. Commun. **87**, 923–937 (2016). https://doi.org/10.1007/s11277-015-2625-6

16. Weihua, G., et al.: Enhanced entropy-based resource searching in unstructured P2P networks. Chin. J. Electron. **24**(2), 229–235 (2015). https://doi.org/10.1049/cje.2015.04.002

An Efficient VM Selection Strategy for Minimization of Migration in Cloud Environment

Nimisha Patel[1,2(✉)] and Hiren Patel[3]

[1] Rai University, Ahmedabad, Gujarat, India
nimishaa_25@yahoo.co.in
[2] Sankalchand Patel College of Engineering, Visnagar, Gujarat, India
[3] LDRP Institute of Technology and Research, Gandhinagar, Gujarat, India
hbpatel1976@gmail.com

Abstract. Cloud Computing has been one of the most emphasized paradigms over the last few years. Increased usage of Cloud Computing has resulted into the augmentation of energy consumption and emission of carbon footprints in the environment. Many researchers have been working in the different directions to address these issues. Out of various facets, efficient allocation of Virtual Machines (VMs) on hosts could be one of the good paths to save energy of data center. Optimized VM allocation process is divided into two phases viz. (i) selection of VMs to be migrated and (ii) placement of VMs on the new host. During the selection phase, minimizing the number of VMs to be migrated would result into improvement in performance and reduction in SLA violation. In this research, we have proposed a modification in an existing Minimization of Migration algorithm. The existing algorithm works for two scenarios viz. (a) single VM selection and (b) multiple VM selections. We find the scope of enhancement in the existing algorithm, especially in the case of multiple VM selection. In such scenario, the existing algorithm selects a combination of VMs which is not the optimum. We propose our algorithm to optimally select the combination of VMs such that number of VMs to be migrated remains minimal and utilization of host, after migration, reaches nearer (and below) to an upper threshold value. The prospect of this research would to enhance utilization of hosts which would result in a reduction in a number of live hosts resulting in saving in energy consumption.

Keywords: Energy efficiency · VM migration · Cloud computing
Consolidation

1 Introduction

Cloud computing (CC) has been a novel paradigm in the field of Information and Communication Technology which offers a different style of computing where users do not own their computing resources but rent and pay for them. NIST [1] defines it as "a model for enabling ubiquitous, convenient, on-demand network access to a shared pool of configurable computing resources (e.g., networks, servers, storage, applications and

© Springer Nature Singapore Pte Ltd. 2018
A. V. Deshpande et al. (Eds.): SmartCom 2017, CCIS 876, pp. 92–101, 2018.
https://doi.org/10.1007/978-981-13-1423-0_11

services) that can be rapidly provisioned and released with minimal management effort or service provider interaction." Hence, resources are provisioned/released to/from the user on demand over the network and payment is made accordingly. This new paradigm has become very popular in recent times.

Out of various challenges faced by Cloud such as security, availability, performance etc., the issue of energy consumption has attracted the attention of many researchers. The issue is being addressed in many facets such as VM Consolidation, Load balancing, VM Migration etc. In this research, we aim to address the issue of energy consumption by optimally selecting (minimum number of) VMs to be migrated from one host to another in such a way that a minimum number of the host are to be kept on, resulting in a reduction in electrical power. Authors of [2] have addressed the issue of minimizing migration but it works fine for the cases where only one VM is to be migrated to consolidate the system. But, in real situation, where a number of hosts in a data center is huge and the number of VMs in a host is large, we need to migrate multiple VMs to stabilize the system. In such scenario, the existing method does not give an optimum solution. Hence, we find the scope of improvement in the existing method and we propose a modified version of minimization of migration algorithm to handle the cases of multiple VM selection.

Proper utilization of hosts leads into keeping an optimum number of hosts alive and rest to be idle resulting in saving in power consumption. VM consolidation is a process of appropriately distributing tasks on VMs and mapping or migrating VMs on or across hosts. The process of VM consolidation is divided among four phases [3] viz. (a) Overloaded host detection (b) VM selection from overloaded host (c) VM placement for selected VMs (d) Underloaded host detection. In this research, we propose a modified minimization of migration algorithm for VM selection (as mentioned in b) for optimally selecting the combination of VMs to be migrated. The Efficient method to select the best combination of VMs would result into significant improvement in power consumption.

The overall paper has been organized as follows. Section 2 discusses related work, followed by our proposed scheme in Sect. 3. Experimentations and results are described in Sect. 4. The overall research has been concluded in Sect. 5 followed by a list of references.

2 Related Work

Anton et al. [2] have been one of the few researchers who worked in the domain of achieving energy efficiency by proper resource allocation. Along with defining an architectural framework and survey of research in energy-efficient computing, the authors have proposed energy-efficient resource allocation policies and scheduling algorithms and claimed significant cost saving and improvement of energy efficiency. Minimization of Migrations (MM) is one of the key contributions by the authors in the direction of selecting a combination of VMs from an overloaded host for subsequent migration. The algorithm covers two aspects of migration viz. (a) single VM selection and (b) multiple VMs selection. The algorithm works efficiently for (a) but there seems to be a scope of improvement in (b) which is one of the main sources of motivation for this research. In [3], authors identified dynamic consolidation of VMs using live migration and switching idle nodes to sleep mode, as the mean to optimize resource usage and reduce energy consumption. Further, the authors propose heuristics for dynamic consolidation of VMs to claim a reduction in energy consumption and maintenance of SLA. Different statistical methods such as (a) Median Absolute Deviation (MAD) (b) Interquartile Range (IQR) (c) Local Regression (LR) and (d) Robust Local Regression (LRR), have been used for detection of the overloaded host. Various methods for VM selection such as (a) Minimum Migration Time (MMT) (b) Random Choice (RC) and (c) Maximum Correlation (MC) have been discussed. Power Aware Best Fit Decreasing (PABFD) policy has been proposed for VM placement. A research paper [4], aimed to maximize utilization and minimize cost by proper management of resources and allocation strategies. Authors proposed performance analysis based resource allocation scheme which follows the best fit strategy for efficient VM allocation. The execution time of CPU and performance of memory are considered as two important factors with a flexibility of assigning weight to resource. Subsequently, authors claimed improvement in resource utilization without compromising the allocation time. In the survey paper, [5] identified resource utilization and energy consumption as two important factors to be considered in the process of VM consolidation. To address the factors, authors have suggested having intelligent workload placement and relocation techniques. Authors have exhaustively described terminology involved such as virtualization, VM migration, VM consolidation (static, dynamic) etc. Authors of [6] proposed a QoS-aware VM consolidation approach (based on resource utilization history of VMs) to improve QoS metrics and energy consumption. Initially, the proposed algorithm detects an overloaded host. Then, VMs are selected for migration from these overloaded hosts. Next, detect underloaded hosts and select all VMs from them for migration. At the end, a new placement is searched for VMs to be migrated. Authors claimed a reduction in energy consumption and SLA violation.

3 Proposed Algorithm: Modified Minimization of Migration

The Minimization of Migration (MM) [2] policy selects the minimum number of VMs to migrate from overloaded hosts to reduce the CPU utilization under the upper utilization threshold. The algorithm tries to selects best possible VM combination that satisfies two conditions viz. (a) keep the number of VMs to be migrated as minimum as possible (b) keep the host utilization under and nearer to the upper threshold, after migration. The algorithm works well where the resultant VM is single. But, there are cases where single VM selection is not sufficient for bringing host utilization under the upper threshold. In such scenarios, MM algorithm selects one VM (by default) with the highest utilization and proceeds to make best possible combination by selecting next VM(s) for bringing the host utilization under the upper threshold. The main issue with the MM algorithm is that it does not provide the optimum combination of VMs which brings the host utilization nearer to the upper threshold. To address this issue, for the cases of multiple VM selection, we have modified existing MM algorithm to maximize utilization of host while keeping the number of VMs to be migrated minimal. We start the selection procedure for a number of VM to be migrated equal to 2 and check whether host utilization (after migration) goes below upper threshold or not. If not, the selection of VM proceeds for all nCr combinations incrementally, where n is total number of VMs in a host and r ranges from 2 to n.

To understand the scenario and to support our claim, we have taken following example values. It is worth noting here that we have taken the example of the scenario where more than one VMs are to be selected for migration. Current Host Utilization $hUtil$ = 85%, Upper Threshold $THRESH\_UP$ = 70% (0.7), Total number of VMs in a host = 4, Utilization of all VM in the host, $vmUtil$ = {13, 11, 9, 5} (sorted in decreasing order based on utilization).

Existing Method (MM) [2]: MM selects first VM (by default) irrespective of its utilization. That means, in this case, first VM with utilization = 13 is selected. Then, the method checks for all other VMs where the difference between (a) and (b) remains minimum and resulted in utilization under to THRESH_UP, where (a) hUtil - THRESH_UP = 85 − 70 = 15 (b) Addition of utilization of all VMs selected. So for the example values given, a combination of {13, 5} shall be selected as the total utilization is 18 where the difference is 3 [(13 + 5) − (85 − 70)] which is minimum and resultant utilization will nearer and under THRESH_UP [85 − (13 + 5) = 67, 67 < 70].

Our Proposal (Modified Minimization of Migration – M3): In our proposal, unlike existing method, we do not select the first VM (by default). On the contrary, we look for all the possible combinations of VMs ranging from 2 to n (until we achieve host utilization below THRESH_UP). In above example, possible combinations are as under. For VM = 2, VM combinations are {13, 11}, {13, 9}, {13, 5}, {11, 9}, {11, 5}, {9, 5}, For VM = 3, VM combinations are {13, 11, 9}, {13, 11, 5}, {11, 9, 5}, For VM = n = 4, VM combination is {13, 11, 9, 5}.

In our proposal, the algorithm selects a pair {11, 5} because while doing so difference between (a) and (b) remains minimum and nearer to THRESH_UP. (a) hUtil - THRESH_UP = 85 − 70 = 15 (b) Addition of utilization of all VMs selected (11 + 5 = 16). So, for this value, the difference is 1 (against 3 in existing method) and hUtil will be 69 (against 67 in existing method). For these case example, as we have identified a pair of VM from the first option only, hence the algorithm would not go for checking other combinations with VM = 3 or VM = 4.

Algorithm: Modified Minimization of Migration (M3)

Input: hostList **Output:** migrationList
for each h in hostList **do**
      vmList ← h.getVmList()
      vmList.sortDecreasingUtilization()
      hUtil←h.getUtil()
      bestFitUtil←MAX
      if hUtil − THRESH_UP > VM.getUtil() **then** goto Multiple_VM_Selection **endif**
Single_VM_Selection:
      while hUtil > THRESH_UP **do**
            for each vm in vmList **do**
                 if vm.getUtil() > hUtil − THRESH_UP **then**
                        t←vm.getUtil() − hUtil + THRESH_UP
                    if t < bestFitUtil **then**
                        bestFitUtil←t
                        bestFitVm←vm
                    endif
                endif
            endfor
            hUtil←hUtil − bestFitVm.getUtil()
            migrationList.add(bestFitVm)
            vmList.remove(bestFitVm)
      endwhile
      goto Update
Multiple_VM_Selection:
      n ← h.getVmSize()
      for each total_Migration from 2 step 1 till n **do**
            bestFitUtil ← MAX
            bestFitCombination ← NULL
            for each Combination of VM starting from 2 step 1 till $_nC_{totalMigration}$ **do**
              totalUtil ← 0
              for each VM in Combination **do**
                 totalUtil = totalUtil + Combination.nextVm.getUtil()
             endfor
             if [totalUtil >= (hUtil − THRESH_UP)] AND [totalUtil <bestFitUtil] **then**
                bestFitUtil ← totalUtil
                bestFitCombination ← Combination
             endif
            endfor
            if bestFitUtil != MAX **then** break **endif**
      endfor
      hUtil ← hUtil − bestFitUtil
      migrationList.add(bestFitCombination.getAllVMs())
      vmList.remove(bestFitCombination.getAllVMs())
Update:
      if hUtil < THRESH_LOW **then**
            migrationList.add(h.getVmList())
            vmList.remove(h.getVmList())
      endif
endfor
return migrationList

Table 1. Data set

Host ID	Host type	Host capacity	VM ID	Core per VM	VM capacity (MIPS)	VM utilization required (%)	MIPS required by VM
1	HpProLiantMl110G5Xeon3075	Total Core = 2 MIPS per Core = 2660 Total Capacity = 5320	101	1	2500	30	750
			102	1	2000	25	500
			103	1	1000	25	250
			104	1	500	30	150
			105	1	1000	20	200
			106	1	2000	35	700
			107	1	1000	35	350
			108	1	2500	25	625
			109	1	500	40	200
2	HpProLiantMl110G4Xeon3040	Total Core = 2 MIPS per Core = 1860 Total Capacity = 3720	201	1	2500	24	600
			202	1	2000	21	420
			203	1	1000	18	180
			204	1	500	17	85
			205	1	1000	13	130
			206	1	2000	7	140
			207	1	1000	35	350
			208	1	2500	30	750
			209	1	500	22	110
			210	1	2000	30	600

(continued)

Table 1. (*continued*)

Host ID	Host type	Host capacity	VM ID	Core per VM	VM capacity (MIPS)	VM utilization required (%)	MIPS required by VM
3	HpProLiantMl110G5Xeon3075	Total Core = 2 MIPS per Core = 2660 Total Capacity = 5320	301	1	2500	50	1250
			302	1	2000	60	1200
			303	1	1000	15	150
			304	1	500	18	90
			305	1	1000	17	170
			306	1	2000	12	240
			307	1	1000	26	260
			308	1	2500	28	700
			309	1	500	31	155
4	HpProLiantMl110G4Xeon3040	Total Core = 2 MIPS per Core = 1860 Total Capacity = 3720	401	1	2500	26	650
			402	1	2000	39	780
			403	1	1000	29	290
			404	1	500	21	105
			405	1	1000	14	150
			406	1	2000	20	400
			407	1	1000	10	100
			408	1	2500	27	675
			409	1	500	27	135
			410	1	2000	17	340

4 Experimentation and Results

In this section, we discuss the analysis of existing Minimization of Migration algorithm along with our proposal, Modified Minimization of Migration. For our experimentation, we have taken dataset as mentioned in Table 1. We have simulated a data center consisting of 4 hosts with 9 to 10 VMs on each. Each host is modeled to have 2 CPU cores with MIPS capacity of either 2660 or 1860 per core. Each VM requires 1 CPU core with utilization requirement as mentioned in Table 1. The CloudSim toolkit [7] has been used as a simulation platform because it supports modeling of on-demand virtualization-enabled resource and application management with a varying workload.

For the described simulation setup, we have carried out series of experimentation and generated the results as mentioned in Table 2 and Fig. 1.

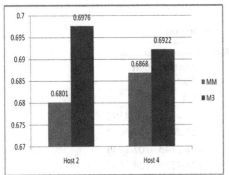

Fig. 1. Host utilization after migration

Fig. 2. Difference (threshold- host utilization after migration)

In our experimentation, the value of the upper threshold is taken as 0.7 which can be calculated dynamically using any of the available statistical methods such as Median Absolute Deviation, Interqurtile Range, Local regression etc. As can be seen from Table 2 that for the case of Host 1 and Host 3, there exists a solution with only one VM selection. So, for both these hosts, both the algorithm results in the same outcome. Hence, these results are not considered for comparison. But, for Host 2 and Host 4, the results are compared in Fig. 1. As shown in the figure, M3 gives resultant host utilization (after migration) nearer to the upper threshold value (here, 0.7). Hence we claim more optimized utilization of available hosts, without compromising the number of VMs to be migrated. Figure 2, the difference between the upper threshold and host utilization after migration has been shown. Lower the difference (nearer to the upper threshold) better the host utilization.

Further, to understand the impact of migration on power consumption, we analyzed the same empirically. Table 3 and Fig. 3 summarize the same. As can be seen from the table and figure, the resultant power gets reduced after migration in both the methods.

Table 2. Results

Host ID	Host utilization (before)	Algorithm	VM selection type	VM selected	Host utilization (after)	Difference (threshold-host utilization after migration)
Host 1	0.7002	MM	Single	104	0.6720	0.0280
		M3	Single	104	0.6720	0.0280
Host 2	0.9046	MM	Multiple	208, 204	0.6801	0.0199
		M3	Multiple	202, 207	0.6976	0.0024
Host 3	0.7923	MM	Single	308	0.6607	0.0393
		M3	Single	308	0.6607	0.0393
Host 4	0.9745	MM	Multiple	402, 403	0.6868	0.0132
		M3	Multiple	401, 406	0.6922	0.0078

Table 3. Power consumption

Host ID	Power consumption before migration (Watts)	Power consumption after migration (Watts)	
		MM	M3
Host 1	108.0075	107.4398	107.4398
Host 2	133.0914	124.2043	124.9032
Host 3	111.6917	107.2143	107.2143
Host 4	134.4892	124.4731	124.6882

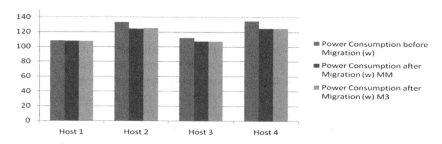

Fig. 3. Power consumption

But, there is a negligible increase in power consumed by M3 as compared to MM. So, we may conclude that without significant increase in power consumption, one may achieve higher utilization using M3.

5 Conclusion

The issues of energy consumption and carbon emission by Cloud data center have attracted the attention of many researchers in recent time. In this research, we have modified an existing algorithm which claimed to minimize the VM migration while keeping the hosts optimally utilized. Our contribution through this research is to identify the best combination of VMs to be migrated in such a way that (a) number of VMs to be migrated is minimizes and (b) host utilization after migration remains below and nearer to the upper threshold. Our results show that the proposed algorithm provides an optimum solution as compared to the existing method.

References

1. Mell, P., Grace, T.: The NIST definition of cloud computing (draft). NIST Special Publication, vol. 800, p. 145 (2011)
2. Beloglazov, A., Abawajy, J., Buyya, R.: Energy-aware resource allocation heuristics for efficient management of data centers for cloud computing. Future Gener. Comput. Syst. **28**(5), 755–768 (2012)
3. Beloglazov, A., Buyya, R.: Optimal online deterministic algorithms and adaptive heuristics for energy and performance efficient dynamic consolidation of virtual machines in cloud data centers. Concurr. Comput.: Pract. Exp. **24**(13), 1397–1420 (2012)
4. Lee, H.M., Jeong, Y.S., Jang, H.J.: Performance analysis based resource allocation for green cloud computing. J. Supercomput. **69**(3), 1013–1026 (2014)
5. Ferdaus, M.H., Murshed, M.: Energy-aware virtual machine consolidation in IaaS cloud computing. In: Mahmood, Z. (ed.) Cloud Computing, pp. 179–208. Springer, Cham (2014). https://doi.org/10.1007/978-3-319-10530-7_8
6. Horri, A., Mozafari, M.S., Dastghaibyfard, G.: Novel resource allocation algorithms to performance and energy efficiency in cloud computing. J. Supercomput. **69**(3), 1445–1461 (2014)
7. Calheiros, R.N., Ranjan, R., Beloglazov, A., De Rose, C.A., Buyya, R.: CloudSim: a toolkit for modeling and simulation of cloud computing environments and evaluation of resource provisioning algorithms. Softw.: Pract. Exp. **41**(1), 23–50 (2011)

Design of High Gain LNA for Wireless Front-End Communication

Ram Kumar[1](✉), Jayendra Kumar[1], F. A. Talukdar[1], Nilanjan Dey[2], Amira S. Ashour[3], and Fuqian Shi[4]

[1] Department of ECE, National Institute of Technology, Silchar 788010, India
`ramkumar.purnea@gmail.com`, `jayendra854330@gmail.com`,
`fatalukdar@gmail.com`
[2] Department of IT, Techno India College of Technology, Kolkata, West Bengal, India
`neelanjandey@gmail.com`
[3] Department of Electronics and Electrical Communications Engineering,
Faculty of Engineering, Tanta University, Tanta, Egypt
`amirasashour@yahoo.com`
[4] Wenzhou Medical University, Wenzhou, People's Republic of China
`fuqian.shi@qq.com`

Abstract. Estimating the input power is an important task in order to design a Low Noise Amplifier (LNA). In the current study, a survey of actual available power in different wireless communication frequency bands is conducted using a wideband low gain micro-strip patch antenna. The circularly polarized low gain antenna is designed and simulated using HFSS. A model of the antenna is fabricated and tested on network analyzer and used for the survey of actual available power. Indoor surroundings as well in outdoor surroundings are considered in the present work to exhibit the significant variations. Based on the minimum available power a high gain LNA is designed considering cascode inductive source degeneration topology. The gain is enhanced by incorporating an inter-stage matching element. The results established 28.21 dB Voltage gain with 0.541 dB noise figure.

Keywords: Cascode · Inductive source degeneration · Low noise amplifier
Patch antenna · Spectrum sensing

1 Introduction

Designing front-end wireless devices is a tremendous challenge to provide increasing number of applications and connectivity. Communication systems of this era operate in a wide range of frequency from few MHz to 100 s of GHz. MICS utilizes 400 MHz band, while, automobile radar systems operate at 77 GHz. Recently, LNA is considered one of the essential element of any communication systems. Typically, LNA should meet several specifications, including high gain, low noise figure, high linearity and good input/output matching. However, the dynamic range of input power has profound effect on the LNA performance.

In the present survey, the actual ambient power available in the GSM, UMTS and LTE bands and a high gain LNA is designed at 2.1 GHz for UMTS band. The UMTS

© Springer Nature Singapore Pte Ltd. 2018
A. V. Deshpande et al. (Eds.): SmartCom 2017, CCIS 876, pp. 102–110, 2018.
https://doi.org/10.1007/978-981-13-1423-0_12

communication system requires a unity gain, omnidirectional, and circularly polarized antenna. The monopole micro-strip patch antenna is a best candidate to meet the requirement of low gain and omnidirectional pattern [1–7]. Recently, designers are concerned with developing circular polarization antennadesign. Numerous methods have been reported in the literature to achieve circular polarization as dual-orthogonal feed and slotted patch [8–11]. In the current work, a plus-shaped slot based circularly polarized antenna is proposed. The circular polarization is enhanced by diagonal arrangement of identical plus shaped slot. Further, the same antenna is used in survey of the ambient power available in different communication bands.

By the Friis's Transmission formula, the noise figure of the first block dominates the noise figure of the entire receiver [12, 13], which is given by:

$$F_{total} = F_{First\ stage} + \frac{\left(F_{subsequent\ stage} - 1\right)}{G_{First\ stage}} \tag{1}$$

Generally, noise optimization plays an important role in the LNA circuit design that depend on the gain of LNA. Thus, an LNA with low noise figure and high gain improves the overall noise figure of the receiver [14]. In this work, the gain of the cascode inductive source degeneration LNA is enhanced using interstage matching between the main transistor and the cascoding transistor.

The proposed LNA is simulated in Cadence SpectreUMC 180 nm CMOS technology. Moreover, antenna optimization is done using HFSS, Version-13. The prototype of the antenna is fabricated and tested as well as the power surveying is done using R&S Spectrum Analyzer.

The organization of the remaining work is as follows. Section 2 describes the antenna design and survey of ambient power. In Sect. 3, the design of inductive source degeneration LNA is discussed with simulation results. Finally, in Sect. 4 conclusion of the work is described.

2 Antenna Design and Structure

In the present work, a wideband circularly polarized patch antenna is designed covering 250 MHz to 2.9 GHz. A low gain antenna that can receive the signal from all directions is proposed. The structure and dimensions of the proposed antenna is shown in Fig. 1. The antenna is built on an FR4 Epoxy dielectric substrate of dielectric constant 4.4, dielectric loss tangent 0.02 and thickness 1.6 mm. A Co-planer Waveguide feeding is used through a 50 Ω SMA connector.

A square patch monopole antenna is selected as a basic configuration due to its miniature structure, ultra-wideband response and good radiation characteristics. However, the ground plane width is optimized to achieve the desired frequency band. The antenna produces circular polarization when two orthogonal field components of equal magnitude and in phase quadrature are radiated [15, 16], which are represented as follows:

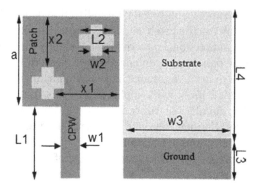

Fig. 1. Configuration of antenna (a = 31 mm, L1 = 17 mm, w1 = 2.38 mm, x2 = 16 mm, x1 = 21.75 mm, L2 = 13 mm, w2 = 3 mm, w3 = 39 mm, L3 = 11.8 mm and L4 = 40.2 mm)

$$|E_x| = |E_y|$$

$$\phi_x - \phi_y = \left(\frac{1}{2} + n\right) \pi \ for \ RHCP$$

$$= -\left(\frac{1}{2} + n\right) \pi \ for \ LHCP \qquad (2)$$

where, n = 0, 1, 2, 3, 4,...

In order to achieve circular polarization, two identical plus-shaped slots are incorporated diagonaly on the patch. These plus-shaped slots introduces two ortagonal field components. In addition, the symmetrical structure of square patch and plus-shaped slots

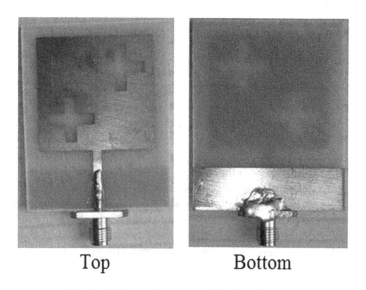

Top   Bottom

Fig. 2. Fabricated prototype of designed antenna

gives in phase quadrature with equal amplitude. A model of the designed antenna is fabricated and tested on the network analyzer as demonstrated in Fig. 2.

The return loss of the antenna is measured on Vector Network Analyzer as shown in Fig. 3. There is excellent agreement between simulated and measured return loss and covering the entire GSM, UMTS and LTE bands. The radiation pattern of the antenna is measured using Spectrum Analyzer and some additional tools at 2.1 GHz and shown in Fig. 4. The 3 dB Axial Ratio bandwidth of the antenna is narrower from 1.5 GHz to 2.5 GHz shown in Fig. 3 with return loss.

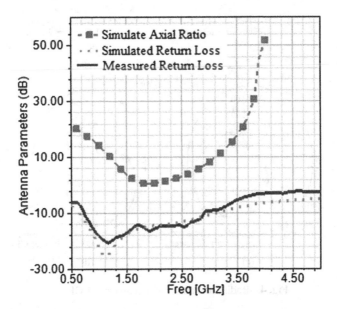

Fig. 3. Return loss and axial ration of designed antenna ($\emptyset = 92°$, $\theta = 0°$)

The survey of the ambient power is done by the designed antenna in indoor as well outdoor surroundings as shown in Fig. 5.

In Fig. 5, the measurement setup is inspired by [17–19]. The indoor surveying is done within a communication laboratory and peak −31.5 dBm, where the power is sensed at UMTS band. The outdoor surveying is done on the 3-story building roof-top, where peak of −24 dBm is sensed at GSM and UMTS bands. Significant variations around (8–10 dBm) is observed due to multipath fading effect.

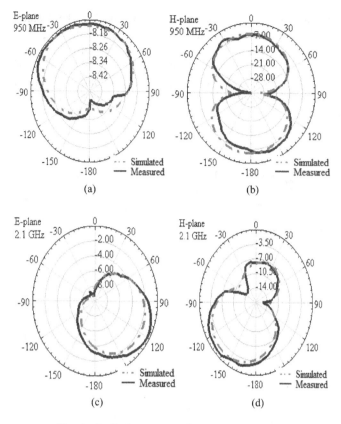

Fig. 4. Radiation pattern of antenna at 2.1 GHz

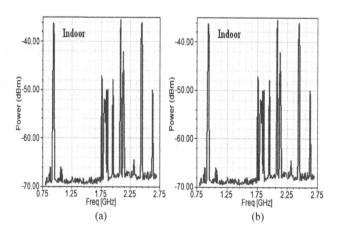

Fig. 5. Actual ambient power received by the designed antenna

3   Design of LNA

The schematic of LNA under study is illustrated in Fig. 6, where L_g, L_s and L_d are on-chip spiral inductors and representing gate, source and drain inductors; respectively. These inductors are used to act the following functions, namely (i) the gate and source inductors are incorporated to tune the input matching with input capacitance, (ii) L_d is used to achieve output resonance with output capacitance and also to improve the LNA gain significantly, and (iii) M1 is the main transistor, and M2 is the Cascading device. The M2 is used to provide isolation between the tuned output and tuned input. Due to the effect of gate-to-drain capacitance of M1, the performance of an LNA is highly affected. This effect of gate-to-drain capacitance is also minimized by the cascading transistor M2 [20]. Furthermore, M3 and R1 form a current mirror which is used for biasing [21].

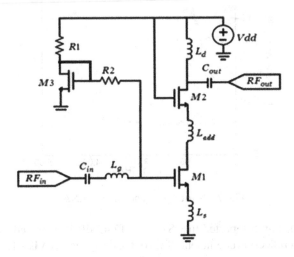

Fig. 6. Schematic of the LNA

3.1   Gain Enhancement Using Inter-stage Matching

The matching network plays an important role in maximum power transfer from one stage to another. Moreover, it helps to improve the signal to noise ratio simultaneously by increasing the signal level. Since the input impedance of common gate MOSFET and output reactance of common source MOSFET is capacitive. Also, for maximum power transfer from MOSFET M1 to M2, the input impedance of M2 must have the complex conjugate of the output impedance of M1 [22]. Moreover, this can be done using the inter-stage matching network.

In this matching series, the inductor is inserted between M1 and M2 [23]. This series inductor L adds and shunted capacitor forms a matching network, which improves the impedance matching between two MOSFETs. It also helps in suppressing the signals of undesired frequency.

3.2   Results and Discussion of LNA

The LNA is designed and simulated for minimum actual received power (−35 dBm) from the antenna explained in earlier section. Based on the minimum possible input power in UMTS band shown in Fig. 5, the LNA performance is studied. This section discusses the simulation results of LNA obtained by Cadence Spectre UMC 180 nm CMOS technology. At 1.8 V power supply, the LNA achieves a gain of 28.21 dB at 2.1 GHz operating frequency as shown in Fig. 7. The noise figure of the designed LNA is found satisfactory (0.541 dB) as demonstrated in Fig. 7.

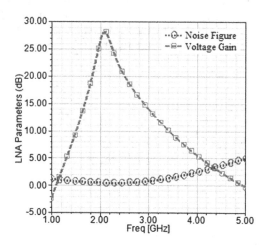

Fig. 7.   Noise figure and Gain of LNA

In this design, Fig. 8 reported that S11 of −17.42 dB is achieved as illustrated in Fig. 8. The output reflection coefficient (S22) of the designed LNA is −15.2 dB as shown in Fig. 8.

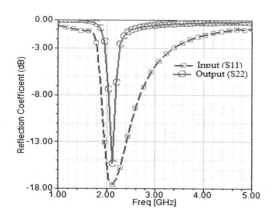

Fig. 8.   Input and output reflection coefficient of LNA

4 Conclusions

A wideband low gain circularly polarized monopole antenna has been designed and excellent agreement is found between simulated and measured results. Survey of actual available ambient power is done using the antenna and significant variations are observed due to multipath fading. Considering the minimum input power at UMTS 2.1 GHz band a high gain LNA is designed.

In the present work, inductive degeneration topology is utilized and applicable in all low noise LNA at 0.18 μm UMC CMOS technology. The inter-stage matching in cascodetopology improved the gain of LNA at 1.8 V power supply.

References

1. Boudaghi, H., Azarmanesh, M., Mehranpour, M.: A frequency-reconfigurable monopole antenna using switchable slotted ground structure. IEEE Antennas Wirel. Propag. Lett. **11**, 655–658 (2012)
2. Hamad, E.K.I., Radwan, A.H.: Compact ultra wideband microstrip-fed printed monopole antenna. In: 30th National Radio Science Conference, Egypt (2013)
3. Foudazi, A., Hassani, H.R., Nezhad, S.M.: Small UWB planar monopole antenna with added GPS/GSM/WLAN bands. IEEE Trans. Antennas Propag. **60**(6), 2987–2992 (2012)
4. Aboufoul, T., Alomainy, A., Parini, C.: Reconfiguring UWB monopole antenna for cognitive radio applications using GaAs FET switches. IEEE Antennas Wirel. Propag. Lett. **11**, 392–394 (2012)
5. Sadeghzadeh-Sheikhan, R.A., Naser-Moghadasi, M., Ebadifallah, E., Rousta, H., Katouli, M., Virdee, B.S.: Planar monopole antenna employing back-plane ladder-shaped resonant structure for ultra-wideband performance. IETMicrowaves Antenna Propag. **4**(9), 1327–1335 (2009)
6. Naghshvarian-Jahromi, M.: Novel wideband planar fractal monopole antenna. IEEE Trans. Antennas Propag. **56**(12), 3844–3849 (2008)
7. Wu, M., Chuang, M.: Multibroadband slotted bow-tie monopole antenna. IEEE Antennas Wirel. Propag. Lett. **14**, 887–890 (2015)
8. Chen, N.Z.N., Qing, X.: Slotted microstrip antennas for circular polarization with compact size. IEEE Antennas Propag. Mag. **55**(2), 124–137 (2013)
9. Chen, N.Z.N., Qing, X.: A compact circularly polarized cross-shaped slotted microstrip antenna. IEEE Trans. Antennas Propag. **60**(03), 6506–6509 (2012)
10. Ushijima, Y., Nishiyama, E., Aikawa, M.: Circular polarization switchable microstrip antenna with SPDT switching circuit. In: IEEE Antennas and Propagation Society International Symposium (APSURSI) (2010). https://doi.org/10.1109/aps.2010.5560951
11. Ushijima, Y., Nishiyama, E., Aikawa, M.: Dual-polarized microstrip array antenna with orthogonal feed circuit. In: IEEE Antennas and Propagation Society International Symposium (APSURSI) (2011). https://doi.org/10.1109/aps.2011.5996770
12. Lee, T.H.: The Design of CMOS Radio-Frequency Integrated Circuits. Cambridge University Press, Cambridge (1998)
13. Lee, T.H.: 5-GHz CMOS wireless LANs. IEEE Trans. Microw. Theory Tech. **50**, 268–280 (2002)
14. Leroux, P., Steyaert, M.: LNA ESD co-design for fully integrated CMOS wireless receivers (2008)

15. Balanis, C.A.: "Fundamental Parameters of Antennas", Antenna Theory, Analysis and Design, 3rd edn. JWS, Hoboken (2005)
16. Garg, R., Bhartia, P., Bahl, I., Ittipiboon, A.: Micro-strip antenna Design Handbook. Artec House, Boston (2001)
17. Habibul Islam, M., et al.: Spectrum survey in Singapore: occupancy measurements and analyses. In: 3rd International Conference on Cognitive Radio Oriented Wireless Networks and Communication 2008 ©IEEE Conference Publications (2008). https://doi.org/10.1109/crowncom.2008.4562457
18. Pedraza, L.F., Forero, F., Paez, I.: Metropolitan spectrum survey in Bogota Colombia. In: WAINA 2013, pp. 548–553. IEEE Computer Society, Bogota (2013)
19. Xue, J., Feng, Z., Chen, K.: Beijing spectrum survey for cognitive radio applications. In: IEEE 78th Vehicular Technology Conference (VTC Fall), 2013 ©IEEE Conference Publications (2013). https://doi.org/10.1109/vtcfall.2013.6692114
20. Razavi, B.: RF Microelectronics. Prentice-Hall PTR, Upper Saddle River (1997)
21. Ellinger, F.: Radio Frequency Integrated Circuits and Technologies, 2nd edn. Springer, Heidelberg (2007). https://doi.org/10.1007/978-3-540-35790-2
22. Rastegar, H., Saryazdi, S., Hakimi, A.: A low power and high linearity UWB low noise amplifier (LNA) for 3.1–10.6 GHz wireless applications in 0.13 um CMOS process. Microelectron. J. **44**, 201–209 (2013)
23. Zhang, C., Huang, D., Lou, D.: Proceedings of the Conference on Electron. Devices and Solid State Circuit (Hong Kong, China, 16–18 December 2003), p. 465 (2003)

Smart Data and IT Innovations

Context-Aware Network for Smart City Services: A Layered Approach

Prathviraj Nagaraj[1(✉)] and Santosh L. Deshpande[2(✉)]

[1] St Joseph Engineering College, Mangaluru, Karnataka, India
Praj151986@gmail.com
[2] Department of PG Studies, VTU, Belagavi, Karnataka, India
sld@vtu.ac.in

Abstract. The smart city service is the collection of heterogeneous services that requires managing and analyzing information from multiple applications. The data collected by one application can be reused by another application if both are developed on common framework. Integration of information from cross application requires integration of data and schema from different application is necessary. The common framework for building any application will overrule the requirement of data and schema integration. This framework minimizes the intermediate computation and data interpretation by human intervention. The service standardization by adopting one city one framework policy will bring all the services of smart city into a single roof.

Keywords: Smart city · Context aware network · Service standardization

1 Introduction

The context in smart city scenario refers to the present situation or status of the city. Here context will be helpful to extract the current status of the city and helpful to make decision based on the current situation. The term context may give different meaning in different places [1]. Four basic categories of context have been mentioned. First one is computing context, relates to geographical area and information related to intra networking, inter networking and CPU, memory, printers etc. Second one is user context like information related users usage log, which includes user's personal information, preferences, current location and potential activity etc. Third one is physical context, which includes location, time, destination, physical and environmental conditions. Last one time context, which give and access information related to time and calendar on a daily, weekly and monthly basis.

There are different kinds of Context-aware application for smart city services [2], which make the environment around us smart for example home, hospital, class room, etc. When a traveler landed in unfamiliar tourist destination, application acts as a travel guide and also it will help traffic police to manage the heavy congested traffic during peak time. In addition, context aware applications manage information repositories, which will be helpful for decision making, to communicate among user and web service (Figs. 1, 2 and 3).

© Springer Nature Singapore Pte Ltd. 2018
A. V. Deshpande et al. (Eds.): SmartCom 2017, CCIS 876, pp. 113–119, 2018.
https://doi.org/10.1007/978-981-13-1423-0_13

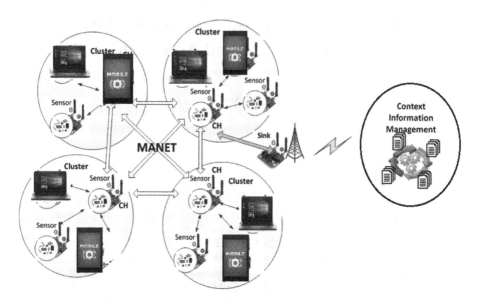

Fig. 1. Context aware network scenario

The smart space may be real or artificial places consists number of artifacts, these artifacts embedded with sensors and actuators in any kind of mobile devices, independent moving vehicles and also humans [3]. The artifacts equipped in smart spaces have their own processing and communication ability to exchange information among individual on mutual consent. These artifacts will be helpful to collect real time information and to make use this information in decision making. Example like smart traffic, smart health, smart governance, and smart home will assist the user in living ambience to make their stay without any difficulties. The context aware applications are also useful in both business and private application areas apart from smart city project implementation by government agencies [5]. Telecom services, as well as energy saving, gaming, chatting, entertainment, information and payment services are exemplary constituents of smart environments.

Implementing a context-aware system for smart city services requires answering many issues like system representing the contextual data internally, combining contextual information with the system and application state, storing context—locally, on the network, or both, relevant data structures and algorithms.

The smart city services which are incorporating Context aware systems should address different requirements from government agencies and business organization [4]. The requirements of smart city services are like heterogeneity of components, ease of use for naive user, protecting privacy of user, flexibility of information modelling and management, scalability from few to many users and devices, reactivity in order to guarantee a real time adaption and a reasonable response time.

1.1 Motivation for Layered Approach

The requirement of the people using smart city services is not only about getting best-effort services also about getting better quality of services. The better quality of service guarantees very high level of quality of experience among the people using smart city services. The smart city services are the horizontal integration of different types of services required to improve the quality of life for citizens. The possibility of integrating MANET with other networks provides an entirely new cross network routing option that enables cost effective applications for a large set of people of smart city service consumer. To efficiently exploit the recent advancements in mobile devices to speed up the smart city services MANET can be effectively utilized as a backbone.

2 Architecture of Context-Aware System for Smart City Services

2.1 User Interaction and Application Layer

The beneficiaries of context aware system for smart city services interact with the smart city application to get different government services. Here beneficiaries may use laptops, smart phones and personal computer or tailor made devices which include sensors to make use of the smart city services. To provide autonomous service without human intervention user interface is customized based on the context and preferences. Context-aware applications act in anticipation of future goals or problems. Context-aware applications not only handle current task, situation and action but also, anticipate future behavior, moving point and problem of user.

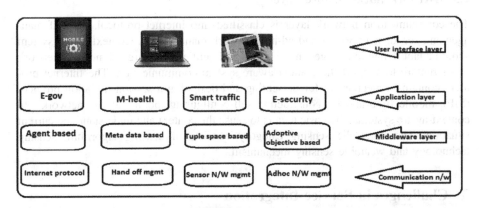

Fig. 2. Layered architecture of context-aware system

2.2 Middleware Layer

The middleware layer collects context information from application, process it and transform into meaningful event. These events will be helpful to enhance the services provided by the application. In context aware system middleware plays a major role in adopting the system to changing contexts by analyzing the contextual information for different logic with respect to changing context. Therefore, the middleware layer acts as context-aware agents for interpreting the context. There are four important categories of middleware that will acts as interpreter of data. First one is agent based, essential part of agent based is mobile agents [6]. Mobile agents come up as a middleware technology suitable to develop context-aware services, and have been developed to implement the needed active infrastructure and the MA-based middleware design and implementation. Second one is metadata middleware that will provide Meta information about context in general. In specific metadata provides information about users, environment, devices, and resources. It is a kind of runtime binding arrangement between the metadata repository and context. Third one is tuple space based have been considered important in sensor networks and works as a black box mechanism that allow us to retrieve partially extracted information. Last one is Adaptive middleware is a middleware for application like smart-home set up. In this scheme, the middleware matches the Quality of Context (QoC) requirements with the QoC available with the sensors. The application's QoC requirements are mapped to a utility function using the QoC attributes of the sensors available.

The rough set approach is used to optimize and analyze the unified preprocessed datasets collected from different services. The Rough Set Theory is to be a useful tool for solving problems in decision analysis, particularly for the analysis of multi-criteria decision problems related to multi criteria sorting problems, multi-criteria multi-sorting problems and multi-criteria description of objects [9]. This will be helpful in setting the benchmark for different smart city scenarios. The attributes of dataset from different smart city services are maintained in a single master table.

2.3 Network Infrastructure Layer

The communication network layer is classified into internet protocol, handoff management, sensor networking and ad-hoc network management. Context-aware system should adapt dynamic changes in the real world entities. So there is a need of network infrastructure to support the context aware system communication. The Internet protocol contains a mechanism for presenting and designing a session initiation protocol (SIP), mobile IPv6 and for constructing self-configuring mobile ad-hoc networks. In context-aware systems, the basic idea is to sense the context and understand the current situation. Therefore, the sensing category consists of sensing algorithm, sensing technology and wearable sensing mechanism.

3 Challenges in Service Integration

3.1 Device Heterogeneity

The common issue raised every time in smart city deployments is the heterogeneity of the device used like sensors, actuators, M2M etc. The outcome of these devices is based on the same principle but due to various protocols and data structures are used by different devices, integration of the heterogeneous devices is tedious job. The possible solution to solve this problem is to come up with standard/common middleware; this will create a new data abstraction layer which provides common data structures to communicate with heterogeneous devices.

3.2 Network Routing

The main challenge is to design a new standardized routing protocol for communication between heterogeneous devices by considering node mobility, energy consumption and quality of Experience in to account. To tackle the problems of citizens of city, while coming up with smart city solution services offered should be user centric; ensure Quality of Service expected by the user of the service. In days to come videos and multimedia information will rule the communication between end users, user platforms and servers. So routing protocols have to consider quality of service as one of the important parameter of effective routing.

3.3 Schema Matching

The information collected from different services/applications should be stored in central repository. To store information in central repository uniformity over the data collected from different applications should be maintained. The uniformity in terms of schemas used in different application should match with all the application/services provided by the smart city project [7]. The traditional integration techniques will leads to taking extra time and no support for extendibility. So the schema design for all application in smart city project should follow common protocol.

4   Service Standardization: One City One Framework

Two barriers currently exist to effective and powerful smart city solutions [8]. First, many current smart city ICT deployments are based on custom systems that are not interoperable, portable across cities, extensible, or cost-effective. Second, a number of architectural design efforts are currently underway (e.g. ISO/IEC JTC1, IEC, IEEE, ITU and consortia) but have not yet converged, creating uncertainty among stakeholders. To reduce these barriers, NIST and its partners are convening an international public working group to compare and distill from these architectural efforts and city stakeholders a consensus framework of common architectural features to enable smart city solutions that meet the needs of modern communities.

The standardization of smart city planning should include following contents:

4.1   Smart City Objectives

The transformation from city to smart city should include set of objectives related to social, economic and better leaving. The government should provide common framework to pro-actively develop the smart system matching with objectives of smart city projects. So in aligned with smart city objectives, a standard framework for the development of intelligent, intensive, green and low carbon city for our future

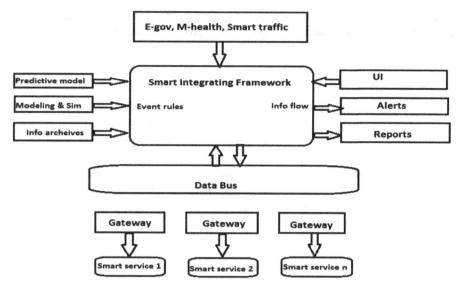

Fig. 3. Smart integrating framework

generation. The end product of this standardization will leads to effective usage of information, smart coordination between different services, smart urban management.

4.2 Policy and Standards

The policy and standardization has become an essential element for all product/service of all countries in the world. The high-level committee for implementing smart city project should come up with common policy to standardize all the service/product provided under smart city project. These policies and standards act as a reference for planning smart cities, standard for developing shared platforms, reference for collaborative application and development.

4.3 Strategic Tasks

The key strategic tasks should be identified in aligned with smart city objectives. The prioritization of key tasks is very important in planning process and implementation methods. For example prioritization of social planning compared to economic planning. The implementation strategy of smart city project is step by step tackling of easier issues first, giving more importance to usability and launching pilot projects to develop, summarize, and to enhance the smart city projects.

4.4 Product/Service Validation

The validation system should be developed for effective measurement of smart city product/service and for setting indicator for the level of competence of the product/service. The evaluation system compares objectives, policies and final outcome of the smart city projects. This procedure has become an effective mode of accessing smart city project implementation and has been great value for solving smart city problems.

5 Conclusion

The critical information is most often placed in different heterogonous systems, across different, disconnected departments, both citizens and governing authorities feel it difficult to coordinate the work. The current smart city services lack a single, integrated view of information, events, crises, and the ability to rapidly share information. Without this city might be unable to deliver services in a sustainable way to protect citizens, or drive economic growth for the future. The independent nature of different services of smart city project is not aligned with the other smart city services. So integration of information collected from different services for decision making in smart governance is critical tasks. The smart city framework is developed in aligned with event rules, information flow and routing protocol. This framework will bring all the services of smart city project into common platform which will avoid different problem like mismatch in event rules, data flow and schema matching.

References

1. Wang, J., Li, C., Xiong, Z., Shan, Z.: Survey of data-centric smart city. J. Comput. Res. Dev. **51**(2), 239–259 (2014)
2. Wang, Y.: Smart city top-down design. ZTE Technol. J. **20**(4) (2014)
3. Wan, B.: Smart city development needs one city one policy. Smart City **8**, 64–65 (2014)
4. Bouk, S.H., Sasase, I., Ahmed, S.H., Javaid, N.: Gateway discovery algorithm based on multiple QoS path parameters between mobile node and gateway node. J. Commun. Netw. **14** (4), 434–442 (2012)
5. Madhavan, J., Bemstein, P.A., Rahm, E.: Generic schema matching with cupid microsoft research. Microsoft Corporation Technical report MSR-TR-2001-58, August 2001
6. Gea, T., Paradells, J., Lamarca, M., Roldana, D.: Smart cities as an application of smart internet of things: experiences and lessons learnt in Barcelona. In: Seventh International Conference on Innovative mobile and Internet Services in Ubiquitous Computing, July 2013. https://doi.org/10.1109/im-is.2013.158
7. Lei, J., Yong, X., Liu, Y., Qin, Y., Tang, H., Zhao, Z.: Using physical-level context awareness to improve service ranking in wireless sensor network. J. Netw. **7**(6), 926 (2012)
8. Baldauf, M., Dustdar, S., Rosenberg, F.: A survey on context-aware system. Int. J. Ad Hoc Ubiquitous Comput. **2**(4), 263–277 (2007)
9. Prathviraj, N., Deshpande, S.L.: Rough set approach for solving multi-constrained QoS routing problems in MANET. In: International Conference on Wireless Communications Signal Processing and Networking (WISPNET), pp. 1150–1153 (2016)

Searching Lead to Better Search Intension for Keyword

Dipalee P. More[✉] and Ujwala M. Patil

R. C. Patel Institute of Technology, Shirpur, India
dipali.p.more26@gmail.com

Abstract. In this world the Internet has become very casual for searching. Ordinary user appears to use it every time; even they need to search keyword from any query information. Also, people use search engine like Google, Bing when they are willing to search something, wants to use some relevant information or go to their synonyms. But searching for correct result requires more time and less execution speed even they produce multiple choices. So, this process is very confusing for users to decide one correct keyword amid the many results as a search engine show overall results. An agglomerative algorithm which is useful in searching better result by their centroid, hence it executes up to their centroid. Intended for the Bisect K means approach is used which aim to generate exact keyword in less time and reducing computational cost. For these reasons, enhance method called Bisect k means approach is very useful for knowing the best result from requiring query candidate.

Keywords: Agglomerative algorithm · Anchor-based pruning solution
Baseline solution · Bisect k-means algorithm

1 Introduction

Searching is one of the best ways to know the information content from structured and semi-structured data, but the user having the knowledge of sophisticated query language [1]. In a process of information retrieval, the node chooses to detect a list of relevant documents For example, when someone is interested to search a particular information purchasing product. The information like Name of person, Mobile Number of people, City of person, Qualification of Pearson for details otherwise in harvests similar AC, Refrigerator, bike for buying, he/she would famine near recognize the other prospect earlier accomplishment the absolute verdict. Trendy this domain, persons effortlessly search further stuffs however solitary once they recognize all around individuals articles. For specimen, Searching information about an AC or refrigerator for going out to the market is tranquil as we recognize a slight tad around these gadgets. That wealth searching receipts in a higher data. Customer Information, the core information chart is the cradles that provide such a high knowledge of product and try to satisfy the need of searching. As most of the folks use seek devices to search keyword and number of keywords are produce hence it require more time. So we presented method centers solitary on display the superlative option and best unconventional which is habitually vital to sort the ending resolution. The user's contains

A. V. Deshpande et al. (Eds.): SmartCom 2017, CCIS 876, pp. 120–128, 2018.
https://doi.org/10.1007/978-981-13-1423-0_14

query which is easier to search intention with query can be identified, a user mutual action may require more time when dataset size is large. To solve this, problem, in existing paper develops a method of diversifying query suggestions to user's based on result to be generated. At the time of performing the users may choose to adapt their original queries based on their return diversify result of query suggestion.

Diversification is one of the methods uses to find the exact search keyword. In the diversification process, firstly deduces the mutually related feature terms of gauging its consequence to unique result then proposed result set. In Existing paper, we produce a number of results from input query keyword. It is very confusing to decide which is useful; hence this method is used to prepare better result.

K-means clustering is the most widely used partition clustering algorithm. It starts by choosing K representative points as the initial centroids. Each point is then assigned to the closest centroid based on a particular proximity measure chosen. Once the clusters are formed, the centroids for each cluster are updated. After that we use an agglomerative algorithm for searching. The agglomerative algorithm works by number of values compounded in unique result, their distance between the data point which required less time and more execution speed. Bisecting K-means clustering is a divisive hierarchical clustering method which uses k-means repeats on the parent cluster C to determine the best possible split to obtain two child Clusters.

2 Related Work

The searching method before is done with structured and semi-structured data has implemented by using the information retrieved. But specifically detecting search keyword was not done yet.

Chen et al. Presented a novel approach to keyword search for structure and semi-structured data, search result generates and improving the search result, by using information integration and analysis. It provides a lightweight method of integration as a database selection by keyword relationship graph, query generation, analytical processing. Also describe the future research model as diverse data model, improve quality for search result and evaluation [1].

Guo et al. Present a method of XML dataset. It describes the problem on efficiently occurred search result using the model structure of the database and semantic of query. Specifically, describe the XML data, the result of a query and ranking method. It also describes the index structures and query evaluation techniques [2].

Sun et al. Present a novel approach of keyword searches on smallest, lowest common ancestor from an XML document by using their anchor node and their properties, also provide incremental multiway common ancestor and at the last analyze this process. The properties of the LCA computation and improved algorithms to solve the traditional KWS problem. The index lookup algorithm is the algorithm of choice when the KWS involves at least one low frequency keyword [3].

Xu et al. Present a novel approach to efficient keyword search, also present the search result on rooting the sub tree. The index lookup eager algorithm for indexing purpose and also uses scan eager algorithm for the scan node list, stack algorithm for merges all keyword lists nodes [4].

The work on keyword search is associated with information retrieval and re-ranking query interpretations in information extraction. Specifically, the most appropriate work is by Clarkel and E. Demidove [5, 6] on real-world datasets demonstrates that search results. Their methods applied redundancy and novelty [5] learned from relevance estimation. In their experimental methods typically can attain normalize discount cumulative gain set up as the standard evaluation method.

Zhuang et al. Present iteration for large database. Which present limited iteration to higher comparing iteration with current dataset. Bisect k-means has the high potential by achieving high efficiency and maintain cluster quality. The former ensures that the differentiation feature set can be easily checked by a user, and the later ensuresthat the comparison based on differentiation feature set correctly reflects the comparison of results [7].

Reddy et al. Present a survey of partition and hierarchical clustering algorithms, which show the various types of clustering algorithms and also present the variation in k-means clustering . Fuzzy C-Means clustering is perform hard assignments. To extract such overlapping structures, fuzzy clustering algorithm can be used. In fuzzy C-means clustering algorithm, membership of points to different clusters. X-Means is a clustering method which can be used to efficiently estimate the value of K [8].

Murugesan et al. Present a hybrid bisect k-means clustering algorithm which shows the divisive clustering algorithm and Unweighted Pair Group Method with Arithmetic Mean (UPGMA) for agglomerative clustering algorithm [9].

3   Methodology

In general, searching the relevant information and objective methods like generation procedure. Optimization seeks values of variables that lead to an optimal value of the function that is to be optimized in Fig. 1. It takes the input as a keyword, then enter into XML database, then procedure to diversification algorithm as baseline algorithm, anchor based algorithm and anchor based parallel sharing after that use the clustering methods as a agglomerative algorithm and bisect k-means algorithm, at the last generate output as qualified search intension in less time.

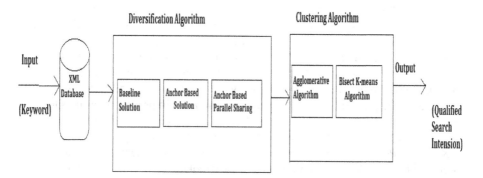

Fig. 1. System structure.

3.1 Baseline Solution

The baseline solution, retrieve the relevant terms with their score. Then, list out the query candidates. The mutual information score is used to search their keyword result.

I. Construct matrix M_{m*n} by using pre-computed relevant feature terms of graph G.
II. Then generate new query q_{new} from matrix M_{m*n} by function GenerateNewQuery ().
III. Then write new query candidate q_{new} in order of descending, according to their score.
IV. Compute the common ancestor result of q_{new} by retrieving the node list of keyword feature terms.
V. Then work out the probable result of causing witnessed query q.
VI. Then compute the common ancestor result of actual result and old result, in order to obtain diversified common ancestor result.
VII. And at the last, compare new result with old result and interchange outright ones in Q.

3.2 Anchor-Based Pruning Solution

By studying the previous method of search result, we can compute the final one execution rate of this resolution done on the determining ancestor result and destroying unnecessary ancestor result from a fresh and old produced outcome set. The anchor-based pruning, solution design to escape gratuitous execution costs by analyzing their interrelationship between intermediate ancestor results.

I. Firstly constructs matrix M_{m*n} of feature terms, retrieve the list of nodes by maintaining their index term.
II. And above, then evaluate q related when the query is q_{new}.
III. Then apply the intermediate common ancestor results of old result as node efficiently computes new ancestor result.
IV. Caused query, we can find the common ancestor consequences expending previously implemented searching method as a baseline solution.
V. The prune result of ancestor is considered as a first query and the list of nodes of the second queries for reducing its cost of evaluation.
VI. Anchor node for every list of nodes of keyword in present fresh query, we grow many active grades of nodes using index term by using the Partition () method.
VII. The common ancestor results are different from the old ancestor node, then they will be canned as new distinguishable result and old ancestor result will remove from the implementing result set.
VIII. At the last, we record the score and result of the new query.

3.3 Agglomerative Algorithm

By analyzing the base paper method, the user involution is useful to fine search value is of keyword queries, a user's searching process may require more time when the size of the pertinent result set is large. In our presented paper use the agglomerative algorithm works by number of values compounded in unique result, their distance between the data point which required less time and more execution speed. In existing paper implementation, the cluster is divided in n number of document with same size [11]. Then, it sets centroid as a maximum number of keyword present in that document, these document values consider as a centroid value. Every document file having one relevance value [12]. After that, centroid matches to those documents that value is similar. And only analyze that document for example, it has total 10 documents Centroid calculates as a maximum number of documents having common value. So, 4 documents having common value as a 5. Hence, only 4 document matches there centroid so remaining 6 not to analyze their value, so the execution process will not carry out and time require to process execution is also less and speed also increases [13]. These system perform step wise process as below.

I. Start.
II. K (0) = 0 and r a categorization value initially is r = 0.
III. Finding lowest distance in running clustering as a pair of (r), (s) allowing to d [(r) (s)] = mn d [(i) (j)] when bottom to all terminated.
IV. r = r + 1
V. Join (r), (s) into single cluster from another cluster m.
VI. K (r) = d [(r)(s)].
VII. Inform reserve value and adding to form new cluster, as a (r, s).
VIII. Stop.

3.4 Bisect K-means Algorithm

By analyzing the base paper method, the user involution is useful to fine search value is of keyword queries, a user's searching process may require more time when the size of the pertinent result set is large. In our proposed method use bisect k-means approach for evaluating the exact result in less time. Bisecting k-Means is like a combination of k-Means and hierarchical clustering. Instead of partitioning the data into 'k' clusters in each iteration, Bisecting k-means splits one cluster into two sub clusters at each bisecting step(by using k-means) describe as below.

I. Pick a cluster to split.
II. Find 2 sub-clusters using the basic K-means algorithm. (Bisecting step)
III. Repeat step 2, the bisecting step, for ITER times and take the split that produces the clustering with the highest overall similarity.
IV. Repeat steps 1, 2 and 3 until the desired number of Clusters are reached.

4 Experimental Results

4.1 Data Source

To perform the experiments of base paper, the data sets are requested from DBLP [14] this is the real data set and XMark [15] is an artificial XML dataset for testing the diversification keyword result. The size of DBLP dataset is 227 MB, it has element

3332130, attribute is 404276, maximum depth is 6 and average depth is 2090228. The size of the artificial XMark dataset is 198 MB, having element 26859, attribute is 5689, maximum depth is 4 and the average depth is 2.668.

4.2 Analysis

We analyze the existing paper method, Baseline solution is to repossess the pertinent piece values with the in elevation score. Then generate list occurred value keyword that is sorted in descending order for the total score. And then, finally compute the common ancestor result for is querying candidate measure their score. Different from other search engine, existing system work need to appraise multiple query candidate and generate entire result set.

By analyzing anchor-based pruning, solution, limitation of baseline solution as more computational cost and time is overcome in the anchor-based solution. Anchor-based parallel sharing solution use by working the similarly by virtue of corresponding of diversification for search keyword and reduction in the perennial scanning of the similar list of nodes, which is a less time-consuming process and more execution speed.

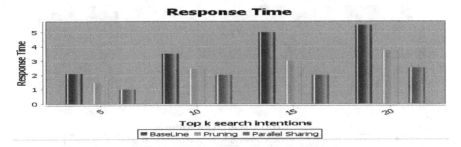

Fig. 2. Average time cost of queries.

In the base paper there is a limitation in Sun et al. A method that, their method many numbers of queries are evaluated using structure value methods. For example, keyword Day generates result as age, epoch, term, period, cycle. But in our method we have overcome this limitation that means our method can generate exact key word in minimum time with high speed. We use the agglomerative algorithm to improve our final result. These methods use the step wise processing as firstly, Assign each object to a separate cluster, then Evaluate all pairwise distances between clusters. In our presented paper, we use an agglomerative algorithm for improving their results as reduce their response time by using the centroid identification method. In the centroid identification method, firstly computes centroid as a maximum result occurred document value. Then it matches only that document. Remaining document is not being analyzed. So, visiting document process is less hence time require also less and execution speed increases. Figure 2 shows the average time cost of queries, using the baseline by using an information retrieval process and removing duplicate results. And anchor-based pruning, solution used by avoiding unqualified ancestor result. Parallel sharing used by partitioning in similar part. So, the result is improved by their method.

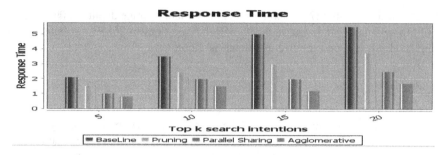

Fig. 3. Comparison result between base paper and agglomerative algorithm.

Figure 3 shows the comparative result between Baseline, Pruning, Parallel Sharing and Agglomerative Algorithm. And Fig. 4 shows the comparative result between Baseline, Pruning, Parallel Sharing, Agglomerative Algorithm and Bisect K-means Algorithm.

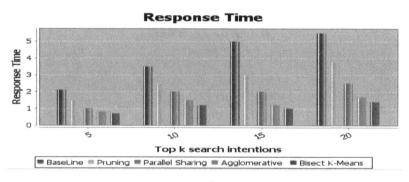

Fig. 4. Comparison result between base paper, agglomerative algorithm and bisect K-means algorithm.

In the base paper there is a limitation in Sun et al. A method that, their method many numbers of queries are evaluated using structure value methods. For example, keyword Day generates result as age, epoch, term, period, cycle. But in our method we have overcome this limitation that means our method can generate exact key word in minimum time with high speed. We use the agglomerative algorithm to improve our final result. These methods use the step wise processing as firstly, Assign each object to a separate cluster, then evaluate all pairwise distances between clusters. In our presented paper, we use an agglomerative algorithm for improving their results as reduce their response time by using the centroid identification method. In the centroid identification method, firstly computes centroid as a maximum result occurred document value. Then it matches only that document. Remaining document is not being analyzed. So, visiting document process is less hence time require also less and execution speed increases.

The Bisect k-means algorithm archives high processing efficiency by limiting the number of iteration for the two means and employs the basic k-means as a refinement after k clusters have been obtain from bisecting process. In Fig. 4 show the enhance result as compare to the existing method result. In agglomerative algorithm use centroid method for execution. In centroid method, only process on centroid match document. In these method less number of document are execute for searching process hence agglomerative method require less time. In Fig. 4, baseline algorithm requires 2.2 s response time for 5 top-k search intension. In anchor-based pruning algorithm require 1.5 s response time for 5 top-k search intension, because these algorithm analyze interrelationship then execute. In parallel sharing algorithm require 0.9 s response time for 5 top-k search intension, because these algorithm exploiting parallelism then execute. In agglomerative algorithm require 0.8 s response time for 5 top-k search intension, because these algorithm use centroid method. In bisect k-means algorithm require 0.6 s response time for 5 top-k search intension. Bisect k-means algorithm, divide one parent node into two child node such as, C is one parent node and it divide into C1 and C2 child node.

5   Conclusions

Searching using a search engine for relevant entity from database for exact result search is may be time consuming and frustrating process. Thus, baseline solution focuses on fetching relevant keyword from large database which means it directly give relevant information. Likewise Anchor-based pruning solution, removing unqualified results from the newly and previously generated result sets. Anchor-based pruning solution is very useful for everyone who computes result in less time by reducing computational cost. Also, the anchor-based parallel sharing solution improved by exploiting the parallelism of keyword diversification and reducing the repeated scanning of the same node list. Agglomerative algorithm is useful for searching best result by their centroid method in less time and also reduces the computational cost. It significantly improves the searching result from the dataset. Bisect K-means Algorithm, which perform clustering up to their optimal result, hence these processes require less time and provide results as exact keyword.

References

1. Chen, Y., Wang, W., Liu, Z., Lin, X.: Keyword search on structured and semi-structured data, In: SIGMOD Conference, pp. b1005–1010 (2009)
2. Guo, L., Shao, F., Botev, C., Shanmugasundaram, J.: XRANK: ranked keyword search over XML documents. In: SIGMOD Conference, pp. 16–27 (2003)
3. Sun, C., Chan, C.Y., Goenka, A.K.: Multiway SLCA based keyword search in XML data. In: WWW, pp. 1043–1052 (2007)
4. Xu, Y., Papakonstantinou, Y.: Efficient keyword search for smallest LCAs in xml databases. In: SIGMOD Conference, pp. 537–538 (2005)
5. Clarke, C.L.A.: Novelty and diversity in information retrieval evaluation. In: SIGIR, pp. 659–666 (2008)

6. Demidova, E., Fankhauser, P., Zhou, X., Nejdl, W.: DivQ: diversification for keyword search over structured databases. In: Proceedings SIGIR, pp. 331–338 (2010)
7. Zhuang, Y., Mao, Y., Chen, X.: A limited-iteration isect K-means for fast clustering large datasets. In: IEEE TrustCom-BigDataSE-ISPA, pp. 2257–2262 (2016)
8. Chandan, K., Raddy, A.: Survey of partitional and hierarchical clustering algorithm, pp. 57–110
9. Murugesan, K. Zhang, J.: Hybride bisect K-means clustering algorithm. In: International Conference on Business Computing and Global Information (2011)
10. Slonim, N. Tishby, N.: Agglomerative Aglorithm Bottlneck
11. Sasirekha, K., Baby, P.: Agglomerative hierarchical clustering algorithm: a review. IJSRP **3** (3), 1–3 (2013)
12. Hasan, M., Mueen, A., Tsotras, V.J., Keogh, E.J.: Diversifying query results on semi-structured data. In: CIKM, pp. 2099–2103 (2012)
13. http://dblp.uni-trier.de/xml/
14. http://monetdb.cwi.nl/xml/

Real Time Surveillance and Object Tracking

Shantanu Rane, Pranav Rane, Kiran Panchal, and Gargi Phadke[✉]

Ramrao Adik Institute of Technology,
DY Patil Vidyanagari, Nerul, Navi Mumbai, India
rane.shantanu29@gmail.com, pranel957@gmail.com,
kiranpanchal731@gmail.com, gargi.phadke@rait.ac.in

Abstract. Object tracking is a challenging task in surveillance and activity analysis. Autonomous video surveillance and monitoring has a rich history in real time object tracking. It has many application in different area like home automation, military, in surveillance monitoring as well as in search-and-rescue operations. Main objective is tracking a particular target or object from real time videos and transmit it to one place to another place. Raspberry pi is used as processor. Video transport has technical challenge when the wireless transmissions require high data rate and low latency.

Keywords: Mean-shift · Bhattacharyya coefficient · Cam-shift

1 Introduction

Tracking are the important and challenging tasks [19]. Its numerous applications include home automation, surveillance, tracking robots vehicles tracking etc. It is one of the best technologies to fight against crimes and terrorist activities and also provides personnel safety. Video tracking is challenging task in computer vision when human and vehicles tracking are required. This work consists of designing of efficient video tracking and surveillance system which works in any kind of environment. In video surveillance for object detection, detection of different kinds of objects from video are important [5]. Detection of moving objects in video streams is first step of tracking. Background subtraction is a very popular approach, but it has different problem when illumination variations, clustering and shadows are in the videos. In [13] author proposed a method which is used for tracking using optical flow. In [9] author has proposed method to overcome illumination variation problem, background cluster and shadows problem is solved by author in [15]. For understanding the human activities detection and tracking of different body parts is important [11, 19]. Due to an increasing demand for intelligent and automated security surveillance systems in public areas such systems have become area of important research in present time. Public areas include railway stations, shopping malls, airports etc. In this paper, for surveillance systems based on the tracking, tracking of moving foreground objects is one of the most important need. For the detection of stationary objects, object tracking based techniques are very useful as the camera used is stationary and works well in variable lightening conditions. It is also popular method for separation of different foreground objects from the frame [12]. In surveillance, feed captured by the camera can be viewed

© Springer Nature Singapore Pte Ltd. 2018
A. V. Deshpande et al. (Eds.): SmartCom 2017, CCIS 876, pp. 129–136, 2018.
https://doi.org/10.1007/978-981-13-1423-0_15

on the display or on group of displays which is monitored by some people. As the events occur, it is not easy for the human operator to detect them. Recently computer vision defined several ways that automatically detects and provides some data to help human operators [6]. Constant flow of information and delivery of packets is an important factor for proper video streaming [6], wireless radio networks are not capable of providing reliability in such service. The problem arises due to the disagreement between the network nodes, as well as due to the interference from external radio waves such as microwaves and the waves generating from the mobile phones etc. [8]. In case of mobile networks, Multi-path fading and shadowing can further increase transmission error rate and linking capacities [17]. The most important benefit of wireless tracking over wired tracking is that we can watch the tracked objects on any devices such as mobiles, computers, laptops, tablets connected to the same network and hence user can move freely from one place to another [6]. Users are also able to communicate with each other using wireless devices that are connected to the network. It also makes it easier to watch the live tracking on different devices connected to the network with the help of the same IP address, as no new cabling is needed [12]. In video tracking video captured by the camera is converted into frames. Then the frames are analyzed by using previously defined algorithms which gives us output as tracked objects. There is large number of algorithms for object tracking. Each algorithm has its own strengths and weaknesses. For tracking different kind of objects such as human bodies, vehicles there are different types of algorithms which differ from each other. In visual tracking system there are two major components: representation of target and localization of target. It also includes the filtering and data association [14]. Target representation and localization is Representation of target and localization is considered as bottom-up process. Variety of tools for identifying the moving objects is provided by these methods. An algorithm plays an important rule in locating and tracking an object successfully. As person's profile changes dynamically blob tracking is used for tracking human movements [19]. Complexity of these algorithms is generally low. Kernel-based tracking (mean shift tracking), contour tracking, cam shift tracking are the algorithms generally used for tracking an object [10].

1.1 Design Challenges

In order to achieve the proper video streaming proper delivery of packets by deadline and steady flow of information is required. The problem arises due to the disagreement between the network nodes, as well as due to the interference from external radio waves such as microwaves and the waves generating from the mobile phones etc. [8]. In case of mobile networks, Multi-path fading increase transmission error rate and linking capacities.

1.2 Advantages of Wireless Streaming

One of the biggest pros of wireless tracking over a wire done is that it grants users the liberty to move around freely within the area of the network and still get a live tracking. Users can also communicate with each other through devices that are connected to the network wirelessly. This proves to be a considerable advantage in terms of time and expense. It also makes it easier to obtain the live feed on various devices connected to the network without cable routing [16]. During video tracking an algorithm analyzes sequential video frames and outputs the movement of targets between the frames. There are two major components of a visual tracking system: target representation and localization, as well as filtering and data association. These methods give a variety of tools for identifying the moving object. Locating and tracking the target object successfully is dependent on the algorithm. Considering the intended use helps in choosing which algorithm to use [3].

1.3   Application of Tracking

Homeland security applications should have the ability to detect a threat in advance and generate alarm in order to allow inform user and allow them to take necessary actions. Military image processing, detection of moving object is important criteria. Lack of ability to detect and track the moving object can be overcome using image processing and video analysis techniques. It is one of the hardest when geographical conditions vary makes it difficult to detect motions [16]. Video tracking is also difficult in fog conditions. It reduces clarity of images. Capra Image Processing Platform eliminates fog. It increases visibility range of image by 30–40% [16].

Video Stabilization, in military applications, real time images and videos are used. Different techniques are proposed by different authors to obtain the desired outputs for motion detection, target detection and object tracking. Here images are acquired from cameras on moving platforms, For further processing, images or videos should be stable. Capras parallel and multi-core programming architecture is used for stabilization is proposed in [2].

In this paper, we proposed method video streaming for tracking using mean shift algorithm. Section 2 gives introduction about mean shift tracking, Sect. 3 gives details of proposed method and last Sect. 4 gives result analysis of the method.

2   Mean Shift Tracking Algorithm

Mean shift is an iterative method for localization based on the maximization of a similarity measure (Bhattacharyya coefficient). In mean shift tracking, target tracking is achieved by choosing a target histogram from the region-of-interest (ROI) corresponding to the object to be tracked in the reference frame example as shown in Fig. 1 [10]. This target histogram is compared with a candidate histogram to obtain the mean shift vector, which gives the target position [7]. The target histogram and candidate histograms are given as,

$$q_u = c_1 \sum_{i=1}^{n} k\left(\|X_i\|^2\right) \delta[b(X_i) - u], \quad \text{and} \tag{1}$$

$$p_u(Y) = c_2 \sum_{i=1}^{n} k\left(\left\|\frac{Y - X_i}{B}\right\|^2\right) \delta[b(X_i) - u]. \tag{2}$$

(a) F1:Normal image   (b) F1:Mean-Shifted image

Fig. 1. Example of mean-shifting

where c_1, c_2 are normalization constants, Y is the target center, (Xi) i = 1; 2...., n are pixel co-ordinates of the target model, B is bandwidth, b is bins of the reflectance component of Vr. Using the target histogram, candidate histogram, and mean shift vector, the center for the target in the next frame is given in Eq. 3.

$$Y = \frac{\sum_{i=1}^{n} X_i z_i g \left(\frac{Y_o - X_i}{B} \right)^2}{\sum_{i=1}^{n} z_i g \left(\frac{Y_o - X_i}{B} \right)^2}, \tag{3}$$

Here 'g' is the negative of derivative of kernel k, and z is the weight calculated from the target and candidate histograms, which are used to calculate the new center of the target. The center of the kernel is then shifted from Y0 to a new center point Y [18]. This is repeated till the candidate model is close to target model. Here we use Bhattacharyya distance for similarity measurement. Target model and candidate histograms [7] are obtained from the reflectance component of each frame, which is invariant to illumination. Hence, the mean shift vector is invariant to illumination [9, 20].

(a) F1:Mean-Shifted image   (b) F1:cam-Shifted image

Fig. 2. Examples (a) mean shift tracker (b) Cam shift tracker, green bounding box indicate tracked result

Camshaft is advanced algorithm than mean shift. Size of window is updated after mean shift converges. It also calculates the orientation of object. Again mean shift center search in new frame is started with new scaled search window and previous window location. It is also iterative process [10] (Fig. 2).

3 Block Diagram

Figure 3 Shows block diagram of proposed method. Camera is used for capturing videos. Using Rasberry Pi video streaming and tracking is done. Implementation and tracking is main part of the proposed method. OpenCV, a computer vision library is used for video capturing and conversion of the video into frame by frame images. The images are sent by using a network shield to the user interface. Raspberry pi, a microcontroller kit buildwith ARM11 board is used to integrate this entire shield and the OpenCV program written in python with the user interface. Feed from camera is given as input to the raspberry pi. Logitech C310 camera is used for video recording. The OpenCV code is compiled on the Pi using Python 3. It is continuously run once the Pi boots.

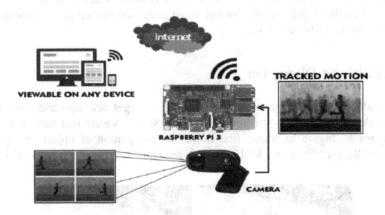

Fig. 3. Block diagram of the proposed method

3.1 Working

Figure 4 shows working of the proposed method. OpenCV, a computer vision library is used for video capturing and conversion of the video into frame by frame images. The images are sent by using a network shield to the user interface. Raspberry pi, a microcontroller kit build with ARM11 board is used to integrate this entire shield and the OpenCV program written in python with the user interface. Feed from camera is given as input to the raspberrypi. Logitech C310 camera is used for video recording. The OpenCV code is compiled on the Pi using Python 3. It is continuously run once the Pi boots.

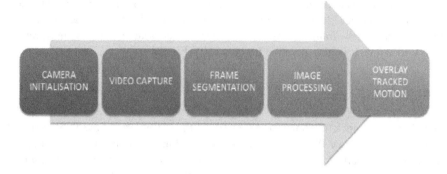

Fig. 4. Flowchart of the proposed method

When a frame is captured by the cam, it is fed to the Pi and the Pi then processes this frame. The user can pause the live feed and specify the Region of Interest (RoI) by using the cursor to specify 4 distinct points. Once, the RoI has been determined, it will be tracked by using cam shift method. The output of this processing is a video feed with the tracking details over layer on the original captured video feed. This video feed can be seen on the display monitor or any smart device connected to the same network as the Raspberry Pi by streaming.

4   Results and Discussion

Here Results are divided into two parts first one is target detection and other one is target tracking using video streaming. Figure 5 Shows Visual real time video with tracking result. Figure 5a shows first frame for recognition of object or region of interest (ROI), Fig. 5b shows ROI selection, remaining figures gives tracking results.

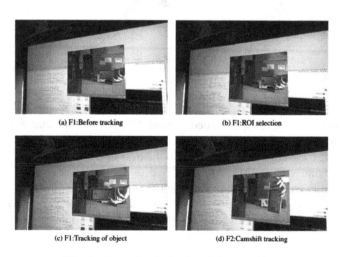

(a) F1:Before tracking

(b) F1:ROI selection

(c) F1:Tracking of object

(d) F2:Camshift tracking

Fig. 5. Example of visual real time tracking

Results show proposed method work in rotation of the ROI. It also works in different attributes in videos like illumination changes, occlusion and complex videos. Different videos are used for result analysis. It is checked with computational time in different conditions.

Table 1 shows result analysis using attributes for different videos.

Table 1. Result analysis of different videos for different attributes using proposed method.

Video	Attributes			
Name	Lighting	Occlusion	Complexity	Computation time
1	Good	No	Less	Very low
2	Bad	Low	Medium	Low
3	Good	Medium	Medium	Medium
4	Excellent	No	Very less	Low
5	Fair	High	Very high	High

5 Conclusion

In this paper we have trying to achieve video real time tracking in different attributes. The system is based on Cam shift algorithm and can handle scaling of target has demonstrated good results over multiple objects in varying conditions. As demonstrated in analysis proposed method works better in different scenario. Here we also proposed tracking in using wireless streaming.

Introducing multiple viewing the scene in different angles would improve the object tracking and classification performance and robustness of the system.

Acknowledgment. We would like to thanks Mumbai university and Ramrao Adik Institute of Technology, Nerul for Financial support.

References

1. Comaniciu, D., Ramesh, V., Meer, P.: Real-time tracking of non-rigid objects using mean shift. In: IEEE Proceedings of CVPR (2000)
2. Zou, X., Wang, W., Kittler, J.: Non-negative matrix factorization for face illumination analysis. The University of Liverpool (2008)
3. Wu, Y., Shen, B., Ling, H.: Visual tracking via online nonnegative matrix factorization. IEEE Trans. Circuits Syst. Video Technol. **24**, 374–383 (2014)
4. Buciu, I., Nafornita, I.: Non-negative matrix factorization methods for face recognition under extreme lighting variations. In: International Symposium on Signals, Circuits and Systems (ISSCS) (2009)
5. Wang, J., Yagi, Y.: Integrating color and shape-texture features for adaptive real-time object tracking **17** (1999)
6. Nawaz, T., Cavallaro, A.: A protocol for evaluating video trackers. In: IEEE Proceedings on ICIP (2011)

7. Hong, L., Ze, Y., Hongbin, Z., Yuexian, Z., Zhang, L.: Robust human tracking based on multi-cue integration and mean-shift. Pattern Recogn. Lett. **30**, 827–837 (2009)
8. Moreno-Noguer, F., Sanfeliu, A., Samaras, D.: Integration of deformable contours and a multiple hypotheses Fisher color model for robust tracking in varying illuminant environments. Image Vis. Comput. **25**, 285–296 (2007)
9. Yu, G., Lu, H.: Illumination invariant object tracking with incremental subspace learning. In: Conference on ICIG (2009)
10. Deilamani, M., Asli, R.: Moving object tracking based on mean shift algorithm and features fusion. In: International Conference on AISP (2011)
11. Xu, Y., Roy-Chowdhury, A.: Integrating motion, illumination, and structure in video sequences with applications in illumination-invariant tracking. IEEE Trans. Pattern Anal. Mach. Intell. **29**, 793–806 (2007)
12. Yang, F., Lu, H., Zhang, W., Yang, G.: Visual tracking via bag of features. IET Image Process. **6**, 115–128 (2012)
13. Freedman, D., Turek, W.: Illumination-invariant tracking via graph cuts. In: IEEE Proceedings of CVPR (2005)
14. Mckenna, S., Raja, Y., Gong, S.: Object tracking using adaptive colour mixture models. In: Asian Conference on Computer Vision, pp. 615–622 (1998)
15. Bales, M., Ryan, F.: Bigbackground-based illumination compensation for surveillance video. Image Video Processing (2011). Hindawi Proceedings
16. Rautaray, S., Agrawal, A.: A real time hand tracking system for interactive applications. Int. J. Comput. Appl. **18**, 28–33 (2011)
17. Huang, K., Wang, L., Tan, T., Maybank, S.: A real-time object detecting and tracking system for outdoor night surveillance. Pattern Recogn. **41**, 432–444 (2008). Sciencedirect Proceedings
18. Ning, J., Zhang, L., Zhang, D., Wu, C.: Robust mean-shift tracking with corrected background-weighted histogram. IET Comput. Vis. **6**, 62–69 (2012)
19. Miller, A., Basharat, A., White, B., Liu, J., Shah, M.: Person and vehicle tracking in surveillance video. In: Stiefelhagen, R., Bowers, R., Fiscus, J. (eds.) CLEAR/RT -2007. LNCS, vol. 4625, pp. 174–178. Springer, Heidelberg (2008). https://doi.org/10.1007/978-3-540-68585-2_14
20. Phadke, G., Velmurgan, R.: Illumination invariant mean-shift tracking. In: IEEE Workshop on Applications of Computer Vision (WACV) (2013)

Hybrid Clustering Based Smart Crawler

Swati G. Bhoi[✉] and Ujwala M. Patil

R. C. Patel Institute of Technology, Shirpur, India
bhoi.swati93@gmail.com

Abstract. Everyone can easily use the Internet because it is the source of information. The Internet holds a tremendous amount of information, get the relevant information and high efficiency is challenging issue. The crawler is helping to extract relevant information easily. We propose smart crawler which provides better results than another crawler. Smart crawler has two stages as site locating and in-site exploring. Site locating can fetch the relevant information and in-site exploring rank the sites as per their relevancy. We implement smart crawler using a hybrid algorithm. The hybrid algorithm is a combination of bisect K-means algorithm and bottom up agglomerative clustering algorithm. The bisect K-means clustering algorithm split cluster into sub clusters and agglomerative algorithm computes the centroid of the clusters and merge them on the basis of similarities or approximate similar centroid value and form singleton cluster hence it is simple to use and provides efficient and better result than K-means clustering algorithm as it generates uniform size clusters.

Keywords: Crawler · FFC · ACHE · Agglomerative · K-means
URLs

1 Introduction

Nowadays the Internet is the part of the daily routine. It holds a large amount of information. The reason behind the user cannot get appropriate information is an availability of vast and different content about one topic. This headache reduces by crawler. The crawler can search relevant information about searching topic. The topic related information extracted by the crawler and divide it by as per its relevancy. The spider, catalog and software are parts of crawler. The site visited, the number of links which included in the pages so spider must visit these links and extract information from them. The catalog has stored the every copy of web pages that crawler finds. If the web page is changed, then it can update information in the database. The software can make arrangement of web pages as per its relevancy to search. In this way, the crawler can work.

There are various types of crawler are Generic Crawler, Form Focus Crawler (FFC) and Adaptive crawler for hidden webs entries (ACHE). Generic crawler does not focus on specific topics because it follows all links present in web pages and copy all content. This problem addressed by Form Focus Crawler, it can search topic related information, but ACHE provides more efficiency of crawler than FFC due to two additional components such as form filtering and adaptive link learner. The accuracy of

A. V. Deshpande et al. (Eds.): SmartCom 2017, CCIS 876, pp. 137–144, 2018.
https://doi.org/10.1007/978-981-13-1423-0_16

FFC is low, hence we implemented smart crawler. Smart crawler has two stages as first is site locating and the second is in-site exploring [2].

Clustering can parse a data and makes its groups by referring information related to data that computed objects and relationships between them. The partitioning method, hierarchical methods, density-based methods and K-Means Clustering are the different clustering methods. The agglomerative and divisive are two types include in hierarchical method. There is a set of data objects and for that, it can create hierarchical decomposition. The result of bottom up means agglomerative method is singleton cluster in which up to the termination it can merge the clusters as per their similarity. The alternate name of top down approach is a divisive method because it can work the reverse of bottom up approach that means it can divide all the clusters into smaller cluster and final output of this method is a single data object. This method finds only, round or spherical shapes clusters, but there are complications to describe an arbitrary shape cluster. K-means algorithm is based on clustering methods. The clustering means it can partition data and group this data object and cluster is a collection of similar data objects [3].

2 Related Work

Olston et al. studied two crawling methods such as batch crawling and incremental crawling. In batch crawling, the crawl order does not contain duplicate occurrences of any page, but if there are new pages are occurring, then the whole crawling process is periodically halted and restart. Whereas in incremental crawling, Web pages may appear multiple times in the crawl order and crawling is an uninterrupted process that conceptually never aborted. The incremental crawling is more powerful than the batch crawling because at different rates the re-visitation of pages is permitted hence [1].

Zhao et al. implemented the smart crawler which has two stages. As the hidden web grows very quickly, hence extracting appropriate information from the web is the challenging issues. To solve such problems author implements smart crawler, which has the first stage is site locating which extract the relevant information from the web; it can rank the website as per related topic. The Second stage is in-site exploring, it can assigns priorities to link. The aim of implementation of author is user getting relevant information from the Internet within the least amount of time [2].

Bangoria et al. studied different clustering methods such as partition methods, hierarchical methods, density-based methods. In partition methods, all clusters computed only once and also data objects are partitioned into non-overlapping clusters. The types of hierarchical method are bottom-up and top down approach, top down starts with each object forming a separate group and bottom up combines small clusters and form single cluster. The third type is density-based method can find only round shaped clusters [3].

Wagsta et al. developed the constrained K-means clustering method. In this method, the set of instance-level constraint provides with background knowledge expressed in the clustering process. In partitioning algorithm, the basic knowledge about instance decides that it is grouped together or not and constraint performs an important role in this whole process. The must link and cannot link are two constraints. If in one cluster two instances are present, then it is called must link constrains but if two instances are present in different clusters then it is known as cannot link constraints [4].

Purohit et al. implemented the new efficient approach for traditional K-means clustering algorithm. This new approach cannot select centroid points randomly rather it selects efficiently k initial centroid. The new approach used algorithm known as enhance algorithm, it forms new data set by using the Euclidian distance method. That means, first of all is starting the closest data object and after that, by using the Euclidian distance it can determine the closest distance between these data objects. At last, it can remove such data points from a population and form a new dataset. This algorithm gives the better result than traditional K-means algorithm and it works better for dense dataset rather than sparse data set [5].

Singh et al. developed hybrid clustering with enhanced K-means clustering. It performed the text clustering on two words by calculating the distance between these words. The hybrid clustering is a combination of partitioning and the agglomerative clustering method. The k-means clustering is an unsupervised method and calculate centroid and forms a number of clusters. Hierarchical clustering added smaller cluster into larger one or splitting larger cluster into smaller one. But when the data is present in the form of heterogeneous multimedia data, then it is unable to work [6].

Sasirekha et al. studied the agglomerative hierarchical clustering algorithm. This algorithm is robust which play an important role in mining appropriate information from the vast database. The agglomerative algorithm forms greedy structure due to its merge and split nature. The bottom-up and top down are two approaches are included in the agglomerative algorithm. The top-down means it can divide the cluster into sub clusters such that each cluster has one of the data item and bottom-up approach work on merge concept that means is can combine some clusters depends on some similar criteria. The advantage of this algorithm is, it can produce an ordering of object which is informative for data display [7].

3 Methodology

The responsibility of the crawler is to provide an appropriate information to the users and smart crawler exactly done that. The seed database provides the sites to classify by the classifier. Firstly, we used naïve bayes classifier. The classifier includes two stages as site locating and in-site exploring as shown in Fig. 1. At the First phase, crawler finds the most relevant website for a given subject and then the second phase will be in-site exploring stage which uncovers searchable content from the site. The first stage is site locating perform reverse searching that means it finds center pages. Site locating has three main sub-stages as site collecting, site ranking and site classification. The site database takes input from seed sites and provides the site to site frontier and adaptive site learner. The site ranker can rank sites which received from site frontier and site classifier classifies sites as per their relevancy. The second stage in-site exploring appropriate pages is extracted from the link by using page fetcher. Form classifier eligible to classify forms and its efficiency, improve due to adaptive link learner.

There are various classifiers are available such as an Artificial Neural Network (ANN), Decision Tree (DC) but we implemented smart crawler using the naive bayes

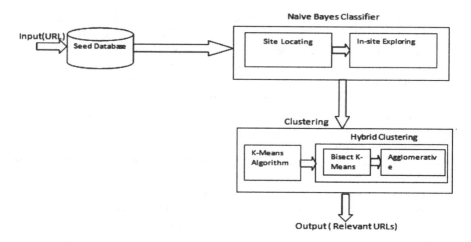

Fig. 1. System architecture

classifier because it is simple to implement and also suitable for our research domains. The ANN is complicated for certain domains due to a large number of nodes and synapses are generated and DT is quite complex because it can produce out of hand number of nodes in some cases. The smart crawler using naïve bayes gives more accurate and better results than. But when the sites are increasing for crawling, then the process becomes slow that means the crawling time required more. Hence, to overcome this problem we use K-means clustering method, in that the number of clusters is formed of similar data items. It can divide the dataset into a number of groups. Center all address text. If there is n number of addresses, then it uses n centered tab and so on. We use the k-means clustering method which collects same data object in one cluster.

3.1   K-means Algorithm

- **Input:** URL.
- **Output:** K Clusters.

1. Any set of K instances chooses as centers of the clusters.
2. Next, each instance assigns to the cluster, which is closest.
3. The cluster centroids are recalculated.
4. This process is iterated until there is not much change in the cluster centroids.

K-means clustering algorithm is too simple to implement, but it works very slow due to the reassignment of the cluster objects also form loose clusters due to the existence of outlier and to compute the mean value there is needed to specify the number of clusters. To overcome this, all problems we implement smart crawler using the hybrid clustering algorithm, which required less time to crawl sites and also provide better results (Table 1).

3.2   Hybrid Clustering Algorithm

Our algorithm uses both the top-down (Bisect K-means) and bottom-up (centroid based) agglomerative hybrid clustering algorithms to address this problem. We pass the K' cluster information (centroids) computed from the bisect K-means algorithm to the bottom up algorithm to correct the inconsistencies occurred due to the wrong decision made while merging or splitting a cluster. First, we ran the bisect K-means algorithm on the searched URLs until K' number of clusters were generated. The generated clusters should not be empty. Then, we compute the centroids for each of the resulting clusters. Each of these centroids represents a cluster and all of its data items in the cluster. The hybrid clustering algorithm as follows:

1. Pick a cluster to split.
2. Find 2 sub clusters using a k-means algorithm.
3. Repeat Steps 1 (Initialization step) and 2 (bisecting step) until the K' > K number of clusters are generated.
4. Compute the centroids for each of the K' clusters such that each document in a collection belongs to one of these centroids.
5. Construct a K' X K' similarity matrix between these centroid clusters.
6. Merge two similar centroid clusters (i.e., place these centroids in the same cluster).
7. Update the centroid clusters similarity matrix.
8. Repeat Steps 6–7 until the K clusters of centroids are generated.
9. If two centroids belong to same centroid clusters, then the document clusters of these centroids will go together as a final cluster (Merging step).

In Steps 5–8, we ran the centroid agglomerative hybrid clustering algorithm on the centroids of these document clusters for a given value of K (given in the algorithm) to generate a set of K' centroid clusters. We used the term centroid clusters to avoid possible confusion with the document clusters. Like document cluster is a cluster of documents, centroid cluster is a cluster of centroids. Hybrid clustering beneficial due to every data object assigned to cluster only once and also required processing time less due to avoiding reallocation.

4   Experimental Results

4.1   Dataset

We evaluate the efficiency of our proposed solution over real web data in 8 representative domains. Form classifier is one of the main components of smart crawler trained by TEL-8 dataset This TEL-8 dataset contains 8 representative domains, which form 3 groups "TEL"- means Travel group, Entertainment group and Living group [8]. Travel group includes Airfare, Auto. Entertainment group includes Book, Movie and Music and Living group include Hotel, Rental, and Apartment. We crawl all these domain sites by smart crawler by naïve bayes, K-means clustering and hybrid clustering algorithm and compare their results.

The existing system contains two stage framework site locating and in-site exploring. The first stage extracts relevant sites and the second stage prioritizes these sites.

Table 1. Eight domains for experiments

Domain	Description
Airfares	Airfare search
Automobiles	Used cars search
Books	Books search
Car rentals	Car search
Car search	Hotel search
Jobs	Job search
Movies	Movie titles and DVDs search
Music records	Music CDs search

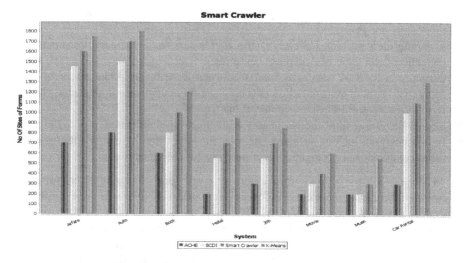

Fig. 2. Efficiency comparison with other systems

Smart crawler provides better results than other crawlers, but the implementation of smart crawler using K-means clustering doesn't have a guarantee for a relevant solution because it works well if and only if the initialization is proper. We used a hybrid clustering algorithm which provides better results within the least amount of time due to its merging nature.

In Fig. 2 we see the hybrid clustering algorithm give better efficiency than other methods and Fig. 3 shows the coverage graph. This graph shows that the hybrid algorithm has wider coverage than other. The Fig. 2 shows graphs of the efficiency of crawler which retrieves the relevant URLs from a set of available URLs.

As Fig. 4 shows the time utilization by all three methods. The naive bayes requires more time for crawling sites because it takes time for training and also for testing data, but K-means forms clusters which require less time than naive bayes classifier. But K-means form clusters of different sizes, hence it takes more time for one cluster testing

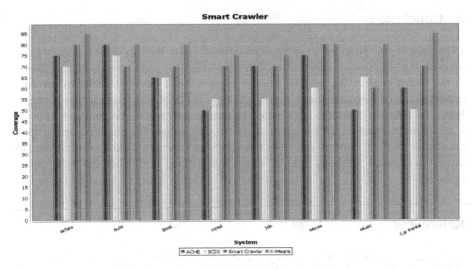

Fig. 3. Coverage comparison with other systems

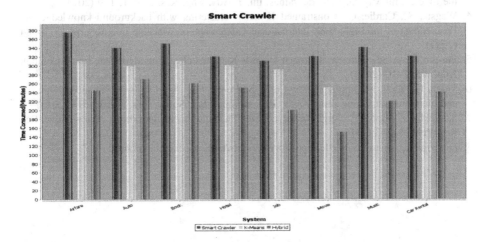

Fig. 4. Time consumption by Naive Bayes, K-means and hybrid clustering

or less time for another cluster as depends on the cluster size, but that's not possible in hybrid clustering because it forms uniform size clusters, merge them and scan this singleton cluster. Hence the hybrid clustering requires less time to crawl a number of sites.

5   Conclusions

The search engine provides an appropriate information to Internet users but many times users do not get relevant information. The crawler is also one of the main components of the search engine. We propose crawler using a naive bayes classifier to get topic related sites. But it requires more time when the number of sites increases for crawling. Hence we enhance crawler using a hybrid clustering, which is the combination of bisect k-means and bottom-up agglomerative clustering algorithm. The bisect clustering splits the cluster into sub clusters and bottom-up approach merges a number of clusters by satisfying centroid similarity criteria. Hence this method is efficient and requires less time.

References

1. Olston, C., Najork, M.: Web crawling. Found. Trends Inf. Retr. **4**, 175–246 (2010)
2. Zhao, F., Zhou, J., Nie, C., Jin, H.: SmartCrawler: a two-stage crawler for efficiently harvesting deep-web interfaces. IEEE Trans. Serv. Comput. **99**, 1–14 (2015)
3. Bangoria, B., Mankad, N., Pambhar, V.: Enhanced K-means clustering algorithm to reduce the time complexity for numeric values. Int. J. Adv. Eng. Res. Dev. **1**, 1–9 (2014)
4. Wagsta, K., Cardie, C.: Constrained K-means clustering with background knowledge. In: Proceedings of the Eighteenth International Conference on Machine Learning, pp. 577–584 (2001)
5. Purohit, P.: A new efficient approach towards K-means clustering algorithm. Int. J. Comput. Appl. **65**, 7–10 (2013)
6. Singh, G., Kaur, N.: Implementation of hybrid clustering algorithm with enhanced K-means and hierarchal clustering. Int. J. Adv. Res. Comput. Sci. Softw. Eng. **3**, 608–618 (2013)
7. Sasirekha, K., Baby, P.: Agglomerative hierarchical clustering algorithm-a review. Int. J. Sci. Res. Publ. **3**, 1–3 (2013)
8. http://metaquerier.cs.uiuc.edu/repository/datasets/tel-8/documentation.html

Binding Affinity Prediction Models for Spinocerebellar Ataxia Using Supervised Learning

P. R. Asha[✉] and M. S. Vijaya

Department of Computer Science, PSGR Krishnammal College for Women,
Coimbatore, India
ashamscsoft@gmail.com, msvijaya@psgrkc.com

Abstract. Spinocerebellar Ataxia (SCA) is an inherited disorder flow in the family, even when one parent is affected. Disorder arises mainly due to mutations in the gene, which affects the gray matter in the brain and causes neuron degeneration. There are certain types of SCA that are caused by repeat mutation in the gene, which produces differences in the formation of protein sequence and structures. Binding affinity is essential to know how tightly the ligand binds to the protein. In this work, the binding affinity prediction model is built using machine learning. To build the model, features like Binding energy, IC_{50}, Torsional energy and surface area for both ligand and protein are extracted from Auto dock, auto dock vina and PYmol from the complex. A total of 17 structures and 18 drugs were used for building the model. This paper proposes a predictive model using applied mathematics, machine learning regression techniques like rectilinear regression, Artificial neural network (ANN) and Random Forest (RF). Experimental results show that the model built using Random Forest outperforms in predicting the binding affinity.

Keywords: Binding affinity · Docking · Ligand · Machine learning
Prediction · Protein · Protein structure

1 Introduction

Spinocerebellar ataxia is a hereditary anarchy portrayed by deviations in grey matter handling its tasks. The disorder is due to mutations in the genes which results in brain and spinal cord degeneration. Each type of SCA features its own symptoms [1]. SCA occurs due to mutations in the genes that produces differences in the formation of protein sequence and structures. SCA1, SCA2, SCA3, SCA6, SCA7, SCA8 and SCA10 are caused by repeat mutaion [2, 3].

Docking is always to forecast the binding modes. An earlier illumination for the ligand-receptor binding procedure could be a lock-and-key principle, wherein the ligand sits into the protein just just like lock and key. After that induced-fit concept, it carries lock-and-key theory a section a lot of, proclaiming that the energetic website of the macromolecule is perpetually reshaped by interactions with the ligands since the ligands communicate with the organic compound [4, 5].

© Springer Nature Singapore Pte Ltd. 2018
A. V. Deshpande et al. (Eds.): SmartCom 2017, CCIS 876, pp. 145–152, 2018.
https://doi.org/10.1007/978-981-13-1423-0_17

Affinity is a measure of the strength of attraction between a receptor and its ligand. The binding affinity of a substance to the receptor is improbably essential, as some amount of the binding energy is employed at intervals the receptor to bring a conformational change. This ends up in altered behavior of associate associated particle channel or the supermolecule.

Ligands like medicine, even have some specificity of the binding web site on the receptor like target supermolecule. Thus the potency of a drug depends on its binding affinity for the binding information processing system additionally as its binding ability to cause the desired effect [6].

This research work is proposed to create a model from which the affinity is predicted. A total of 17 structures and 18 drugs were used for building the model. The purpose has been studied and therefore the want is known from literature survey.

Li et al., proposed a method for prediction of binding affinity in docked complex. They collected data from PDBBind. To predict affinity, machine learning scoring was used and the features like physiochemical properties and gauss have been extracted. In this paper to predict affinity, number of models has been used their performance results have been compared and random forest outperforms other models [7].

Li et al., proposed a method for automatic protein-protein affinity binding based on svr-ensemble. Two-layer support vector regression (TLSVR) model is employed to implicitly capture, binding contributions that square measure exhausting to expressly model. The TLSVR circumvents both the descriptor compatibility problem and the need for problematic modeling assumptions. Input features for TLSVR in the first layer are scores of 2209 interacting atom pairs within each distance bin [8].

Su et al., planned a way for qualitative prediction of protein-protein affinity prediction by volume correction. The dataset used here was X-ray structures of macromolecule-protein complexes from macromolecule data bank. to evaluate the prediction ability for protein–protein binding affinity, six check sets ar examined. Sets 1–5 were used as check set in five disclosed studies, severally, and set half-dozen was the union set of sets 1–5, with a whole of eighty six protein–protein complexes [9].

Durrant and McCammon projected a neural network primarily based analysis, perform called the NN - score to predict affinity binding. to form Associate in Nursing data of protein−ligand complexes of legendary binding affinity, we've got an inclination to better-known X-ray crystal and resonance structures of the supermolecule data Bank (PDB) that had Kd values listed at intervals the MOAD and PDBbind-CN databases [10].

From the background study it had been perceived that the bulk of the works were supported the advanced that binding affinity was provided by the info. This emphasizes the need for more research on affinity prediction with known structures and unknown drugs by planning and accounts the effective options for generating new model.

2 Methodology

The research work is initiated by structure, acquisition from gene cards, which contains a structure that is mapped with six types of SCA. The structure is docked with the drugs to get essential features to build the model which predicts binding affinity. Training dataset is prepared from docked complexes and features are extracted. Affinity prediction models are built by employing linear regression, neural networks and random forest.

A model is created for training and testing to predict the binding affinity. To create the model, the feature values are essential and the values are engaged from complexes which are docked using auto dock. Docking is performed with 17 structures and 18 drugs that is each structure is docked with 18 drugs. The data set contains 27 attributes and 306 instances. The dataset is used to build the model which predicts binding affinity.

2.1 Docking

Docking is performed by preparing receptor (protein) and ligand (drug). Protein is manufactured by converting the protein into pdbq format that is by adding hydrogen, computing geastier charge and kolman charges are added. Protein.pdbq is converted to pdbqt by not adding partial charges. Ligand is prepared by converting the ligand into pdbqt format that is by detecting root in torsion tree. The docking log file is essential to check the docking results. The docking conformation is chosen based on which confirmation is high and provide better results. Docking results are shown in Fig. 1.

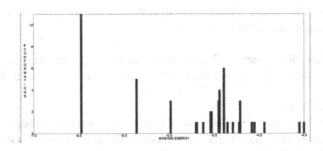

Fig. 1. Docking result

The feature values that are engaged from various tools plays vital role in building model that predicts affinity in an effective way. The predictor variable and their values are taken from tools like auto dock, auto dock vina and PYmol are explained below.

- Binding energy range
  The binding energy range describes at which cluster the binding energy falls.
- Binding energy
  Binding energy is a live of the affinity of ligand-protein advanced, or is that the distinction between the energy of advanced and therefore the total of energies of every molecule singly.
- Ligand Efficiency
  Ligand efficiency is binding energy per atom of ligand to protein.

- Inhibition Constant (pIC50)
  It is a sign of however, potentially AN matter is; it's the concentration needed to supply 0.5 most inhibition.
- Intermolecular Energy
  Intermolecular energy is the energy between non-bonded atoms that is the energy between atoms separated by 3–4 bonds or between atoms in different molecules.
- Desolvation Energy
  Desolvation energy is that the static and/or van der Waals energy, lose of the interaction between substance or organic compound and solvent upon binding.
- Electrostatic Energy
  Electrostatic energy is that the non-bonded energy, that is totally different from electricity desolvation energy and it's the amendment on the electricity non delimited energy of substance or supermolecule upon binding.
- Total internal energy
  Total energy is that the total of changes of all energetic terms enclosed in rating operates of matter or supermolecule upon binding, and the changes upon binding of the entropic terms.
- Torsional energy
  Torsion energy is related to dihedral term of internal energy.
- clRMS
  It is the rms distinction between current conformation and also the lowest energy conformation in its cluster.
- refRMS
  It is the rms distinction between current conformation coordinates and current reference structure. By default the input substance is employed as a results of the reference.
- Binding Affinity
  Affinity is a measure of the strength of attraction between a molecule and legend. High affinity binding has strong intermolecular force, whereas low affinity binding has weak intermolecular force.
- RMSD
  RMSD values area unit calculated relative to the easy mode and use only movable important atoms. a pair of variants of RMSD metrics area unit provided, rmsd/lb (RMSD lower bound) and rmsd/ub (RMSD higher bound), differing in but the atoms area unit matched at intervals the gap calculation: rmsd/ub matches each atom in one conformation with itself at intervals the various conformation.

3 Model Generation

Binding affinity is taken as the response variable and other independent variables are engaged from auto dock and pyMOL are treated as independent variables. The three variants of regression specifically artificial neural networks and random forest square measure enforced for building the models.

3.1   Linear Regression

In a regression toward the mean model, the variable of interest the supposed variable quantity Associate in Nursingticipated – from k completely different variables the supposed freelance variables using an equation. If Y denotes the variable, and X1, ..., Xk, area unit the freelance variables, then the belief is that the worth of Y at time t or row t within the info sample is prepared by the equation.

$$Y_t = \beta_0 + \beta_1 X_{1t} + \beta_2 X_{2t} + \ldots + \beta_k X_{kt} + \varepsilon_t$$

The corresponding equation for predicting Yt from the corresponding values of the X's is thus

$$y_t = b_0 + b_1 X_{1t} + b_2 X_{2t} + \ldots + b_k X_{kt}$$

Where the b's whole group estimates of the betas obtained by least-squares, i.e., minimizing the square prediction error inside the sample [11].

3.2   Artificial Neural Network

An artificial neural network subsist of an associate input layer of neurons, one or 2 hidden layers of neurons, and a final layer of output neurons. Every affiliation is related to a numeric variable referred to as weight. During this work by applying artificial neural network a perceptron usually has several inputs and these inputs are on an individual basis weighted. These weighted signals are then intercalary along and passed into the activation perform. The activation performs is employed to convert the input into an additional helpful output. To improve the model, back propogation is used. In this method weights are adjusted to decrease the margin of errors. The weights are adjusted between hidden layer and output layer [12, 13].

3.3   Random Forest

Random forests or random decision forests unit of measurement AN ensemble learning technique for classification, regression and numerous tasks, that operate by constructing AN outsized vary of call trees at the coaching time and outputting the category that's the mode of the classes' classification or mean prediction regression of the individual trees. The rule of random forest is like bootstrapping with call tree CART model. It'll take random sample and each that means chosen initial variables produce a CART model and so the strategy repeats to form a final prediction. The final word prediction is mean of each prediction [14].

4   Experiments and Results

Experiments unit of measurement administered within the R setting to form the models for affinity prediction by implementing machine learning formula. The dataset with 306 instances unit of measurement prepared from docked sophisticated. Statistical procedure, Artificial Neural network and Random forest unit of measurement used for model generation and conjointly the models unit of measurement evaluated for his or her performance. The analysis measures just like the basis mean sq. error and correlation unit of measurement used for performance analysis of affinity model.

4.1 Evaluation Measures

Correlation is also a homogenous selection that describes, but closely the two variables unit of measurement connected. The statistic endlessly lies between -1 and one. A relentless of 1 representing sensible correlation, zero represents no correlation, and -1 represents sensible correlation. Statistic measures the applied mathematical correlation between the actual values ai and expected values pi exploitation the formula,

$$\text{Correlation Coefficient} = S_{PA}/\sqrt{S_P S_A}$$
$$\text{where } S_{PA} = \frac{\sum_i (p_i - \bar{p})(a_i - \bar{a})}{n-1}, \ Sp = \frac{\sum_i (p_i - \bar{p})^2}{n-1}$$
$$\text{and } S_A = \frac{(a_i - \bar{a})^2}{n-1}$$

Error term is that the excellence between the regression line and actual data points accustomed construct the road and root mean sq. error is evaluated pattern,

$$RMSE = \frac{\sqrt{(p_1 - a_1)^2 + \ldots\ldots + (p_n - a_n)^2}}{n}$$

Higher Correlation and least error values ar expected for the foremost effective prediction accuracy. Except for data point and RMSE there square measure fully completely different measures like mean absolute error-MAE, relative absolute error-RAE, and root relative sq. error-RRSE. Mean absolute error is employed to live however shut forecasts or predictions unit to the last word outcomes. The mean absolute error is given by

$$MAE = 1/n + \sum_{i=1}^{n} |f_i - y_i| = 1/n \sum_{i=1}^{n} |e_i|$$

Mean absolute error is a median of absolutely the errors $|e_i| = |f_i - y_i|$, wherever fi is that the prediction. The relative sq. error takes the whole sq. error and normalizes it by dividing by the whole sq. error of the easy predictor. The concept relative sq. error Ei of a personal program i is evaluated by the equation:

$$E_i = \sqrt{\frac{\sum_{j-1}^{n} \left(P_{(ij)} - T_j\right)^2}{\sum_{j-1}^{n} \left(T_j - \bar{T}\right)^2}}$$

where P(ij) is that value|the worth|the value – foretold by the individual program i for sample case j (out of n sample cases); Tj is that the target value for sample case j; and is given by the formula:

$$\bar{T} = \frac{1}{n} \sum_{j-1}^{n} T_j$$

The constant of correlation between the actual values and expected values of affinity for the 3 regression models are analyzed beside RMSE and thus the comparative results ar tabulated in Table 1 and illustrated in Fig. 2.

Table 1. Performance of affinity models

Models	RMSE	Correlation coefficient	MAE	RAE (%)	RRSE (%)
LR	0.6064	0.88	0.4788	47.8691	47.32
ANN	0.8051	0.7998	0.5924	59.2175	62.82
RF	0.5105	0.9186	0.405	40.4848	39.83

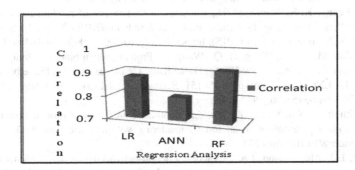

Fig. 2. Performance evaluation

A correlation larger than zero is usually delineated as robust correlation, whereas a correlation, but zero. 5 area unit thought-about as weak correlation. In Table 1 the correlation of the RF model offers robust correlation and it outperforms the opposite 2 models. Compared with the opposite 2 models error rate is significantly low in RF model. So, it's evident from the estimates that the model generated victimization RF furnish higher correct ends up in predicting affinity binding with reduced error and most coefficient of correlation.

5 Conclusion

This analytical work demonstrates the modelling of affinity prediction and implementation victimization machine learning algorithms. Supervised machine learning paradigms, particularly simple regression, artificial neural network and random forest area unit adapted to construct the models. It's discovered from the experimental results that the random forest regression model is additional economical than the opposite 2 models in predicting binding affinity. In future the analysis are often applied victimisation sizable amount of complicated with correlative options. The models that were engineered are often integrated to make an ensemble model thus on improving the prediction result.

References

1. Weiss, T.C.: Ataxia Spinocerebellar: SCA Facts and Information (2010)
2. Bird, T.D.: Hereditary Ataxia Overview, 3 March 2016
3. Whaley, N.R., Fujioka, S., Wszolek, Z.K.: Autosomal dominant cerebellar ataxia type I: a review of the phenotypic and genotypic characteristics. https://doi.org/10.1186/1750-1172-6-33. Accessed 28 May 2011
4. Fischer, E.: Einfluss der configuration auf die working derenzyme. Ber. Dt. Chem. Ges. **27**, 2985–2993 (1894)
5. Koshland Jr., D.E.: Correlation of structure and function in enzyme action. Science **142**, 1533–1541 (1963)
6. http://chemistry.tutorvista.com/inorganic-chemistry/binding-affinity.html
7. Li, H., Leung, K.-S., Wong, M.-H., Ballester, P.J.: The use of random forest to predict binding affinity in docking. In: Ortuño, F., Rojas, I. (eds.) IWBBIO 2015. LNCS, vol. 9044, pp. 238–247. Springer, Cham (2015). https://doi.org/10.1007/978-3-319-16480-9_24
8. Li, X., Zhu, M., Li, X., Wang, H.-Q., Wang, S.: Protein-protein binding affinity prediction based on an SVR ensemble. In: Huang, D.-S., Jiang, C., Bevilacqua, V., Figueroa, J.C. (eds.) ICIC 2012. LNCS, vol. 7389, pp. 145–151. Springer, Heidelberg (2012). https://doi.org/10.1007/978-3-642-31588-6_19
9. Su, Y., Zhou, A., Xia, X., Li, W., Sun, Z.: Quantitative prediction of protein–protein binding affinity with a potential of mean force considering volume correction, 1 October 2009. https://doi.org/10.1002/pro.257
10. Durrant, J.D., McCammon, J.A.: NNScore: a neural-network-based scoring function for the characterization of protein−ligand complexes. J. Chem. Inf. Modell. **50**(10), 1865–1871 (2010)
11. Montgomery, D.C., Peck, E.A., Vining, G.G.: Introduction to Linear Regression Analysis. Series in Probability and Statistics. Wiley, Hoboken (2012)
12. Jacobson, L.: Intorduction to Artificial Neural Networks. The Project Spot, 5 December 2013
13. Miller, S.: How to build a neural network, 10 August 2015
14. Louppe, G.: Understanding random forests, University of Liege, Ph.D. dissertation, July 2014

A Load Aware Routing Technique
Using AODV Modification

Bharat Pahadiya(✉) ⓘ and Jitendra Sharma ⓘ

Shri Vaishnav Vidhyapeeth Vishwavidyalaya, Indore, MP, India
bharat_adil43@yahoo.com, jsl5052013@gmail.com

Abstract. Wireless mobile ad hoc network is a combination of free mobile devices, able to communicate using wireless channel. In addition of that, the mobile devices are direction independent. Therefore, routing is backbone of new generation wireless communication technology. That is also responsible for network organization, and governances of network. These devices are developed with limited resources such as battery power and computational ability. Therefore, utilization of these resources is required to optimize for less resource consumption. The presented paper, introduces a new routing strategy for minimizing the energy consumption in wireless ad hoc network Using CPR routing technique with the help of traditional AODV routing technology. Additionally that include the implementation of the proposed routing technique and results analysis is also provided. According to the archived results, the performance of the traditional AODV routing is improved in terms of energy consumption and packet delivery ratio.

Keywords: Load aware routing · CPR · AODV · Routing protocol
Energy consumption

1 Introduction

Wireless ad hoc network is self-defining and having its own features; it is self-concern, wireless communication manner which is not restricted by topologies and self-created. Due to the self-concern nature of the network policies and mobile nature it is still an area of new challenges & idea exploration. There are various performance problems arises in the network i.e. security, performance and simulation Due to lack of dependent network. While it is an important feature required to be accepted in different application of data transfer and network monitoring. The wireless and free topology makes it costlier in order of applications and network utilities. It includes WSN (Wireless Sensor Networks), MANET, and wireless enabled short range communication [3].

There are number of techniques and previous work available for improving routing strategies. The routing techniques use different parameter for evaluation of load on routing devices. On the basis of load parameter the wireless network decides prominent route for delivery of packets, considerably which improves network performance.

The most effective and considerable work found during literature in [1]. Author uses Node energy as a most valuable parameter for calculating network load because energy once consumed cannot recover. Author proposed energy consumption and its

A. V. Deshpande et al. (Eds.): SmartCom 2017, CCIS 876, pp. 153–160, 2018.
https://doi.org/10.1007/978-981-13-1423-0_18

related routing technique for better performance. But it can be made more efficient and effective by using some more parameter.

2 Proposed Work

This section involved the demonstration of the problem identification, solution and the algorithm design which is further implemented to optimize the performance of routing.

MANET is characterized by their ad hoc nature, due to this various issues of performance and security is arises. Routing is played as backbone of the network. Therefore routing techniques are responsible for topology formation and communication. The objective of the proposed work is to provide efficient routing policy which provides reliability and effectiveness in the network communication with limited energy and high traffic over the available network.

MANET is basically a wireless network, where devices having the limited resources such as energy, processing capability and connectivity. Energy is main focus on the presented paper. The amount of energy consumed is never recovered during the mobility of devices. Additionally, for each event i.e. packet sending, receiving and routing a fixed amount of energy is consumed that is not recoverable. Additionally, in wireless communication the connectivity is limited, in other words the available bandwidth is limited. Therefore if the network density is increases than the throughput of network is also affected. Therefore a new solution for MANET is required to find for optimizing the performance of network in terms of network throughput and energy consumption by node.

To overcome the above discussed issues a new solution is proposed for implementing routing policy. To discover the route from source to destination with the help of load parameter, a node with minimum energy and overloaded routers are considered. Therefore the proposed technique considers important factors based on load aware routing, it also includes free nature of nodes and provides efficient routing during overloaded traffic.

In proposed work, calculation of the load is done on the basis of the energy consumed by the nodes. It means each node have some initial energy and amount of energy consumed during packet transfer and routing.so the work totally focused on two important factors, first when energy is below the limit i.e. Node is not available for communication and required to eliminate from the routing network, while second factor is if node consume more energy it means it is overloaded hence node is full of data and not able to handle more data.

So an efficient routing method is required, which is based on load awareness to be implemented using AODV routing technique. That can be implementing using buffer length and threshold level of available nodes energy [5], which help in finding efficient route between communicating nodes.so the proposed routing policy helps to provides efficient and effective route discovery.

3   Proposed Algorithm

This section describes a new routing algorithm for enhancing the energy consumption in mobile ad hoc network; the algorithm is given by the following steps.

Algorithm:

```
For each neighbouring node
Cost to progress ratio (CPR) is calculated as
```

$$CPR = \frac{Cost(CA)}{|CD| - |AD|}$$

```
If (CPR ≤ energy)
{
Not selected as route; // due to low energy
}
If (buffer != null)
{
    Not selected as route; // due to load
}
Else if (CPR ≥ energy)
{
    If (buffer available)
    {
        Select as next hop;
    }
}
```

The proposed routing technique is enhancement on a traditional routing protocol, for that purpose a small change of existing routing protocol is performed according to the above given algorithm steps. In order to send data to a targeted node, first required discovering an optimum route between source and sink. During this process first control message exchange is performed using the RREQ and RREP packets. After that the shortest path is evaluated for finding the optimum path, for that purpose the router first estimate the cost progress ratio according to the CPR routing protocol [2] the after that cost progress ratio is compared with the energy level of node if the node not having the sufficient energy then node is not chosen for routing, in addition of that the current buffer length is compared for finding the load free node. If the buffer size is full that means the node is already processing some requests and that is busy. Therefore that node is also not selected for routing. Finally if the node energy is higher than the threshold limit and queue is free, the node having sufficient energy level, and free processing unit for routing the data packets The flow of decisions and control is given using Fig. 1.

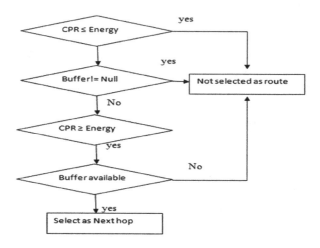

Fig. 1. Algorithm's flow chart

The above derived idea is taken from CPR routing technique, where the CPR routing is described as that is based on Fig. 2:

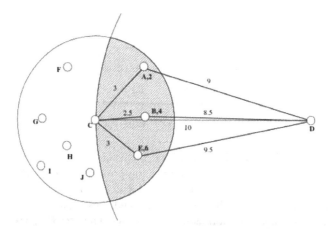

Fig. 2. CPR routing scenario [1]

A localized CPR (Cost over Progress Ratio) framework [1] for designing network layer protocols, this framework may be applied in geographic routing to optimize cost as follows. Suppose that each edge has a cost measure. Node C, currently holding the packet, will forward it to neighbour A, closer to destination D than itself, which minimizes the objective function (the ratio of cost over progress):

$$F_{CPR} = \frac{Cost(CA)}{|CD| - |AD|} \tag{1}$$

While progress clearly measures the advance of A toward D in the CPR framework, the cost measure can be hop count (from A to D), power, reluctance, power reluctance, delay, and expected hop count, etc., depending on the assumptions and metrics used [6]. In the context of load balancing, we have Cost (CA) = Load (A). The CPR framework gives effective results for different network optimization factors and provides efficient result for that. But it can be more evaluated and it can give more efficient results for various range of application. In particular, there is no performance evaluation in load balancing setting [1].

4   Implementation

The proposed algorithm is implemented using the NS2 network simulator. This section provides the implementation details using three modules. First, network setup, secondly simulation scenarios and finally results and performance evaluation.

4.1   Simulation Setup

For successfully evaluation of the desired routing protocol, Table (1) provides the network configuration.

Table 1. Simulation parameters

Channel	Wireless channel
Network interface	Phy/wireless
Queue length	50
No. of node	15
Traffic	CBR(constant bit rate)
Antenna	Omni antenna
Routing protocol	AODV/ELA
Energy model	EnergyModel
Simulation area	1000 X 1000
Simulation time	60 s

Using the above network configuration the network animator provides the Fig. 3 network.

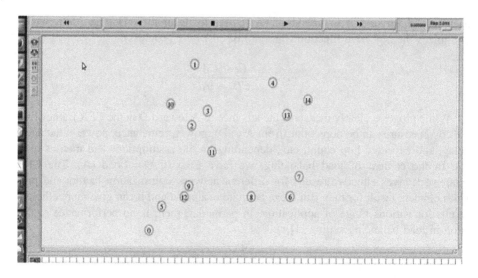

Fig. 3. Initial simulation

4.2   Simulation Scenario

There are a simple network is designed using the Table (1) network configuration. The given network is a used for comparing the two routing protocol therefore, here with similar network configuration and different routing techniques the desired simulation is performed and performance is evaluated.

4.3   Performance Analysis

The performance of the designed routing protocol is evaluated using different network parameters such as PDR and energy utilization.

4.3.1   Energy Consumption

The energy consumed during different communication sessions is given using Fig. 4. Energy consumption is referred as the total energy consumed during the data sending, receiving and transfer of a data packets. For each event an amount of energy is used, therefore here consumption of energy is provided.

In the above given diagram red line represents energy consumption of AODV routing and green line shows the energy consumption using the modified AODV routing protocol. Where X axis represents simulation time and Y axis provide the node residual energy. From the above result that is found the amount of energy is less consumed during enhanced algorithm. On the other hand the energy is consumed frequently during the experiments with AODV routing.

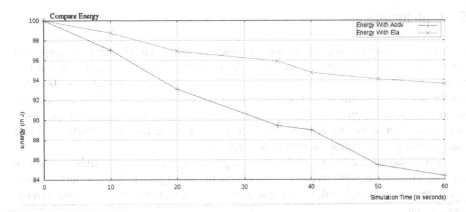

Fig. 4. Comparison of energy consumption between AODV and proposed ELA method. (Color figure online)

4.3.2 Packet Delivery Ratio

The amount of packet is delivered during a communication session is defined as packet delivery ratio. It is given in terms of percentage. In the given Fig. 5 the comparison of packet delivery ratio is provided where red line provides the packet deliver by AODV and green line represents packet delivery by the enhanced AODV routing.

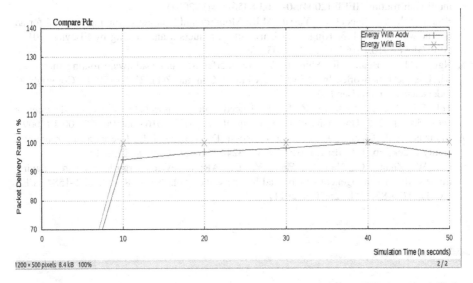

Fig. 5. Comparison of packet delivery ratio between AODV and proposed ELA method (Color figure online)

From the above given results that is found that the amount of packet delivered is also optimized due to implementation of enhanced routing protocol.

5 Conclusions

In this work a better load aware routing technique is presented. The given routing is an extension of AODV traditional routing to optimize the network performance. For that purpose an additional algorithm is developed for finding the optimal route between source and sink with minimum energy consumption and routing cost. The simulation of the desired routing protocol is performed using NS2 discrete event simulator. After implementation of routing algorithm the performance of the routing algorithm is found more efficient than traditional routing algorithms.

In near future that is extendable for energy saving options and MANET security aspects, using cross layer technique and for energy saving technique can further more optimize able through additional parameter consideration such as connectivity, mobility etc.

References

1. Li, X., Mitton, N., Nayak, A., Stojmenovic, I.: Localized load balancing for geographic routing in wireless ad hoc networks. In: Wireless Networks Symposium (IEEE ICC-WNS 2012), pp. 5478–5482 (2012). 978-1-4577-2053-6/12/$30
2. Stojmenovic, I.: Localized network layer protocols in sensor networks based on optimizing cost over progress ratio. IEEE Netw. **20**(1), 21–27 (2006)
3. Ganjali, Y., Keshavarzian, A.: Load balancing in ad hoc networks: single-path routing vs. multi-path routing. IEEE (2004). 0-7803-8356-7/04©(2004)
4. Khamayseh, Y., Obiedat, G., Yassin, M.B.: Mobility and load aware routing protocol for ad hoc networks, 105–113. King Saud University. Production and hosting by Elsevier (2011). https://doi.org/10.1016/j.jksuci.2011.05.006
5. Nguyen, L.T., Beuran, R., Shinoda, Y.: An interference and load aware routing metric for wireless mesh networks. Int. J. Ad Hoc Ubiquit. Comput. **7**(1), 25–37 (2011). Copyright © Inderscience Enterprises Ltd
6. Toh, C.K., Le, A.-N., Cho, Y.-Z.: Load balanced routing protocols for ad hoc mobile wireless networks, pp. 2–8. University of Hong Kong. IEEE (2009). 0163-6804/09/$25.00 ©(2009)
7. Bianzino, A.P., Chaudet, C., Larroca, F., Rossi, D., Rougier, J.-L.: Energy-aware routing: a reality check, pp. 1–6. IEEE (2010). 978-1-4244-8864-3/10/$26.00 ©(2010)
8. Liu, W., Zhang, C., Yao, G., Fang, Y.: DELAR: a device-energy-load aware relaying framework for heterogeneous mobile ad hoc networks, vol. 29, no. 8, pp. 1572–1584. IEEE (2011). 0733-8716/11/$25.00 ©(2011)

Multiple Independent Path Finding Algorithm for Concurrent Data Transmission in Dual Frequency and Dual Polarized MANETs

Sandhya Chilukuri[✉], Kaustubh Nabar, and Govind Kadambi

M. S. Ramaiah University of Applied Sciences, Bangalore, 560058, Karnataka, India
reachsandhyach@gmail.com, nabarkaustubh@yahoo.com,
pvc.research@msruas.ac.in

Abstract. This paper presents a Recursive Search Independent Multipath Finding Algorithm (RSIMFA) to determine possible independent paths to support Space-Frequency-Polarisation (SFP) reuse in MANETs. The concept of various reuse techniques like Space-Frequency (SF), Space-Polarisation (SP) and SFP are emerging as promising research avenues for throughput improvement in MANETs. The use of SF/SP/SFP reuse facilitates the provision of multiple independent links for concurrent data transmission along a single or multiple independent paths. In most of the existing literature on MANETs with single frequency and single polarization, the data transmission is realized along a single path, while the alternate multiple paths serve as a backup in the event of a failure of a chosen route. To facilitate the concurrent data transmission along multiple paths using the concept of SFP, there is a need for an efficient algorithm to determine multiple independent paths. A detailed formulation for RSIMFA with the following four main functions: Multipath Finding, Path Ranking, Sorting Logic and Decision Making is presented with requisite analytical and simulation results. The results of MATLAB simulations reveal that RSIMFA delivers a throughput improvement by a factor of about 3.9 with SFP as compared to a conventional data transmission through a single path using single frequency and polarisation.

Keywords: Mobile ad hoc networks · Antennas · Space polarisation
Space frequency polarisation · Multipath routing · Throughput · Radiation pattern
Microstrip antenna

1 Introduction

Traditionally, routing from source (S) to destination (D) nodes is realised through omni directional antenna with vertical polarisation. Even for the omni directional routing, alternate multiple paths are computed and stored as a back up to deal with the potential breakage of routes due to node mobility [1, 2]. In the traditional MANET with single frequency and single polarisation operation using omni mode, there is a lack of provision to simultaneously route the data through multiple paths due to interference between the adjacent co-located paths.

In past two decades, a significant research avenue in MANET is the advent of directional antennas. Even with the use of directional antennas in MANET [3, 4], the

© Springer Nature Singapore Pte Ltd. 2018
A. V. Deshpande et al. (Eds.): SmartCom 2017, CCIS 876, pp. 161–177, 2018.
https://doi.org/10.1007/978-981-13-1423-0_19

preference for data routing is still over single path [5]. Even though the interference between the adjacent co-located paths is relatively less severe in directional mode, the alternate paths are computed and stored only to use them as back up paths [6]. Directional mode of data routing is proved to be more energy efficient compared to the omni mode [7]. Most of the existing research on MANET is directed towards the concept of dual polarisation and directional antenna [8]. The research work carried out in [8] has provisions for two independent links along a single path for possible throughput improvement. However, the routing of data is realized through a single path. The concurrent transmission utilising both the Vertical Polarisation (VP) and Horizontal Polarisation (HP) using a single path or multiple paths associated with multi hop has not been addressed in [8]. While using the dual polarisation directional antenna for concurrent transmission of data, it is desirable to have independent multiple paths so that the links established are likely to perform satisfactorily in an actual scenario. Further, since the research on routing of data (both in omni as well as directional modes) is predominantly restricted to single frequency and single polarisation, the feasibility of simultaneous monitoring the route for maintenance and sustenance purposes remains unexplored. For the provision of route monitoring as well as concurrent transmission of data, the multiple paths must be independent. One feature of the independence of multiple paths in the above context is the absence of common intermediate nodes. In view of the above consideration, a new scheme for the multipath finding algorithm to determine all possible independent paths needs to be explored for the proposed reuse techniques involving space, polarisation and frequency.

2   Definition of Space-Frequency Reuse, Space-Polarisation Reuse and Space-Frequency Polarisation Reuse

This section defines the concept and various classifications of space reuse. The term 'space reuse' is meant to imply the sharing of the available space or space between any two nodes for the multi-mode operation of the link. The multi-mode operation may involve different frequencies giving rise to SF reuse. It may also include different polarisations leading to SP reuse or different frequencies along with different polarisations simultaneously forming SFP reuse. To support SF reuse, one needs two antennas operating at different frequencies with or without differing polarisation and hence it provides two independent links between S and D nodes with one link operating at first frequency and the second link operating at a second frequency. For SP reuse, two antennas operating at two polarisation (preferably orthogonal to each other) with or without differing frequencies are required. SP also offers two independent paths between S and D nodes with the first link operating at first polarisation (E.g. VP) and the second link at second polarisation (E.g. HP). For SFP reuse, four antennas are needed with two antennas operating at the first frequency but one in VP and the other in HP while the other two antenna operates at second frequency, one in VP and other in HP. Therefore, SFP reuse offers four independent links between S and D nodes with the first link operating at the first frequency and first polarisation (E.g. VP). The second link operates at the first frequency and second polarisation (E.g. HP) with the third link operating at second frequency and VP. The fourth link operating at second frequency and HP. Hence, SFP reuse offers four Degrees of Freedom (DoF) to simultaneously transmit data along four independent paths between a given S and D nodes. Ideally, it is desirable to have four independent paths to completely harness the potential of SFP reuse concept. To facilitate the SFP reuse concept, this paper presents the formulation to determine multiple independent paths between S and D node with RSIMFA.

3   Principles of Proposed RSIMFA

Given the S and D nodes, determination of all potential multipath for data transfer is an important step in MANET routing. In this paper, a Recursive Search Independent Multipath Finding Algorithm (RSIMFA) to determine possible multiple paths between S and D is presented. RSIMFA is similar to the traditional Ad-hoc On-demand Distance Vector (AODV) protocol [9]. The fundamental difference between RSIMFA and AODV is that unlike AODV, RSIMFA derives all possible multi-paths available between S and D using Depth First search (DFS) technique [10]. The proposed RSIMFA consists of following four functional blocks as shown in Fig. 1.

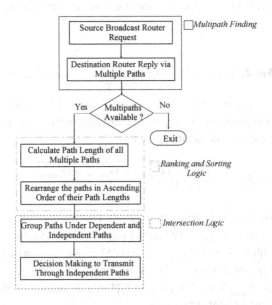

Fig. 1. Flow chart of the system (RSIMFA)

1. Algorithm for finding multiple paths
2. Ranking of multiple paths in the ascending order of their total path distance
3. Sorting logic to categorise multiple paths into paths with and without common intermediate nodes
4. Decision logic for the ranking and selection of multiple paths for concurrent or simultaneous data transmission using SP- Frequency Reuse techniques

To illustrate the concept of RSIMFA, the MANET topology of 53 nodes is considered as shown in Fig. 2. The S and D in the topology are node 11 and node 29 respectively.

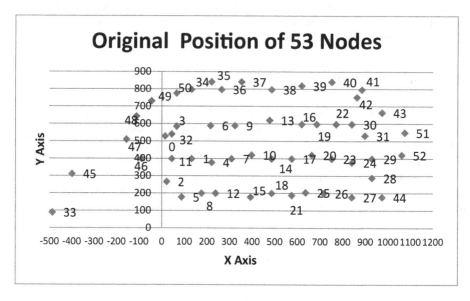

Fig. 2. Positional co-ordinates of 53 nodes in a network

Like in AODV, initially paths are formed based on the omni directional communication range. The maximum omni directional communication range, max_R_{omni} is calculated using Friss transmission formula given by:

$$max\_R_{omni} = \left[\frac{\lambda}{4\pi}\right]\sqrt{\frac{P_{Tomni} * G_{Tomni} * G_{Romni}}{RSS}} \tag{1}$$

Where, λ is wavelength of operation; P_{Tomni} is Transmitter Power; G_{Tomni} is Gain of Transmit Omni Antenna; G_{Romni} is the Gain of Receive Omni Antenna; RSS is Received Signal Strength. With RSS $= -73$ dBm, $\lambda = 0.057$ m, $P_{Tomni} = 40\,mW$, $G_{Tomni} = 1dBi$, $G_{Romni} = 1dBi$ the maximum omni communication range $max\_R_{omni} = 161.72$ m (at 5.25 GHz) and max_R_{omni} 346.55 m (at 2.45 GHz). The functional blocks of RSIMFA is explained in the subsequent subsections.

3.1 Algorithm to Discover Multiple Paths

Given a MANET topology, when S node wants to communicate with a particular D node, S broadcasts Route Request (RREQ) packets to its neighbouring nodes. RREQ packets contain Broadcast ID, Source ID, Route ID (RI) list, Destination ID, Node Distance and the energy list. Broadcast ID is unique ID generated by the source while broadcasting RREQ to avoid duplicate packet reception from other sources. Route ID

(RI) list contains the list of node IDs the RREQ packet had to travel through to reach the D node. Initially the RI list will be empty. Node Distance field calculates the inter node distance between each hop along a path and the energy list contains the nodes residual energy information. The intermediate nodes on receiving the RREQ packet checks for the address of D. If the address is not found then it checks RI list for the presence of its own node ID. If it already has its ID then it simply neglects the packet, else it updates its Node ID in RI list and forwards the packet to its immediate neighbours.

This technique avoids the packet over flow in the network and also helps in retrieving all the possible routes to the D. When the D receives the RREQ packets, it replies to the S with Route Reply (RREP) packet along the reverse path that is generated in RI list during RREQ. On the reception of RREP, the S waits for the specific interval of time to receive from all possible paths. Once the S has the list of all paths to the D, the next step is to decide the optimal or appropriate paths for reliable data transfer. Figure 3 illustrates bidirectional broadcast nature of RREQ packets from the S to among all the consequent neighbouring nodes.

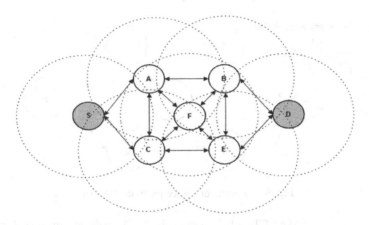

Fig. 3. Example of broadcast RREQs

For example, if Node F receives RREQs along (S A F) and (S C F), Node F will accept both RREQs and broadcasts them. Whereas, if RREQ repeats through (S A F B F) or (S C F E B F), Node F will simply discard both the packet as its ID (i.e., F) is already present in the RI list of RREQ packet. Figure 4 elucidates few example routes through which D receives RREQ.

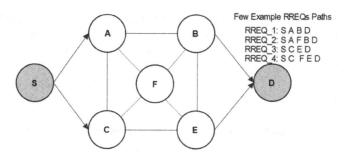

Fig. 4. Example of destination node receiving RREQs

Similarly Fig. 5 illustrates a few possible RREPs that S node receives from D. On receiving the RREP, S will have information of RI, residual energy and hop count of the obtained paths. From the received RREP in Fig. 5, examples of multiple paths are: (S A B D); (S A F B D); (S C E D); (S C F E D).

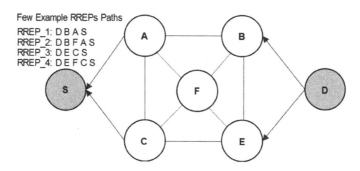

Fig. 5. Example of source receiving RREPs

For the scenario of MANET with 53 nodes (Fig. 2), Fig. 6 depicts the first 30 resulting paths out of 280 paths obtained through the proposed path finding algorithm of RSIMFA.

```
RESULTPATH  0    PATH:11  1  4  7  10  14  17  20  23  24  28  29
RESULTPATH  1    PATH:11  1  4  7  10  14  17  20  23  24  29
RESULTPATH  2    PATH:11  2  5  8  12  15  18  21  25  26  27  28  24  29
RESULTPATH  3    PATH:11  2  5  8  12  15  18  21  25  26  27  28  29
RESULTPATH  4    PATH:11  2  5  8  12  15  18  21  25  26  27  44  28  24  29
RESULTPATH  5    PATH:11  2  5  8  12  15  18  21  25  26  27  44  28  29
RESULTPATH  6    PATH:11  2  5  8  12  15  18  21  26  27  28  24  29
RESULTPATH  7    PATH:11  2  5  8  12  15  18  21  26  27  28  29
RESULTPATH  8    PATH:11  2  5  8  12  15  18  21  26  27  44  28  24  29
RESULTPATH  9    PATH:11  2  5  8  12  15  18  21  26  27  44  28  29
RESULTPATH  10   PATH:11  2  5  8  12  15  18  25  21  26  27  28  24  29
RESULTPATH  11   PATH:11  2  5  8  12  15  18  25  21  26  27  28  29
RESULTPATH  12   PATH:11  2  5  8  12  15  18  25  21  26  27  44  28  24  29
RESULTPATH  13   PATH:11  2  5  8  12  15  18  25  21  26  27  44  28  29
RESULTPATH  14   PATH:11  2  5  8  12  15  18  25  26  27  28  24  29
RESULTPATH  15   PATH:11  2  5  8  12  15  18  25  26  27  28  29
RESULTPATH  16   PATH:11  2  5  8  12  15  18  25  26  27  44  28  24  29
RESULTPATH  17   PATH:11  2  5  8  12  15  18  25  26  27  44  28  29
RESULTPATH  18   PATH:11  2  5  12  15  18  21  25  26  27  28  24  29
RESULTPATH  19   PATH:11  2  5  12  15  18  21  25  26  27  28  29
RESULTPATH  20   PATH:11  2  5  12  15  18  21  25  26  27  44  28  24  29
RESULTPATH  21   PATH:11  2  5  12  15  18  21  25  26  27  44  28  29
RESULTPATH  22   PATH:11  2  5  12  15  18  21  26  27  28  24  29
RESULTPATH  23   PATH:11  2  5  12  15  18  21  26  27  28  29
RESULTPATH  24   PATH:11  2  5  12  15  18  21  26  27  44  28  24  29
RESULTPATH  25   PATH:11  2  5  12  15  18  21  26  27  44  28  29
RESULTPATH  26   PATH:11  2  5  12  15  18  25  21  26  27  28  24  29
RESULTPATH  27   PATH:11  2  5  12  15  18  25  21  26  27  28  29
RESULTPATH  28   PATH:11  2  5  12  15  18  25  21  26  27  44  28  24  29
RESULTPATH  29   PATH:11  2  5  12  15  18  25  21  26  27  44  28  29
RESULTPATH  30   PATH:11  2  5  12  15  18  25  26  27  28  24  29
```

Fig. 6. List of some of the available multiple paths

3.2   Ranking of Paths

After determination of the multi paths, the next step is to rank them based on its total path distance. The individual path distance which is nothing but the total distance that the path covers to reach the D is calculated. It requires inputs from RREP packet about the inter node distances along a path. For illustration purposes, the total path distance of the randomly selected four paths with respective path indices are shown in Table 1. Path index is the path number assigned to each path sequentially on obtaining the paths. The path index is fixed and unique to each path. The highest path index indicates the total number of multiple paths obtained.

Table 1. Path distance calculation

Path Index	Paths	Range (m)
0	11 1 4 7 10 14 17 20 23 24 28 29	1051.3
1	11 1 4 7 10 14 17 20 23 24 29	906.73
2	11 2 5 8 12 15 18 21 25 26 27 28 24 29	1367.18
3	11 2 5 8 12 15 18 21 25 26 27 28 29	1261.44

3.3   Path Sorting Function

After calculating the path length (distance) of all the available paths, the path are sorted in ascending order of their path lengths to get the path with the lowest range. The obtained path with lowest range is the path with shortest distance to reach D node 29. The sorting technique using insertion logic is shown in Table 2.

Table 2. Sorting technique on path lengths

	Input Range	Step 1	Step 2	Step 3	Step 4 (Output)
N1	1051.3	1051.3	906.73	906.73	906.73
N2	906.73	906.73	1051.3	1051.3	1051.3
N3	1367.18	1367.18	1367.18	1367.18	1261.44
N4	1261.44	1261.44	1261.44	1261.44	1367.18
	Pointer Position	N2	N3	N4	

In Table 2, the sorting logic is applied to the input range array {1051.3, 906.73, 1367.18 and 1261.44} to get the ascending ordered sorted array {906.73, 1051.3, 1261.44, and 1367.18}. The sorting procedure terminates with the determination of ascending ordered array, irrespective of how many number of steps are involved in the exchange. For example, in the first step of Table 2, the first two range values are compared to find the smaller among the two namely $N1 = 1051.3$ and $N2 = 906.73$. On comparison, the lower N value should be moved up. Now with N2 being the lower value, the values of N1 and N2 are swapped so that now $N1 = 906.73$ and $N2 = 1051.3$. Now the pointer for comparison moves down by one step in step 2 between $N2 = 1051.3$ and $N3 = 1367.18$. Since in step 2, the upper positioned N2 being the lower value when compared to N3, the corresponding value position is retained. The process of comparison or sorting continues till all the multiple paths are arranged in the ascending order of the path distance. Table 3 depicts paths of Table 2 sorted in ascending order of path lengths. Range index enables the sequential numbering of the sorted paths.

Table 3. Sorted paths in ascending order of path length

Sorting paths According to its Sorted Ranges			
Path Index	Paths	Range (m)	Range Index
1	11 1 4 7 10 14 17 20 23 24 29	906.73	0
0	11 1 4 7 10 14 17 20 23 24 28 29	1051.3	1
3	11 2 5 8 12 15 18 21 25 26 27 28 29	1261.44	2
2	11 2 5 8 12 15 18 21 25 26 27 28 24 29	1367.18	3

For a scenario of 53 nodes, Fig. 7 shows the list of resultant sorted paths in ascending order of path lengths.

```
        Path(Ascending Order of DISTANCE)
 1) RESULT PATH:   1  DISTANCE: '906.726074'  ELEMENTS:  [ 11 1 4 7 10 14 17 20 23 24 29 ]
 2) RESULT PATH:   0  DISTANCE: '1051.301270' ELEMENTS:  [ 11 1 4 7 10 14 17 20 23 24 28 29 ]
 3) RESULT PATH:  44  DISTANCE: '1180.463745' ELEMENTS:  [ 11 32 3 6 9 13 16 19 22 31 29 ]
 4) RESULT PATH:  82  DISTANCE: '1180.463745' ELEMENTS:  [ 11 32 3 6 9 13 16 22 31 29 ]
 5) RESULT PATH:  34  DISTANCE: '1194.425171' ELEMENTS:  [ 11 32 3 6 9 13 16 19 22 30 31 29 ]
 6) RESULT PATH:  52  DISTANCE: '1194.425171' ELEMENTS:  [ 11 32 3 6 9 13 16 19 30 31 29 ]
 7) RESULT PATH:  72  DISTANCE: '1194.425171' ELEMENTS:  [ 11 32 3 6 9 13 16 22 30 31 29 ]
 8) RESULT PATH:  31  DISTANCE: '1257.634399' ELEMENTS:  [ 11 2 5 12 15 18 25 26 27 28 29 ]
 9) RESULT PATH:  23  DISTANCE: '1258.659424' ELEMENTS:  [ 11 2 5 12 15 18 21 26 27 28 29 ]
10) RESULT PATH:  15  DISTANCE: '1258.740479' ELEMENTS:  [ 11 2 5 8 12 15 18 25 26 27 28 29 ]
11) RESULT PATH:   7  DISTANCE: '1259.765503' ELEMENTS:  [ 11 2 5 8 12 15 18 21 26 27 28 29 ]
12) RESULT PATH:  19  DISTANCE: '1260.330322' ELEMENTS:  [ 11 2 5 12 15 18 21 25 26 27 28 29 ]
13) RESULT PATH:   3  DISTANCE: '1261.436401' ELEMENTS:  [ 11 2 5 8 12 15 18 21 25 26 27 28 29 ]
14) RESULT PATH:  50  DISTANCE: '1318.523926' ELEMENTS:  [ 11 32 3 6 9 13 16 19 30 22 31 29 ]
15) RESULT PATH:  30  DISTANCE: '1363.375000' ELEMENTS:  [ 11 2 5 12 15 18 25 26 27 28 24 29 ]
16) RESULT PATH:  22  DISTANCE: '1364.400024' ELEMENTS:  [ 11 2 5 12 15 18 21 26 27 28 24 29 ]
17) RESULT PATH:  14  DISTANCE: '1364.481079' ELEMENTS:  [ 11 2 5 8 12 15 18 25 26 27 28 24 29 ]
18) RESULT PATH:   6  DISTANCE: '1365.506104' ELEMENTS:  [ 11 2 5 8 12 15 18 21 26 27 28 24 29 ]
19) RESULT PATH:  18  DISTANCE: '1366.070923' ELEMENTS:  [ 11 2 5 12 15 18 21 25 26 27 28 24 29 ]
20) RESULT PATH:  62  DISTANCE: '1366.105225' ELEMENTS:  [ 11 32 3 6 9 13 16 22 19 30 31 29 ]
21) RESULT PATH:   2  DISTANCE: '1367.177002' ELEMENTS:  [ 11 2 5 8 12 15 18 21 25 26 27 28 24 29 ]
22) RESULT PATH:  33  DISTANCE: '1367.856079' ELEMENTS:  [ 11 2 5 12 15 18 25 26 27 44 28 29 ]
23) RESULT PATH:  25  DISTANCE: '1368.880981' ELEMENTS:  [ 11 2 5 12 15 18 21 26 27 44 28 29 ]
24) RESULT PATH:  17  DISTANCE: '1368.962158' ELEMENTS:  [ 11 2 5 8 12 15 18 25 26 27 44 28 29 ]
25) RESULT PATH:   9  DISTANCE: '1369.987183' ELEMENTS:  [ 11 2 5 8 12 15 18 21 26 27 44 28 29 ]
26) RESULT PATH:  21  DISTANCE: '1370.551880' ELEMENTS:  [ 11 2 5 12 15 18 21 25 26 27 44 28 29 ]
27) RESULT PATH:   5  DISTANCE: '1371.658081' ELEMENTS:  [ 11 2 5 8 12 15 18 21 25 26 27 44 28 29 ]
28) RESULT PATH:  27  DISTANCE: '1383.894287' ELEMENTS:  [ 11 2 5 12 15 18 25 21 26 27 28 29 ]
29) RESULT PATH:  11  DISTANCE: '1385.000366' ELEMENTS:  [ 11 2 5 8 12 15 18 25 21 26 27 28 29 ]
30) RESULT PATH:  42  DISTANCE: '1407.578613' ELEMENTS:  [ 11 32 3 6 9 13 16 19 22 30 43 31 29 ]
```

Fig. 7. List of sorted paths in ascending order of the path lengths

3.4 Intersection Logic to Categorise Multi-paths into Paths with and Without Common Intermediate Nodes

A flow chart to determine independent and dependent paths from the sorted multiple paths is shown in Fig. 8. The input to the intersection logic is the sorted multi paths in accordance with range. The intersection logic helps in identifying common elements/ nodes on comparison. The path with Range index R (0) which implies the shortest route to the destination is fixed for comparison. Each ranked path elements (Node ID) are compared with the elements of R (0) path sequentially. This requires the input from RI list containing all the Node IDs along the path from RREP. On comparing the elements, all sorted multiple paths are categorised under dependent or independent paths. Independent are the paths that do not contain any common node when compared to the nodes of all the obtained and ranked multiple paths. Whereas, dependent paths have one or more nodes in common when compared to the elements of paths in independent path list. Sorting and intersection logic helps in prioritising the paths and classifying the available paths into independent paths and dependent paths as shown in Figs. 8 and 9. It is important to note that when intersection logic is applied, the 1st and the last elements (S and D nodes) in a path can be neglected as all the paths will have those two elements in common.

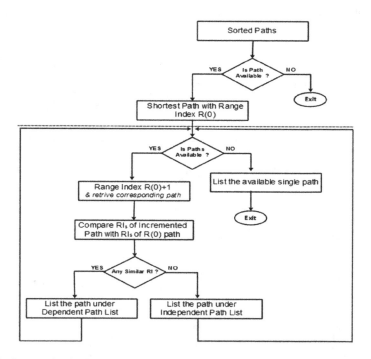

Fig. 8. Intersection logic to classify multiple-paths into independent and dependent paths

For a given MANET topology in Fig. 2, there are four possible independent paths obtained as illustrated in Fig. 9. Paths with indices 1, 44, 31 and 183 are the independent paths, this infers that the intermediate elements of path 1, 44, 31 and 183 should be unique. In case, if there are no independent paths present between the given S and D, the next priority is to choose the dependent paths based on decision weight.

```
            List of independent paths
 1) RESULT PATH:   1  DISTANCE: '906.726074' ELEMENTS:  [11 1 4 7 10 14 17 20 23 24 29 ]
 2) RESULT PATH:  44  DISTANCE: '1180.463745' ELEMENTS:  [11 32 3 6 9 13 16 19 22 31 29 ]
 3) RESULT PATH:  31  DISTANCE: '1257.634399' ELEMENTS:  [11 2 5 12 15 18 25 26 27 28 29 ]
 4) RESULT PATH: 183  DISTANCE: '2042.656738' ELEMENTS:  [11 46 47 48 49 50 34 35 37 38 39 40 42 43 51 52 29 ]

            List of normal paths
 1) RESULT PATH:   0  DISTANCE: '1051.301270' ELEMENTS:  [11 1 4 7 10 14 17 20 23 24 28 29 ]
 2) RESULT PATH:  82  DISTANCE: '1180.463745' ELEMENTS:  [11 32 3 6 9 13 16 22 31 29 ]
 3) RESULT PATH:  34  DISTANCE: '1194.425171' ELEMENTS:  [11 32 3 6 9 13 16 19 22 30 31 29 ]
 4) RESULT PATH:  52  DISTANCE: '1194.425171' ELEMENTS:  [11 32 3 6 9 13 16 19 30 31 29 ]
 5) RESULT PATH:  72  DISTANCE: '1194.425171' ELEMENTS:  [11 32 3 6 9 13 16 22 30 31 29 ]
 6) RESULT PATH:  23  DISTANCE: '1258.659424' ELEMENTS:  [11 2 5 12 15 18 21 26 27 28 29 ]
 7) RESULT PATH:  15  DISTANCE: '1258.740479' ELEMENTS:  [11 2 5 8 12 15 18 25 26 27 28 29 ]
 8) RESULT PATH:   7  DISTANCE: '1259.765503' ELEMENTS:  [11 2 5 8 12 15 18 21 26 27 28 29 ]
 9) RESULT PATH:  19  DISTANCE: '1260.330322' ELEMENTS:  [11 2 5 12 15 18 21 25 26 27 28 29 ]
10) RESULT PATH:   3  DISTANCE: '1261.436401' ELEMENTS:  [11 2 5 8 12 15 18 21 25 26 27 28 29 ]
11) RESULT PATH:  50  DISTANCE: '1318.523926' ELEMENTS:  [11 32 3 6 9 13 16 19 30 22 31 29 ]
12) RESULT PATH:  30  DISTANCE: '1363.375000' ELEMENTS:  [11 2 5 12 15 18 25 26 27 28 24 29 ]
13) RESULT PATH:  22  DISTANCE: '1364.400024' ELEMENTS:  [11 2 5 12 15 18 21 26 27 28 24 29 ]
14) RESULT PATH:  14  DISTANCE: '1364.481079' ELEMENTS:  [11 2 5 8 12 15 18 25 26 27 28 24 29 ]
15) RESULT PATH:   6  DISTANCE: '1365.506104' ELEMENTS:  [11 2 5 8 12 15 18 21 26 27 28 24 29 ]
16) RESULT PATH:  18  DISTANCE: '1366.070923' ELEMENTS:  [11 2 5 12 15 18 21 25 26 27 28 24 29 ]
17) RESULT PATH:  62  DISTANCE: '1366.105225' ELEMENTS:  [11 32 3 6 9 13 16 22 19 30 31 29 ]
18) RESULT PATH:   2  DISTANCE: '1367.177002' ELEMENTS:  [11 2 5 8 12 15 18 21 25 26 27 28 24 29 ]
19) RESULT PATH:  33  DISTANCE: '1367.856079' ELEMENTS:  [11 2 5 12 15 18 25 26 27 44 28 29 ]
20) RESULT PATH:  25  DISTANCE: '1368.880981' ELEMENTS:  [11 2 5 12 15 18 21 26 27 44 28 29 ]
21) RESULT PATH:  17  DISTANCE: '1368.962158' ELEMENTS:  [11 2 5 8 12 15 18 25 26 27 44 28 29 ]
22) RESULT PATH:   9  DISTANCE: '1369.987183' ELEMENTS:  [11 2 5 8 12 15 18 21 26 27 44 28 29 ]
23) RESULT PATH:  21  DISTANCE: '1370.551880' ELEMENTS:  [11 2 5 12 15 18 21 25 26 27 44 28 29 ]
24) RESULT PATH:   5  DISTANCE: '1371.658081' ELEMENTS:  [11 2 5 8 12 15 18 21 25 26 27 44 28 29 ]
25) RESULT PATH:  27  DISTANCE: '1383.894287' ELEMENTS:  [11 2 5 12 15 18 25 21 26 27 28 29 ]
26) RESULT PATH:  11  DISTANCE: '1385.000366' ELEMENTS:  [11 2 5 8 12 15 18 25 21 26 27 28 29 ]
27) RESULT PATH:  42  DISTANCE: '1407.578613' ELEMENTS:  [11 32 3 6 9 13 16 19 22 30 43 31 29 ]
28) RESULT PATH:  60  DISTANCE: '1407.578613' ELEMENTS:  [11 32 3 6 9 13 16 19 30 43 31 29 ]
29) RESULT PATH:  80  DISTANCE: '1407.578613' ELEMENTS:  [11 32 3 6 9 13 16 22 30 43 31 29 ]
30) RESULT PATH:  32  DISTANCE: '1473.596680' ELEMENTS:  [11 2 5 12 15 18 25 26 27 44 28 24 29 ]
```

Fig. 9. List of independent paths and paths with common intermediate nodes

3.5 Decision Making Logic to Rank and Select the Independent Paths for Data Transmission

Once the independent paths are found, any one of the below computation options or the combination of all or if required, any additional computation can be chosen to assign the decision weight.

1. Residual energy of each independent path must be determined from RREP packet which means the sum of residual energies of each node in that path. Path is considered only if all the nodes along a path satisfy a specific user-defined threshold residual energy criteria
2. Battery Energy required to transmit Data (B.E Data) is calculated for all the paths
3. Residue of residual energy of each path must be known which the resultant of residual energy – B.E Data.
4. Hop count of each path should be known from RREP packet

With the choice of the combination of all the four parameters, the decision weight for each of the paths is determined by the formula,

$$DecisionWeight[i] = \left[\frac{\alpha_1 \times ResidueofResidualEnergy}{\alpha_2 \times HopCount + \alpha_3 \times B.E_{Data}} \right] \tag{2}$$

Where i denotes i^{th} path, α_1, α_2 and α_3 are the associated weights such that $\alpha_1 + \alpha_2 + \alpha_3 = 1$.

The four independent paths with maximum decision weights are to be selected (meaning 1st four highest weighted paths). The residual energy of each node in the selected path is checked in RREP Packet. If any node in the selected path has residual energy less than the B.E_Data, then that path is replaced by the next highest decision weighted path. If many paths have the same decision weights as well as satisfy the threshold criteria, then the path which is first among them in the list is selected.

However, modifications or additional factors needed to be considered for the implementation of concurrent transmission of data along multipath load sharing as well as load balancing (consideration of maximum communication range, range of the path, mobility as well as residual battery energy). This has been addressed in the ongoing research work of the current authors. This has not been included since it is beyond the scope of this paper.

The concurrent data transmission along a single path using SFP is feasible. However, it is preferable to have independent multiple paths so that the links established along such independent paths are likely to perform relatively better in an actual scenario.

4   Simulation Results and Analysis

This section presents simulation results to substantiate the utility of SFP reuse concept for the improved performance of MANET. As stated while explaining the concept SFP reuse, two antennas operating in the first frequency with one of them in VP and the other in HP are needed. In addition, two more antennas radiating in the second frequency with one of them in VP and the other in HP are required. The two frequencies chosen for the simulation are 2.45 GHz and 5.2 GHz. The configuration of 4 microstrip antennas developed to implement the SFP reuse concept are shown in Fig. 10. Since microstrip antenna exhibits directional radiation pattern associated with defined main beam, the configuration shown in Fig. 10 is termed as directional mode for SFP.

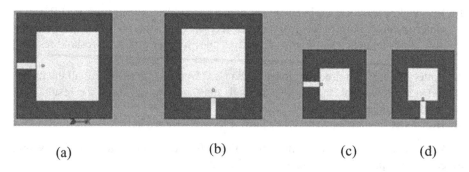

(a)   (b)   (c)   (d)

Fig. 10.   Configuration of 4 microstrip antennas in dual frequency and dual polarisation (DFDP) configuration for SFP reuse

The two antennas designed for the operating frequency of 2.45 GHz are shown in Fig. 10(a) and (b). Figure 10(a) depicts the microstrip antenna radiating in 2.45 GHz with HP. The microstrip antenna operating in 2.45 GHz with VP is shown in Fig. 10(b).

The combination of antenna shown in Fig. 10(a) and (b) results in Dual-Polarisation (DP) concept at 2.45 GHz. Similarly, Fig. 10(c) is the design configuration of the microstrip antenna at 5.2 GHz in HP. The microstrip antenna radiating at 5.25 GHz in VP is shown in Fig. 10(d). The combination of antennas shown in Fig. 10(c) and (d) results in DP concept at 5.2 GHz. DP at 2.45 GHz and DP at 5.2 GHz results in DFDP microstrip antenna configuration required for SFP reuse concept. All the four antennas are simulated for simultaneous operation required in concurrent transmission of data along multiple paths in MANET with each path operating at a specified frequency and polarisation and not interfering with other paths.

The inter distance between successive antennas in the above configuration is less than 25 mm. The radiation pattern of the antenna in the azimuth plane operating with HP in 2.45 GHz is shown in Fig. 11(a). The results of the Fig. 11(a) indicate a co polarisation (HP) gain of 4.50 dBi and the cross polarisation (VP) along the direction of main beam is less than −50 dBi clearly indicating polarisation discrimination. The results shown in Fig. 10(b) depict the radiation pattern of the antenna operating at 2.45 GHz with VP as co polarisation. The co polarisation (VP) gain is better than 5 dBi and the cross polarisation (HP) along the direction of the main beam is less than −22 dBi.

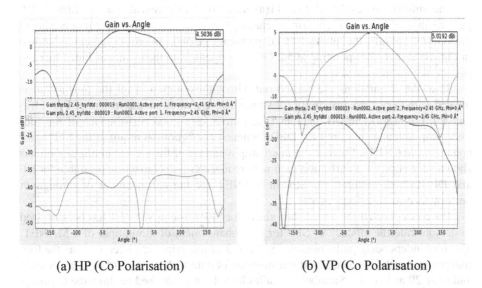

(a) HP (Co Polarisation)   (b) VP (Co Polarisation)

Fig. 11. Radiation patterns in azimuth plane of microstrip antennas operating at 2.45 GHz

The corresponding radiation patterns of the microstrip antenna at 5.2 GHz are shown Fig. 12. The radiation pattern of the microstrip antenna (Fig. 10 (d)) in the azimuth plane with HP as co polarisation is shown in Fig. 12(a). The results of Fig. 12(a) reveal that for the microstrip antenna operating at 5.2 GHz, the co-polarisation (HP) gain is better than 6 dBi with the cross polarisation (VP) along the main beam less than −20 dBi. The results of Fig. 12(b) reveal that the gain of microstrip antenna (Fig. 10(c)) operating at 5.2 GHz with VP as a co-polarisation has a gain of 6.37 dBi with the cross polarisation along the main beam less than −22 dBi.

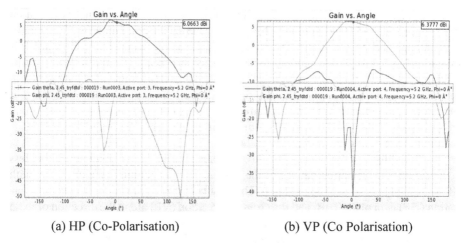

(a) HP (Co-Polarisation)   (b) VP (Co Polarisation)

Fig. 12. Radiation patterns in azimuth plane of microstrip antennas operating at 5.2 GHz.

The simulation results of Fig. 11(a) and (b) clearly reveal the satisfactory DP performance of the two microstrip antennas (shown in Fig. 10(a) and (b)) operating at 2.45 GHz. Similarly, the satisfactory DP performance of the microstrip antennas (shown in Fig. 10(c) and (d)) operating at 5.2 GHz is evident from the results of Fig. 12(a) and (b).

Since the simulations are carried out with the excitation of all the four antennas located with very close proximity for simultaneous operation, the results of Fig. 11(a) and (b), Fig. 12(a) and (b) together constitute a very good performance of the four microstrip antennas required for DFDP antenna configuration required for SFP reuse concept in MANETs. Each of the microstrip antennas of the arrived configuration has shown very good co-polarisation gain with reduced cross polarisation desirable for DF and DP features required for SFP in MANET for the enhancement of throughput performance in directional mode.

The concept of DFDP established above for SFP reuse in MANET has been utilised to demonstrate the efficacy of SFP for the enhancement of throughput of a MANET. The four independent paths obtained in Sect. 3 of this paper has been used as the four independent paths for concurrent transmission of data with node 11 of Fig. 2 as S node and node 29 as D node. Simulation studies have been performed to show the improvement in the throughput of the MANET with the application of SFP reuse. The proposed SFP reuse concept is not amenable for implementation in commercial simulators like QUALNET and NS-2. A source code has been developed in MATLAB to carry out the simulation of a MANET with SFP reuse concept. For the simulation, the first independent path (path index 1) has been assigned the frequency of 2.45 GHz and VP. The second independent path (path index 44) has been assigned 2.45 GHz and HP. The third independent path (path index 31) has been assigned the frequency of 5.2 GHz and VP. The fourth independent path (path index 183) has been assigned the frequency of 5.2 GHz and HP. Table 4 depicts the throughput performance of a MANET with 53 nodes with a topology shown in Fig. 2 when the SFP reuse concept is applied for various channel conditions expressed through SNR. The gain performance of the 4 microstrip antennas discussed in Figs. 11 and 12 has been utilised in the directional mode of concurrent transmission of data along the four independent paths. In the simulation results shown in Table 4, the data size of 4 MB has been distributed equally amongst the four independent paths. The size of each packet is 512 Bytes and the assigned data rate is 1 Mbps.

Table 4. Throughput with SFP Reuse (with four independent paths)

Throughput (TP) in Kbps					
SNR (dB)	TP (Path 1)	TP (Path 2)	TP (Path 3)	TP (Path 4)	TP (System)	Relative improvement factor in TP
0	943.9	944.2	899.1	868.8	3646	3.862
10	971.5	970.2	969.4	967.9	3879	3.993
15	979.3	978.2	972.5	969.3	3899	3.982

System throughput stated in Table 4 is the sum of the throughput of all the four paths in lieu of the concurrent transmission of data along the four independent paths. The relative improvement factor in Throughput (TP) stated is the ratio system throughput to the throughput for data transmission through a single path. The ideal TP improvement factor for this specific scenario is 4 because of four independent paths. The comparative performance of the TP shown in Table 4 has also been illustrated in Fig. 13.

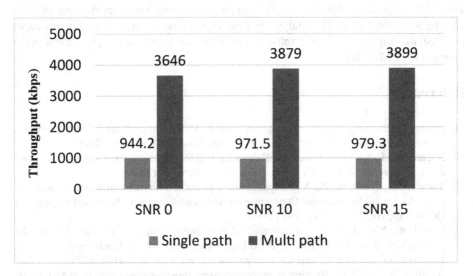

Fig. 13. Comparison of throughput with data transmission through single path and 4 paths

The throughput improvement factor derived for varying SNR conditions are 3.862 (SNR = 0), 3.993 (SNR = 10) and 3.982 (SNR = 15) which compares favorably with the ideal throughput improvement factor of 4. As a consequence, the significance of SFP reuse or DFDP for the significant improvement in the throughput of MANET is established.

5   Conclusions

This paper has presented the need and justification for an algorithm to find the multiple independent paths for concurrent transmission of data in MANET that SFP reuse concept for enhanced throughput. The inadequacy of the existing protocols and the associated multipath finding scheme for the proposed application of SFP reuse concept in MANET has been clearly highlighted. The requirement of additional sorting technique to classify the obtained multipath into independent paths and dependent paths is also clearly explained. The various steps in the development of proposed RSIMFA have been explained in requisite analytical details. The configuration of 4 microstrip antennas which typically satisfies the requirement of SFP in directional mode has been proposed. Through simulation studies, the configuration of the four microstrip antennas developed has been proved to satisfy the desirable features both the good co-polar gain and low cross polarisation required for SFP reuse in MANET. The consequent advantage of the application of SFP for the improved throughput performance of a MANET has been illustrated through a comparative performance of a MANET with data transmission through a single path and four independent paths. The average improvement factor in Throughput realised through transmission of data through four independent paths is about 3.9 which compares favourably with an ideal throughput improvement of 4 for varying SNR conditions. The analysis and the simulation results presented in this paper establish the importance of SFP reuse or DFDP for the significant improvement in the throughput of MANET.

References

1. Prabha, R., Ramaraj, N.: An improved multipath MANET routing using link estimation and swarm intelligence. EURASIP J. Wirel. Commun. Netw. **2015**, 90–173 (2015)
2. Nagaratna, M., NarasimhaRao, V.G.: Rebroadcasting for minimization of routing based upon neighbor coverage in MANET's. Int. J. Sci. Res. **4**, 616–620 (2015)
3. Yonghui, C., Chunfeng, Z.: A multipath routing protocol with path compression for ad hoc networks. In: 3rd International Conference on Advanced Computer Theory and Engineering (ICA CTE), vol. 20, no. 5, pp. 1–5 (2010)
4. Roy, C.R., Nitin H.V.: Performance of ad hoc routing using directional antennas. In: Proceedings of the Fourth Annual IEEE Communications Society Conference on Sensor, University of Illinois at Urbana Champaign, vol. 22, no. 5, pp. 401–410 (2007)
5. Amith, K.S., David, B.: Routing improvement using directional antennas in MANETs. In: IEEE International Conference on Mobile Ad hoc Networks 2005, Fort Lauderdale, Florida, pp. 304–313 (2016)
6. Ramanathan, R., Redi, J., Santivanez, C., Wiggins, D., Polit, S.: Ad hoc networking with directional antennas. A complete system solution. IEEE J. Commun. **23**(3), 496–506 (2005)
7. Sandhya, Ch.: Design and development of an energy efficient multipath routing protocol using directional antenna for MANETs, M.Sc. (Engg) thesis, Coventry University, UK (2012)

8. Rinki, S.: Simulation studies on effects of dual polarisation and directivity of antennas on the performance of MANETs, Ph.D. thesis, Coventry University, UK (2014)
9. Taneja, S., Kush, A., Makkar, A.: Experimental analysis of DSR, AODV using speed and pause time. Int. J. Innov. Manag. Technol. 1(5), 453–458 (2010). ISSN 2010-0248
10. Korf, R.E.: Depth-first iterative-deepening, an optimal admissible tree search. Artif. Intell. 27, 97–109 (1985)

Analyzing the Effect of Database Dimensionality on Performance of Adaptive Apriori Algorithm

Shubhangi D. Patil[1(✉)], Ratnadeep R. Deshmukh[2],
Dnyaneshwar K. Kirange[3], and Swapnil Waghmare[2]

[1] Department of Information Technology,
Government Polytechnic, Jalgaon, India
sdkirange@gmail.com
[2] Department of Computer Science and IT,
Dr. Babasaheb Ambedkar Marathwada University, Aurangabaad, India
[3] Department of Computer Engineering, J. T. Mahajan College of Engineering,
Faizpur, Jalgaon, India
dkirange@gmail.com

Abstract. Obtaining frequent itemsets from the dataset is one of the most promising areas of data mining. The Apriori algorithm is one of the most important algorithms for obtaining frequent itemsets from the dataset. But the algorithm fails in terms of time required as well as number of database scans. Hence a new improved version of Apriori is proposed in this paper which is efficient in terms of time required as well as number of database scans than the Apriori algorithm. It is well known that the size of the database for defining candidates has great effect on running time and memory need. The usefulness of the adaptive apriori algorithm in terms of dimensionality of the dataset is demonstrated. We presented experimental results, showing that the proposed algorithm always outperform Apriori. To evaluate the performance of the proposed algorithm, we have tested it on Turkey student's database of faculty evaluations.

Keywords: Database scans · Apriori · Data mining

1 Introduction

In Data Mining, for location and fascination of relations in variables in large databases, Association Rule Mining is a standard and well researched technique. Before applying various data mining techniques such as classification, clustering and prediction, for data analysis, association rule mining is used. The association rule mining was first proposed by Agrawal et al. [1]. It is one of the most recommended research area which is applicable in most of the fields like analysis of market trends, forecasting and detection of faults. The process of association rule mining is divided in two steps; first find all frequent items from the dataset and then discovering the relationships among the items

© Springer Nature Singapore Pte Ltd. 2018
A. V. Deshpande et al. (Eds.): SmartCom 2017, CCIS 876, pp. 178–185, 2018.
https://doi.org/10.1007/978-981-13-1423-0_20

in the database. Itemset denotes a set of items. Itemsets with support count more than the minimum support threshold are referred as frequent itemsets. Mostly the performance of the association rule mining is affected by the first step, as next step of association rule mining is simple [2]. Hence mostly association rule mining is mostly called as frequent itemset mining also.

The two most frequently used algorithms of association rule mining are Apriori and FP-Growth [3, 4]. Both of these algorithms are having different approaches for finding frequent itemsets. In this paper the Apriori algorithm is improved in terms of time required as well as number of database scans. The intermediate dynamic dataset is created separately using MATLAB by using the database transactions at each level separately. Thus instead of scanning the entire database, we need to scan only the extracted rows and columns at each level. The proposed improved Apriori algorithm outperforms the basic Apriori because at each level, the transactions with minimum support are eliminated. Hence not considered for higher levels. This helps to reduce the size of the database at each level which saves a lot of time, and a noticeable improvement in the speed by reducing the frequent database scans. Here, in this paper we have demonstrated the efficiency of the adaptive apriori algorithm in terms of various dimensionalities of the databases.

2 Related Work

In the DHP algorithm proposed by Park et al. [8] the algorithm is based on dynamic hash hashing algorithms and pruning algorithm. Here the transactions that are not involved in generating frequent itemsets are not considered while traversing the database. Thus the efficiency for frequent itemset mining is improved.

The dynamic itemset counting algorithm proposed by Brin [9] requires less number of database scans. In this algorithm the transaction database is divided in to data blocks of same size.

MapReduce [10] framework produced by Googlein 2004 is able to handle the big data. In the similar way, Hadoop based on MapReduce, cluster based parallel data mining are some of works for big data mining. Various classical data mining algorithms are based on Hadoop. Various parallel algorithms using Apriori such as SPC, FPC and DPC [11] are proposed by Lin et al. These are based on MapReduce. The parallel frequent itemset mining algorithm proposed by Li et al. [12] scans the transactions database for counting the frequent itemsets in the Map stage, and the statistical operations are performed for obtaining frequent itemsets in the Reduce phase Hammoud [13] proposed a parallel in each round of the iterative procedure, where cut datasets are alloted to every Map hub and measurable competitor incessant itemsets, then converging to get continuous itemsets in the Reduce stage. Spark is a memory-based parallel registering system, and it can incredibly enhance the ongoing information handling and guarantee the group's high adaptation to internal failure and high versatility [14] in enormous information situations. A parallel Apriori algorithm was introduced by Qiu H et al which is related to Spark YAFIM [15]. The results obtained using SPARt are more promising than that using Hadoop.

3 Apriori Algorithm

3.1 Apriori Algorithm

Apriori algorithm was the first algorithm for finding the frequent itemsets and association rule mining. The Apriori algorithm is divided in two major steps: join and prune.

The new candidate seta is generated in the join step. Depending on the support count, the candidate set can be defined as frequent or infrequent. For generating higher level candidate itemsets (Ci) previous level frequent itemsets Li-1 are joined. In the pruning step, the infrequent candidate item sets are filtered out. This step ensures that every subset of a frequent itemset is also frequent. Hence, if the candidate item set contains more infrequent item sets, will be removed from the process of frequent itemset and association mining [4]. This process is called pruning.

The Apriori algorithmic program takes longer time for candidate generation technique. The Apriori algorithmic program needs many scans of the database. Many trivial rules are derived and it will be hard to extract the most interesting rules. Rules can be inexplicable and fine grained. Redundant rules are generated.

3.2 Adaptive Apriori Algorithm

The Adaptive Apriori algorithm proposed here is able to overcome the basic Apriori algorithm in terms of number of database scans as well as time required. The size of the database is reduced at each level. This algorithm uses a dynamic technique to reduce the time required for candidate itemset generation. It is claimed that the size of the database is reduced at each level starting from last to first and hence the time required for candidate itemset generation is reduced as compared with basic Apriori algorithm. Here we generate the dynamic intermediate database for each level separately.

For example, when scanning each transaction in the database find all the transactions which contain all items. These transactions are considered for generation for level K itemset. The same transactions are also considered for generating level 1 to level k−1 itemsets. So these are copied for all these levels. Now the database is updated by deleting all these transactions. This updated database is again considered for generating level L k−1 itemsets. Hence the size of the database is reduced at level of candidate itemset generation as well as the time required is also minimized.

Algorithm:
Input D, a database of transactions
    Min_sup, the minimum threshold support
Output L_k Maximal frequent itemsets in D
      C_k Set of Candidate k-itemsets.
Method:
1. Generate the Intermediate Database
   a. Find all transactions to be considered for level K containing all itemsets.
   b. Copy these transactions in the database to be considered for level 1 to K
   c. Delete these transactions from the database D and update the database.
   d. Now consider this updated (reduced in size) database for finding all transactions for level 1 to K-1
   e. Repeat the steps subsequently and update the database.
2. Consider this updated database for candidate itemset generation at each step.
3. L_1 =Frequent items of length 1.
4. For(k=1;L_k!=ϕ;k++) do.
5. Consider D as intermediate updated database for level k
6. C_{k+1}=candidates generated from L_k.
7. For each transaction t in database D do.
8. Increment the count of all candidates in C_{k+1} that are contained in t.
9. L_{k+1} =candidates in C_{k+1} with minimum support
10. end do
11. Return the set L_k as the set of all possible frequent itemsets

In this algorithm, the intermediate database is generated to reduce the time required for candidate itemset generation.

4   Analysis and Evaluation

Apriori Algorithm used to check the database thrice yet this paper exhibits a change on it by utilizing versatile calculation and the idea of moderate database scans. The examination demonstrates that the time expended and number of database scans required in enhanced Apriori in each group of transactions is less than the first Apriori. The memory space is lessened by utilizing the dynamic database approach which segments the first database at first and select one specific database out of this. It is a change as prior the calculation took exponential time however now it is decreased incredibly.

4.1   Analysis and Evaluation of the Adaptive Apriori for Number of Database Scans

The first experiment compares the number of database scans of original Apriori, and our improved algorithm by applying the Turkiye student's evaluation database [16] considering various dimensionality in the implementation. Table 1 shows that the improved Apriori reduce the number of database scans from the original Apriori.

Table 1. Evaluation of number of database scans for dimensionality of the data

Dimensionality	Number of transactions	Average number of database scans	
		Apriori	Adaptive apriori
5	100	6300	**3800**
	300	18900	**11400**
	500	19000	**31500**
	1000	63000	**38000**
	1500	94500	**57000**
10	100	204700	**103500**
	300	614100	**3010500**
	500	1023500	**517500**
	1000	2047000	**1035000**
	1500	3070500	**1552500**

Table 2. Execution time for 5 dimensional dataset

Support	Execution time for dimensionality = 5						
		100	300	500	1000	1500	Performance
0.1	Adaptive apriori	**1.78**	**5.21**	8.75	25.42	26.41	
	Apriori	2.04	5.61	**8.72**	**24.85**	**26.16**	√
0.2	Adaptive apriori	1.74	5.14	9.70	27.24	26.39	
	Apriori	**1.72**	**5.07**	**8.71**	**25.04**	**26.12**	√
0.3	Adaptive apriori	1.76	6.07	**8.70**	25.43	26.64	
	Apriori	**1.73**	**5.16**	8.72	**24.87**	**26.06**	√
0.4	Adaptive apriori	1.78	5.17	8.74	25.62	27.01	
	Apriori	**1.74**	**5.12**	**8.68**	**24.83**	**26.09**	√
0.5	Adaptive apriori	1.74	**5.14**	9.08	25.43	32.61	
	Apriori	**1.71**	5.15	**8.70**	**24.74**	**26.39**	√
0.6	Adaptive apriori	1.72	5.54	8.76	25.40	26.54	
	Apriori	**1.70**	**5.15**	**8.72**	**24.92**	**26.02**	√
0.7	Adaptive apriori	1.79	5.23	8.79	25.56	26.33	
	Apriori	**1.73**	**5.16**	**8.67**	**24.88**	**25.73**	√
0.8	Adaptive apriori	1.79	**5.11**	9.11	25.53	29.06	
	Apriori	**1.79**	5.14	**8.65**	**24.92**	**27.45**	√
0.9	Adaptive apriori	**1.73**	5.41	8.72	25.48	28.19	
	Apriori	1.73	**5.06**	**8.67**	**24.93**	**27.23**	√
1.0	Adaptive apriori	1.72	5.22	8.72	25.70	**27.33**	
	Apriori	**1.70**	**5.17**	**8.68**	**24.88**	27.35	√

4.2   Analysis and Evaluation of the Adaptive Apriori for Execution Time

As shown in Table 2, the execution time required for basic apriori algorithm is less as compared to adaptive apriori algorithm if the dimensionality of the dataset is 5. But in real time or in many applications, we need the dimensionality of the dataset to be more than 5.

As shown in Table 3, the execution time required for adaptive apriori is less as compared to basic apriori for support values greater than 0.3. By considering various number of transactions, if we consider the dimensionality of the dataset to be 10, the adaptive apriori algorithm is faster than basic apriori.

Table 3. Execution time for 10 dimensional dataset

Support	Execution time for dimensionality = 10						
		100	300	500	1000	1500	Performance
0.1	Adaptive apriori	649.2056	1619.555	**3554.324**	4773.694	**8855.127**	
	Apriori	**648.8535**	**1566.181**	3563.96	**4742.727**	8903.619	√
0.2	Adaptive apriori	654.7472	1686.096	**3552.79**	4943.852	9379.062	
	Apriori	**649.8377**	**1648.411**	3561.927	**4822.311**	**8857.793**	√
0.3	Adaptive apriori	**651.1549**	**1508.606**	3546.318	**4783.323**	8863.988	√
	Apriori	765.6032	1545.419	3570.253	4851.56	9002.406	
0.4	Adaptive apriori	**648.6697**	1647.063	**3549.455**	4834.075	**8919.802**	√
	Apriori	751.9009	**1592.73**	4741.744	**4822.59**	8987.67	
0.5	Adaptive apriori	**649.1094**	**1614.312**	**3544.177**	4875.973	**8854.327**	√
	Apriori	754.0942	1709.107	3556.594	**4857.307**	8974.088	
0.6	Adaptive apriori	**651.6117**	**1593.247**	3555.141	**4848.513**	**8859.67**	√
	Apriori	751.2995	1605.491	**3554.041**	4866.288	8969.633	
0.7	Adaptive apriori	**652.9595**	1557.227	**3564.79**	**4878.745**	**8938.141**	√
	Apriori	750.8612	**1556.755**	3579.224	4902.723	8988.605	
0.8	Adaptive apriori	**650.563**	1617.032	**3580.356**	**4873.193**	**8967.364**	√
	Apriori	751.3451	**1594.051**	3588.731	4878.262	9046.656	
0.9	Adaptive apriori	**652.0687**	1659.602	**3606.023**	**4863.328**	**8974.902**	√
	Apriori	753.1749	**1658.427**	3570.957	4886.018	9020.493	
1.0	Adaptive apriori	**655.5711**	**1661.588**	**3581.665**	**4895.289**	16593.79	√
	Apriori	750.5311	1691.652	3598.664	4883.936	**13020.72**	

Table 4. Evaluation of adaptive apriori algorithm for dimensionality of the data

Dimensionality	Number of transactions	Suggested faster algorithm
5	100	Apriori
	300	Apriori
	500	Apriori
	1000	Apriori
	1500	Apriori
10	100	Adaptive apriori
	300	Adaptive apriori
	500	Adaptive apriori
	1000	Adaptive apriori
	1500	Adaptive apriori

We have evaluated the performance of the adaptive apriori algorithm by considering various number of transactions of the same Turkiye students' evaluation dataset. As summarized in Table 4 from above Tables 2 and 3, for all various dataset size, the adaptive apriori algorithm is faster if the dimensionality of the dataset is greater than 5.

5   Conclusion

Association rule mining plays the major role in the field of data mining. The association rule mining is divided in two steps. Firstly it finds all frequent itemsets and then it generated the association rules. Apriori algorithm is one of the most important algorithms proposed for frequent itemset mining. But the Apriori algorithm required more time for generation of frequent itemsets as well as the number of database scans is more.

In this paper the improved Apriori algorithm is proposed which is more efficient in terms of time as well as number of database scans. In this algorithm, the intermediate database is created at each level. Hence scanning the entire database at each subsequent level is avoided. Which reduces the time required for candidate itemset generation as well as the number of database scans. The performance of the proposed algorithm is evaluated using the Turkiye standard student faculty evaluation dataset as well as the real time dataset.

References

1. Agrawal, R., Imielinski, T., Swami, A.: Mining association rules between sets of items in large databases. In: Proceedings of the 1993 ACM SIGMOD International Conference on Management of Data, SIGMOD 1993, New York, NY, USA, pp. 207–216 (1993)
2. Han, J., Kamber, M.: Data Mining. Concepts and Techniques, 2nd edn. Morgan Kaufmann, Burlington (2006)

3. Agrawal, R., Srikant, R.: Fast algorithms for mining association rules in large databases. In: Proceedings of the 20th International Conference on Very Large Data Bases, VLDB 1994, San Francisco, CA, USA, pp. 487–499. Morgan Kaufmann Publishers Inc. (1994)

4. Han, J., Pei, J., Yin, Y.: Mining frequent patterns without candidate generation. In: Proceedings of the 2000 ACM SIGMOD International Conference on Management of Data, SIGMOD 2000, New York, NY, USA, pp. 1–12 (2000)

5. Pavon, J., Viana, S., Gomez, S.: Matrix apriori: speeding up the search for frequent patterns. In: Proceedings of the 24th IASTED International Conference on Database and Applications, DBA 2006, Anaheim, CA, USA, pp. 75–82. ACTA Press (2006)

6. Yildiz, B., Ergenc, B.: Comparison of two association rule mining algorithms without candidate generation. In: Proceedings of the 10th IASTED International Conference on Artificial Intelligence and Applications, SIGMOD 1993, pp. 450–457. ACM (2010)

7. Agrawal, R., Srikant, R.: Fast algorithm for mining association rules. In: Proceedings of 20th International Conference on Very Large Data Bases (VLDB), pp. 487–499. Morgan Kaufman Press (1994)

8. Park, J.S., Chen, M.S., Yu, P.S.: Efficient parallel data mining of association rules. In: 4th International Conference on Information and Knowledge Management, vol. 11, pp. 233–235 (1995)

9. Brin, S., et al.: Dynamic itemset counting and implication rules for market basket data. In: Proceedings of the ACM SIGMOD International Conference on Management of Data, pp. 123–140 (1997)

10. Dean, J., Ghemawat, S.: "Map/reduce: simplified", data processing on large clusters. In: Sixth Symposium on Operating System Design and Implementation, OSDI 2004 (2004)

11. Lin, M., Lee, P., Hsueh, S.: Apriori-based frequent itemset mining algorithms on MapReduce. In: Proceedings of the 16th International Conference on Ubiquitous Information Management and Communication (ICUIMC 2012). ACM, New York (2012). Article No. 76

12. Li, N., Zeng, L., He, Q., Shi, Z.: Parallel implementation of apriori algorithm based on MapReduce. In: Proceedings of the 13th ACM International Conference on Software Engineering, Artificial Intelligence, Networking and Parallel and Distributed Computing (SNPD 2012), pp. 236–241. IEEE, Kyoto (2012)

13. Hammoud, S.: MapReduce network enabled algorithms for classification based on association rules, Thesis (2011)

14. Gao, Y.: Data Processing with Spark Technology, Application and Performance Optimization, vol. 11, pp. 1–2. China Machine Press (2014)

15. Qiu, H., Gu, R., Yuan, C., et al.: YAFIM: a parallel frequent itemset mining algorithm with spark. In: 2014 IEEE International Parallel and Distributed Processing" Symposium Workshops (IPDPSW), pp. 1664–1671. IEEE (2014)

16. Gunduz, G., Fokoue, E.: UCI Machine Learning Repository. University of California, School of Information and Computer Science, Irvine (2012)

Public Auditing Schemes (PAS) for Dynamic Data in Cloud: A Review

Dipa Dharamadhikari[1(✉)] and Sharvaree Tamne[2]

[1] Department of Computer Science and Engineering,
Marathwada Institute of Technology, Aurangabad, Maharashtra, India
dipa.dharmadhikari@gmail.com
[2] Department of Information Technology,
Jawaharlal Nehru Engineering College, Aurangabad, Maharashtra, India
sharvaree73@yahoo.com

Abstract. With the manifestation of cloud computing, storage on the cloud has become a rising trend. It facilates users to store their data on remote server. Security being one of the most concern issue in cloud computing. The principles of security applied for stored data is blooming topic of research. Various methods have been reported in literature for secure & efficient public audit scheme. but, these methods are not secure against various attacks like sybil, resource depletion & cloud storage leakage. It is found that several schemes can provide an efficient public auditing scheme based on vector commitment, verifier-local revocation, group signature. The present paper focuses on different schemes available for maintaining security in case of dynamic data in the cloud.

Keywords: Cloud computing · Public Auditing Schemes · Vector commitment
Group user revocation

1 Introduction

Cloud computing promotes organization and enterprises to subcontract their data to third party cloud service providers, which will improve the storage limitation of resource confine local devices [1]. Cloud computing is biggest innovation which uses advanced computational power & improves data sharing & data storing capabilities. Cloud is large group of interrelated computers, which is major change in how information is stored & applications are run. Cloud storage services are simple storage service (S3) [2], Dropbox [3], Google drive [4], on-line backup services of Amazon, Sugarsync [5], Version Control Systems are built as cloud application. Due to the hardware or software failures it is likely for the cloud servers to provide unexpected results. Sometimes human maintenance and malicious attack may also lead to problems. A novel form of data integrity is needed to protect the security of cloud user's data.

Cloud storage is significant service of cloud computing, which allows cloud users to store their data in the cloud and have benefit of demanding data to the cloud server. With the development of cloud computing and storage services data is not only stored in the cloud but also is regularly shared among a large number of users in a group and updated by the users through modification, insertion and deletion. To provide the security aspects

© Springer Nature Singapore Pte Ltd. 2018
A. V. Deshpande et al. (Eds.): SmartCom 2017, CCIS 876, pp. 186–191, 2018.
https://doi.org/10.1007/978-981-13-1423-0_21

like integrity, confidentiality, security, privacy. Several solutions have been found [6–8]. Dynamic data is the data obtained during data transfer between users on cloud computing. Public Auditing schemes support the dynamic data operation so that each data modification operation is performed by an authorized group member only. When the integrity check can be performed by data owners as well as additional third party auditor, this scheme is referred as public verifiable scheme. TPA can audit information of data owner thus reliving the overhead of managing data only by data owner.

2 Literature Survey

Several methods have been proposed for Public Auditing schemes. Amongst the published works few are reviewed and the details are given in the Table 1 below.

Table 1. Literature survey for public auditing scheme for dynamic data in cloud

Author & Year	Title	Methodology	Disadvantages
Anh Le et al. June 2015	Auditing for distributed storage systems [9]	Discussed new data integrity checking scheme based on cryptography, which is developed for coding-based network system. The imajor component of new cryptography audit design is a combination of SpaceMac which is homomarp meaasge authentication code for network coding and Ncrypt which is cnosen plaingtext attack gthat preserves the correcteness of spaceMac	Data arbitration time between server and audit is not yet focused
Jianfeng Wang 2015	Verifiable auditing for outsourced database in cloud computing [10]	The author designed a new verifiable auditing scheme for outsourced database achieving correctness, and Security	Confidentiality of the data is not maintained
Luo Yuchuan et al. November, 2014	Enable data dynamics for algebraic signatures based remote data possession checking in the cloud storage [11]	An auditing framework comprised of algebraic signature based remote data possession is proposed	File insert operation consumes higher computational time

(continued)

Table 1. (*continued*)

Author & Year	Title	Methodology	Disadvantages
Boyang Wang December, 2014	Efficient public verification on the integrity of multi-owner data in the cloud [12]	Each block of data is under the control of multi-owner.and each owner holds possesses signature to maintain data integrity	As the no. of owners increases, the computation of key increases
Boyang Wang et al. January–March 2014	Oruta: privacy-preserving public auditing for shared data in the cloud [13]	Oruta consider, audit the integrity of shared data in cloud with static group. Group is predefined before shared data created in cloud. Membership of users is constant in the group. Original user decides who is able to share data to the cloud before outsourcing	-Auditing the integrity of shared data in cloud with dynamic group. -Higher number of re-computation involves higher no. of signatures in batch auditing processes
J. Yuan and S. Yu April 2014	Efficient public integrity checking for cloud data sharing with multi-user modification, [14]	The author discussed about data integrity auditing scheme with group user revocation. Design polynomial authentication tag and adopt proxy tag update technique. If data owner shares group key with group users and defection or revocation occurs, a group user will have to force other group users to update their shared key	Error detection probability rate is higher and post- processing the files includes higher computational cost because of its irrelevant data
Cong wang et al. February 2013	Privacy-preserving public auditing for secure cloud storage [15]	The concept of multi-user was introduced to ensure the integrity and confidentiality of the data	The soundness property is not focused
Cong Wang et al. May 2012	Toward secure and dependable storage services in cloud computing [16]	Erasure coded data techniques to provide data integrity in distributed cloud environment	Leads to data dependability
Qian Wang et al. May 2011	Enabling public auditability and data dynamics for storage security in cloud computing [17]	Discussed the integrity of the data storage in cloud computing using Merkle Hash Tree system was used for providing better authentication systems at lower expenses	Make use of higher computational tasks

3 Public Auditing Schemes for Dynamic Data

Data owner can create several groups. Each group can have n no of users. Data owner decides the accessibility of data to these groups. The group users are not allowed to modify or update the data. To maintain this data integrity, data owner audit the data quite often. To retrieve from auditing overhead the data owner can provide a TPA to audit the data. Several auditing schemes in order to check the data integrity have been projected in the literature.

The author has projected Vector Commitment Schemes in [18]. Data modification attacks are carried out by the illegitimate users who intend to modify the data by acting as legitimate users. Thus, data security should be focused and it is achieved by the mechanism of Vector Commitment Schemes based on commitments and hiding. Another method of Asymmetric group key agreement is proposed in [19]. Group key plays vital role in the public communication networks. Confidentiality and Aggregate are the main security parameters examined among the group of users. Proposal of a generic construction of one-round Asymmetric group key agreement is based on a new primitive referred to as Aggregate Signature-Based Broadcast, in which the public key can be simultaneously used to verify signatures and encrypt messages while any signature can be used to decrypt ciphertext under this public key.

The author has proposed Identity-Based Authenticated Asymmetric Group Key Agreement protocol (IBAAGKP) [20]. The purpose of the identity based cryptosystem is to solve the issues in public key cryptosystem. Double security of ciphertext data base update among group users is considered as the main parameter in identity based Cryptosystem. In that paradigm, key agreement protocols relied on the entities obtaining each other's certificates, extracting each other's public keys, checking certificate chains and finally generating a shared session key.

Short signature scheme is based on the Computational Diffie-Hellman assumption on certain elliptic and hyper-elliptic curves. The signature length is half the size of a Digital Signature Algorithm signature for a similar level of security is discussed in [21]. The author has proposed Group signature [22] that provides anonymity for signers, where each group member has a private key that enables the user to sign messages. The resulting signature keeps the identity of the signer secret. Third party auditor conducts the signature anonymity using a special trapdoor. Some systems support revocation where group membership can be disabled without affecting the signing ability of unrevoked users. An efficient group signature with verifier-local revocation has been proposed. The scheme provides the properties of group signature such as selfless-anonymity. Also, the scheme is a short signature scheme where user revocation only requires sending revocation information to signature verifiers is discussed in [23].

4 Discussion and Conclusion

The cloud security models are viewed as 'supply chain issues' i.e. relationships between different service provider and their dependencies. Presently, the concept of Third Party Management has been introduced between the cloud server and cloud client. The task of Third Party Management (TPM) is to balance the services requested by the clients as well as response to those request in terms of data access services, defining security levels etc. Also, during Group User Revocation the TPM maintains revocation list that contains details of the revoked users. Commitment and Hiding property of vector commitment scheme hold a strong security value which is hard to compromise by the illegitimate users; instantiation of a one-round ASGKA protocol may strictly reduce to the decision Bilinear Diffie-Hellman Exponentiation (BDHE) assumption in the standard model. Also, Identity-Based Authenticated Asymmetric Group Key Agreement protocol (IBAAGKP) provides double Security which is considered as the main parameter in identity based cryptosystem. It lacks to identify & prevent the attacks like Resource Depletion attack & Sybil attack. This list is commonly referred to secure the data from revoked users. There is a need for robust scheme to achieve different security parameters like efficiency, confidentiality, integrity along with traceability, accountability, privacy and to secure the data against several attacks.

References

1. Shuchengyu, Y.J.: Public integrity auditing for dynamic data sharing with multi-user modification. In: Proceedings of IEEE Transactions on Information Forensics and Security, vol. 8, pp. 1717–1726 (2015)
2. Sugarsync. https://www.sugarsync.com/business
3. Amazon simple storage service (s3). http://aws.amazon.com/s3
4. Dropbox. https://www.dropbox.com
5. Google drive. http://drive.google.com
6. Juels, A., Kalisk, B.S.: PORS proof of retrievability for large files. In: 14th ACM Conference on Computation and Communications Security, pp. 584–597, October 2007
7. Wang, C., Wang, Q.: Privacy-preserving public auditing for data storage security in cloud computing. In: Proceedings of IEEE INFOCOM, pp. 525–533, March 2010
8. Wang, B., Baochum, L.: Public auditing for shared with efficient user revocation in the cloud. In: Proceedings of IEEE INFOCOM, pp. 2904–2912, April 2013
9. Le, A.: Äuditing for distributed storage system. IEEE Trans. Netw. **24**, 1–36 (2015)
10. Wang, J., Chen, X.: Verifiable auditing for outsourced database in cloud computing. IEEE Trans. Comput. **64**, 3293–3303 (2015)
11. Yuchuan, L., Shaojing, F.: Enable data dynamics for algebraic signatures based remote data possession checking in the cloud storage. IEEE China Commun. **11**, 114–124 (2014)
12. Wang, B., Hui, L.: Efficient public verification on the integrity of multi-owner data in the cloud. J. Commun. Netw. **16**, 592–599 (2014)
13. Wang, B., Baochun, L., Li, H.: Oruta: privacy-preserving public auditing for shared data in the cloud. Proc. IEEE Trans. Cloud Comput. **2**(1), 43–56 (2014)
14. Yuan, J., Yu, C.: Efficient public integrity checking for cloud data sharing with multi-user modification. In: Proceedings of IEEE INFOCOM Toronto, Canada, pp. 2121–2129, April 2014
15. Wang, C., Sherman, S.M.: Privacy-preserving public auditing for secure cloud storage. IEEE Trans. Comput. **62**, 362–375 (2013)
16. Wang, C., Wang, Q.: Toward secure and dependable storage services in cloud computing. IEEE Trans. Serv. Comput. **5**, 220–232 (2012)
17. Wang, Q., Wang, C.: Enabling public auditability and data dynamics for storage security in cloud computing. Proc. IEEE Trans. Parallel Distrib. Syst. **22**, 847–859 (2011)

18. Catalano, D., Fiore, D.: Vector commitments and their applications. In: Kurosawa, K., Hanaoka, G. (eds.) PKC 2013. LNCS, vol. 7778, pp. 55–72. Springer, Heidelberg (2013). https://doi.org/10.1007/978-3-642-36362-7_5
19. Wu, Q., Mu, Y., Susilo, W., Qin, B., Domingo-Ferrer, J.: Asymmetric group key agreement. In: Joux, A. (ed.) EUROCRYPT 2009. LNCS, vol. 5479, pp. 153–170. Springer, Heidelberg (2009). https://doi.org/10.1007/978-3-642-01001-9_9
20. Zhang, L., Wu, Q., Qin, B., Domingo-Ferrer, J.: Identity-based authenticated asymmetric group key agreement protocol. In: Thai, My T., Sahni, S. (eds.) COCOON 2010. LNCS, vol. 6196, pp. 510–519. Springer, Heidelberg (2010). https://doi.org/10.1007/978-3-642-14031-0_54
21. Boneh, D., Lynn, B., Shacham, H.: Short signatures from the weil pairing. In: Boyd, C. (ed.) ASIACRYPT 2001. LNCS, vol. 2248, pp. 514–532. Springer, Heidelberg (2001). https://doi.org/10.1007/3-540-45682-1_30
22. Chaum, D., van Heyst, E.: Group signatures. In: Davies, Donald W. (ed.) EUROCRYPT 1991. LNCS, vol. 547, pp. 257–265. Springer, Heidelberg (1991). https://doi.org/10.1007/3-540-46416-6_22
23. Dan, B., Hovav, S.: Group signatures with-local revocation. In: Proceedings of ACM Conference on Computer and Communications Security, pp. 168–177, 25–29 October 2004

Advanced LTE (5G) in Medical IOT-Research, Future and Scope

R. Dhaya[1(✉)], S. Suganth Maharaja[1], J. Sowmya[1], and R. Kanthavel[2]

[1] Department of CSE, Rajalakshmi Engineering College, Chennai, India
dhayavel2005@gmail.com, suganth2331@gmail.com,
sowmyajayaraaman@gmail.com
[2] Department of ECE, Rajalakshmi Institute of Technology, Chennai, India

Abstract. 5G, the Fifth Generation is the major juncture in the telecom network. 5G provides unified global framework. 5G makes life more lively, interactive and beneficial by catering all the demands of the users as well as organizations. 5g enables Anywhere Anytime Anyone Anything (4A) connectivity. The development in Internet and Mobile communication have paved the way to the advancement in technology. Such technologies have been applied in medical field for the welfare of the patients. This paper presents the merits of 5G, its influence in the medical field and also expresses the new innovations in the Healthcare system. The purpose of this paper is to explain the overview of technologies in the health domain with 5G characteristics.

Keywords: IOT · Health care · LTE · Internet

1 Introduction

The transformation from one generation to the next generation is mainly to enhance the data rate (Bandwidth) and increase the pace over the network. The First Generation (1G) of mobile communication used the standard Advanced Mobile Phone System (AMPS) but had poor voice links and less security. The Second Generation (2G) used Global System for Mobile Communication (GSM) for providing services like call forwarding/waiting, SMS, Long distance calls and some others. Encryption was used for security. The 2.5G, using packet switching doesn't serve to the level of service as expected. The Third Generation (3G) uses International Telecommunication Union (ITU) and International Mobile Telecommunication (IMT) Standards for video conference, games, multimedia, location based services and others [7]. Then, IP based network system exercised a new technology known as 4g for high quality, low cost and high speed services [9]. But however due to the extravagant demand of the users lead to the need for a new technology known as 5G. This technology works by splitting the Network Layer into two layers as Upper Layer for Mobile Terminal and Lower Layer for Interfacing. Open Transport Protocol (OTP) is exerted to reduce the bit loss in 5g [8]. 5G aims in creating a hyper connected society where Person-to-Person (or) Person-to-Machine communication is made stronger. The "G" in 5G refers to the term that "Cellular Wireless Generation". 5G supports very high frequency in the range (3–300 GHz) thus, enabling us to use large spectrum giving higher transmission rate. Even

© Springer Nature Singapore Pte Ltd. 2018
A. V. Deshpande et al. (Eds.): SmartCom 2017, CCIS 876, pp. 192–200, 2018.
https://doi.org/10.1007/978-981-13-1423-0_22

the HD movies could be downloaded within seconds with 1000 times more capacity. South Korea has invested USD 1.5 Billion for 5Gresearch. The idea behind this 5G technology is that the researchers use self-flying air craft's at high altitudes to offers fast internet access. 5G Network infrastructure supports large data capacity and less number of terminals with high connection requests. Some of the services offered by the 5G are diagnostics by the doctors in the remote areas, availability of data anytime and any-where, making education easier, increasing parallelism and so on. Here, we explore the challenges and prospective opportunities of 5G in Health Care Systems. The Future scenario for 5G in health system is management of patient database, tracking the hospitals, robotics-assisted tele-surgery, monitoring remote patients etc.

2 Literature Survey

The authors [1] presented a state-of-the-art review of the literature to show how researchers are using and considering the use of multiple antennas in small cells. Attention is given to current generation networks; and with SBSs being a dominant technology necessary for 5G and also provided insights into the design challenges in such possible future networks. The authors [2] reviewed emerging optical access network technologies that aim to support 5G wireless with high capacity, low latency, and low cost and power per bit. Advances in high-capacity passive optical networks (PONs), such as 100 Gbit/s PON, would be reviewed and also discussed the need for coordination between RAN and PON to simplify the overall network, reduce the network latency, and improve the network cost efficiency and power efficiency. The authors [3] defined a methodology for managing such handover traffic in a Wi-Fi network. The approach integrates and leverages aspects of three quality control mechanisms to enable stable, higher quality delivery of enhanced Wi-Fi network ser-vices. It combined (i) information adduced from a theoretical model with (ii) a low complexity Quality of Experience metric that was quick and easy to estimate and (iii) a queue management scheme. The authors [4] first discussed the new architectural changes associated with the radio access network (RAN) design, including air inter-faces, smart antennas, cloud and heterogeneous RAN. Next, the details of MAC layer protocols and multiplexing schemes needed to efficiently support this new physical layer are discussed and also looked into the killer applications, considered as the major driving force behind 5G. As understanding the current status of 5G implementation was important for its eventual commercialization. The authors [5] summarized the deter-minants for future e- Health network and IT infrastructures in the health care envi-ronment and also provided a broad overview over the implications of the e-Health domain to provide inputs in ongoing discussion on 5G characteristics. The authors [6] proposed the system that exploited Transparent Interconnection of Lots of Links (TRILL) protocol for mobility management and data packet delivery. In addition, each evolved node B (eNB) acted as a routing bridge (RB), where data delivery operations were achieved between RB using TRILL mechanism. Moreover, a scheme for mobility management is also proposed that was used for mapping identifies (IP address) and MAC address of RB. The following table shows the related works of LTE. The Table 1 shows the mechanisms used in 5G Networks.

Table 1. Mechanisms used in 5G networks

S No	Title of the journal/conference	Title of the paper	Mechanism/techniques used
1	MELECON 2016 - Conference	5G and the Fog - survey of related technologies and research directions	-Fog computing -Cloud computing (mobile computing)
2	IEEE/OSA journal of optical communications and networking	Emerging optical access network Technologies for 5G wireless	-MAC scheduling between RAN-MAC and Pon-Mac. -Upstream and downstream modulation of passive optical network. -Cloud radio access network via coordinated multipoint
3	Wireless on - demand network Systems and services ONS, 2017 conference	Ensuring quality services on wi-fi networks for offloaded cellular traffic	-Quality queue management algorithm (QQM) -Quality of experience metric
4	Green computing and internet of things ICGCIOT, 2015 International Conference	5G: revolution of future communication technology	-All-ip set of connections (AIPN) -Radio access technologies (RAT). -Cloud and computer resources -Reconfigurable multi technology core (RMTC)
5	signals, systems and computers, 2016	5G new radio and ultra low latency applications: a physical implementation perspective	-Ultra low delay concept (URLLC) Novel frame structure -Implementation of physical & MAC layer using software defined radio platform (SDR)
6	Vehicular Technology Conference	Channel coding for ultra-reliable low-latency	-Channel coding schemes (turbo code, polarcode, convolution code, peg-ldpc codes)
7	VTC-IEEE fall, 2016	Communication in 5G systems	-Block error rate (bler) Performance
8	IEEE access	A survey of the challenges, opportunities and use of multiple antennas in current and future 5G small cell base stations	-Usage of multiple antennas. -Use of multiple input multiple output (MIMO) technique. -Spatial correlation & antenna mutual coupling

(continued)

Table 1. (*continued*)

S No	Title of the journal/conference	Title of the paper	Mechanism/techniques used
9	Globecom workshops, 2016 IEEE	The access procedure design for low latency in 5 g Cellular network	-Access procedure Radio bearer
10	IEEE communication on surveys & tutorials	Next generation 5 g wireless networks: a comprehensive survey	-Cloud on heterogeneous RAN. -Massive multiple input multiple output technology
11	IEEE/ACM transactions on networking	Toward 5G: Fi-wi enhanced LTE-a HETNETS with Reliable low - latency fiber backhaul Sharing and wi-fi offloading	-Decentralized routing algorithm. -Capacity centric fiber-wireless (FIWI) Broadband access networks
12	IEEE Conference - standards for communications and networking (CSCN), 2016	Network slice selection, assignment and routing Within 5G networks	-Network function virtualization (NFV). -Routine path algorithm
13	IEEE Sarnoff symposium, 2016	Ultra- wideband signals for high-resolution Cognitive positioning techniques in 5G wireless	-Ultra wide band technique -Cognitive positioning technique
14	20th IEEE international workshop CAMAD, 2015	Challenges and possibilities for flexible duplexing in 5G networks	-Full duplex relaying. - Full duplex in D2D
15	IEEE transactions on vehicular technology	Power - fractionizing mechanism: achieving joint user scheduling and Power allocation via geometric programming	-Geometric programming -User scheduling algorithm -Power fractionizing mechanism (PFM)
16	19th international – ICACT 2017	Slot based radio resource management for low latency in LTE- advanced system	-Slot transmission time interval (TTI). -Enhanced physical downlink control channel (EPDCCH)

3 Difference Between 4G and 5G

The evolution from 4G to 5G may lower the battery utilization provides wide coverage, gives rapid speed and higher bandwidth. Here are some of the differences between them (Table 2):

Table 2. Differences between 4G and 5G

Specifications	4G	5G
Full form	Fourth generation	Fifth generation
Frequency	2–8 GHz	3–300 GHz
Standards	Convergence including OFDMA, MC-CDMA, network-LMPS	CDMA, BDMA
Multiple access	Orthogonal multiple access	Non orthogonal multiple access
Bandwidth	2 Mbps to 1 Gbps	More than 1 Gbps speed

Fourth generation uses Orthogonal Frequency Division Multiplexing (OFDM), Ultra Wide Band (UWB) and millimeter wireless standards. The bandwidth problem in 3G is overcome in 4G. However this 4G is enough to meet today's requirements, but not for the upcoming new applications in the near future. Thus 5G acts as backbone for the Internet Of Things (IoT) and is a part of the Information Technology (IT [10]). Thus 5g is 1000 times faster than today's cellular system.

4 5G Enabled IoT

With 5G in Health protection the human imagination comes true such as pursuing treatment from home, handling surgery in remote areas and so on [12]. The Internet of Things (IOT) aims in providing communication between interconnected physical objects, devices, human-beings, smart phones, wearable's, tablets, sensors, Implantable Medical Devices (IMD) through complete connections between them. With this IoT technology, the patients don't have the need to visit the doctor directly, instead they can consult and get treated without much expense. The doctor – patient interaction is made simple universally through the 5G networking services [11]. The physicians can examine the patient from distance via Digital Image processing and other techniques. The victims can also get second opinion easily without having to travel long. The cloud technique facilitate the patient information to be readily accessible anywhere and at anytime. All the devices connected in the IoT environment must be sustainable for the full duration until the treatment gets completed. Employing 5G with IoT could probably resolve all health services [13].

Mobile Health focus on offering health solutions; patient information and monitoring them through smart phones, tablets and other smart devices [14]. The 5G acts as a platform and may provide fast access between doctor and patient. The Digital Medicine allows access to images and enables sharing of information across the globe my minimizing the distance and time [16]. The patient in remote areas usually do not have easy approach to high level specialist. Hence, they are extremely benefited by this mobile IoT [15].

5 General Architecture of IOT in Healthcare System

The following Fig. 1 shows the General architecture of IOT in healthcare system:

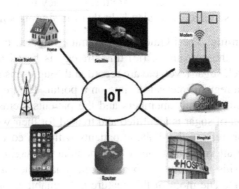

Fig. 1. General architecture of IOT in healthcare system

The establishment of 5G in health system minimizes the global cost as well as retains the Quality of Service (QoS). Here, we have analyzed the recent inventions made both technically and socially in the Health care System [18]. 5G will play a major role in connecting billions of devices and machines in several health issues. The 5G network offers Machine to Machine (M2M) and Device to Device communication (D2D) on large scale for better solutions in health systems [17]. The victims can get opinions from the doctors by sending their medical image or their test reports with much ease. The employment of 5G in medical field would decrease flaws and increase the efficiency of health services [19]. Figure 2 shows the working architecture of healthcare systems using 5G enabled IoT.

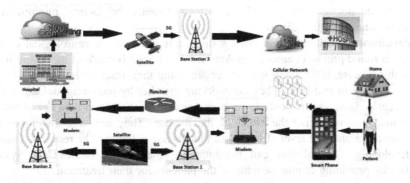

Fig. 2. Working architecture of healthcare system using 5G enabled IOT

6 5G Influence in Medical Care

The patients can be monitored with ease by establishing connection between the devices through IoT network. The greatest benefit among the researchers on implementing the 5G enabled IoT health care system is that they have enough patients' data to analyze on the disease effects and also help them in finding solutions.

- **i-Glucose Programme:** The i-Glucose programme initiated by the Vodafone had great value among the customers. (ie) this strategy is based on the idea that the person's blood level, sugar level, etc are recorded through sensors like Smart Meter and is updated at a regular interval of time on a portal. The portal can be accessed by a group of doctors, family members and the patients themselves. The patients with abnormal level of sugar is identified and treated for their well being. Thus, this idea works fine for treating the diabetic patients with less cost.
- **Hike Run:** As we all know that, one of the popular messaging applications is the Hike messenger. This messenger app has recently launched a new feature called **"Hike Run (Beta)".** The moto of this feature is to enable people burn their fat in terms of calories. It works by tracking the number of steps walked by every individual by using devices called as accelerometer. At the end of the day, this application generates a report with attributes like total calories burnt, number of steps walked, Ranking. The Ranking factor in this feature may stimulate the individuals to compete with their friends in reducing their weights. The drawback of this new feature is that the steps may be counted even when a jerk in the phone is detected. So, with all these features there is an another accurate Health application known as **"Fisto",** which serves the proposed purpose successfully.
- **Asthma:** Asthma is a persistent disease found in humans in a varying range. The number of people affected by asthma may differ from country to country. The impact of this disease is severe. We are in need of finding some methodology for curing this disease. Here comes the IoT technology which transforms the healthcare system for the welfare of the patients suffering from asthma. The patients can get connected with the doctors through the IoT network. The tests can be taken even at their homes and the doctors can examine the reports via the cloud Technology. Then, the doctors can give advice to their patients and thereby minimizing the severe impact of this disease.
- **Parkinson's Disorder:** Parkinson's disease is a hereditary neurological disorder that is found prevalent among the Americans, who die because of the severe impact of this disease. IBM along with Pfizer are doing their research to drastically lower this disease in real-time. They are working together by recording and analysis the patient's data. The patients have been injected with sensors and are monitored regularly to minimize the effect of the disease. They are kept under complete medication until the level of impact of this disease is found to be reduced. Thus, the developing Technologies can revolutinalize the Global Health-Care Systems, thereby providing atmost benefits to the patients for their treatment.

7 Conclusion

Now, this is the era for Fifth Generation Mobile Networks. The complete establishment of 5G has been planned by the year 2020. There are enormous open doors through 5G over an assortment of parts to associate the social insurance world in inventive ways. The utilization of cell phones, sensors, and remote checking hardware will develop and there will be an emotional progression in patients getting imaging, finding, or treatment through advanced innovation. To guarantee the greater part of this turns into a reality, however, work should be done to encourage a conclusion to-end framework. Gadgets must associate with systems and the cloud in ways that are interoperable and secure. That will empower wellbeing suppliers and patients to get the advantages of computerized development for health and human services. On the off chance that we can overcome these hindrances, both human services customers and suppliers will see significant advances in therapeutic treatment.

8 Future Scope

There are enormous open doors through 5G over an assortment of parts to associate the social insurance world in inventive ways. The utilization of cell phones, sensors, and remote checking hardware will develop and there will be an emotional progression in patients getting imaging, finding, or treatment through advanced innovation. To guarantee the greater part of this turns into a reality, however, work should be done to encourage a conclusion to-end framework. Gadgets must associate with systems and the cloud in ways that are interoperable and secure. That will empower wellbeing suppliers and patients to get the advantages of computerized development for health and human services. On the off chance that we can overcome these hindrances, both human services customers and suppliers will see significant advances in therapeutic treatment.

References

1. Muirhead, D., Imran, A., Arshad, K.: A survey of the challenges, opportunities and use of multiple antennas in current and future 5G small cell base stations. In: IEEE Conference, pp. 1–14 (2016)
2. Liu, X., Effenberger, F.: Emerging optical access network technologies for 5G wireless. IEEE/OSA J. Opt. Commun. Netw. 8(12), B70–B79 (2016)
3. Pibiri, G., Mc Goldrick, C., Huggard, M.: Ensuring quality services on WiFi networks for offloaded cellular traffic. In: IEEE Conference on Wireless On-Demand Network Systems and Services (2017)
4. Agiwal, M., Roy, A., Saxena, N.: Next generation 5G wireless networks: a comprehensive survey. IEEE Commun. Surv. Tutorials 18(3), 1617–1655 (2016)
5. Thuemmler, C., Paulin, A., Lim, A.K.: Determinants of next generation e-Health network and architecture specifications. In: IEEE Conference on e-Health Networking, Applications and Services (2016)

6. Din, S., Paul, A., Ahmad, A., Rho, S.: Emerging mobile communication technologies for healthcare system in 5G Network. In: IEEE Conference DASC/PiCom/DataCom/Cyber SciTech (2016)
7. Sarda, B.: Vision from Orange Healthcare on 5G. Orange Healthcare (2017)
8. Adebomehin, A.A., Walker, S.D.: Ultra-wideband signals for high- resolution cognitive positioning techniques in 5G wireless. In: Sarnoff Symposium (2017)
9. Beyranvand, H., Lévesque, M., Maier, M., Salehi, J.A., Verikoukis, C., Tipper, D.: Toward 5G: FiWi enhanced LTE-A HetNets with reliable low-latency fiber backhaul sharing and WiFi offloading. IEEE/ACM Trans. Netw. 25(2), 690–707 (2017)
10. Brito, J.M.C.: Trends in wireless communications towards 5G networks – the influence of e-health and IoT applications. In: 2016 International Multidisciplinary Conference on Computer and Energy Science (2016)
11. Wirth, T., Mehlhose, M., Pilz, J., Holfeld, B., Wieruch, D.: Fraunhofer Heinrich Hertz Institute, Einsteinufer: 5G new radio and ultra low latency applications: a PHY implementation perspective, signals, systems and computers (2016)
12. Sybis, M., Wesołowski, K., Jayasinghe, K., Venkatasubramanian, V., Vukadinovic, V.: Channel coding for ultra-reliable low- latency communication in 5G systems. In: Vehicular Technology Conference (2016)
13. Pirinen, P.: Challenges and possibilities for flexible duplexing in 5G networks. In: IEEE Computer Aided Modelling and Design of Communication Links and Networks (2015)
14. Lee, J., Kwak, Y.: G Standard Development: Technology and Roadmap, Signal Processing for 5G, pp. 561–576 (2016)
15. Kumar, S., Gupta, G., Singh, K.R.: 5G: revolution of future communication technology. In: International Conference on Green Computing and Internet of Things (2015)
16. Kitanov, S., Monteiro, E., Janevski, T.: 5G and the fog - survey of related technologies and research directions. In: 2016 18th Mediterranean Electrotechnical Conference (MELECON) (2016)
17. Choyi, V.K., Abdel-Hamid, A., Shah, Y., Ferdi, S., Brusilovsky, A.: Network slice selection, assignment and routing within 5G networks. In: IEEE Conference on Standards for Communications and Networking (CSCN) (2016)
18. Fu, S., Wen, H., Wu, B.: Power-fractionizing mechanism: achieving joint user scheduling and power allocation via geometric programming. IEEE Trans. Veh. Technol. 1(99), 2025–2034 (2017)
19. Jin, R., Zhong, X., Zhou, S.: The access procedure design for low latency in 5G cellular network. In: Globecom Workshops (2016)

Decision Tree Based Model
for the Classification of Pathogenic Gene
Sequences Causing ASD

V. Pream Sudha[(⊠)] and M. S. Vijaya

PSGR Krishnammal College for Women, Coimbatore, India
preamsudha@psgrkc.ac.in

Abstract. Pathogenic gene identification is an important research problem in biomedical domain. The genetic cause of ASD, which is a multifaceted developmental disability is hard to research. Hence, there is a critical need for inventive approaches to further portray the genetic basis of ASD which will enable better filtering and specific therapies. This paper adopts machine learning techniques to classify gene sequences which are the significant drivers of syndromic and asyndromic ASD. The synthetic dataset with 150 sequences of six different categories of genes were prepared and coding measures of gene sequences were taken as attributes for gene identification. Pattern learning algorithms like support vector machine, decision tree and Multiplayer perceptron were used to train the model. The model was evaluated using 10 fold cross validation and the results are reported. The study reveals that Decision trees outperform other classifiers with an accuracy of 97.33%

Keywords: Disease gene identification · Machine learning
Multilayer perceptron · Support vector machines · Decision tree induction

1 Introduction

The enormous amount of sequence data available today has increased the real need for accurate and fast techniques to analyze these sequences and to elucidate the genetic basis for common diseases. Prediction of pretentious genes that underlie a disease is a significant challenge in biomedical research. Autism-spectrum disorder (ASD) is a developmental disorder characterised by atypical social behavior, weak communication and typecast behavior. The signs of ASD usually emerge during early days and person suffering from ASD is unable to communicate and interact with others. ASD is defined by a range of conditions and behaviors that affect persons to varied degrees. Some of the indications associated with autism include deferred learning of language, complicatedness in making eye contact or making a conversation, monotonous behaviors and limited interests or activities, difficulty with executive functioning, deprived motor skills and sensory sensitivities.

This paper focuses on the genetics of ASDs, as the percentage of occurrence is found to be high among twins and siblings. The incidence rate of ASD is 73–95% among monozygotic twins, the transmissible rate is 90%, risk of incidence in siblings is

© Springer Nature Singapore Pte Ltd. 2018
A. V. Deshpande et al. (Eds.): SmartCom 2017, CCIS 876, pp. 201–212, 2018.
https://doi.org/10.1007/978-981-13-1423-0_23

5–6%. The occurrence of mild autistic qualities in the close relatives of people with autism shows a strong genetic component in ASD. The genetic markers for the disease are so unusual and hard to match from patient to patient.

This paper aims to recognize the associated genes of ASD using machine learning approaches. Existing methods require further developments so that they augment perceptions of the genetic cause of the disease and become precious in a clinical disease risk prognostic situation. An early and accurate diagnosis of ASD markers would help in appropriate therapy selection. As machine learning models provide accuracy and interpretability, this study utilizes supervised learning techniques such as Decision Tree Learning, Multi Layer Perceptron and Support Vector Machines in predicting genes causing Autism-spectrum disorder.

The genetic ground of this comprehensive developmental disability is very difficult to research. Even though there is no identified distinct basis of autism, recent studies show that a range of genetic methods may be involved in the development of ASD like gene disorder, copy-number dissimilarity and polygenic mechanisms. Research shows that alleles of multiple genes, each of little consequence, may trigger ASD. Many genes and environmental factors play a major role in ASD, making it complicated to segregate diseased genes. Hence this study focuses on spotting the diseased genes causing ASD.

There are two types of ASD, syndromic and non-syndromic. Syndromic ASD occurs in concurrence with additional phenotypes and dysmorphic features. The reasons for syndromic ASD may engage chromosomal abnormalities, copy number variations, and mutations in a single gene. Mutations in FMR1, MECP2, TSC1, CACNA1C, PTEN lead to Fragile X syndrome, Rett syndrome, tuberous sclerosis complex, Timothy syndrome and macrocephaly syndrome respectively. Non-syndromic ASD refers to classic autism where additional symptoms are not present.

Human genetic variations are caused by nucleotide polymorphisms that occur in nucleotide bases in the human population. When gene mutations occur, one or more of the proteins are stopped from working appropriately. The gene's code for making a protein is altered by the mutation which causes the protein to malfunction. When a mutation alters a protein that has a major role in the body, it can interrupt normal development or cause a disorder. This research work aims to identify ASD driver genes that are affected by mutations using machine learning techniques.

Machine learning techniques have been effectively used to resolve various important biomedical problems like genome annotation, inference of gene regulatory networks [1], classification of microarray data [2], prediction of drug-target and discovery of gene-gene interaction in disease data [3]. In particular, they have been applied to recognize disease linked genes. Primarily, the problem is formulated as a supervised learning problem, where the task is to gain knowledge from training data. The learned classifier is used to forecast whether a gene is a diseased gene or not.

[1] investigated the occurrence of autism using efficient brain connectivity measures resulting from EEG of children through face perception tasks. Samples were obtained from EEG signals for typical children and children affected by ASD. In each class, 12 subjects were used for the extraction of connectivity features from joyful, sad and scared faces. The discriminant analysis and support vector machine with polynomial kernels were investigated for the classification task. 94.7% accuracy was

reported in the leave one out cross-validation of the SVM with sensitivity and specificity values as 85.7% and 100% respectively.

[2] explored the most important genes which are strictly related to autism using gene expression microarrays. The paper applied different methods of gene selection, to select the most representative input attributes for an ensemble of classifiers. The authors developed a two stage ensemble system of automatic recognition of autism on the basis of gene microarray. The results of selection combined with a genetic algorithm and SVM classifier showed increased accuracy of autism recognition.

[3] used a machine-learning approach based on a human brain-specific functional gene interaction network to present a genome-wide prediction of autism-associated genes, including candidate genes for which there is minimal or no prior genetic evidence. The work was validated in an independent case-control sequencing study of approximately 2,500 families. A statistical model was built that captured the connectivity patterns of known autism genes in the brain-specific network. This model was used to predict whether each of the other unlabeled genes in the network resembled an autism gene based on its connectivity in the network. It also recognized probable pathogenic genes with most common autism-associated copy-number-variants (CNVs) and reported genes and pathways that are possible mediators of autism across multiple CNVs. The work involved an evidence-weighted linear support vector machine (SVM) classifier.

Further studies reveal that mutations play a major role in ASD [4–9] and also that research has been done to identify integrated gene networks for ASD [10–12]. The above literature survey indicates that there are only few works involved in the recognition of diseased genes of ASD. Hence it is significant to propose a discriminative model to identify precisely the type of gene causing ASD. The proposed model will be crucial in a clinical environment as it provides a better understanding of the affected gene sequences aiding early therapies and focused treatment. The coding regions of diseased gene sequences are utilized to extract features which are helpful in training the machine learning based multi-class classification model. The model acquires knowledge of the sequences by studying the reviewed sequences, and the same properties were used by the model for identification of the unknown gene sequence.

2   Proposed Work

The work was divided into the following parts: the establishment of data sets, feature extraction, model building and performance evaluation of gene classification models. The framework of the proposed model is depicted in Fig. 1.

2.1   Data Preprocessing

The establishment of the dataset is significant for the subsequent gene identification. The mutated gene sequences are not explicitly available for this complicated disease and hence the dataset is prepared by simulating diseased gene sequences causing syndromic and non-syndromic ASD. The reference gene sequences of SHANK3,

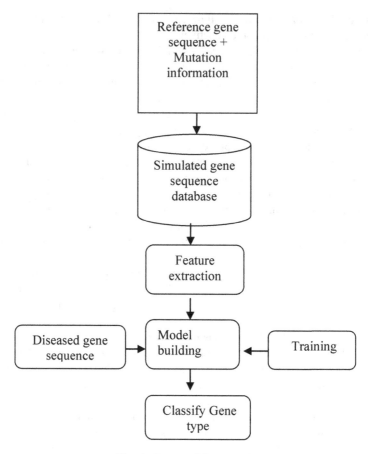

Fig. 1. Proposed framework

CNTNAP2, MECP2 responsible for syndromic ASD and that of CHD8, FOXP2, GABRB3 accounting for non-syndromic ASD were retrieved from OMIM [13], HGMD database[1]. Table 1 depicts the genes taken for study and their associated behavior. Most of the known genetic discrepancies that are associated to inherited human diseases are due to gene mutations that cause amino acid alterations. The developmental disorder of ASD is caused by different mutations that affect the gene sequences. Four types of mutations namely missense, nonsense, synonymous and frameshift have been considered for generating mutated sequences. R coding is used for simulating these mutations with the help of mutation information derived from SFARI [14] gene database[2]. 25 mutated gene sequences are generated accounting for each of the six types of gene and the total dataset comprises of 150 mutated gene sequences causing syndromic and asyndromic ASD.

---

[1] http://www.hgmd.cf.ac.uk.

[2] https://sfari.org/.

Table 1. Clinical features due to gene disorders

Type of ASD	Genes taken for study	Associated behavior
Syndromic ASD	SHANK3	Impulsivity, social anxiety, biting, obsessive chewing
	CNTNAP2	Behavioral deficits associated with ASD, hyperactivity, epilepsy
	MECP2	Gaze avoidance, limited facial expression, atypical socialization
Asyndromic ASD	CHD8	Gastrointestinal (GI) problems, persistent constipation, sleep problems
	FOXP2	Speech and language abnormalities
	GABRB3	Unexplained Epilepsy and Intellectual or Developmental Disabilities

2.2 Feature Extraction

Feature extraction is one of the important steps in data analysis, mainly influencing the accomplishment of any machine learning task. A good data depiction is very domain specific and correlated to accessible measurements. Studies reveal that combination of intrinsic and extrinsic features enhance gene identification problems. The study investigated a total of 43 attributes in both intrinsic and extrinsic categories are considered as the contributing features for representing the mutated gene sequences. Many gene recognition algorithms use one or more coding measures that compute attributes interrelated with protein coding function. These coding measures are dissimilar in different gene families and hence this trait is a well-chosen descriptor for specifying different gene families. The features taken into consideration for gene identification are nucleotide composition, GC content, Rho values of biwords, Z scores of biwords, Alignment score, Number of exons, Number of donor sites, Number of acceptor sites, CpG percent, ratio of CpG percent/expected.

The number of occurrence of individual nucleotides exhibit noteworthy variations in eukaryotic genes. The A, C, G, T nucleotide variations are extracted as features since such dissimilarity result from differential mutational pressures and from the incidence of specific regulatory motifs, like transcription sites. Similarly GC content is an essential property of a genome sequenc, which indicates the portion of the sequence which contains Gs and Cs.

$$\textbf{GC content} = (\textbf{count of Gs} + \textbf{count of Cs}) * \textbf{100}/(\textbf{genome length}).$$

The variations in GC content inside the genome sequence can provide motivating information like biases in mutation. Hence GC content is considered as an important feature in identifying the gene type.

The work also investigates DNA words that are two nucleotides long and are over-represented or under-represented. If a DNA word is over-represented in a sequence, probably it occurs many more times in the sequence than expected whereas when it is under-represented in a sequence, it is present less number of times in the sequence than expected. Statistical measures Rho and z − scores are used to measure over-representation or under-representation of a particular DNA word which also contributes in classifying the genes. For a DNA word that is two nucleotides long, Rho is calculated as:

$$\mathbf{Rho(xy) = f(xy) / (fx * fy)}$$

The z-score of biwords is computed by finding the difference between the mean divided by the standard deviation. For a single gene sequence, 16 rho values and 16 z–score values are obtained.

One of the non- consensus property, alignment score is used to compare the simulated gene sequences with a library of sequences and to spot library sequences that is similar to the query sequence. BLAST aligned similarity score is computed and taken into account for building the model. The number of introns an organism's genes hold is absolutely linked to its complexity. Thus the number of expressed sequences, exons and average length of exons are also employed as descriptors.

Splicing requires a donor site and an acceptor site within introns. Hence the number of donors and acceptors are recognized as essential discriminators. The incidence of a CpG island is used to help in the prediction and annotation of genes. The CpG sites are DNA portions where a guanine nucleotide occurs after a cytosine nucleotide in the linear sequence of bases along its 5' $\rightarrow$ 3' direction. The observed-to-expected CpG ratio is computed as:

$$\mathbf{Observed\, CpG \,=\, No.\, of\, CpG}$$

$$\mathbf{Expected\, CpG \,=\, No.\, of\, C \,*\, no.\, of\, G \,/\, length\, of\, sequence}$$

In summary, a total of 43 features including intrinsic and extrinsic properties of each gene sequence were defined. The training set for the multi-class classification problem includes 150 feature vectors with a dimension 43.

2.3   Machine Learning

Machine learning learns previously unknown regularities and trends from varied datasets, employing machines to carry out the tiresome task of acquiring knowledge from experimental data. It includes an extensive variety of techniques used for the detection of rules and relationships in datasets. It also produces a simplification of these relationships that can be used to understand new unseen data. The system gains knowledge from examples of given data and represents it in the form of structural description. These descriptions recapitulate knowledge learned by the system and can be represented in different ways.

In this study it is intended to construct a genotype–phenotype model by training the system with genetic blueprints from a labeled set of instances that will offer accurate phenotypic predictions in fresh cases with analogous genetic conditions. The model built is focused on maximizing the predictive power at the level of individuals, to provide individualized risk prediction based on personal genetic profiles. Three commonly used pattern classification algorithms such as Multi Layer perceptron (MLP), Decision tree, Support Vector Machines (SVM) are used in the work for building the gene identification model.

Multi Layer Perceptron (MLP)

Multi Layer perceptron (MLP) consists of one or more layers between input and output layer and is a feed forward neural network. Feed forward signifies that data flows in one direction from input to output layer. Back propagation learning algorithm is used to train this network. MLPs are used for pattern classification, prediction and approximation as it is capable of solving problems which are non-linearly separable. Similarly an N - layer neural networks is trained with the same ideas of single layer networks. The output cost functionis minimized by adjusting the network weights. It is only the output of the final layer that emerges in the output error function. The eearlier layers of weight decide the final layer output and the learning algorithm will adjust all of them. The learning algorithm repeatedly adjusts the outputs of the earlier layers so that they form appropriate intermediary depictions.

Decision Tree Induction

Decision tree induction is the method of learning decision trees from labelled training instances. The classification algorithm constructs a binary tree like structure known as decision tree. The non leaf nodes indicate a check on an attribute whereas a branch symbolizes a result of the test. The leaf node or terminal node contains a class label. The root node is the uppermost node in a tree. A decision tree model comprises rules which are used to predict the class label. The class label of a new instance is predicted by testing the attribute values of the instance against the decision tree. The class label of data is predicted by going through the path from the root node to a leaf node. The selection of the best split of attributes is done based on impurity measures. The split tries to decrease the impurity of the parent node. If $(E_1, E_2, ..., E_k)$ are splits induced on the set of records E, a splitting criterion that makes use of the impurity measure I is given as

$$\Delta = I(E) - \sum (|E_i| / |E|).I(E_i), \text{ where } i = 1 \text{ to } k.$$

Support Vector Machine (SVM)

Support vector machine (SVM) can handle noise and large datasets and hence has achieved recognition than other machine learning methods. In SVM, classwise separation of points in the input variable space is done by the best hyperplane. SVMs are not influenced by local minima and do not experience the problem of dimensionality. The position of the dividing hyper plane is decided by support vectors that are the decisive elements of the training set. The optimal line that can divide the two classes is the line with the largest margin and is known as the Maximal-Margin hyperplane. The margin is considered as the perpendicular distance from the line to the nearest points. Support vectors are the points pertinent in defining the line and in building the classifier.

3   Results and Discussion

Experiments have been carried out by implementing standard supervised machine learning techniques, namely Decision tree induction, Multilayer Perceptron and Support vector machine (SVM). The dataset with features as described in Sect. 2 is employed for learning the model. The dataset is split into training and testing sets and a standard 10- fold cross-validation technique is used to estimate their impact on the prediction performance for unknown samples. The results obtained from the learned classifiers were analyzed through Precision, Recall, F- measure, Accuracy, Sensitivity, Specificity and ROC area as the performance analysis measures. The performance analysis is tabulated in Table 2 which shows the precision, recall and F-measure obtained when three types of machine learning approaches are performed on the same data set and is illustrated in Fig. 4.

Table 2. Performance comparison of classifiers

Classifier	Precision	Recall	F Measure
Multilayer perceptron	0.967	0.957	0.967
Support vector machines	0.958	0.953	0.953
Decision tree	0.974	0.973	0.973

Figures 2 and 3 depicts the precision and recall of the classifiers. As indicated in Fig. 4 Decision trees fares well when compared with other techniques. The highest precision and recall was achieved by decision tree classifier (0.974 and 0.973). Table 3 indicates the Kappa statistic, Mean absolute error and accuracy values of the classifiers studied.

As illustrated in Table 3 the mean absolute error of Decision tree is least (0.0125) when compared to other techniques. SVM attained 0.2233 mean absolute error whereas MLP has attained 0.0176. Kappa statistic of the three classifiers are 0.952 (MLP), 0.943 (SVM) and 0.967 (Decision tree).

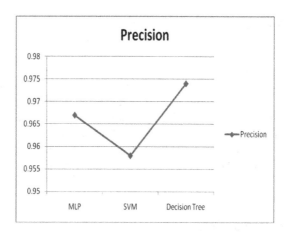

Fig. 2. Precision of classifiers

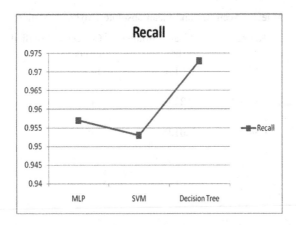

Fig. 3. Recall of classifiers

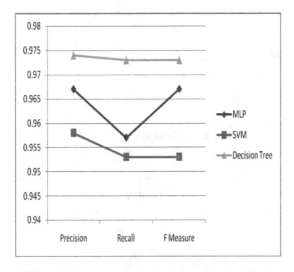

Fig. 4. Precision, recall, F measure of classifiers

Decision tree has correctly classified 146 instances and its accuracy is 97.33% whereas MLP and SVM has an accuracy of 96.66 and 95.33 respectively. Figures 5 and 6 depicts the kappa statistic, mean absolute error and accuracy of the 3 classifiers.

Table 4 illustrates that Decision tree gives a prominent score value for the sensitivity (0.973) than SVM (0.739) and Multilayer Perceptron (0.96).Similarly specificity is comparatively high in Decision tree (0.095) than other learning techniques. Matthews Correlation coefficient (MCC) of Decision tree is 0.97 and its ROC area is 0.991

The comparative results point out that Decision tree based classification model shows a better performance when compared with other models. In comparison with

Table 3. Accuracy and mean absolute error of classifiers

Classifier	Kappa statistic	Mean absolute error	Correctly classified instances	Accuracy
Multilayer perceptron	0.952	0.0176	145	96.66
Support vector machines	0.943	0.2233	143	95.33
Decision tree	0.967	0.0125	146	97.33

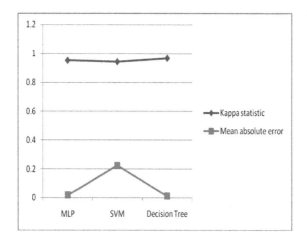

Fig. 5. Performance of classifiers

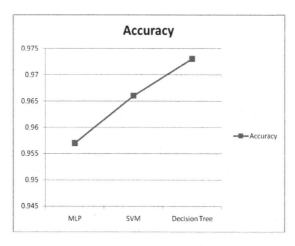

Fig. 6. Accuracy of classifiers

other previously mentioned works and methods, the proposed method has the following advantages.

(1) The study involves both categories of syndromic and non-syndromic ASD and the dataset contains diseased gene sequences of genes that belong to these categories.
(2) The result confirms that the model has a better sensitivity and predictive accuracy to identify diseased ASD gene.
(3) The model can be used to predict the genes of more candidate sequences and to verify the correlation between them with biological experiments.

Table 4. Sensitiviy and Specificity of Classifiers

Evaluation	MLP	SVM	Decision Tree
Sensitivity	0.967	0.739	0.973
Specificity	0.094	0.092	0.095
MCC	0.96	0.946	0.97
ROC area	0.985	0.988	0.991

4 Conclusion

Recognition of pretentious genes which are the basis for disease-related phenotypes in humans is a key problem of medical genetics. It is complicated to identify a single gene causing ASD as a multitude of genes and their variants underlie diseases like Autism spectrum disorder (ASD). Hence powerful Machine Learning models are the need of the hour. The study investigated the development of machine learning model for disease gene classification of ASD genes. The problem is formulated as a multi-class classification problem using simulated gene sequences. The gene coding measures are extracted as features and a model is built by employing supervised machine learning algorithms such as MLP, Decision Tree and SVM. The performance of the learning methods was evaluated and the experiment results showed that Decision trees performed best with respect to various performance measures. In future, the problem can be extended by exploring different feature set and investigating alternate machine learning methods.

References

1. Jamal, W., et al.: Classification of autism spectrum disorder using supervised learning of brain connectivity measures extracted from synchrostates. J. Neural Eng. **11**(4), 046019 (2014)
2. Latkowski, T., Osowski, S.: Computerized system for recognition of autism on the basis of gene expression microarray data. Comput. Biol. Med. **56**, 82–88 (2015). https://doi.org/10.1016/j.compbiomed.2014.11.004
3. Krishnan, A., et al.: Genome-wide prediction and functional characterization of the genetic basis of autism spectrum disorder. Nat. Neurosci. **19**, 1454–1462 (2016). https://doi.org/10.1038/nn.4353

4. Ronemus, M., Iossifov, I., Levy, D., Wigler, M.: The role of de novo mutations in the genetics of autism spectrum disorders. Nat. Rev. Genet. **15**, 133–141 (2014)
5. De Rubeis, S., et al.: Synaptic, transcriptional and chromatin genes disrupted in autism. Nature **515**, 209–215 (2014)
6. Sanders, S.J., et al.: Insights into autism spectrum disorder genomic architecture and biology from 71 risk loci. Neuron **87**, 1215–1233 (2015)
7. He, X., et al.: Integrated model of de novo and inherited genetic variants yields greater power to identify risk genes. PLoS Genet. **9**, e1003671 (2013)
8. Gilman, S.R., et al.: Rare de novo variants associated with autism implicate a large functional network of genes involved in formation and function of synapses. Neuron **70**, 898–907 (2011)
9. Chang, J., Gilman, S.R., Chiang, A.H., Sanders, S.J., Vitkup, D.: Genotype to phenotype relationships in autism spectrum disorders. Nat. Neurosci. **18**, 191–198 (2015)
10. Liu, L., Lei, J., Roeder, K.: Network assisted analysis to reveal the genetic basis of autism. Ann. Appl. Stat. **9**, 1571–1600 (2015)
11. Hormozdiari, F., Penn, O., Borenstein, E., Eichler, E.E.: The discovery of integrated gene networks for autism and related disorders. Genome Res. **25**, 142–154 (2015)
12. Cotney, J., et al.: The autism-associated chromatin modifier CHD8 regulates other autism risk genes during human neurodevelopment. Nat. Commun. **6**, 6404 (2015)
13. Hamosh, A., Scott, A.F., Amberger, J.S., Bocchini, C.A., McKusick, V.A.: Online mendelian inheritance in man (OMIM), a knowledgebase of human genes and genetic disorders. Nucleic Acids Res. **33**, D514–D517 (2005)
14. Abrahams, B.S., et al.: SFARI gene 2.0: a community-driven knowledgebase for the autism spectrum disorders (ASDs). Mol. Autism **4**, 36 (2013)

Noise Removal Framework for Market Basket Analysis

Roshan Gangurde[1(✉)], Binod Kumar[2], and Sharad D. Gore[1]

[1] Department of Computer Science, Savitribai Phule Pune University, Pune, India
roshanant@gmail.com, sharaddgore@gmail.com
[2] JSPM's Jayawant Institute of Computer Applications, Pune, India
binod.istar.1970@gmail.com

Abstract. Rapid development in data analysis domain causes an ever growing demand for Market Basket Analysis. However, predefined methods in this domain emphasize on different techniques which concentrate to select appropriate items. In this paper, we tried to develop a framework for cleaning the dataset that depends on the proposition that "Better noise removal brings out better data analysis". Eliminating noisy objects is an essential goal of data preprocessing as noise hampers data analysis. Data cleaning techniques which are recently developed concentrates on noise removals that are the consequences of low-level data errors. It causes due to defective data gathering process, but data objects that are clearly connected or related only at some particular time or unrelated/unimportant can also be significantly interfere with data analysis. Thus, in order to improve the data analysis to a greater extent, noisy data with respect to the underlying analysis must be removed at data preprocessing which is one of the steps of Knowledge Discovery in Databases (KDD). Hence to remove all types of noise, there is a need of data cleaning strategies. Because data sets can contain enormous measures of noise, these methods also need to be able to remove extensive portion of the data. To augment data analysis in existence of high noise intensity, this paper find method meant for noise removal.

Keywords: Data analysis · Data cleaning · Hyperclique pattern
Market Basket Analysis · Noise removal · Prediction model

1 Introduction

Data cleaning is nothing but the data scrubbing or cleansing, deals with eliminating and detecting errors and inconsistencies from data in order to enhance the quality of data. Database quality issues are found in single data accumulations, for example, databases and documents e.g., missing data, unused symbols, space or invalid data. At the point when number of data sources should be incorporated, e.g., in data warehouse, world-wide online data frameworks or combined database frameworks, the requirement for data cleaning increments essentially. That's way the sources often contain redundant data in distinct representations. Keeping in mind the end goal to offer access to steady and exact data, gathering of various data representation and end of copy data become

© Springer Nature Singapore Pte Ltd. 2018
A. V. Deshpande et al. (Eds.): SmartCom 2017, CCIS 876, pp. 213–224, 2018.
https://doi.org/10.1007/978-981-13-1423-0_24

necessary. Noise is nothing but the irrelevant or meaningless data. For recently developed data cleaning techniques, the focus is on locating and destroying the noisy data (low-level data errors) that is the result of a blemished data accumulation process. In any case, at least in the context of a particular analysis, general data objects that are unrelated or only weakly connected with or related to a particular data analysis can also significantly interfere with the data analysis, and consequently, such data objects should be measured as noise. Thus, there is a prerequisite for data cleaning strategies that evacuate a wide range of noise. Sometimes, the measure of noise in the process of data collection is moderately low. For instance, it has been proclaim that field error rates for business are around 7% or less if an association specifically takes measures to disregard data blunders. In this way, data cleaning systems for the upgrade of data analysis likewise should have the capacity to dispose a conceivably vast division of the data [1].

The invention of electronic Point of Sale (PoS) system has led to collection of huge amount of data coming into the enterprise with different attributes which is in turn useful for Market Basket Analysis. The prediction model based on the Market Basket Analysis technique can be used to generate the association rules that can be adopted on recommendation system to make the functionality more operational. Better and effective rule mining techniques can be used for better performance of the recommendation system. The knowledge discovered from Market Basket Analysis is useful for the industries engaged in retailing business for their decision making process [2]. Hence forth, data quality development is a progressing experiment which should be performed to deal with the inconsistency that accompanies the expanding information. To improve data quality is a very tedious task with lots of physical efforts in creating new rules and dictionaries. Domain expert creates these dictionaries and rules and they change across customers.

The rest of the paper is organized as follows: Sect. 2 discusses about the related work. The proposed approach has been detailed out in Sect. 3. The implementation of the proposed approach is discussed in Sect. 4. The results and analysis of the proposed approach are stated in Sect. 5. The article is concluded in the last section.

2   Related Work

In this section, we review recent methods of noise removing. The methods studied are from 2008 to 2016.

Matthias Jacob (2008)
In [3], author introduced a method of architecture and business system that not just accumulate data pre- formatted by other web services, additionally gives a self-developed name Entity Recognition algorithm for removing the names of superstars from particular data sources and after that process them by his mash-up application.

Wei-Heng Zhu (2010)
In [4] author defined methods to self-automatic information cleansing and extraction for data. At first experiment, outcomes demonstrate that, with reasonable manual contribution, it can successfully gather data from raw semi-structured Chinese texts gathered from e-business applications.

Hasimah Hj Mohamed, Tee Leong Kheng (2011)

In [5], author tried to prepare quality data by processing the raw data. Data cleaning, additionally called data purifying or scouring, manages identifying and eliminating errors and irregularities from data with a specific end goal to improve the quality of data. Data cleaning framework are expected to support any accommodation in the structure, portrayal or substance of data. The author defined three sections in the cleaning procedure, i.e. separate the invalid value, coordinating qualities with valid values and data cleaning algorithm. The framework utilizes the transform, load model and extract take as main system process handle model to fill in as a rule for the execution of the framework. Other than that, parsing methods are additionally used for the distinguishing proof of grimy data. The technique that the author decided for coordinating properties is standard expression. Among these data cleaning algorithms, k-Nearest Neighbor algorithm is chosen for the data cleaning some portion of this venture since it is easy to comprehend and simple to implement.

K. Hima Prasad (2011)

According to [6], improved data quality is one of the important aspects of data management. The features of data under analysis may change as per the user or domain requirement for improving data quality which is a challenging task. This process mainly involves removal of duplicate data which are present within the data. In this paper, author introduced a tool which identify variant for given entity present in the data set. For maintaining data quality rules, he presented a ripple down rule which helps to reduce the service efforts for adding new rules. The Author also offered one of the work-flow which is used to data quality improvement method. The results of the research and analysis on the usefulness of the tools are also presented by reducing service efforts in a data quality improvement.

Gonzalo Mateos (2013)

In [7], author developed a novel load cleansing and imputation scheme to sparse nature of "bad data". Principal Component Pursuit (PCP) which is a robust estimator is adopted which effects a twofold sparsity-promoting regularization through a norm of the outliers and the nuclear norms of the nominal load profiles. To carry out the imputation and cleansing tasks, distributed (D-) PCP algorithms is developed using networked devices which encompass the so-termed advanced metering infrastructure. If D-PCP converges and a qualification inequality is satisfied, the novel distributed estimator provably attains the performance of its centralized PCP counterpart, which has access to all network wide data. The convergence and effectiveness of the novel D-PCP algorithm supports computer simulations and tests with real load curve data.

Boye A. Høverstad (2011)

In [8], author trusts that preprocessing filters, for example, cleansing should prompt more robustness or potentially accuracy in the consequent handling step. However, load cleansing system try to make the popular assumption of independently and normally distributed noise in the time series. Author states that the existing work is incorrect at the diurnal level, due to power consumption of the characteristic pattern, with couple peak load between daytime and a nighttime trough. Author further illustrates empirical evidence that a preprocessing step based on this assumption fails to contribute positively to the performance of the subsequent prediction steps. To correct this problem, they suggested minimizing the average power load consumption in a provided period before cleansing. Data cleansing and load forecast is performed by a framework that hunts out parameters utilizing a transformative approach.

Wei-Shinn Ku (2013)

In [9], author developed a framework based on "Bayesian inference" to clean RFID raw data by primarily designing an n-state detection model. Author tried to prove that the three-state model can maximize the system performance. Then, he extended the n-state model to compute the likelihood efficiently and support two-dimensional RFID reader arrays. What's more, to clean RFID information with more exactness and proficiency, he devised a Metropolis-Hastings sampler with requirements, which incorporate limitation administration. Additionally, to help constant question observing, they demonstrate the gushing Bayesian surmising method to adapt to continuous RFID information streams. At long last, he figured the execution of his answers through broad tests.

Anpeng Huang (2013)

In [10], author proposed a way to deal with clean clinical features from ECG unused data in light of principle crease learning, called the Manifold-based ECG-includes purification algorithm. His clinical trials rate of up to 94% which extremely improves in consistently health-risk alert applications. Most importantly, the practical results shows that the WE-CARE system enabled by his proposal can increase system reliability by minimum two times and reduce false negative rates to 0.76% in the system integration level and also extend the battery life by 40.54%.

Erhard Rahm (2014)

In [11], author partitioned data quality issues that are addressed by data cleaning and provided a review of the principle arrangement approaches. Data cleaning is particularly needs when incorporating diverse data sources and should be addressed together with schema related data transformation. Data cleaning is one of the significant parts of the purported ETL process. Author additionally discussed about current tool which is supported for data cleaning.

Hui Xiong (2010)

In [1], author characterized four techniques expected for noise removal to improve data analysis within the sight of noise levels. Out of four methods, three of these methods are chip away at conventional exception discovery systems: bunching based, separate based and an approach in view of the Local Outlier Factor (LOF) of a protest. The author proposed a hyper clique circle - based data cleaner (HCleaner) which is another technique. These methods are evaluated in terms of analysis significantly and clustering and association analysis with their impact on the subsequent data. The results upon experiment proved that the techniques proposed the author can provide better performance over clustering and higher quality association patterns as the substantial amount of noise being removed, in spite of the fact that HCleaner by and large prompts enhanced grouping execution and good quality relationship than the other three strategies for binary data.

T. Redman (2003)

In [12], author tried to present the impact of poor data on enterprise. Customer dissatisfaction, less effective decision-making, increased operational cost and a minimized ability to make and execute strategy are included in impacts. Making consciousness of a problem and its impact is a critical first step towards resolution of the problem. The needed awareness of the poor data quality is not yet achieved in many enterprises.

W. Eckerson (2002)

In [13], author discussed the sources of poor quality data. In data entry processes, the most frequent data quality problems, and systems interfaces are occurs. Misspellings, incorrect or missing codes, transposition of numerals, data placed in the wrong fields and unrecognizable names, nicknames, abbreviations or acronyms are examples of errors. These types of errors are minimizing the accuracy of work so author tries to improve quality of data.

J. Chen, W. Li, A. Lau, J. Cao (2010)

In [14], author presented the two smoothing techniques which are B-Spline smoothing and Kernel smoothing which automatically cleanses corrupted and missing data. A man–machine dialogue procedure is implementing, proposed to enhance the performance.

V. Raman and J. M. Hellerstein (2001)

In [15], authors discussed an interactive data cleaning system that discrepancy detection and tightly integrates transformation. By adding or undoing transforms on spreadsheet-like interface users gradually create transformations to clean the data. These transforms are specified either through simple graphical operations, or by showing the desired effects on example data values.

J. I. Maletic and A. Marcus (2000)

In [16], author tried to analyze the problem of automatically recognize potential errors in data sets and data cleansing. An overview of the small amount of existing literature concerning data cleansing is given. Methods for error detection that go beyond integrity analysis are presented and reviewed. They provide brief results supporting the use of such methods are given.

3 Methodology

In this section, we discuss our proposed algorithm and the methodology used.

3.1 Basics of Market Basket Analysis (MBA)

Market basket analysis enlightens the combinations of products that frequently co-occur in transactions. For example, people who purchase bread and eggs, also tend to buy butter as many of them are planning to make an omelette. Marketing team should target customers who buy bread and eggs with offers on butter, to persuade them to spend more on their shopping basket.

It is also known as "Affinity Analysis" or "Association Rule Mining". The problem of Association rule mining is defined as:

Let I = {i1, i2, i3, ..., in} be a set of n binary attributes called items.

Let D = {t1, t2, t3, ..., tm} be a set of transactions called database.

Each transaction in D has a unique transaction ID and contains a subset of the items I.

A rule is defined as an implication of the form: X => Y where X, Y is subset of I and X intersection Y = NULL.

Every rule is composed by two different set of items, also known as itemsets, X and Y where X is called antecedent or left-hand-side (LHS) and Y consequent or right-hand-side (RHS).

Association Rules are used for discovering regularities between products in big transactional databases.

A transaction is an event involving one or more of the products (items) in the business or domain. For example buying of goods by a consumer in a super market is a transaction.

A set of items is usually referred as "itemset", and an itemset with "k" number of items is called "k-itemset".

The general form of an association rule is X => Y, where X and Y are two disjoint itemsets.

A given association rule X => Y is considered significant and useful, if it has high support and confidence values. Interestingness measures of association rules are support and confidence.

Support(S): It is defined as the ratio of occurrence of two items and total number of transactions.

S (X, Y) = (No. of Transactions containing both X and Y/(Total No. of Transactions).

Confidence(C): It is defined as ratio that how many instances satisfy the rule of an antecedent.

C(Y/X) = (No. of Transactions containing both X and Y)/(No. of Transactions containing X).

The user will specify a threshold value for support and confidence, so that different degrees of significance can be observed based on these threshold values.

3.2   Data Cleaning Techniques

Data cleaning deals with a variety of problems on data quality which includes noise and outliers, inconsistent data, duplicate data, and missing values. Data cleaning techniques can be categorized as the techniques that apply at data collection stage and the techniques that apply at data analysis stage.

3.2.1   Data Cleaning Techniques at Data Collection Stage

Most typical data errors at Data Collection Stage are due to the misuse of abbreviations, data entry mistakes, duplicate records, missing values, spelling errors, outdated codes, etc. Data cleaning techniques applied at the data collection stage are focused on detecting and removing low-level errors and irregularities due to an imperfect data collection process [1].

3.2.2 Data Cleaning Techniques at Data Analysis Stage

At data analysis stage, the primary function of data cleaning techniques is to eliminate data objects that are irrelevant or only weakly-relevant to the underlying data analysis. Its purpose is to improve the results of the data analysis.

The key contribution of this research paper is to propose a data cleaning technique which addresses at both data collection stage as well as data analysis stage.

3.2.3 Hyperclique Pattern

Hyperclique patterns [1] are the patterns which consist of objects that are strongly similar to each other. In particular, each pair of objects within a hyperclique pattern is guaranteed to have a cosine similarity above a certain level. The cosine similarity measure is also known as the uncentered Pearson's correlation coefficient, a measure of association that depicts the strength or magnitude of a association between two objects. The hyperclique patterns can be used as a filter to remove data objects that are not strongly connected to other data objects in the data set. Such patterns generate a new kind of association patterns that contains objects that are highly associated with each other. This means that every pair of objects within a pattern is guaranteed to have a cosine similarity (uncentered Pearson's correlation coefficient) above a certain level. If a data object do not belongs to any hyperclique pattern, then it is likely to be comparatively unrelated to other objects, and thus, potentially noisy objects.

The h-confidence measure is exclusively designed to capture the strength of this association.

Definition 1: The h-confidence of a pattern $X = \{i1, i2, ..., im\}$, denoted as hconf(X), is a measure that reflects the overall affinity among items within the pattern. This measure is defined as min (conf($\{i1\}$ → $\{i2, ..., im\}$), conf($\{i2\}$ → $\{i1, i3, ..., im\}$), ..., conf($\{im\}$ → $\{i1, ..., im-1\}$)), where conf is the confidence of association rule as given above.

3.3 Algorithm

The dataset used for our experiment is related to retail industry. The dataset contains information of each transaction with the transaction ids. Each row represents a single transaction, i.e. purchased items' information of a single customer.

For example, if a row present the data like {Potato, coffee, Milk, Egg, Butter}, it means this customer has purchased these mentioned items in a single transaction.

Following is the proposed **Noise Removal Algorithm**

Extended HCleaner Algorithm (E-Cleaner)

```
Input: Transaction set T
Result: Set of noise points N, Set of non-noise points P

for  i = 1 to ntrans do
          if T[i].contain(HTMLcharcters) then
                    T[i].remove(HTMLcharacter)
          end
          if T[i].contain(StopWords) then
                    T[i].remove(StopWords)
          end
          if T[i].contain(Expression) then
                    T[i].remove(Expression)
          end
          if T[i].contain(Punctuation) then
                    T[i].remove(Expression)
          end
          if T[i].contain(URLs) then
                    T[i].remove(URL)
          end
end

HCS ← HypercliqueMiner(T) //HC: Hyperclique Set;
T[1...ntrans].covered ← false;
len_hc ← size(HCS);
for  i = 1 to len_hc do
          for j = 1 to ntrans do
                    if ((!T[j].covered)&&contains(T[j],HCS[i])) then
                        T[j].covered ← true;
                    end
          end
end
N ← {};
P ← {};
for  i = 1 to ntrans do
          if T[i].covered then
                    P ← P ∪ T[i];
          end
          else
                    N ← N ∪ T[i];
          end
end
return N, P;
```

We introduce the Extended Hyperclique Based Data Cleaner (ECleaner). The basic model of E-Cleaner can be recap as follows:

At first, we preprocess each transaction in which we remove html characters, stop words, expressions, URLs and punctuation. These preprocessed transactions are then used to search hyperclique patterns as per given support and h-confidence threshold. This helps to eliminate any objects that are not a part of any hyperclique pattern. The set of hyperclique patterns for any data set depends upon the value of support and h-confidence thresholds. Wherever possible, we set the support threshold to be zero and employ the h-confidence threshold to control the number of objects that are designated as noise. However, setting the support threshold to zero leads to an explosion in the number of hyperclique patterns. For this reason, we use a low support threshold which is high enough to reduce the number of hyperclique patterns to a controllable level.

4   Implementation

In this section, we discuss GUI developed and results of our proposed technique. The GUI shown in Fig. 1 contains four buttons. Browse button is used to browse the specified dataset file. The file path is set to the text box as shown in Fig. 1.

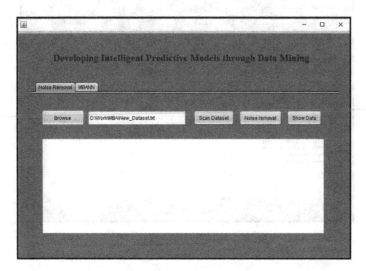

Fig. 1.   GUI of the proposed model

Scan Dataset button is used to read appropriate data set file line by line and displays all transactions in text area as shown in Fig. 2.

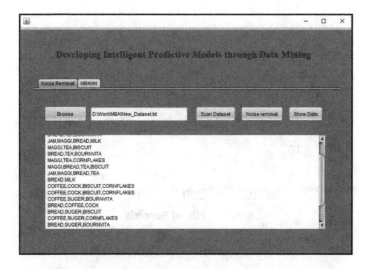

Fig. 2.   Browse dataset

The Noise Removal button is used to apply proposed algorithm on dataset. Then Show Data button displays data objects without noise. Now data without noise is shown in Fig. 3.

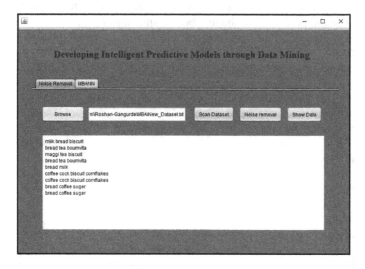

Fig. 3. Data objects after applying algorithm

5   Results and Analysis

As shown in Fig. 4, the x-axis shows number of records in dataset and y-axis shows time required to remove noise from dataset. Time is directly propositional to the size of data

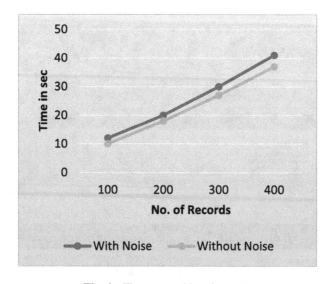

Fig. 4. Time versus No. of records

set. In below graph, we show that dataset without noise required less time to any processing as compared to dataset with noise. Here we compare both file performance with respect to time.

As showing in Fig. 5, the x-axis shows noise percentage in dataset and y-axis shows accuracy of result. Accuracy is directly propositional to the noise percentage. If we remove maximum noise from dataset then we would get more accurate results.

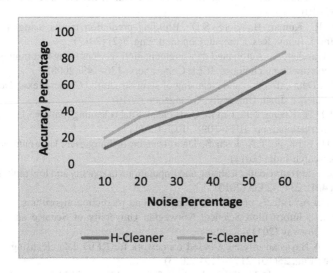

Fig. 5. Accuracy versus noise percentage

After applying proposed noise removal algorithm, data set size reduced by 272 bytes so it contains 55% of noise. With respect to space and time, noise free dataset is better for data analysis. Following Table 1 shows the data set size before and after applying the noise removal algorithm.

Table 1. Dataset size comparison

	Before	After
Dataset	460 bytes	188 bytes

6 Conclusion

The main aim of the proposed work in this paper is to increase the quality of data analytics, by minimizing the consequences of noise at the stage data analysis. This may be noise not only because of the deficiencies in data gathering process but also due to data objects that are relevant in some specific time period or irrelevant information objects. Noisy data for no good reason increases the volume of storage space needed and can also badly affect the results of any data mining analysis. Our focus was on the dataset without noise because quality decisions must be based on quality data. We provide a structure for ascertaining the adequacy of noise elimination techniques for better data analysis that depends on steps defined in Sect. 3.

References

1. Xiong, H.: Enhancing data analysis with noise removal. IEEE Trans. Knowl. Data Eng. **18**, 304–319 (2010)
2. Gangurde, R., Kumar, B., Gore, S.D.: Building prediction model using market basket analysis. Int. J. Innov. Res. Comput. Commun. Eng. **5**(2) (2017)
3. Jacob, M., Kuscher, A.: Automated data augmentation services using text mining, data clean singand web crawling techniques. IEEE Congr. Serv. 136–143 (2008)
4. Zhu, W.-H.: Data extraction and cleansing of semi-structured Chinese texts, Department of Computer Science. Jinan University, Guangzhou (2010)
5. Mohamed, H.H., Kheng, T.L., Collin, C.: E-clean: a data cleaning framework for patient data. In: IEEE International, pp. 1093–1098. IEEE (2011)
6. Prasad, K.H., Faruquie, T.A., Joshi, S.: Data cleansing techniques for large enterprise datasets. In: IBM Research-India (2011)
7. Mateos, G.: Load curve data cleansing and imputation via sparsity and low rank. IEEE Trans. Smartgrid **4**(4), 2347–2355 (2013)
8. Høverstad, B.A.: Effects of data cleansing on load prediction algorithms, Department of Computer and Information Science. Norwegian University of Science and Technology, Trondheim, Norway (2011)
9. Ku, W.-S.: A Bayesian inference-based framework for RFID data cleansing. IEEE Trans. Knowl. Data Eng. **25**(10), 2177–2191 (2013)
10. Huang, A.: System light-loading technology for mhealth: manifold-learning-based medical data cleansing and clinical trials in WE-CARE project. IEEE J. Biomed. Health Inf. **18**(5), 1581–1589 (2014)
11. Rahm, E.: Data cleaning: problems and current approaches. University of Leipzig, Germany (2014)
12. Redman, T.: The impact of poor data quality on the typical enterprise. Commun. ACM **2**, 79–82 (2003)
13. Eckerson, W.: Data quality and the bottom line: achieving business success through a commitment to high quality data. Technical report, The Data Warehousing Institute (2002)
14. Chen, J., Li, W., Lau, A., Cao, J., Wang, K.: Automated load curve data cleansing in powers ystems. IEEE Trans. Smartgrid **1**, 213–221 (2010)
15. Raman, V., Hellerstein, J.M.: Potter's wheel: an interactive framework for data transformation and cleaning. In: Proceedings of the 27th VLDB Conference, Roma, Italy (2001)
16. Maletic, J.I., Marcus, A.: Data cleansing: beyond integrity analysis. In: Proceedings of the Conference on Information Quality (2000)

Load Balanced Efficient Routing Technique for Mobility Based RPL

K. Sneha[1(✉)] and B. G. Prasad[2]

[1] BNM Institute of Technology, Bengaluru, India
`sneha.ky30@gmail.com`
[2] BMS College of Engineering, Bengaluru, India
`drbgprasad@gmail.com`

Abstract. We are living in the era of Internet of Things (IoT) where each and every object is connected to network and therefore able to send and receive data. The devices used here such as sensors are low power devices which are interconnected through different links. Low power and Lossy Networks (LLNs) are a class of network which mostly consists of low power devices. The IETF standard proposed routing protocol known as RPL (Routing protocol for Low power and Lossy network) is a protocol which has been designed basically for low power networks where nodes are static in nature. Mobility and load balancing are the issues in such networks. In this paper we have proposed a technique known as LBER-RPL (Load Balanced – Efficient Routing Technique) which leverages the lifetime of the RPL network by balancing the load and provides an efficient routing for dynamic environment. The simulation is carried out using Cooja Network Simulator. The performance analysis of LBER-RPL is carried out by comparing it with the standard RPL and the former outperforms with respect to packet delivery ratio, handoff and route formation delay.

Keywords: LLNs · RPL · Delay · Hand-off optimization · Load balancing

1 Introduction

Low-Power and Lossy Networks (LLNs) are a class of network in which the routers and their interconnect are constrained. It consists largely of constrained nodes with limited processing power, memory, and sometimes energy when they are battery operated [1]. LLNs operate with a hard and very small bound on state [2]. Routing protocol for Low power and Lossy networks (RPL) is an IPv6 distance vector routing protocol for LLNs. It is designed to operate with low memory devices, and low data traffic. It has been introduced at the IETF in 2008 as a proposed standard routing protocol for LLNs [3]. RPL is designed for static networks. The standard RPL protocol [4, 5] does not emphasize on mobility issue as its goal and hence researchers [6–9] have made effort to introduce mobility with RPL.

In this paper, mobility based routing technique with the load balancing method has been developed that intends to optimize the major routing constraints of mobile WSNs, such as dynamic topology variation, routing efficiency in terms of packet delivery ratio, delay. Here, to enable best forwarding route selection the route stability oriented hand-

© Springer Nature Singapore Pte Ltd. 2018
A. V. Deshpande et al. (Eds.): SmartCom 2017, CCIS 876, pp. 225–235, 2018.
https://doi.org/10.1007/978-981-13-1423-0_25

off optimization has been done. Our proposed model achieves the best route selection with a balanced load in the network. The handoff-scheduling is carried out using multiple timers which has strengthened the proposed model to achieve best route in the mobility based RPL. The remaining sections are divided as follows. Section 2 discusses the overview of RPL routing protocol, which is followed by the discussion of the mobility based low power lossy network in Sect. 3. The technique of load balancing and the hand-off optimization based RPL routing scheme for best route selection is discussed in Sect. 4. Section 5 presents the results and discussions followed by conclusion in Sect. 6. Finally the references are mentioned.

2 Background

2.1 RPL Overview

RPL is a routing protocol specified to support LLNs. It operates specifically with low power, low memory devices and in low data-traffic. Since it is constrained, it has one entry to reach root node while building the network. The network comprises of group of nodes, in which some nodes are roots. The topology is acyclic where network doesn't contain cycles and the edges are directed and hence called as DAG (Directed Acyclic Graph). In such a graph, if there is single root for entire group of nodes, it is called DODAG (Destination Oriented DAG). The root node contains all inward edges but no outgoing edges. DODAG construction requires knowing Objective function which determines how RPL nodes select the optimal path towards the DODAG root in a network.

2.2 RPL Parameters

RPL has parameters such as RPL Instance ID, DODAG ID, DODAG Version ID and Rank. Each parameter has its own scope.

- **RPL Instance ID:** It uniquely identifies a network. It may consist of several DODAGs. RPL instances may be local or global. Each DODAG will have same RPL Instance ID but different DODAG ID.
- **DODAG ID:** It uniquely identifies each DODAG. DODAGs within the RPL instance have same RPL instance. It is identified by tuple <RPL Instance ID, DODAG ID>.
- **DODAG Version ID:** Whenever there is a change in network, DODAG updates itself and gives a new version number to it. Version number increments sequentially and this is done by root. It is identified by tuple <RPL Instance ID, DODAG ID, DODAG Version Number>.
- **Rank:** It is the relative position of a node with respect to root node. Rank is computed using objective function. Typically a root node is at Rank 0 always. Rank increments when going away from root and decrements when going towards the root [1].

2.3 RPL Control Messages

RPL has four control messages namely

- **DIS [DODAG Information Solicitation]:** The DODAG Information Solicitation (DIS) message may be used to solicit a DODAG Information Object from a RPL node [10].
- **DIO [DODAG Information Object]:** The DODAG Information Object carries information that allows a node to discover a RPL Instance, learn its configuration parameters, select a DODAG parent set, and maintain the DODAG [10].
- **DAO [Destination Advertisement Object]:** The Destination Advertisement Object (DAO) is used to propagate destination information upward along the DODAG. In Storing mode, the DAO message is unicast by the child to the selected parent(s).In Non-Storing mode, the DAO message is unicast to the DODAG root [10].
- **DAO-ACK [DAO Acknowledgment]:** The DAO-ACK message is sent as a unicast packet by a DAO recipient (a DAO parent or DODAG root) in response to a unicast DAO message [10].

3 Mobility Enabled Low Power and Lossy Networks

Low Power Lossy Wireless Sensor Networks (LPWNs) also called LLNs have emerged as a potential solution for low cost communication system [6]. Based on application scenarios, LLNs has to face varied topological variations, especially due to node mobility. Due to the lossy nature of wireless communication and changing radio environment the link node set might also change because of various physical conditions [10]. The mobility in communication network introduces numerous challenges due to continuous topological variation. The existing mobility based techniques [11] focuses either on routing or load balancing. The proposed mobility based RPL protocol focuses on best route selection along with the load balancing method in mobile scenarios. To achieve best route selection in mobile RPL network, we have considered a route stability model which involves selection of best parent through average received signal strength (ARSSI) and number of children attached to the node. It also exhibits efficient hand-off mechanism to select the best route. This technique uses two phases

1. Neighbor discovery and best path selection.
2. Data Transmission.

The first phase encompasses neighbor discovery by sending control packets from source to destination. Initially the mobile node will be disconnected from all other neighboring nodes in the network. The mobile node initiates sending the beacon messages and receives messages from its neighboring nodes based on which the route discovery and path selection takes place. The received messages contain the average received signal strength (ARSSI) of the node based on which the best path is selected by the mobile node. After selecting the best route the mobile node data transmission is initiated. Here we have considered three operational factors such as the frequency of route link, hysteresis margin and threshold which is used in the selection of the best route.

3.1 Route Link Frequency

The frequency of link monitoring determines how frequently the link monitoring needs to be done which is represented using the variable F_W (frame width). The frame width represents the number of packets needed to measure link quality for certain defined time period. Here, we have fixed the frequency of link monitoring at 33 Hz and the inter-packet interval has been defined at 10 s. Smaller frame size signifies higher sampling frequency that can be effective to provide link quality information in dynamic conditions. An optimal frame size selection has been done here in order to avoid unwanted hand-offs and link establishment. In this paper F_W has been selected as 3.

3.2 Hysteresis Margin

The second parameter considered is hysteresis margin to construct best routing link. The hysteresis margin value plays an important role in the hand-off performance. It is represented as H_M. In route discovery process, the mobile node transmits beacon message at certain defined interval F_W, which is then replied by neighboring nodes stating average RSSI of the received beacons message.

3.3 Threshold

The third parameter is the threshold T used to derive the optimal threshold $T_S = T + H_M$ where H_M is used in conjunction with threshold T. The mobile node continues discovering the node meeting threshold criteria $T > T_S$ to create a route.

3.4 Handoff Procedures

In LLN networks, the threshold (T) and H_M estimation can be done by means of the transition region analysis that varies across the wireless links. To construct best routing link if the neighboring node has higher threshold (T), the mobile node creates a path with that node considering it as the best node having the highest link quality and thus completes its data transmission. The least possible threshold is affected by the boundaries of the transitional region. Most of the links greater than 50% are used to be in the transitional region and the precise thresholding can be done by considering the transitional region analysis. If the threshold is too high, the mobile node suffers from extreme hand-offs and beacon exchange, thus exhausting the network. We have defined the transition region as [−90 dBm, −80 dBm] [10] based on the IEEE 802.15.4 CC2420 radio transceiver. The hysteresis margin H_M cope up with the dynamism in LLNs. Similar to the threshold definition, in case of tool low H_M, there can be significant unwanted hand-offs between two nodes and in case of too high H_M the duration of route establishment can be too long that it may result into higher delay and throughput reduction. To deal with mobility scenario in RPL, the periodic transmission of the control packets is performed, which is scheduled by Trickle algorithm that detects the topological variations. In this approach, RPL can re-initiate certain global routing update mechanism but at the cost of increased computational complexity and overheads.

Considering the overall approaches, it can be found that transmitting-receiving DIS and DAO, and acquiring dynamic link quality (ARSSI) for parent node selection require efficient hand-off process. The effective transmission scheduling of DIS and DAO messages can also affect overall effectiveness of the network. Unlike standard RPL, in our work, four distinct timers have been introduced that significantly assist for enhancing the hand-off process and enabling the best route formation in mobile LLN. The timer used here are connectivity timer, hand-off timer, response timer and mobility detection timer.

The connectivity timer T_C allows the mobile node to continuously monitor the channel activity so as to detect any packet reception from connected nodes. Each mobile node executes a "connectivity monitoring timer" to enhance the responsiveness of the RPL routing. We have defined the connectivity timer based on the highest trickle interval TR_{MAX}. It determines whether the mobile node is connected to the parent node. If it is still connected then the data transmission takes place else if the mobile node finds a non responding parent it initiates the neighbor discovery process which gets terminated once detecting any response or packet reception (DIO message) from connected node and is followed by resetting of the timer.

The hand-off timer T_H is to minimize the data exchange and the delay caused due to hand-off during best routing path formation. It regulates the periodicity of DIS beaconing. It has been applied in such a manner that it enables accommodating DIS with maximum feasible transmission rate and reception of the intermittent responses from the neighboring nodes. In our approach, the DIO responses are gathered soon after transmitting individual burst. The parent nodes schedule the response transmission using CSMA MAC that significantly reduces the collision probability.

In our approach response timer T_R is used for two scenarios initially when neighbor discovery is carried out and also to avoid any probable collision. Hence the response time is estimated with respect to three parameters given as $(F_W - C) \times T_{DIS}$. Here C represents the DIS packet counter within individual frame width (F_W) and T_{DIS} gives the DIS interval. In our proposed approach, the response time is varied adaptively as per new packet arrival.

Mobility detection timer T_{MD} has been decided as per the rate of data generation at the mobile node.

4 LBER-Load Balanced Efficient Routing

The proposed load balanced efficient routing considers two features

- It leverages the lifetime of the network by balancing the load of the network
- It proposes an efficient routing technique for a mobility based RPL node.

In Algorithm 1 the mobile node initially starts multicasting the DIS messages. On receiving the DIS messages the nodes unicasts the DIO messages to the mobile node. The received DIO messages are buffered to have a count of the DIO messages arriving represented as L. The mobile node reduces the number of DIS messages by half on receiving the DIO messages if the maximum limit L_M has exceeded. If the count is lesser than the set limit then continue sending the DIS control messages. DIO packets reception is examined until the response timer expires. The timer is reset and a neighbor discovery is again initiated.

> **Algorithm1: DIS control message in Mobile RPL**
> Initiate transmission of DIS control messages from mobile node
> **begin**
>   **if** DIO packets received then
> Reset Response timer T_R
> // Save in buffer to have the count L
>   **if** $L > L_M$ //L_M is the maximum DIO packets allowed.
>   Reduce sending of DIS message by half to balance
>   the load
>   **else**
>   continue sending burst of DIS messages
>   **end**
> **else**
> Send the DIS packets until the response timer expires
> **end**
> **end**

Algorithm 2 is described as follows. The received DIO messages are examined for the average received signal strength (ARSSI) value and total number of children attached to sender node $T_{CHILDREN}$. $T_{CHILDREN}$ is considered for load balancing during the parent selection and route formation. The ARSSI and $T_{CHILDREN}$ are compared against the maximum threshold and maximum children allowed. If the condition is satisfied then the mobile node selects the parent node and best route selection is done and data transmission phase is initiated. If the mobility detection timer T_{MD} expires then the burst transmission of DIS is initiated and the process is repeated. If the connectivity timer T_C expires the neighbor discovery phase is initiated.

Algorithm2: Load Balanced Best Route Selection in Mobile RPL
begin
    if DIO packet is received then
        reset Connectivity Timer T_C;
        Extract and verify DIO ARSSI value and children count;
        if ARSSI< T_s and $T_{CHILDREN}$ > Count_max
          //Count_max represents the maximum children
            count allowed.
          Initiate Neighbour discovery (ND);
        else if ARSSI< T_s and $T_{CHILDREN}$ < Count_max
        Current Parent Node is Unstable or unreliable;
          Initiate ND;
        else if ARSSI> T_s and $T_{CHILDREN}$ > Count_max
        Current Parent Node is Unstable or unreliable;
        else
          Current Parent node is stable and reliable;
          ARSSI> T_s and $T_{CHILDREN}$ < Count_max
        Construct DODAG for Best Route Selection;
        Continue data transmission;
    end
    else if Mobility detection timer T_{MD} expires then
        reset T_{MD};
        Send burst of DIS; //Multicast
        reset handoff-timer T_H;
        go to begin;
    else if T_C expires then
        initiate discovery phase;
    end

end

The results obtained for the proposed load balanced hand-off optimization based best route selection algorithm for mobile RPL are discussed in the following section.

5 Results and Discussions

In this paper, to implement the load balanced and route selection strategy for mobile RPL network, we have used InstantContiki-2.7 operating system that supports advanced Cooja simulator. Contiki is a lightweight, highly portable open source operating system and dedicated for WSNs and IoT. The Cooja simulator has the accessibility of RPL/6LoWPAN, hardware compatibility and availability of mobility plugin [12]. Table 1 represents the simulation environment of the developed mobility based RPL protocol for load balanced efficient route selection.

Table 1. Test environment

Test environment	
OS	Instant Contiki-2.7
Simulator	Cooja
Radio	Unit disk graph medium (distance loss)
Motes	Tmote sky
Network	Routing (RPL)
	Adaption (6LoWPAN)
Data link	CSMA
Physical	IEEE 802.15.4
Mobility pattern	Physical mobility (random walk, pedestrian model)

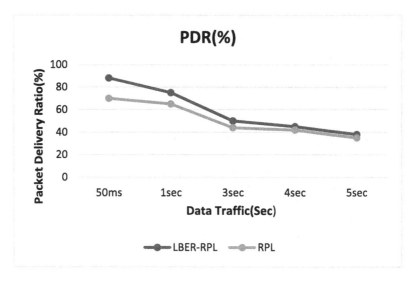

Fig. 1. Packet delivery ratio (LBER-RPL Vs RPL)

The overall performance has been assessed in terms of packet delivery ratio (PDR), DIO control messages, handoff and route formation delay, delay caused due to load balancing and network overheads due to hand-offs and load balancing. Figure 1 represents the PDR that compares the total packet transmitted by source node against the total packet received by the destination nodes. Here, it can be seen that even with the load balancing and stabilized route formation LBER-RPL outperforms with respect to packet delivery ratio compared to standard RPL since in standard RPL there is load imbalance caused due to the congestion at some sensor nodes. Figure 2 represents the number of DIOs and DAO messages received and sent by the mobile node. These control messages play an important role in best route discovery and selection. Figure 3 represents the hand-off and route formation delay, where it can be observed that in LBER-RPL, increase in the traffic elevates the delay. Increasing traffic does have impact on parent node discovery and hence results into elevated delay in route formation or selection. But its performance is better than RPL protocol where delay is found to be still higher due to the congestion caused. Figure 4 represents the delay caused due to load balancing in LBER-RPL. Since the mobile node need to compare the count of the child node of each DIO packet the delay is seen during parent selection procedure. Figure 5 represents the network overhead in LBER-RPL which has been estimated in terms of the control messages transmitted during best path selection. Since frequent hand-offs take place due to mobility in LBER-RPL the overhead is more compared to standard RPL that needs to be optimized.

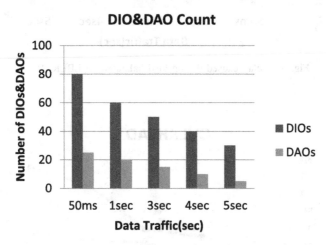

Fig. 2. Number of DIOs and DAOs

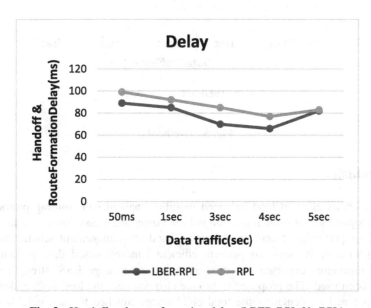

Fig. 3. Handoff and route formation delay (LBER-RPL Vs RPL)

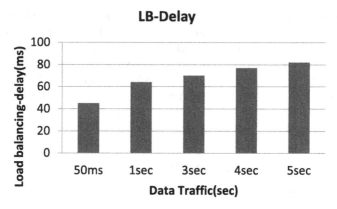

Fig. 4. Delay caused during load balancing in LBER-RPL

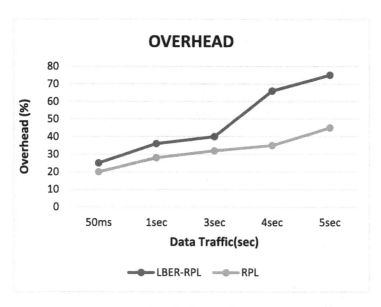

Fig. 5. Overhead

6 Conclusion

In this paper, an efficient load balanced mobility enabled RPL routing protocol has been developed for best route formation in Low Power and Lossy Networks. In order to identify best preferable parent node a novel hand-off management scheme and load balancing strategy is used. To perform efficient hand-off based data exchange and DODAG formation, expected transmission count and average RSSI strength of each node has been used. The proposed technique also balances the load before identifying the best parent by calculating the total child nodes attached to each neighbor node.

The result has exhibited higher packet delivery ratio, minimum hand-off delay in comparison with the standard RPL. DIO and DAO counts for best path selection or formation is identified. The additive complexities incurred through hand-offs, load balancing and other associated functions have elevated the overheads in LBER-RPL compared to standard RPL that in future can be optimized using scheduling measures, using better timers and control messages for dynamic link quality estimation.

References

1. Winter, T., Thubert, P.: RPL: IPv6 routing protocol for low power and lossy networks. IETF Internet-Draft draft-dt-roll-rpl.txt, vol. 3 (2010)
2. Sneha, K., Prasad, B.G.: A survey on routing requirements of IPv6 based low power and lossy network applications. IJSER 4(9) (2013)
3. Vasseur, J.P.: Terminology in Low power And Lossy Networks. draftietf-roll-terminology-06.txt, September 2011
4. Winter, T., et al.: RPL: IPv6 routing protocol for low power and lossy networks. RFC 6550, IETF ROLL WG, March 2012
5. Vasseur, J., Dunkels, A.: Interconnecting Smart Objects with IP: The Next Internet, 1st edn. Morgan Kaufmann, Burlington (2010)
6. El Korbi, I., Brahim, M.B., Adjih, C., Saidane, L.A.: Mobility enhanced RPL for wireless sensor networks. In: 2012 IEEE Conference on Network of the Future, NOF (2012)
7. Fotouhi, H., Moreira, D., Alves, M.: mRPL: boosting mobility in the Internet of Things. J. AdHoc Netw. 26, 17–35 (2015)
8. Somaa, F., El Korbi, I., Adjih, C., Saidane, L.A.: A modified RPL for Wireless Sensor Networks with Bayesian inference mobility prediction. In: 2016 International Wireless Communications and Mobile Computing Conference, IWCMC, pp. 690–695 (2016). ISSN 2376-6506
9. Lee, K.C., et al.: A comprehensive evaluation of RPL under mobility. Int. J. Veh. Technol. 2012 (2012). Hindawi Publishing Corporation
10. Shelby, Z., Chakrabarti, S., Nordmark, E.: Neighbor discovery optimization for low power and lossy networks (6LoWPAN). IETF draft-ietf-6lowpan-nd-18 (2011, Work in progress)
11. Sneha, K., Prasad, B.G.: Comparative study of mobility support techniques for IPv6 based RPL. IJSER 7(7), 483–491 (2016)
12. Contiki OS and Cooja Simulator. http://www.contiki-os.org/

A Formal Approach for Evaluating Data Warehouse Metrics

Anjana Gosain and Jaspreeti Singh[✉]

University School of Information, Communication and Technology,
GGS Indraprastha University, Dwarka 110078, New Delhi, India
anjana_gosain@yahoo.com, jaspreeti_singh@yahoo.com

Abstract. In the last decade, the multidimensional (conceptual) modeling has gained popularity. Some structural metrics exist in the literature for evaluating data warehouse multidimensional (DWMD) model quality. Authors have previously proposed structural metrics involving important concepts related to dimension hierarchies, their sharing and relationship among parent-child hierarchy levels in multidimensional models. However, any quality metric can be widely adopted only if one can ascertain its validity. Therefore, this paper provides formal (theoretical) validation of our previously proposed metrics using a measurement-theoretic framework. The obtained results indicate that these quality metrics are useful for data warehouse development.

Keywords: Quality metrics · Theoretical validation · Data warehouse
Multidimensional models · Zuse framework

1 Background

Multidimensional modeling provides ways to symbolize data using fundamental constructs like facts, dimensions and hierarchies [1]. Analyzing multidimensional models for evaluating quality of data warehouse is becoming increasingly important as the conceptual (multidimensional) modeling continues to gain popularity [2–4]. Metrics helps in measuring the structural complexity of software artifacts and thereby helps in predicting software's external quality [5]. DWMD models are indeed software artifacts and their quality can be determined using metrics [6, 7]. Some metrics [6, 8–13] exist in the literature for evaluating the quality of these models. However, any quality metric can be widely adopted only if one can ascertain its validity, theoretically as well as empirically [5, 6].

Theoretical validation involves studying metrics' mathematical properties for demonstrating that metric is really computing what it claims to compute. Empirical validation helps in demonstrating that the metric is practically useful to measure external attributes like maintainability, analyzability etc. [5, 6]. To this end, proper validation of DWMD model quality metrics is essential to demonstrate that (a) they correctly determine the aspects of multidimensional model they were designed to determine, (b) they

© Springer Nature Singapore Pte Ltd. 2018
A. V. Deshpande et al. (Eds.): SmartCom 2017, CCIS 876, pp. 236–243, 2018.
https://doi.org/10.1007/978-981-13-1423-0_26

are associated with external quality attributes in expected ways. Without proper validation, one would not be able to meaningfully conclude about the results obtained from analysis of metrics data.

This paper considers authors' previously defined structural metrics for DWMD models [13]. They involve important concepts related to dimension hierarchies in multi-dimensional modeling like sharing of dimension hierarchy levels; relationships between parent-child levels of a hierarchy; count of hierarchical/non-hierarchical dimensions etc. (refer Sect. 2).

This paper aims to formally validate our structural metrics [13]. Several frameworks are available in the literature for formal (theoretical) validation of the metrics. They can be classified on the basis of concept used as: (a) the ones using the concept of axioms (for instance, [14]), and (b) the ones using the concept of measurement theory (for instance, [15]). We have already validated our metrics theoretically using Briand's framework [14] (which is based on (a) above) and empirically using statistical techniques (correlation and linear regression) revealing their relationship with multidimensional model understandability [16]. Notably, this paper utilizes the concept of measurement theory to further validate these metrics and get insight into the scale to which the metrics belong.

The benefit of measurement-theoretic approach is that it involves formulating empirical conditions which are then used to derive hypothesis of reality [15]. We have utilized the formal framework of Zuse [15] for describing our metrics' [13] mathematical properties. This framework has been used by research community for formal validation of data warehouse metrics [6, 7].

This paper is structured as follows: the metrics considered in this paper are defined in Sect. 2, Sect. 3 provides the detailed evaluation using Zuse framework, Sect. 4 provides conclusion and future work.

2 Metrics Under Consideration

The structural metrics [13] for DWMD models considered in this paper are provided in Fig. 1. These metrics are based on significant concepts of dimension hierarchies like sharing of hierarchy levels within and across fact schemes, many-to-many relationship between parent-child hierarchy levels etc.

Metrics	Definition
NNHD	*Number of non-hierarchical dimensions in a multidimensional model*
NHD	*Number of hierarchical dimensions in a multidimensional model*
NSLWD	*Number of levels shared among hierarchies, within the dimensions of a multidimensional model*
NSLBD	*Number of levels shared among hierarchies associated to different dimensions within a fact scheme, for all the fact schemes in a multidimensional model*
NSLAF	*Number of levels shared among hierarchies associated to different dimensions across the fact schemes in a multidimensional model*
NNSH	*Number of non-strict hierarchies for all the fact schemes in a multidimensional model*

Fig. 1. Metrics definition [13]

3   Validation Using Zuse Framework

Using Zuse's framework [15], the following provides description of the properties fulfilled by our structural metrics. This framework applies measurement theory concepts to find the scale corresponding to the metric. In this approach, individuals tend to determine empirical relations like *"lower than"*, *"equally lower than"*, *"higher than"* etc. among objects. Consider an empirical relational system, say, $(X, \bullet \geq, \circ)$. In this system, X is a set of objects which is not empty, $\bullet \geq$ is a binary empirical relation to X and $\circ$ is a closed binary operation (concatenation) on X. Now, consider a numerical relational system, say, $(Y, \geq, +)$. In this system, Y is a set of real numbers, $\geq$ is a binary relation to Y and $+$ is a binary operation on Y. So, a mapping function can be defined for the measure m as:

$m: X \rightarrow Y$ such that $\forall X_1, X_2 \in X$ the following two conditions are true:

(i) $X_1 \bullet \geq X_2 \Longleftrightarrow m(X_1) \geq m(X_2)$, and (ii) $m(X_1 \circ X_2) = m(X_1) + m(X_2)$.

Therefore, (X, Y, m) is termed as the scale pertaining to measure m.

Zuse [15] applied the concept of extensive structures to define three set of properties for software measures, namely, *"Modified Extensive Structures* (MES)", *"Independence Conditions* (IC)", and *"Modified Relation of Belief* (MRB)". The important mathematical structures relating this framework are shown in Fig. 2. One can determine the scale of a metric on the basis of these mathematical structures. For a metric which fulfills the properties of MES, it belongs to the ratio scale. In the case it fulfills ICs (and not MES), then the metric relates to ordinal scale. Finally, if the metric fulfills properties associated to MRB, then it belongs to *"above"* ordinal scale. For a metric to be useful, it is primarily important to characterize it *"above"* ordinal scale as not much analysis can be carried out with ordinal numbers [15].

Modified Extensive Structure	Independence Conditions	Modified Relation of Belief
Axiom1: (Weak Order)(A, •≥)	C1:A1≈A2 ⟹ A1∘A≈ A2∘A and A1≈A2 ⟹A∘A1≈ A∘A2	MRB1: (Completeness) ∀ A, B
Axiom2: (Positivity)A1∘A2 •≥ A1	C2:A1≈A2⟺A1∘A≈A2∘A and A1≈A2⟺ A∘A1≈ A∘A2	∈ℑ : A•≥B or B•≥A
Axiom3:(Weak Associativity.) (A1∘A2)∘A3 ≈ A1∘(A2∘A3)	C3: A1•≥A2⟹A1∘A•≥A2∘A and A1•≥A2⟹A∘A1•≥A∘A2	MRB2: (Transitivity) ∀ A, B, C
Axiom4:(Weak Commutativity) A1∘A2 ≈ A2∘A1	C4:A1•≥A2⟺A1∘A•≥A2∘A and A1•≥A2⟺A∘A1•≥A∘A2	∈ℑ: A•≥B or B•≥C ⟹ A•≥C
Axiom5:(Weak Monotonicity) If A1•≥A2 ⟹A1∘A•≥A2∘A	where A1≈A2 iff A1•≥A2 and	MRB3: (Dominance) ∀ A ⊇ B⟹ A •≥ B
Axiom6: (Archimedian Axiom) If A3•>A4, then for any A1 and A2 there exists a natural number n such that A1∘nA3•>A2∘nA4	A2•≥A1 and A1•>A2 iffA1•≥A2 and not (A2•≥A1)	MRB4: (Partial Monotonicity) ∀A⊃B,A∩C=ϕ ⟹ (A•≥B ⟹AUC•>BUC)
		MRB5: (Positivity) ∀A∈ℑ : A•≥ 0

Fig. 2. Zuse framework [15] properties (courtesy [6])

For validation of our metrics, consider an empirical relational system denoted as $S = (S, • ≥, ∘)$, where S represents set of fact schemes (a non-empty set), $• ≥$ represents an empirical relation *"equally or more complex"* on S and $∘$ represents a closed binary operation (concatenation) on S. The fact scheme further comprises of a fact and the dimensions corresponding to that fact. In accordance with Zuse [15], new concatenation operations can be introduced to describe an empirical relation. Following this, *Schema-Concat* is defined as a closed binary concatenation operation $∘$. Figure 3 shows the concatenation of fact schemes S_1 and S_2 using this operation leading to a fact scheme S which comprises all the features of S_1 and S_2, suppressing commonalities (if any) in the original fact schemes, that is, the common features appear only once in the resulting fact scheme S.

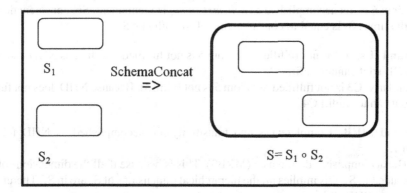

Fig. 3. Concatenation operation on two fact schemes: *SchemeConcat*

The theoretical validation of two metrics, namely, NHD and NSLBD is provided in sub-sections below. Analogously, the formalization of other four metrics (NNHD, NSLWD, NSLAF and NNSH) is done.

3.1   Characterization of NHD

NHD is described as a mapping function *NHD: S -> R* (*S* and *R* represents sets of fact schemes and real numbers respectively), such that the following is true for all fact schemes S_m and $S_n \in$ S: $S_m \bullet \geq S_n \Leftrightarrow NHD\ (S_m) \geq NHD\ (S_n)$.

Also, the rule for concatenation is defined as: $NHD\ (S_m \circ S_n) = NHD\ (S_m) + NHD\ (S_n) - c$, that is, the no. of hierarchical dimensions obtained after concatenation of S_m and S_n equals the total of the no. of hierarchical dimensions of S_m and S_n, considering the hierarchical dimensions common to S_m and S_n only once.

NHD and MES. NHD accomplishes the weak order by its definition. Consider 3 fact schemes S_1, S_2 and S_3 of a multidimensional model. Obviously, $NHD\ (S_1) \geq NHD\ (S_2)$ or $NHD\ (S_2) \geq NHD\ (S_1)$. Besides, if $NHD\ (S_1) \geq NHD\ (S_2)$ and $NHD\ (S_2) \geq NHD\ (S_3)$, this implies that $NHD\ (S_1) \geq NHD\ (S_3)$.

Positivity (axiom 2) is also accomplished by the definition of this metric. $NHD\ (S_1 \circ S_2)$ is always greater than or equal to $NHD\ (S_1)$. If there are no hierarchical dimension in S_2, then $NHD\ (S_1 \circ S_2) = NHD\ (S_1)$, or else, $NHD\ (S_1 \circ S_2) > NHD\ (S_1)$.

As the count of hierarchical dimensions is independent of the order in which fact schemes are concatenated using *SchemeConcat*, so axiom 3 is also fulfilled by NHD.

Axiom 4 is also fulfilled. Consider the definition of *SchemeConcat*, the sequence followed for concatenation of fact schemes has no affect on NHD value

Axiom 5 is not fulfilled. Suppose, $NHD\ (S_1) \geq NHD\ (S_2)$. Now, on concatenating S to both S_1 and S_2, NHD $(S_1 \circ S)$ may not be greater than or equal to NHD $(S_2 \circ S)$ as there may be some hierarchy dimensions of S common to S_1 and not S_2, leading to suppressing the value of NHD $(S_1 \circ S)$ in comparison to NHD $(S_2 \circ S)$.

Axiom 6 is not accomplished as *SchemeConcat* is idempotent. So, concatenation of S_1 with *i* times S_2 is equal to concatenation of S_1 with one S_2.

NHD and ICs. C1 is not fulfilled as axiom 5 is not fulfilled. Further, as NHD does not fulfill C1, so it cannot fulfill C2.

Similarly, C3 is not fulfilled as axiom 5 is not fulfilled. Because NHD does not fulfill C3, so it cannot fulfill C4.

NHD and MRB. Completeness and transitivity are accomplished as NHD fulfills axiom 1.

NHD accomplishes dominance (MRB3). This is because if all the dimensions of S_2 are included in S_1, this implies all the hierarchical dimensions of S_2 are in S_1. Therefore, $NHD\ (S_1 \geq NHD\ (S_2)$.

MRB4 is accomplished because if $S_1 \subset S_2$, then $NHD\ (S_1) > NHD\ (S_2)$. Now, let us consider S_3 having no common hierarchical dimensions with S_1. Then, S_3 cannot have hierarchical dimensions common with S_2 also. So, $NHD\ (S_1 \circ S_3) > NHD\ (S_2 \circ S_3)$.

MRB5 is accomplished. This is because if S has no hierarchical dimension, then $NHD (S) = 0$, but it cannot take negative value.

So, NHD is "*above*" the ordinal scale. As already mentioned, the validation of NNHD and NNSH can be carried out analogously.

3.2   Characterization of NSLBD

NSLBD is described as a mapping function $NSLBD: S -> R$ (S and R represents sets of fact schemes and real numbers respectively), such that the following is true for relations between fact schemes S_m and $S_n \in S$: $S_m \bullet \geq S_n \Leftrightarrow NSLBD (S_m) \geq NSLBD (S_n)$.

Also, the rule for concatenation is defined as: $NSLBD (S_m \circ S_n) = NSLBD (S_m) + NSLBD (S_n) + c$, that is, the number of shared levels between dimensions obtained after concatenation of S_m and S_n equals the total of shared levels between dimensions belonging to S_m and those of S_n, adding the number of levels shared across the fact schemes S_m and S_n. Here, $c = 0$ if there is no sharing of hierarchy levels across these fact schemes.

NSLBD and MES.   This metric accomplishes the first axiom by its definition.

Positivity is also accomplished by its definition. $NSLBD (S_1 \circ S_2)$ is always more than or equal to $NSLBD (S_1)$.

As the value of NSLBD is independent of the order of the fact schemes on applying SchemeConcat, so axiom 3 is also accomplished by this metric.

Axiom 4 is also fulfilled. Consider the definition of SchemeConcat, the sequence followed for concatenation of fact schemes has no affect on NSLBD value.

Axiom 5 is not fulfilled. Suppose $NSLBD (S_1) \geq NSLBD (S_2)$. Now, on concatenating S to both S_1 and S_2, $NSLBD (S_1 \circ S)$ may not be greater than or equal to $NSLBD (S_2 \circ S)$. This may happen when the hierarchy levels are shared across S_2 and S, which now become shared between dimensions of the resultant fact scheme obtained after applying concatenation operation $NSLBD (S_2 \circ S)$.

Axiom 6 is not accomplished as SchemeConcat is idempotent. So, concatenation of S_1 with i times S_2 is equal to concatenation of S_1 with one S_2.

NSLBD and ICs.   C1 is not accomplished as axiom 5 is not satisfied. Further, as NSLBD does not fulfill C1, so it cannot fulfill C2.

Similarly, C3 is not fulfilled as axiom 5 is not satisfied. Because NSLBD does not fulfill C3, so it cannot fulfill C4.

NSLBD and MRB.   Completeness and transitivity are satisfied as NSLBD satisfies axiom 1.

NSLBD accomplishes dominance. This is because if all the dimensions of S_2 are included in S_1, this implies all the hierarchy levels shared between dimensions of S_2 are also included in S_1. Therefore, $NSLBD (S_1) \geq NSLBD (S_2)$.

MRB4 is satisfied because if $S_1 \subset S_2$, this implies $NSLBD (S_1) > NSLBD (S_2)$. Now, let us consider S_3 having no hierarchy levels shared with S_1. Then, S_3 cannot have hierarchy levels shared with S_2 also. So, $NSLBD (S_1 \circ S_3) > NSLBD (S_2 \circ S_3)$.

Positivity is accomplished due to the reason that if S has no hierarchy levels shared between its dimensions, then *NSLBD (S) = 0*, but can never be negative.

So, NSLBD is "*above*" the ordinal scale. As already mentioned, the validation of NSLWD and NSLAF can be carried out analogously.

To summarize, we can characterize all the six metrics considered in this paper as "*above*" ordinal scale; thereby they are theoretically valid and useful metrics. As rightly said by Zuse [15], it is imperative to characterization metrics "*above*" the ordinal scale as not much analysis can be carried with ordinal numbers.

4   Conclusion and Future Work

Metrics play significant role in determining DWMD model quality. This paper considers authors' previously proposed structural metrics based on important concepts of dimension hierarchies and sharing of hierarchy levels within/across fact schemes in DWMD models. Thorough validation of metrics can ensure their practical usefulness. So, the detailed formal validation of our metrics using a measurement-theoretic framework (given by Zuse) is carried out. The obtained results of formal evaluation suggest that all these metrics are "*above*" the ordinal scale; thereby they are theoretically valid and useful metrics. As a future work, the empirical validation of these metrics would be done to find their relationship to various external quality attributes.

References

1. Adamson, C.: The Star Schema Handbook: The Complete Reference to Dimensional Data Warehouse Design. Wiley, Hoboken (2009)
2. Abelló, A., Samos, J., Saltor, F.: A framework for the classification and description of multidimensional data models. In: Mayr, Heinrich C., Lazansky, J., Quirchmayr, G., Vogel, P. (eds.) DEXA 2001. LNCS, vol. 2113, pp. 668–677. Springer, Heidelberg (2001). https://doi.org/10.1007/3-540-44759-8_65
3. Trujillo, J., Palomar, M., Gomez, J., Song, I.Y.: Designing data warehouses with OO conceptual models. IEEE Comput. **34**(12), 66–75 (2001). Special issue on Data Warehouses
4. Gosain, A., Singh, J.: Conceptual multidimensional modeling for data warehouses: a survey. In: Satapathy, S.C., Biswal, B.N., Udgata, S.K., Mandal, J.K. (eds.) Proceedings of the 3rd International Conference on Frontiers of Intelligent Computing: Theory and Applications (FICTA) 2014. AISC, vol. 327, pp. 305–316. Springer, Cham (2015). https://doi.org/10.1007/978-3-319-11933-5_33
5. Fenton, N.E.: Software metrics: theory, tools and validation. Softw. Eng. J. **5**(1), 65–78 (1990)
6. Calero, C., Piattini, M., Pascual, C., Serrano, M.: Towards data warehouse quality metrics. In: Proceedings of Third International Workshop on Design and Management of Data Warehouse, Interlaken, Switzerland (2001)
7. Serrano, M., Calero, C., Sahraouli, H., Piattini, M.: Empirical studies to assess the understandability of data warehouse schemas using structural metrics. Softw. Qual. J. **16**(1), 79–106 (2008)
8. Cherfi, S.S.-S., Prat, N.: Multidimensional schemas quality: assessing and balancing analyzability and simplicity. In: Jeusfeld, M.A., Pastor, Ó. (eds.) ER 2003. LNCS, vol. 2814, pp. 140–151. Springer, Heidelberg (2003). https://doi.org/10.1007/978-3-540-39597-3_14

9. Serrano, M: Definition of a set of metrics for assuring data warehouse quality, Univerisity of Castilla, La Mancha, Spain (2004)
10. Berenguer, G., Romero, R., Trujillo, J., Serrano, M., Piattini, M.: A set of quality indicators and their corresponding metrics for conceptual models of data warehouses. In: Tjoa, A.M., Trujillo, J. (eds.) DaWaK 2005. LNCS, vol. 3589, pp. 95–104. Springer, Heidelberg (2005). https://doi.org/10.1007/11546849_10
11. Gosain, A., Nagpal, S., Sabharwal, S.: Quality metrics for conceptual models for data warehouse focusing on dimension hierarchies. ACM SIGSOFT Softw. Eng. Notes **36**(4), 1–5 (2011)
12. Nagpal, S., Gosain, A., Sabharwal, S.: Complexity metric for multidimensional models for data warehouse. In: Proceedings of the CUBE International Information Technology Conference, pp. 360–365. ACM (2012)
13. Gosain, A., Singh, J.: Quality metrics for data warehouse multidimensional models with focus on dimension hierarchy sharing. In: El-Alfy, E.S., Thampi, S., Takagi, H., Piramuthu, S., Hanne, T. (eds.) Advances in Intelligent Informatics. AISC, vol. 320, pp. 429–443. Springer, Cham (2015). https://doi.org/10.1007/978-3-319-11218-3_39
14. Briand, L.C., Morasca, S., Basili, V.R.: Property based software engineering measurement. IEEE Trans. Softw. Eng. **22**, 68–86 (1996)
15. Zuse, H.: A Framework of Software Measurement. Walter de Gruyter, Berlin (1998)
16. Gosain, A., Singh, J.: Quality metrics emphasizing dimension hierarchy sharing in multidimensional models for data warehouse: a theoretical and empirical evaluation. Int. J. Syst. Assur. Eng. Manag. **8**, 1672–1688 (2017). https://doi.org/10.1007/s13198-017-0641-5

Financial Data Mining: Appropriate Selection of Tools, Techniques and Algorithms

Akash Saxena[1], Navneet Sharma[2], Khushoo Saxena[3], and Satyen M. Parikh[4(✉)]

[1] Compucom Institute of Information Technology and Management, Jaipur, India
akash27saxena@gmail.com
[2] The IIS University, Jaipur, India
navneet.sharma@iisuniv.ac.in
[3] Institute of Science and Technology Bhopal, Bhopal, India
kskhushboosaxena26@gmail.com
[4] Ganpat University, Kherva, India
parikhsatyen@yahoo.com

Abstract. In finance domain, to make any decision data mining is required. The application of data mining in finance includes measuring credibility for loan, identifying fraud transactions, Correctness of information provided at the time of Insurance, Select the right stock for investment decision etc. Selections of data mining algorithm and also data mining tools/techniques are critical decision and very important to achieve desired outcomes. This paper is aimed to help users in this selection by mapping his business requirement. Three different aspects of selection are considered. First aspect is comparative strength of algorithms and requirement, while second is mapping of tool as per clarity in vision and execution ability and finally third aspect is based on statistics of survey reports from social media (global users' feedback). This paper discussed these three aspects in-depth. One can map his requirements with details provided and complete decision related to selection of data mining for financial application needs.

Keywords: Data mining · Neural network · Social media · Data science
Big data

1 Introduction

Data mining, uncover the hidden information from large databases, is a concrete latest technology. The intension of Data mining is to collect required related information from large data base. As the requirement of Data analytics is increased companies are searching for more and more reliable application of data mining and business intelligence [1, 2]. The use of data-mining is diversified. The following list shows the list of data mining in finance: [3, 4]

(i) Market Analysis
(ii) Credit and other Fraud Detection
(iii) Customer Relation Management
(iv) Finance

© Springer Nature Singapore Pte Ltd. 2018
A. V. Deshpande et al. (Eds.): SmartCom 2017, CCIS 876, pp. 244–251, 2018.
https://doi.org/10.1007/978-981-13-1423-0_27

(v) Production Management
(vi) Science Investigation.

The main role of data mining is to facilitate effective decision making using classi-fication, ranking and forecasting algorithms depends on requirements. As financial domain is an important leader in worldwide businesses, enormous applications of data-mining used in finance for data-analysis, data interpretation, data processing, data science, data visualization and even for data breach protection. Here we will discuss about the comparisons of Data Mining methods used for Financial Task. Many Tech-niques and algorithms are available now a days because of that we become confuse that which techniques, algorithm should be used that fulfill our requirements. Financial Prediction related to financial market and relevant products like stock market, exchange rate in currency market, Classification is needed to differentiate Non-performing assets is essential to understand and manage financial risk [5].

Ranking is needed to identify appropriate stock of company based on versatile parameters to and it has ability to addressed most of the challenges of market dynamics using data-mining model of big data [6].

Select of particular tool or algorithm to address the problem is critical decision. In this paper we are going to discuss basically three methodologies for selecting tool or algorithm well-matched with the requirements.

First we are going to discuss and compare the various algorithms based on their basic characteristics. It helps us to match required parameter with the featured available in existing algorithms and choose an appropriate algorithm. Another classification is based on data mining tools classification as Challengers, Leaders, Niche players and Visiona-ries. These classifications are given by Gartner, and may be useful to decide a tool of interest. At last we discuss about feedback on particular tools or technology on the basis of social media feedback. This survey results is also play an important role to take final decision [7].

2 Data Mining Algorithms

Various Financial algorithms are available, which are used in data-mining requirement of business requirement. Let take brief about it and compare, so one can opt a particular algorithm of his/her choice [7].

The widely used tools/techniques are:

1. Artificial Neural Networks
2. Genetic Algorithms
3. Statistical Interference
4. Rule Induction.

However each of these technique has different role like ANN is best suited for classification and forecasting applications, while Genetic algorithm is best suited for search algorithm, Statistical inference used to make proposition about the population, while rule induction used in deep learning where rules are extracted from set of obser-vations [8].

Artificial Neural Networks: An artificial neural network (ANN) is mathematical model based on our biological human neural networks. Like biological neural networks, ANN consists of interconnected group of artificial neurons, which can collectively processes information. ANN has ability to learn from information and use it further for application purposes. Neural networks applications broadly include ranking, classifications, machine learning and forecasting to the data mining industry. Due to its precise prediction ability than the statistical methods, many financial applications prefer to use ANN [9].

Genetic Algorithms: Genetic algorithm is inspired by Darwin's theory of evolution and provides powerful search technique and widely used in search application, which empowers knowledge discovery from the datasets. Genetic Algorithms is based on chromosomes theory, in which different chromosomes forms a genotype with characteristics genes.

Statistical Interference: Statistical Interference method is based on parameters of population results and consistency of statistical interaction on the basis of random sampling.

Rule Induction: Rule Induction is the symbolic demonstration of facts resulting from data. It is natural and easy method. Based on human inspection and analysis concept, it applies to get the solution.

2.1 Comparative Study

Comparison of these algorithms based on important parameters like coding complexity, Flexibility, independence, Interpretability, Ability to optimize, Scalability, Accessibility give more clarity about the selection of particular algorithm, hence compare advantage and disadvantage of particular algorithm [10].

	Artificial neural networks	Genetic algorithms	Statistical interference	Rule induction
Accessibility	High	Low	Very high	High
Coding complexity	High	Very high	Low	Very low
Flexibility	High	Medium	Medium	Low
Independence	High	High	Low	Low
Interpretability	Very low	High	Medium	Very high
Optimization ability	Medium	High	Medium	Medium
Scalability	Very high	Medium	Medium	Very low

3   Classification of Data Mining Tools

Based on Gartner report classification is based on data mining tools as Challengers, Leaders, Niche players and Visionaries. Someone may found this classification useful to decide a specific tool of interest (Fig. 1).

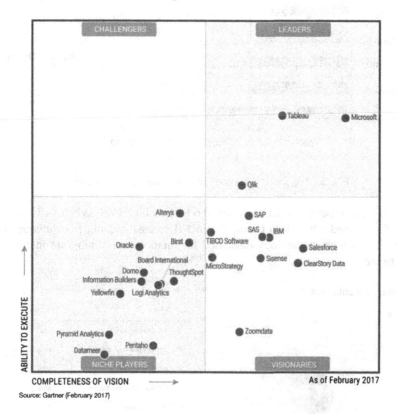

Fig. 1. Classification of data mining tools (source Gartner report feb-2017)

4   Social Media Tools Preference for Data Mining Tools/Technology

In this section we are presenting the details of feedback on particular tools or technology on the based on social media survey. We believe that this survey results plays an important role to take final decision [11].

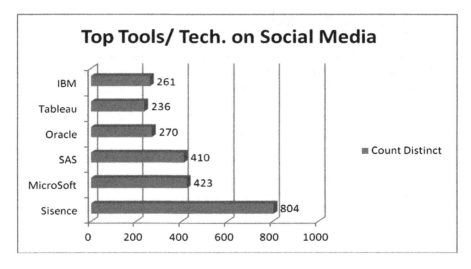

Fig. 2. Top tools/technology discusses based on social media

Based on top count distinct we selected 6 tools, which were as below.

On Social media based on Count Distinct (Discussion count from unique author/source), The top six technology discussed for finance data mining are mentioned in above figure.

What drives Sentiment ?

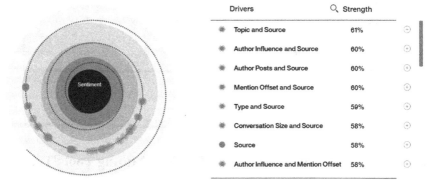

Fig. 3. Sentiments drivers on social media analysis for finance data mining

The following figure gives the details of top parameters, which drive sentiments about tool/technology on social media.

The following figure gives the generalize idea that which users sentiments drive the selection of finance data mining tool as a result of survey of various social media sources.

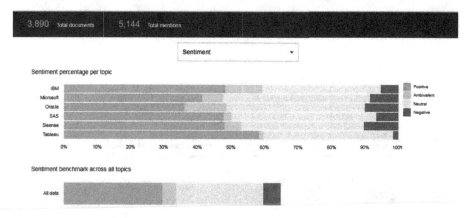

Fig. 4. Sentiments for tools of finance data mining on social media

The above figure shows analysis of users sentiments for top tools/techniques based in social media.

The details of different social media used in survey can be obtained from the following graph.

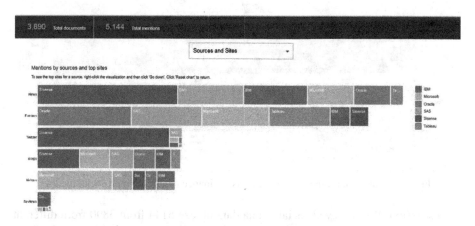

Fig. 5. Source of data with mentioned tools of finance data mining on social media

Different social media sources provide the details of all tools/techniques, News on Web, Twitter, Blogs, and reviews has maximum discussion for Sisence, while Forums has maximum content for Oracle.

The following graph gives idea about users discussion about tools/technology along with the time.

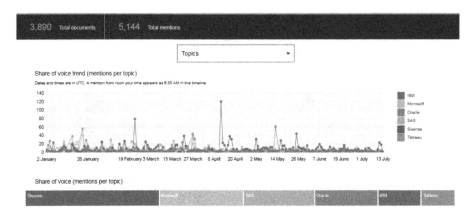

Fig. 6. Details of data on finance data mining tools on social media with time

Demographic participation is described by the following figure:

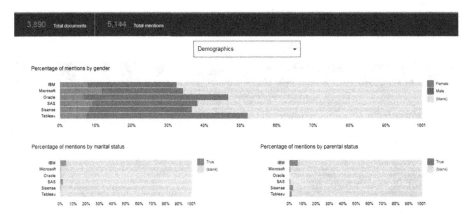

Fig. 7. Demographic sentiments for tools of finance data mining on social media

Discussion: We surveyed social media data of size 5144 from 3890 from different sources using IBM Watson Analytics tool for six months data specified from 1st Jan 2017 to 13 July 2017 and all the figure mentioned in Sect. 4 are showing the details of finance data mining tools discussed on social media. In social media "Sisence" is most discussed tool found in survey (Fig. 2). The sentiment to select tool is mostly influenced by topic and source of social media (Fig. 3). Tableau tool has maximum positive discussion, while Sisence has maximum negative sentiments in collected sample. However all leader tools has more positive sentiments than the negative or neutral sentiments (Fig. 4). The details of sample in different sources can be analyzed from Fig. 5. The details of social media sample for different tool can be viewed for the duration Jan 2017 to July 2017. Tableau was mostly discussed in January and March month, while Sisence was widely discussed in February and April (Fig. 6). The details of sentiments for demography on social media in Fig. 7, Most of female discussed about Microsoft tools, while most of the male discussed about tableau. IBM is most discussed by experienced people, as marital and parental status statistics are favorable for it.

5   Conclusion

The selection of particular tool/technology for data-mining is based on requirement. The paper details compared the technicalities of algorithm; classification of tools based on reports and finally presented details of social media survey. Authors assume that all these approaches collectively helps to understand and match the requirement and select appropriate algorithm, tools and technology well suited with requirements. The details of demographic and source etc. helps to understand the sentiments among the users.

The study is confined within financial domain only. It can be extend to selection of data mining algorithm, tool/techniques in other domains. The paper aimed to help this selection at generalize used. The further work of successive researchers may be helpful to decide further similar decision based on specialized application requirement like identification of credit fraud, prediction of stock value, forecasting of NPS etc.

References

1. Berry, M.J., Linoff, G.: Data Mining Techniques: For Marketing, Sales, and Customer Support. Wiley, Hoboken (1997)
2. Mhetre, N.A., Deshpande, A.V., Mahalle, P.N.: Trust management model based on fuzzy approach for ubiquitous computing. Int. J. Ambient Comput. Intell. (IJACI) 7(2), 33–46 (2016)
3. Shaw, M.J., et al.: Knowledge management and data mining for marketing. Decis. Support Syst. 31(1), 127–137 (2001)
4. Zhang, D., Zhou, L.: Discovering golden nuggets: data mining in financial application. IEEE Trans. Syst. Man Cybern. Part C 34, 513–522 (2004)
5. Nakhaeizadeh, G., Steurer, E., Bartlmae, K.: Banking and Finance. Handbook of Data Mining and Knowledge Discovery. Oxford University Press Inc, Oxford (2002)
6. Parikh, S., Darji, D.N.: Big data analytics model for comprehensive stock market anatomization. Data Min. Knowl. Eng. 9(5), 89–92 (2017)
7. Omand, D.: Social media intelligence (SOCMINT). In: Dover, R., Dylan, H., Goodman, Michael S. (eds.) The Palgrave Handbook of Security, Risk and Intelligence, pp. 355–371. Palgrave Macmillan UK, London (2017). https://doi.org/10.1057/978-1-137-53675-4_20
8. Acharjya, D., Anitha, A.: A comparative study of statistical and rough computing models in predictive data analysis. Int. J. Ambient Comput. Intell. (IJACI) 8(2), 32–51 (2017)
9. Parikh, S.M.: Analysis and modeling a distributed co-operative multi agent system for scaling-up business intelligence. Dissertation Saurashtra University (2008)
10. Han, J., Pei, J., Kamber, M.: Data mining: concepts and techniques. Elsevier, New York (2011)
11. Hoyt, R.E., et al.: IBM Watson analytics: automating visualization, descriptive, and predictive statistics. JMIR Public Health Surveill., 2(2) (2016)
12. Karaa, W.B.A., Dey, N.: Mining Multimedia Documents. CRC Press, Boca Raton (2017)

Smart and Service Computing

Forecasting Energy Consumption from Smart Home Sensor Network by Deep Learning

Nilanjan Dey[1(✉)], Simon Fong[2], Wei Song[3], and Kyungeun Cho[4]

[1] Department of Information Technology, Techno India College of Technology, Kolkata, India
nilanjan.dey@tict.edu.in
[2] Department of Computer and Information Science, University of Macau, Taipa, Macau SAR
ccfong@umac.mo
[3] Department of Digital Media Technology, North China University of Technology,
Beijing, China
sw@ncut.edu.cn
[4] Department of Multimedia Engineering, Dongguk University,
Seoul, South Korea
cke@dongguk.edu

Abstract. Modern smart homes would be equipped with ZigBee sensors that connect home appliances via IoT network. Forecasting the future use of energy for the home appliances would be useful and practical for the home users. Since IoT sensors are designed to collect information in real-time from the home appliances, that include energy usage, indoor/outdoor temperatures and relative humidity measures, the data for harvesting insights should be abundant. Computationally a challenge is to seek for a most appropriate time-series forecasting algorithm that can produce the most accurate results. The difference between the traditional time-series forecasting algorithms and the one that involves IoT data is the ability to learn from the sheer volume of IoT data, which is known as big data nowadays. The sensor data can amount to a huge volume, and the energy drawn from an appliance, for example, air-conditioner can depend on multiple factors – the temperature/humidity of surrounding regions as well as the current weather at the time of the day. In this paper, such forecasting is tested with a range of time-series algorithms including the classical ones in comparison with deep learning which is acclaimed as a suitable prediction tool for learning over very non-linear and complex patterns.

Keywords: IoT smart home · Energy prediction · Time-series forecasting
Deep learning

1 Introduction

Wireless sensor network technology such as those with a low-cost ZigBee standard, are becoming increasingly popular and affordable [1]. It enables ubiquitous connectivity within individual households and wide urban or rural areas, linking up data feeds from users' end-appliances to some central data repository, via sinks, gateways and cloud technologies [2]. This emerging ICT technological trend known as Internet of Things

© Springer Nature Singapore Pte Ltd. 2018
A. V. Deshpande et al. (Eds.): SmartCom 2017, CCIS 876, pp. 255–265, 2018.
https://doi.org/10.1007/978-981-13-1423-0_28

(IoT) facilitates smart controlling system for home appliances for smart home applications is ever prevalent [3, 4]. Some typical IoT solutions include traffic scheduling and control, emergency and healthcare services provisions [5], that involve mobile data sources or data generators. One application that has a profound potential economic impact is on energy management, where the consumers' appliances, via IoT devices are remotely linked up into an energy management system [6, 7]. With the infrastructure in place and energy monitoring applications up and running, massive amounts of data are accumulated, awaiting suitable data mining algorithms to be applied and to discover useful insights [8].

Sensor data or sensor data streams which are continuous in nature, are one of the big data. While a large volume of telemetry data from multitude of sensors over the monitoring objects (such as electricity uses, atmospheric measures and localization information) are generated and received, it is essential for suitable real-time analytic tools to analyze/forecast the conditions of the functioning objects and their surroundings. From the perspective of data analytics, one of the two important purposes from analyzing such sensor data specifically in energy management is to understand the energy consumption patterns which reflect about the users' behaviors and lifestyles. Being able to model and forecast accurately about the future usage patterns, the electricity load generation and their distributions can be optimized, meeting precisely the demands by the controlled supplies. This is usually done at the back-end, crunching over a large archive of big data accumulated over a long time, so to learn the overall longitudinal patterns and perhaps seasonally changing patterns. The other purpose, is to understand from the data prediction model the importance of factors that lead to such a forecast, be it high or low. Knowing the relative importance of each factor or attribute of the data because it offers insights about what actually caused the rise or fall of the usage trend. Especially in smart home environment, where different areas of the house are installed with different sensors, the changes in electricity usage at the appliance (for example, air-conditioner or heater) may depend on multiple factors. For instance a heavy usage of occupancy of a room may imply the opposite of the other rooms, assuming the home users (a family) exhibit certain lifestyle or patterns of moving around rooms which are never random. Interdependency, correlations and even causality should be paid attention to.

2 Related Work

In the literature, many machine learning models have been studied for predicting energy uses. For instance, Mocanu et al. [9], compared the stochastic model, namely the Conditional Restricted Boltzmann Machine, to Hidden Markov Models and Artificial Neural Networks, for time-series prediction of energy consumption. The dataset is real, taken from a Dutch office building over seven weeks of electricity consumption sampled at hourly resolution. Parra Jr. and Kiekintveld [10], attempted to predict customers' demand in an energy market using a Trading Agent Competition system called PowerTAC. The machine learning was done using a Weka toolkit, with algorithms such as k-Nearest Neighbors Online, Linear regression, and various versions of decision trees. The prediction problem which they put forth is to predict how much energy a specific consumer will use at a future time slot. They have found that the forecasting is more than a time-series forecasting problem as in the real life, the electricity usage by a consumer depends on many different factors such as the weather, time of the day, and the consumer's complex living conditions which do change over time etc. Sahai [11], used other machine learning methods such as Support Vector Machines and Artificial Neural Network, as well as suggesting using Gibbs sampling, Ridge regression, Mean field value, RBF kernel. He used Principal Component Analysis (PCA) which is based on generating linearly uncorrelated variables called principal components to find relations between the factors from a data set of multiple correlated variables. He tried to find correlation amongst different weather parameters and green energy availability, etc. Lachut et al. [12], studied the same problem but by investigating the predictability of power consumption of individual appliances and house energy consumption at four future time scales, hourly, quarter-daily, full daily, and weekly. Popular machine learning methods were used, k-Nearest Neighbor (naïve version), Bayesian Network, Support Vector Machine and a classical time-series forecasting method called Autoregression and Moving Average. The power consumption dataset that Lachut et al. produced come from appliances and whole house energy draws that are sequentially gathered over three years, across seven houses from Arkansas, Maryland, and California. The houses are equipped with solar panels while some are powered entirely by power grid. What all these datasets used most of the works in the literature which we reviewed above are based on full historical weather data and full archive of energy consumption datasets over a certain long period of time.

To this end, it is worth noting that most of the studies of energy prediction using machine learning tools are based on static historical records. As sensor data are known to be big data, they potentially amount to infinity without bound. Recently some researchers turned their attentions to deep learning, which is characterized by having many hidden layers in a neural network. The advantage of deep learning model is its ability to learn complex and non-linear patterns over a large volume of data. To the best of the authors' knowledge, there is no performance evaluation work published about using deep learning neural network to be used over energy data stream for IoT smart home scenario. A technical challenge in this type of big energy pattern data forecasting is to find a most appropriate time-series forecasting algorithm that can produce the most accurate results. The difference between the traditional time-series forecasting algorithms and the one that involves IoT big data is the ability to learn from the sheer volume of IoT data, which is known to be archived at big data repository nowadays. In this paper, such forecasting is experimented using a range of time-series algorithms including the classical algorithms in comparison with deep learning. In this experiment, an evolving deep learning model is used. Since we do not know in advance how complex the time-series is going to be, it is neither known how many hidden layers nor how large the neural network configuration should scale up to. Therefore an evolutionary type of neural network called Group Method Data Handling (GMDH) is used. GMDH expands the network complexity iteratively until the additional growth yields no further performance improvement.

The reminder of the paper is structured as follow, after the introduction and related work discussed above: The GMDH model is described in Sect. 3. Section 4 presents the experiment and description of the energy dataset that is subject to the performance evaluation using some popular time-series forecasting algorithms and GMDH neural network. Section 5 shows the experiment results followed by the discussion of the results. Section 6 concludes the paper.

3   GMDH as Evolving Deep Learning Neural Network

Originally invented by Ivakhnenko in [13], GMDH is regarded as an earliest prototype of deep learning model. It is powered by predictive modeling mechanism that evolves a neural network until it reaches the maximum possible accuracy at the marginal model complexity. GMDH works by self-tuning the model's coefficients and parameters via data sampling across an iterative and evolutionary process which incrementally enlarges the network size. One can expect that under the hood of GMDH it is an evolutionary type of optimization process which heuristically improve and complicate the model by increasing its neurons under the observation of marginal performance improvement. The simplified form of such iterative optimization could be represented by Eq. 1 where the candidate model increases its performance with minimum scaling up of complexity.

$$\overline{\zeta} = \arg \min_{\zeta \subseteq Z} Opt(\zeta) \tag{1}$$

where $Opt(\zeta)$ is an external optimization process which monitors the increment of accuracy or the decrement of the optimal model ζ, from the collection of candidate models Z. Serving as construction blocks, the GMDH candidate models can be viewed as some nonlinear multi-parametric equation: $y = h(x_1, \ldots, x_n)$. The function $h()$ maps the relation between the n input variables, $x_1, \ldots, x_n$ which forms a vector $\overline{x}$, and the estimated output of y. For computing the coefficients which are variables that represent the links between neurons as "weights", the equation can be extended into a polynomial series. This is the format of mapping or model which a GMDH model takes, and it is shown in Eq. 2.

$$y = a_0 + \sum_i a_i x_i + \sum_i \sum_j a_{i,j} x_i x_j + \sum_i \sum_j \sum_k a_{i,j,k} x_i x_j x_k + \ldots \tag{2}$$

This polynomial series is named after the Kolmogorov-Gabor's polynomial which is later developed into the concept of GMDH which stands for Group-method-data-handling approach. It is designed based on the basic theorem which tells that any function $y = h(\overline{x})$ could be induced by a vector of coefficients $\overline{a}$. Such vector of coefficient vector is supposed to be found out from the GMDH process by establishing an accurate regression polynomial series. Given the appropriate coefficients Computed by the GMDH process, when the suitable coefficients values are used, they can be associated with $\overline{x}$, which are the observation variables in the polynomial equation, an outcome y is then forecasted as a result.

Two common variants of implementation of GMDH are Combinatorial GMDH called COMBI [14] and Polynomial Neural Networks called Multilayer Iterative GMDH or just MIA [15]. They differ in the learning logics that govern how GMDH evolves. It could come in a simple combinatorial type which rises up the power as the polynomial extends. The other variant expands the configuration of a feed-forward neural network iteratively starting with only 2 neurons to a complex structure of deep learning network. Readers are referred to [15] for more details about the two versions of GMDH.

4   Comparison Experiment

The computer simulation experiment reported in this paper has two objectives: firstly we compare the performance between classical time-series forecasting algorithms and deep learning by GMDH over IoT big data time-series; and secondly we investigate the relative importance of factors that lead to the forecasted result. A total of 10 time-series forecasting algorithms are used in the performance evaluations, including the variants of the GMDH deep learning family. They are: (1) Single Exponential Smoothing, (2) ARIMA, (3) Linear Regression, (4) Support Vector Machine, (5) Feed-forward Neural Network, (6) Random Forest, (7) GMDH-Combi, (8) GMDH-MIA-linear, (9) GMDH-MIA-first-order and (10) GMDH-MIA-power-series. It is noted that the algorithms 1 and 2 are classical time-series forecasting algorithms; algorithms from 3 to 6 are typical machine learning algorithms which are commonly used to model the relations between inputs and output in order to infer a future forecast; the last group of algorithms are deep learning of several variants. GMDH-Combi is the polynomial type of evolutionary neural network that is based on increasing the coefficient values of a polynomial formula for implementing up a deep learning model. As the coefficient values and multitude increase, the model becomes more complicated. The remaining three algorithms are variants of GMDH truly neural network configurations – MIA-linear is based on a linear equation, MIA-first order has a parabola shape and the MIA-power raises the powers of the x sample values to a high degree. Apparently, these variants of MIA are able to model hence learn the relationship between the input variables or samples and the prediction target. The high power learns the most non-linear relationships; MIA-first-order copes with data learning with moderate non-linearity, MIA-linear takes care of the mild or little non-linearity.

In the first experiment, the objective is to compare how accurate the energy prediction performed by different time-series algorithms would be in terms of root mean squared error (RMSE). A 5% hold-out validation method was used for estimating the prediction errors. The dataset is downloaded from UCI data repository; it is donated by Dr. Luis Miguel Candanedo of University of Mons. The dataset is about appliances energy consumption measured at a low energy building, over a period of four and half months at rate of one record per 10 min. The atmospheric data such as temperature and humidity conditions were recorded through a wireless sensor network of ZigBee protocols. The energy use data was wirelessly logged by m-bus indoor energy meters. The indoor data were collected in synchronization with outdoor weather conditions that were obtained from a weather station situated at Chievres Airport, near the building. Two random variables that have no predictive values were added to the data, for the purpose of escalating the challenges for the prediction model. On top of that, the dataset was perpetuated with a random noise generator at 10% noise level – the noises are simulated by modifying the target class values randomly, up to 10% difference from the true values. There are a total of 19735 data instances characterized by 28 attributes. The attributes contain the target value called Appliances which records the energy used in Wh in the past 10 min. The energy usage has minimum and maximum values at 10 Wh and 1080 Wh respectively. The mean is 97.695 Wh and standard deviation is 102.525 Wh. The other attributes are sensor recordings with labels of Tx and RH_x, where x is the identifier of the sensor which is installed in some particular locations of the house. T and RH are variables of temperature and relative humidity readings respectively. The locations of the sensors of various IDs are visualized in Fig. 1.

Fig. 1. (a) Left: blueprint of the first floor of the low energy home; (b) Right: second floor. Image courtesy by https://github.com/LuisM78/Appliances-energy-prediction-data

From the sensor data, it can be seen that the attribute which is also the predication target variable called Appliance has certain seasonality, using auto-correlation analysis by Pearson coefficient. It is shown in Fig. 2.

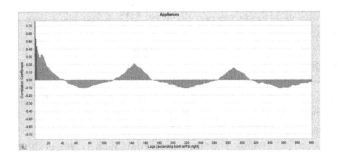

Fig. 2. The time-series called appliances is seasonal.

The other attributes however are non-seasonal. This implies the electricity consumption by probably an air-conditioner fluctuates according to the changes of seasons in an overall scale. The data distributions of the temperature attributes are charted in histogram, shown in Fig. 3.

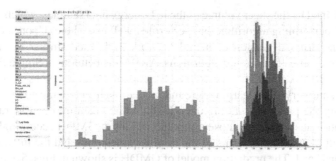

Fig. 3. Data distributions of the temperature attributes

Interestingly, it can be seen that the sensor data T6 has a wide variety in data spread, while the others are relatively tall and narrow. T6 is the only sensor installed outdoor at the patio, the rest of the sensors are indoor. That explains the shapes of the distributions. Given such statistical properties of the data by the different attributes, the data are loaded into the algorithms; the results in RMSE are generated and discussed in Table 1 in the following section.

Table 1. The performance results of energy forecast by using various algorithms in RMSE.

Algorithm type	Name	RMSE
Univariate forecasting	Single exponential smoothing	71.78
Univariate forecasting	ARIMA	65.86
Multivariate modeling	Linear regression	66.92
Multivariate modeling	Support vector machine	66.24
Multivariate modeling	Feed-forward neural network	69.68
Multivariate modeling	Random forest	84.64
Deep learning	GMDH-Combi	68.1
Deep learning	GMDH-MIA-linear	63.23
Deep learning	GMDH-MIA-first-order	64.48
Deep learning	GMDH-MIA-power-series	85.99

5   Results and Discussion

It can be observed clearly from Table 1 that GMDH-MIA-linear achieves the lowest error in RMSE in the forecasting experiment; it indicates that the deep learning by formulating a neural network with linear expansion on its configuration works best for this particular IoT energy dataset. Other types of deep learning in this case do not show advantage. Especially GMDH-MIA that grows by power series has overfit the data badly, resulting in the highest of all at 85.99. Among the machine learning types of algorithms which take the training data as multivariate data, considering over all the attributes, do not however offer superior results in RMSE. In particular, Random Forest falls short of modeling an accurate model despite that it tries out a number of candidate trees each of which was trained with a subset of training data. The under-performance may be explained by the sheer volume of the IoT energy data samples, which overwhelm even a good performing algorithm that performed well elsewhere. Upon such big data, SVM and the original version of neural network performed similar to the standard univariate time-series forecasting algorithms. ARIMA is better than Single Exponential Smoothing; ARIMA actually outperformed the machine learning types of algorithms in this case. In summary, deep learning is found favourable in achieving good performance upon learning the patterns from big data. It should be taken into consideration of the extent of non-linearity, so to choose a suitable variant of GMDH accordingly.

The result of ARIMA in terms of the original time-series and the fitted time-series is depicted in Fig. 4. The prediction model of GMDH is shown in Figs. 5, 6 and 7 which are the original and fitted model, the fitted model only and their forecasting residuals.

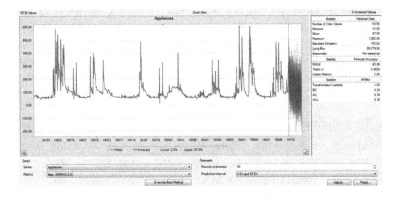

Fig. 4. Prediction model by ARIMA

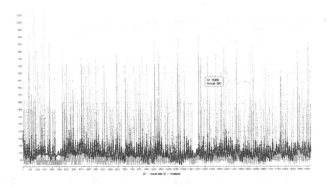

Fig. 5. Prediction model by deep learning GMDH-MIA-linear

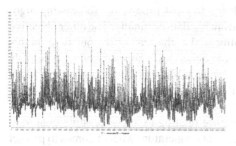 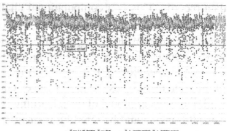

Fig. 6. Model without showing actual data by GMDH-MIA-linear

Fig. 7. Forecasting residuals by GMDH-MIA-linear

From the deep learning neural network, it can offer extra result as the relative importance for the significant variables. In a nutshell, the significant variables are defined by how often they have been used in training up the neural network; it is based on the assumption that the more often the variables have been referred to, when it comes to training/learning and updating the weights which fire the activation function, the variable gets a score. So the results of this case study are telling us that: RH1, RH2 and Lights, each scores 20; RH7 scores 16 and RH8 scores 4. Viewing the sensor positions in Fig. 1, RH1 and RH2 come from sensor 1 and sensor 2 respectively. These sensors are situated at the living room and the dining area of the house. So more relevantly the electricity consumption is related to the occupancy of the users at these two areas. They are the most relevant deciding factors on how much or little energy would be used to power possibly an air-conditioner (cooler or heater). It is therefore inferred that when the users are at home, they would stay there most of the time, while the air-conditioner stays switched on. The third deciding factor is Lights, which hints about whether the users are at home or out of the house. Having the lights on mean that they are home and often using the air-conditioner. Sensors 7 and 8 are installed at the bedroom and ensuite bathroom. Again these are common areas especially at night sleeping, the users would be there. When these areas are occupied, the appliance was turned on drawing electricity. One interesting phenomenon observed is that none o these factors are of temperature. They are rather, relative humidity measures. This implies that temperature is less of a key factor to justify turning on an air-conditioner. It is in fact the humidity; high humidity is known to relate to discomfort as how our human skin feels so. This infers again that electricity consumption by air-conditioner (the so called appliance) has a strong relation to the humidity in air in our surrounding areas.

6   Conclusion

By the recent advances of ZigBee wireless sensor technology, IoT-based smart controlling system for home appliances becomes affordable and popular supporting smart home applications. Data are feeding in continuously, archived in some remote big data waiting for suitable data mining techniques to extract useful intelligence. One important goal of analyzing such sensor data is to forecast the future values based on the big volume of data records. This is a computational challenge to most time-series forecasting algorithms as they were not designed to forecast from big data originally. The other objective is to understand which data attributes are influential to the forecasting outcome. In this paper, a comparison by computer simulation is done in the hope of finding a suitable forecasting technique for accurately forecasting from big data. A comprehensive range of different techniques are tested verses GMDH deep learning methods. It is found that a mild non-linear model of deep learning is able to achieve the lowest error in this case. The attributes could be rated by their importance relating to the forecasting goal. It is found that humidity is a more deciding factor than temperature when it comes to predict about electricity consumption in an appliance. Also sensors that are installed in areas where are frequented by the home users, such as living room, kitchen and bedroom, have greater impact than sensors from other areas with respect to energy forecast.

Acknowledgments. The authors are thankful for the Research Grant "A Scalable Data Stream Mining Methodology", FDCT/126/2014/A3, by Macau government.

References

1. Song, T.-W., Yang, C.-S.: A connectivity improving mechanism for ZigBee wireless sensor networks. In: IEEE/IFIP International Conference on Embedded and Ubiquitous Computing, EUC 2008, 17–20 December 2008, pp. 495–500 (2008)
2. Maity, S., Park, J.H.: Powering IoT devices: a novel design and analysis technique. J. Converg. **7**(2016), 1–18 (2016)
3. Kang, W.M., Moon, S.Y., Park, J.H.: An enhanced security framework for home appliances in smart home. Hum.-Centric Comput. Inf. Sci. **7**(6), 1–12 (2017)
4. Candanedo, L.M., Feldheim, V., Deramaix, D.: Data driven prediction models of energy use of appliances in a low-energy house. Energy Build. **140**(1), 81–97 (2017)
5. Verma, P., Sood, S.K., Kalra, S.: Cloud-centric IoT based student healthcare monitoring framework. J. Ambient Intell. Human. Comput. 1–17 (2017). https://doi.org/10.1007/s12652-017-0520-6
6. Pughat, A., Sharma, V.: A review on stochastic approach for dynamic power management in wireless sensor networks. Hum.-Centric Comput. Inf. Sci. **5**(4), 1–14 (2015)
7. Egarter, D., Monacchi, A., Khatib, T., Elmenreich, W.: Integration of legacy appliances into home energy management systems. J. Ambient Intell. Human. Comput. **7**(2), 171–185 (2016)
8. Finogeev, A.G., Parygin, D.S., Finogeev, A.A.: The convergence computing model for big sensor data mining and knowledge discovery. Hum.-Centric Comput. Inf. Sci. **7**(11), 1–16 (2017)
9. Mocanu, E., Nguyen, P.H., Gibescu, M., Kling, W.L.: Comparison of machine learning methods for estimating energy consumption in buildings. In: 2014 International Conference on Probabilistic Methods Applied to Power Systems (PMAPS), 7–10 July 2014, pp. 1–6 (2014)
10. Parra Jr., J., Kiekintveld, C.: Initial exploration of machine learning to predict customer demand in an energy market simulation. In: Trading Agent Design and Analysis: Papers from the AAAI 2013 Workshop, pp. 29–32 (2013)
11. Sahai, A.: Evaluation of machine learning techniques for green energy prediction. arXiv preprint arXiv:1406.3726, 14 June 2014

12. Lachut, D., Banerjee, N., Rollins, S.: Predictability of energy use in homes. In: 2014 International Green Computing Conference (IGCC), 3–5 November 2014, pp. 1–10 (2014)
13. Ivakhnenko, A.G.: Heuristic self-organization in problems of engineering cybernetics. Automatica **6**, 207–219 (1970)
14. Ivakhnenko, A.G., Zholnarskiy, A.A.: Estimating the coefficients of polynomials in parametric GMDH algorithms by the improved instrumental variables method. J. Autom. Inf. Sci. c/c Avtomatika **25**(3), 25–32 (1992)
15. Fong, S., Nannan, Z., Wong, R.K., Yang, X.-S.: Rare events forecasting using a residual-feedback GMDH neural network. In: IEEE 12th International Conference on Data Mining, OEDM, Brussels, 10 December 2012, pp. 464–473. IEEE (2012)

Predicted Call and Residual Lifetime Based Channel Allocation Model for Primary User Equivalent QoS in Cognitive Radio Cellular Network

Neeta Nathani[1($\boxtimes$)] and G. C. Manna[2]

[1] Department of Electronics Engineering, G.H. Raisoni College of Engineering,
Nagpur, India
neeta_nathani@yahoo.com
[2] Indian Telecommunication Service, BSNL, Jabalpur, India
gcmanna@gmail.com

Abstract. Primary network channels follow binary on-off states with random time duration. Primary User (PU) traffic is observed each hour for channel allocation to secondary user (SU). As per available research works, on placement of SU call request at an instant, the channel allocation processor has to input (a) hourly call arrival rate (λ) of available channels till preceding hour to predict λ for current hour using SARIMA method, (b) Average call holding time in fraction of an hour from channel occupancy statistics and calculate blocking probability of different channels to offer to SU. Further, some optimistic research works excludes busy channels at the instant of SU call offer and selects some particular free channel based on prediction of 'off period lifetime'. All the calculations are based on hourly traffic measurement where as call holding time is in minutes. The allocation of specific PU channel to SU cannot guarantee reliable Quality of Service (QoS). In present paper, PU traffic has been observed each minute for finer analysis. Minute-wise channel occupancy traffic is bumpy in nature, hence, present paper predicts λ using Holt Winters method. Also, at the instant of SU channel request, the channel allocation processor inputs all PU channel status minute-wise, calculates actual mean residual lifetime in minutes for each vacant channel and selects the channel with highest predicted free time. A simulation program runs on data collected from mobile switch of cellular network which creates pseudo-live environment for channel allocation. The present work has compared the MRL method with the other researchers using probabilistic method of channel allocation and MRL method has established as more accurate. The obtained result shows that QoS obtainable to SU is equivalent to PU even during busy hours.

Keywords: Mean residual life time · Cognitive radio · Quality of Service
Channel allocation

© Springer Nature Singapore Pte Ltd. 2018
A. V. Deshpande et al. (Eds.): SmartCom 2017, CCIS 876, pp. 266–278, 2018.
https://doi.org/10.1007/978-981-13-1423-0_29

1 Introduction

With increase of primary user (PU) customer base, the licensed channels have become heavily loaded. Even then, sufficient number of quasi-permanently vacant channels is available [1] which can be deployed as Cognitive Control Channel for out-of-band signaling. In addition, there are dynamically available vacant channels [2] which can be fully allocated for secondary user (SU) traffic.

Allocation of channels to secondary users are done which fulfill certain criterion e.g. interference, spectral efficiency, fairness, energy/battery consumption etc. [3]. Carrier to Interference and Noise Ratio (CINR) is the major factor for throughput and others can be derived. CINR is the ratio of received power from desired transmitter at a distance to that of sum of the received powers from other transmitters at their individual distances plus environmental noise [4]. The Secondary Users (SUs) shall be able to transmit with maximum power, if the CINR at the neighboring receivers is below a threshold i.e. receiver sensitivity, which assumes that the SU has knowledge of the CINR of the neighbouring Primary Users (PUs) [3]. Based on primary CINR received from each secondary user over all channels, a heuristic centralized scheme has been proposed in [5] to assign channels to different secondary users for sensing. The channels list which meet the requirements of missed detection and false alarm probabilities are considered as eligible for cognitive radio. In this analysis, it is assumed that the server running channel allocation algorithm has the knowledge of CINR and channels with poor CINR is excluded from eligible list of data transaction. Having decided the list of eligible channels for a duration, a greedy channel algorithm is set by the central server to allocate channels to each base station [5]. In the present paper, the authors accept the list of eligible channels as basic input of their model for further processing and channel allocation.

In GSM, co-channel interference is taken into consideration at spectrum boundary, but has no effect for timeslot based channel provided timing advance parameter is taken into calculation. In contrast, CDMA is designed to take interference into consideration and SU operation can safely continue as underlay network so-long as the interference is within limit [6]. In the present paper, the authors proposes to utilize traffic data of this part of licensed bands in general and GSM in particular as it is maximum loaded and any calculation based on PU traffic observation shall lead to pessimistic results.

In present paper, SU monitor the call arrivals of PU and stores the traffic information. When a SU has to handle a call, the channel allocation algorithm selects a channel from eligible channel list, check if it is free, estimates the number of PU calls likely to be offered during the hour and their holding time; and assess mean free life time likely to be available for service of SU. This method is repeated for all eligible channels to select the channel with maximum mean free life time. Recent works on channel availability prediction, user holding time prediction and channel residual lifetime prediction algorithms have been discussed in Literature Survey in Sect. 2.

The SUs may function with or without infrastructure. In present paper, we consider SUs as nomadic, less computing intensive and consume least power to have maximum lifetime leaving the responsibilities to infrastructure network. In infrastructure based Cognitive Radio (CR), SUs are located around the Cognitive Radio Base Station

(CR-BS). In response to the service request of SU, one or multiple channels, which have predicted maximum free life time, are allotted by the central server. Cognitive Radio Network architectures are classified as: (a) Cognitive Radio AdHoc Network (CRAHN), (b) Cognitive Wireless Local Area Network (CWLAN), (c) Cognitive Radio Cellular Network (CRCN), (d) Cognitive Wireless Mesh Network (CWMN) and (e) Cognitive Radio Sensor Network (CRSN) [7]. Based on the results obtained in [1, 2], out of band signaling using Cognitive Common Control (CCC) channel [8] can be taken in MAC layer of the CR network. In present paper, a combined evolved CRCN and CRSN network model in Sect. 3 is proposed.

An algorithm has been developed to accept SU service requests with different classified Quality of Service (QoS) [9] from a set of PU channels. Allocation of a PU vacant channel on SU call request is done based on prediction that the channel will remain vacant for more than the assessed holding time of SU. The channel allocation model works based on inputs from (1) the channel call arrival rate prediction model and (2) SU holding time assessment model and has been discussed in Sect. 4. Section 5 discusses logging of live data for several days from channels and active users. The models of Sect. 4 accepts collected data in Sect. 6 as input in time serial manner for running through residual lifetime based prediction model program. The comparison of proposed work has also been done with the model proposed by the authors of [10] and its results and conclusion has been discussed in Sect. 6.

2 Literature Survey

Cognitive Radio utilizes the vacant primary channels which are time varying due to random PU activities. Even after identification of a vacant channel and offered to SU for transmission, selection of the same channel by PU forces SU to switch to another vacant channel for continuation of transmission. However, PU traffic stochastic parameters varies slowly and hence, for a particular period of SU call holding time, channel vacant time can be estimated from channel record data as given in [10]. The authors have studied variation of traffic data during a day consisting of 24 h. A prediction algorithm has been devised for assessment of the probability of no call arrival during the average holding time of SU based on several days data. This algorithm does not include bumpy traffic. The authors have compared their result as equivalent to SARIMA model but claimed their own model as simpler. In addition, the authors have studied the holding time behavior of the channels and arrived at a threshold probability of vacant period above which a free channel can be declared as eligible for handling an incoming SU call. Although a list of eligible channels for offer to SU can be calculated by this method, the preferable channels for allocation to SU in order of merit.

In [11], the authors have modeled the statistical distribution of the availability duration of PU channels as a binary linear programming (BLP) problem which is NP hard and hence computing intensive. The authors have also taken the probability of idle lifetime distribution of vacant channels. Simulation results show no dependence of probability of success on probability of idle lifetime under assumed threshold conditions and hence may be redundant. Prediction of idle times for deterministic and stochastic traffic for maximum likely (ML) time has been considered by authors in [12].

The authors modeled different prediction method for different traffic patterns. This method concentrates on ON/OFF traffic patterns and probable channel switching in a statistical manner only. Spectrum hole prediction based channel allocation scheme has been carried out by the authors in [13]. The authors had predicted non appearance of PU following exponential distribution but linearly added two time periods. Each channel has been divided into small time slots and spectrum holes has been expressed in terms of these time slots. The paper has assumed spectrum holes as multiple of call arrival rate which may not be in order with practical situation.

In [14], the authors have considered an infrastructure based CR network where they have adopted non co-operative spectrum sensing scheme at each CR user. The CR users only send their PU activity monitored data to the base station for further processing. This needs recharging at frequent intervals making it unsuitable for sensors network with long battery life. The authors consider the interference effect on primary as negligible. The use of CR technology by Wireless Sensors has been explained by authors of [15] in Cognitive Radio Sensor Network (CRSN). The network architecture envisages energy sensitive wireless sensors in exclusive clusters with cluster head (CH) as coordinator. CH communicates with CR-BS with a fixed local Common Control Channel (CCC). Channel allocation is done based on optimum energy consumption of SU and no consideration has been done for lifetime to serve SU service request. In [16], for CRSN, the authors has established that channel selection with Reinforcement Learning (RL) system is better than random channel selection method for next generation sensors but threw no light about the lifetime of the selected channel.

In [17], the authors had captured 92 days (2,208 h) of traffic data to study calling behavior of users. They concluded that (1) time scales finer than an hour (minute) are too small to record the calling activity since a call usually lasts 3–5 min, (2) time scales larger than an hour (day) are too coarse to capture. Hence, the common metric employed in telecommunication industry is the hourly number of calls. Accordingly, existing literatures have indicated the need for counting free lifetime of a channel as a probabilistic parameter based on hourly occupied time and hence unaware about residual lifetime, particularly in case of ON/OFF traffic channel conditions.

From above discussion, it is established that no literature has dealt with channel allotment algorithm to SU's based on instantaneous channel status and Residual Mean Lifetime (RML) of the channel and the user holding time behavior. Further, the CR technology is likely to be standardized for infrastructure based sensor network where clusters will communicate on ISM band and using 6LowPAN based sensor to Gateway (Cluster Head-CH) protocol but available literatures are silent about this phenomenon. Present article shall address both these issues and validate the results through live data collected from working mobile network.

3   Evolved Network Architecture

The network architecture is shown in Fig. 1. CR nodes may be combined in exclusive clusters or PANs. The clusters will have a Cluster Head (CH) or Gateway (GW). The CR-GW shall internally coordinate with sensor nodes using standard 6LowPAN based protocols and CR- MAC protocol for GW to CR-BS communication where it will use the vacant channels of licensed band. The GW will be able to handle multi channel multi radio for communication with BS. It will also have a dedicated RF scanner for monitoring licensed channels and inform channel status change to BS at next CCC frame. At the time of access for traffic data, GW-SU transmitter ensures that the access of PU channel do not interfere with PU functioning and CINR at Base Station. Network operators defines various traffic accumulation data counters at BS. These parameters are polled at regular intervals for dynamic record of various RF parameters usually on hourly basis (T) and stored in Operation and Maintenance Centre for Radio (OMC-R) [fusion centre in present case]. One hour time is too long for critical ON/OFF activity observation. Hence, channel status acquisition information need to be polled and updated at fusion centre at rate $\gg \lambda$ (call arrival rate) of the channels, or, in other words, polling time $(\tau) \ll 1/\lambda$ i.e. channel occupancy repetition time. In addition to periodic polling, both (i) the status of the channel change from free state to occupied state and, (ii) SU channel allocation request should be interrupt driven and get instantly registered in Fusion Centre. Channel allocation shall be made by fusion centre from available list of channels for each channel based on: (a) instantaneous channel status i.e. free state; (b) amount of time passed since the channel was free; (c) channel free time behavior prediction during the hour from data warehouse and (d) User call holding time prediction during the hour from data warehouse. Eligible list of channels is thus prepared in order of merit and allocation is made by the switching centre depending upon the user service type request and QoS eligibility of the user.

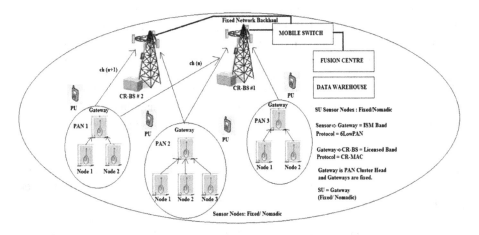

Fig. 1. Cognitive radio cellular and sensor network

4   Channel Allocation Model

The PU channel state shall be considered as $\{H_o, H_1\}$ where, H_o = free and H_1 = occupied. The primary status as sensed or predicted by the SU is shown in Fig. 2. False alarm and missed detection occurs during assessment which leads either to an inefficient system or interference with PU.

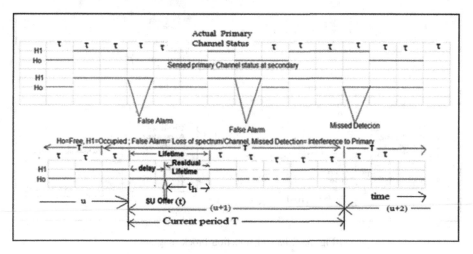

Fig. 2. Channel occupancy in binary state.

Let us consider an unit of time 'τ' which is small enough and minimum time period such that BS can upload scan RF data to Mobile Switching Centre (MSC) and fusion centre without affecting routine CR operation. 'T' is the time period during which the traffic is recorded from pulled data from different counters and used for statistical records e.g. number of seizures of a channel per hour, total holding time of the channel per hour etc. A SU can request for a channel anytime within τ. The request is conveyed to the fusion center where the decision for allocation of a suitable channel is taken based on RML as in Fig. 2 and particular requesting SU's channel holding time profile.

Let λ is the number of calls arrived on a particular traffic data acquisition interval T. If th is the call holding time of a SU requesting a free PU channel at any time t, then the probability that the channel will not be occupied by a PU till t = t + t_h is given by Eq. 1 as:

$$p_0 = \exp\{-(\widehat{\lambda}/T) * \widehat{t_h}\} \text{ for } t_h > \tau \,\&\, t_h > h_p, \tag{1}$$

Where, $\widehat{\lambda}$ = predicted call arrival rate at time t to be determined by Holt-Winter's method,

h_p = predicted optimal holding (service) time, and, $\widehat{t_h}$ = mean of all residual life time (t_h).

As per [17], T will be taken as an hour and (1/λ) in minutes. It is also considered that 'τ' is in minutes. We will further consider that,

(a) τ is the atomic unit of time and further decomposition of it is not practically feasible,
(b) MSC is updated by BS every τ units of time,
(c) MSC updates warehouse every T units of time,
(d) MSC updates SU traffic data in warehouse every T units of time,
(e) Channel occupancy request (PU&SU) is instantly passed on by the BS to MSC in real time t.

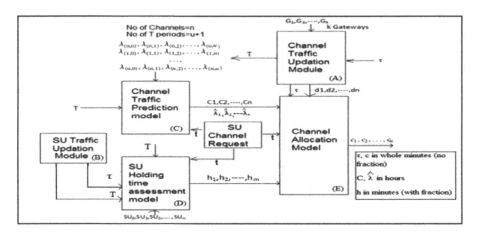

Fig. 3. Channel selection block diagram

The interworking of different blocks for channel allocation is shown in Fig. 3 and is described below:

(A) Channel Traffic Updation: The Gateways (GWs) of Fig. 1 monitor PU activities using dedicated RF scanners. $G_1, G_2, \ldots, G_k$ are responsible for monitoring PU activities as well as for SUs. Any change in channel occupancy is passed on by GW to CR-BS and MSC in real time t. BS maintains several counters for traffic recording purposes. The counts of the counters are polled by MSC every 'τ' interval and then the counters are reset. When $T = k\tau$ where, $k = 2, 3, \ldots$, MSC prepares a table for the call arrival rate for T interval for each channel and deposit to the warehouse where the data is stored in format $\lambda_{(j,u)}$ where, j = channel number and u = current T period number. This module also provides idle time information $d_1, d_2, \ldots, d_3$ etc. in τ units since a channel is free.

(B) SU Traffic Updation Module: SU traffic information is recorded in the billing register after the completion of each call. The traffic details in respect of each SU is stored in warehouse. It is used for predicting holding time of SU at the time of service request.

(C) Channel Traffic Prediction: Primary channel is allotted by network operator according to demand. The channel occupancy is recorded during each T. The traffic pattern of each channel is seasonal in terms of daily traffic. A study of channel occupancy pattern shows that the occupancy varies every hour in a day and again daily occupancy pattern has variations over the days of a week. Seasonal Auto Regressive Integrated Moving Average (SARIMA) uses moving average and auto regression methods which assures sample variations from predicted channel occupancy rate $\widehat{\lambda}_{(j,t)}$ profile as white noise. For further accurate prediction of channel occupancy rate $\widehat{\lambda}_{(j,t)}$ for jth channel at time t shall include three exponential smoothening factors using the Holt-Winters (HW) additive technique.

Thus, the predicted value for $\widehat{\lambda}_{(j,u+1)}$ using HW technique for time period u + 1 for jth channel is given as:

$$\widehat{\lambda}_{(u+1)} = a_u + \tau\, b_u + s_u \tag{2}$$

where,

  a_u is the smoothed estimate of the level at time u,
  b_u is the smoothed estimate of the change in the trend value at time u,
  s_u is the smoothed estimate of the appropriate seasonal component at u.

The list of channels $\{C_1, C_2,...\}$ which satisfies the above condition are predicted during the last hour and are then transferred to the channel allocation model for assessment of holding time during the current hour of allocation.

(D) Channel Allocation model: The proposed work uses empirical Mean Residual Life (MRL) which is defined as:

$$m_n(t) = \frac{\sum_{i=k+1}^{n}(T_{in} - t)}{(n - k)} \text{ for te } \epsilon \left[\Gamma_{kn},\ \Gamma_{(k+1)n}\right] \tag{3}$$

and,

$$m_n(t) = 0 \text{ for } t_e \geq \Gamma_{nn} \text{ and } k = 0, 1, 2, \ldots, (n - 1) \tag{4}$$

where, $m_n(t_e)|_j$ = mean residual lifetime of jth channel which has 'n' number of vacant intervals at observation instant 't' which can be offered a SU call.

  Here, t_e is the time which has elapsed since it became free;
  Γ_j = mean residual lifetime of jth channel at an instant t of SU call offer, and j = 1, 2, ..., r with r = total number of vacant channels at an instant 't' of offer.
  The set of eligible channels are with residual lifetime:

$$t_j = \Gamma_j - h_p > 0 \tag{5}$$

where, h_p = service time needed by SU at time t.
  The eligible channel set $\{c_1, c_2, \ldots, c_r\}$ is arranged and the probability of the success in the offered jth channel shall be:

$$p_{0j} = \exp[-\{\widehat{\lambda}_{(u+1)}/T\} * t_j] \tag{6}$$

  Greedy channel allocation algorithm shall select the channel with highest probability of success as:

$$p_{alloc} = p_{0j} \tag{7}$$

where, $[p_{0j} \geq p_{0,1}; p_{0,2}; p_{0,3}; \ldots; p_{0,r}]$.

5 Simulation Program Flow

The data was chosen at busy hours for various channels ranging from 15 to 50 and minutewise occupancy for 300 min calls is taken for simulation purpose. A program has been developed for real time offering and verification if the call request succeeds or fails for the duration demanded by SU. The program calculates the predicted λ upto last hour at background and has been included in simulation program as offline. Similarly, holding time needed for SU has also been imprinted interactively. The program accepts any number of PU channels upto 50 selectively at the time of trial. The position of occupancy can be seen on screen starting from any instant after 60 min upto 300 min for any duration. Also, one or more SU calls can be offered to the system and minute by minute observation of SU call progress can be monitored on screen.

Traffic data acquisitioned on line each minute is collected in a table in OMC-R. SU can raise service request at any time. To serve channel allocation engine inputs,

(a) At the beginning of each hour, for all channels predicted call arrival rate $\widehat{\lambda}(j, t)$ for the current hour from channel prediction model;
(b) Estimated holding time in minutes for the service request from SU holding time assessment model, and
(c) All channel occupancy status is 'free' or 'busy' mode for last 60 min starting from current minute from channel traffic updation module is taken.

Finally channels with highest probability of survival are selected for offer to the incoming SU traffic.

(I) *PU Call Arrival Rate Prediction*: To produce hourly forecast of call arrival rate, the Holt-Winters (HW) method estimates three components: (1) The current value of call arrival rate (λ) that remains after it is deseasonalized and removal of the effect of random factors (noise), (2) the current trend in call arrival rate, (3) the seasonal index for the forecasting period. As soon as a new predicted value of call arrival rate is available, HW updates its estimates of the level, trend, and seasonal index for that hour. It does this by taking a weighted average of the previous estimates of the component's value and the value suggested by the predicted values of $\widehat{\lambda}$. For each component (level, trend, seasonal) there is a smoothing constant that falls between zero and one. Larger smoothing constants mean more weight is placed on the value suggested by the new predicted value and less on the previous estimate. This means that the method will adapt more quickly to genuine changes in the call arrival pattern.

To compute the predicted value of $\widehat{\lambda}$ using HW method, total number of calls for 46 days was taken for analysis, out of which 35 days of data was taken for prediction of total number of calls for next 11 days, and is shown in Table 1. The predicted data obtained by the set of equations from 2, 3 and 4 was compared with SARIMA in Fig. 4. The trend in HW method with RMS deviation of 38.15 shows that the HW method contains more noisy environment or contains more variation in data as compared to SARIMA with RMS deviation of 50.72 which contains only white Gaussian noise.

Table 1. Call arrival rate prediction using Holt Winter's method.

	AlphaHWA	0.265894368						MSE(HW)	744.2959962
	BetaHWA	0.056342726							
Orig. Data	GammaHWA	1.200591777							
Total Days	Day No.	Week No.	Yt (No. of calls)	at	bt	St	Ft	Et	Et*Et
1	1	1	109			16.2857			
2	2	.	78			-14.714			
3	3	.	51			-41.714			
4	4	.	136			43.2857			
5	5	.	77			-15.714			
6	6	.	95			2.28571			
7	7	.	103	92.7143	-2.7143	10.2857			
8	1	2	65	79.0224	-3.3328	-20.102	106.286	-41.28571429	1704.510204
9	2	.	95	84.7365	-2.8231	15.2738	60.9753	34.02472044	1157.681601
.	.	.	.	.	.	.	.	.	.
.	.	.	.	.	.	.	.	.	.
42	7	.	84	55.1	-1.3973	24.4256	114.385	-30.38541783	923.2736165
43	1	7	79	52.71	-1.4532	25.7402	82.7335	-3.733471251	13.93880759
44	2	.	89	57.2197	-1.1172	35.0827	66.5743	22.42571414	502.9126545
45	3	.	37	54.8814	-1.186	-18.558	41.592	-4.592021712	21.0866634
46	4		50	46.9384	-1.5667	-0.6805	75.4123	-25.41232972	645.7865018

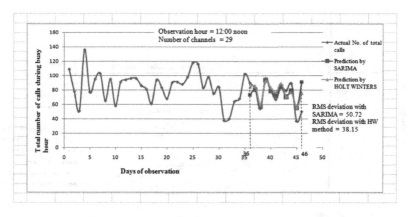

Fig. 4. Hourly traffic prediction and comparison.

(II) *Channel Allocation Process*: The proposed work has compared its method with the methods as described by the authors in [10]. They have used the concept of accessing the channel for SU which is vacant with maximum duration. The program computes probability of success using the method [10], i.e., without MRL and with MRL as proposed in this work. Figure 5 depicts the probability of success with and without MRL for various trunk servers as used by [10] vs. time demanded by CR.

The Fig. 5 clearly depicts that the proposed model using MRL method is superior than the method used by previous researchers [10].

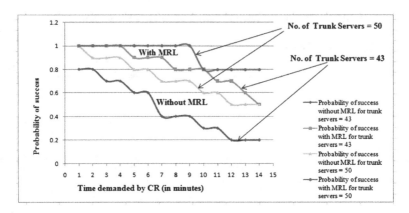

Fig. 5. Comparison of probability of success with and without MRL vs. time demanded by CR for trunk servers = 43 and 50

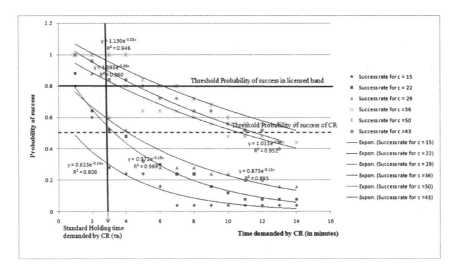

Fig. 6. Probability of success rate vs. time demanded by CR for various trunk servers

(III) *Probability of success under different occupancy*: The program was run repetitively and at random, under various channel availability conditions and differently demanded holding time. The result has been plotted in Fig. 6 where the probability of success (or Quality of Service: QoS) using MRL method has been calculated as:

Probability of success (or QoS) = Number of times call success/Total number of trials,

where, number of trials were 25 times for each run condition at random input time.

In case if the threshold probability in licensed band is taken to be 0.8, the success rate for CR users is still achieved if the channels are equal to greater than 36 with minimum holding time of 2.5 min demanded by the SU. Similarly if the threshold probability for SU is taken to be 0.5, the success rate is achieved if the channels are equal to greater than 22 with minimum holding time of 2.5 min demanded by the SU. The channel occupancy is almost 50% and another 50% is available with instantaneous blocking probability ≤ 0.02, where 0.02 is industry standard for 2% blocking. Thus, the CR-BS will be capable of providing vacant channel to the SU. Grade of Service (GoS) of SU is at par with GoS standard specified for PU when traffic intensity is below 50%. Success rate of channel allocation is increased as number of channels increases in the system.

6 Results and Conclusion

In the present paper, the authors have introduced an evolved CR Personal Area Network architecture to accommodate low traffic long lived sensors which uses ISM band for Sensor-Gateway communication. Hence, unused Primary traffic channels shall be used only for allocation to CR traffic between Gateway and CR-BS. SARIMA model is presently used to predict telecom traffic. The traffic forecasting model used in this paper is based on Holt-Winter's method which has been established to be more accurate than SARIMA model. Also, for PU channel allocation to a requesting SU, the mean residual lifetime (MRL) of the free channels were computed based on requesting SU call holding and the channel with highest MRL is allocated. Results established that CR implementation in PU network based on MRL is competent to provide PU-equivalent Quality of Service and is a superior method as compared to the method used by other researchers. The probability of success increases as the trunk servers increases. Also, the success rate of channel allocation increases as the number of channels increases in the system. The model can be implemented in CR-MAC layer in future with suitable access technologies.

References

1. Nathani, N., Manna, G.C., Mule, S.: An empirical assessment of quasi-permanently vacant channels in mobile communication bands for cognitive radio. In: ICACT Transactions on Advanced Communications Technology (TACT), vol. 3, no. 1, pp. 389–394 (2014)
2. Nathani, N., Manna, G.C., Mule, S.: Dynamically available channel model for cognitive radio in GSM band. In: Proceedings of National Conference on Trends in Signal Processing and Communication (TSPC 2014), 12th–14th April 2014, pp. 8–12 (2014). ISBN: 978-93-83842-40-7
3. Tragos, E.Z., Zeadally, S., Fragkiadakis, A.G., Siris, V.A.: Spectrum assignment in cognitive radio networks: a comprehensive survey. IEEE Commun. Surv. Tutor. 15(3), 1–28 (2013)
4. Katzela, I., Naghshineh, M.: Channel assignment schemes for cellular mobile telecommunication systems. IEEE Commun. Surv. Tutor. 3(2), 10–31 (2009)

5. Wang, W., Behzad, K., Jun, C., Attahiru, S.: Channel assignment of cooperative spectrum sensing in multi-channel cognitive radio networks. In: IEEE ICC 2011 Proceedings, IEEE Communications Society (2011)
6. Xin, Q., Xiang, J.: Joint QoS-aware Admission Control, Channel Assignment, and Power Allocation for Cognitive Radio Cellular Networks. IEEE Xplore (2009)
7. Ahmed, E., Gani, A., Abolfazli, S., Jie Yao, L., Khan, S.: Channel assignment algorithms in cognitive radio networks: taxonomy, open issues, and challenges. IEEE Commun. Surv. Tutor. **18**(1), 795–823 (2016)
8. Kim, W., Kassler, A., Di Felice, M., Gerla, M.: Urban-X: towards distributed channel assignment in cognitive multi-radio mesh networks. In: 2010 IFIP Wireless Days (WD) (2010)
9. Nathani, N., Manna, G.C.: Quality of service challenges for mobile cognitive radio. In: International Conference on Computer Science and Environmental Engineering, Beijing, China, 17–18 May, pp. 967–998. DEStech Publications, Inc. (2015). ISBN 978-1-60595-240-6
10. Li, X., (Reza) Zekavat, S.A.: Cognitive radio based spectrum sharing: evaluating channel availability via traffic pattern prediction. J. Commun. Netw. **11**(2), 104–114 (2009)
11. Haythem, A., Salameh, B.: Probabilistic spectrum assignment for QoS-constrained cognitive radios with parallel transmission capability. IEEE (2012)
12. Hoyhtya, M., Pollin, S., Mammela, A.: Improving the performance of cognitive radios through classification, learning, and predictive channel selection. Adv. Electron. Telecommun. **2**(4), 28–38 (2011)
13. Lee, J., Park, H.: Channel prediction-based channel allocation scheme for multichannel cognitive radio networks. J. Commun. Netw. **16**(2), 209–216 (2014)
14. Canberk, B., Akyildiz, I.F., Oktug, S.: Primary user activity modeling using first-difference filter clustering and correlation in cognitive radio networks. IEEE/ACM Trans. Netw. **19**(1), 170–183 (2011)
15. Li, X., Wang, D., McNair, J., Chen, J.: Residual energy aware channel assignment in cognitive radio sensor networks. In: IEEE WCNC 2011-MAC (2011)
16. Abolarinwa, J., Latiff, N.M.A.A., Yusof, S.K.S., Fisal, N.: Channel decision in cognitive radio enabled sensor networks: a reinforcement learning approach. Int. J. Eng. Technol. (IJET) **7**(4), 1394–1404 (2015)
17. Chen, H., Trajkovic, L.: Trunked radio systems: traffic prediction based on user clusters. In: International Conference on Wireless Communication Systems, September 2004

A Binary Classification Approach to Lead Identification and Qualification

Prasad Gokhale[✉] and Pratima Joshi

Vishwakarma Institute of Technology, Pune, Maharashtra, India
prasad.gokhale@vit.edu, pajoshi@yahoo.com

Abstract. Small and medium sized businesses (SMBs) with a business model of selling their products and services to other SMBs, called as Business-to-Business (B2B) model, are in constant search of new business opportunities and leads. Their prospects and leads identification and qualification process is mostly manual and heavily relies on human intuition and cognitive capabilities. The set of criteria used by sales and marketing teams to identify and qualify leads are limited by the free and public lead information availability. These businesses cannot afford the purchase and licensing costs of traditional Customer Relationship Management (CRM) or Software-as-a-Service tools. Also, the low data volume and limited set of attributes do not justify the investment into such tools. This technical paper proposes a framework to automate the lead identification and qualification process by the combination of a set of automation scripts and data analytics and machine learning models. The proposed framework consists of (a) sales data acquisition, cleansing and pre-processing, (b) data storage, (c) applying classification on stored sales data, and (d) predicting the class of unseen sales data based on the knowledge acquired during training. The paper presents a comparative study of five industry-standard classification and regression algorithms, and also suggests a set of Two-Class Classification algorithms based on the results of experiments performed using low volume as well as high volume data sets.

Keywords: Sales pipeline analytics · Sales pipeline prediction
Business-to-Business · B2B · Classification · Two-class classifiers

1 Introduction

Small and medium sized businesses (SMBs) with a business model of selling services and/or products to other businesses (B2B) are always on the lookout for new business opportunities for their growth. They have to employ a number of techniques to identify and qualify business leads and prospects. Traditionally, the lead identification and qualification has been a manual and time consuming process that relies on human intuition and cognitive capabilities. The sales and marketing teams in SMBs devote most of their time in lead identification and qualification by using a set of criteria. These criteria include but are not limited to budget, authority, need, time frame and urgency of hiring/purchasing requirement, connections between executives, revenue, behavioral study of the Target Company, interaction score between executives, and

© Springer Nature Singapore Pte Ltd. 2018
A. V. Deshpande et al. (Eds.): SmartCom 2017, CCIS 876, pp. 279–291, 2018.
https://doi.org/10.1007/978-981-13-1423-0_30

interest level of the target company. They rely on data mining, analytics and Customer Relationship Management (CRM) softwares for this process.

For SMBs in Business-to-Customer (B2C) space, the CRM or Software-as-a-Service tools are useful. However, for SMBs in B2B space, the purchase and licensing costs of these tools are not justified because of data volume and veracity: (1) with record set of around few hundred to a few thousand records and (2) limited set of attributes. As a result, the sales and marketing teams in a B2B, such as a software services firm, have to spend significant amount of time and energy in the groundwork for identification and qualification of leads. Only after the groundwork is complete, they are able to establish business relations with the right set of leads.

At present, to our best knowledge, there is no single affordable solution available for lead identification and qualification for a SMB operating in B2B services industry. This technical paper proposes a framework that facilitates lead identification and qualification. The proposed system also includes prediction of qualification score of unseen leads based on the intelligence gathered through the training data. The proposed system design includes: (a) sales lead data acquisition via web crawling, extracting information from social media and job portals, (b) data pre-processing, cleansing and storage, (c) applying classification algorithms on stored training data, and (d) predicting the class of unseen data based on the knowledge gathered during training.

The problem statement at hand warrants for two-class classification and prediction of class of unseen data. There are a number of industry standard two-class classification algorithms as mentioned in [1]. Some of the popular Two-class classifiers are: (i) Two-class averaged perceptron, (ii) Two-class Bayes Point Machine, (iii) Two-Class Decision Tree, Decision Forest and Decision Jungle, (iv) Two-Class SVM, (v) Two-class Neural Network, and (vi) Two-Class Logistic Regression. Some of these algorithms, such as SVM or Decision Jungle, are more suited for continuous variables, large volume of data and a large number of features (millions of records, each with hundreds of features). Since the leads information was represented with a limited number of features (less than 10) and the initial data volume was in terms of hundreds of rows, we finalized on the following set of algorithms: (i) Linear Regression, (ii) Two-Class Logistic Regression, (iii) Two-class Boosted Decision Tree, (iv) Two-class Decision Forest, and (v) Two-class Neural Network.

The rest of the paper is organized as follows: Sect. 2 presents the literature survey in two major areas: (a) Data acquisition and preprocessing in B2B, and (b) different classification and prediction approaches for leads/opportunities in B2B. Section 3 elaborates on design and architecture of the proposed framework. Section 4 explains the experimental setup required for the proposed solution along with the results. Section 5 presents the observations and concluding remarks.

2   Literature Survey

For the problem area under consideration for this paper, we reviewed number of technical papers that discussed different models for sales pipeline identification and win prediction for both business-to-business (B2B) and business-to-customer (B2C) scenarios. We also compared a number of commercially available products that leverage data from CRM and present a number of insights about the prospects.

The authors of [2] propose a regression approach to sales pipeline win propensity prediction. In the current market where big data is prominent and drives most of the functioning of the businesses, data driven predictive analytics models drive better sales performance in business-to-business as well as business-to-customer scenarios. The authors propose a two-step approach to determine the win propensity of sales leads: (i) Collection of training dataset to classify the leads as "win", "lose" and "pending" types for a given time window(say a fiscal quarter) and (ii) Using the trained model to estimate the win propensity of leads which are in "pending" status. For each pending lead, the sales person determines a time frame by which the lead should be won (say a quarter). The authors propose two types of features to design the systematic approach of sales leads analytics: (a) unary features and (b) interdependent features. For upcoming lead data, since most of the features remain unchanged, except the time stamp, the model can predict the win propensity using training data. The authors have proposed using (a) Support Vector Machine (SVM), (b) Artificial Neural Network (ANN), and (c) Logistic Regression (LR) as training algorithms. They have trained their model using Logistic Regression on a dataset from different geographies and using just the service lead data instead of whole product line data. The authors have used Gain score as a performance measure for the model. It is calculated as a percentage of total actual "wins" to the number of leads contacted in a given quarter. The models proposed are suitable for high volume of data with temporal features as opposed to the low volume and sparse feature set available in most B2B services environments.

In [3], the authors propose a machine learning based model to predict the sales pipeline win propensity over time. The model proposes that each lead be updated weekly with its win likelihood within next two weeks until the end of current quarter. The updates include static features such as deal size, geography, sector, and product as well as dynamic seller interaction information. The model uses multidimensional Hawkes Process to find patterns from seller-pipeline interaction. The authors have tested the proposed model on a Fortune 500 multinational technology company's sales pipeline data and they also claim that the model can be extended to other domains such as asset management, client purchase lifecycle management.

In [4, 5], the authors have explained the N-Gram based text categorization and how it is used in document classification. These are generic techniques that can be applied to part of the solution for sales pipeline analytics. The target company's description, profile of lead from social media and other text can be classified using N-Gram based text categorization to derive some of the features.

While working with B2B data, a number of important attributes or features need to be considered, namely, Tenure (for an existing customer), Recent Activity (purchase, enquiry or change request by a lead or customer), Revenue (of target company), Product or service usage, and Geography. These features are a fraction of the business customer or prospect data that characterizes the strength of a business. These features, along with demographic data such as company size (by revenue or head count) and vertical classification, decide the business customer segmentation as suggested in [6]. This paper suggests a number of clustering techniques such as between-groups, average linkage and complete linkage for customer segmentation with smaller datasets. For larger datasets, the author recommends K-means clustering.

An opportunity scoring engine that considers thousands of signals from structured CRM data, unstructured text data (Natural Language Processing), government filings, and job postings has been proposed by a company named C9 Inc. [7]. This engine enables the creation of a number of models such as win/loss model, duration model and influencer model. Each model uses different algorithms for opportunity scoring. Win/loss model uses random forest classifiers. Each classifier model is built with varying parameters and cross-validated against historic data to achieve the best classification. The duration model uses Poisson distribution to predict the probability of closing an opportunity within a given quarter. The influencer model uses Generalized Linear Model (GLM) to interpret the probability of win and also the set of influencing features that contribute to the closure. For the sales forecasting, the author proposes bottom-up, top-down and hybrid forecasting methods. The bottom-up forecasting method sums up the amounts of all open opportunities that can be closed in a given time (e.g. a quarter). The top-down forecasting method uses traditional forecasting methods to get trained on historical data and predicts the final revenue of a given quarter based on the learning. The hybrid model combines the top-down and bottom-up methods to arrive at 'quality' of current sales pipeline and how it compares with previous quarter, seasonality, cyclicality etc.

These approaches help in solving different parts of the lead qualification problem each using different types and sets of features such as short descriptions of prospect companies, company type, and industry/vertical, connection "strength" of the executives, location, and urgency of the need. Also, each of them proposes different ways of classification or clustering of data.

Although these methods propose a variety of solutions, we have found that: (a) these methods rely on a variety of structured and unstructured data including temporal or firmographic data of leads. (b) There is no cohesive lead qualification and scoring/ranking system available for SMBs. There are a number of software product/platform companies focused on sales pipeline analytics, and marketing data analytics, but most of them are yet to explore AI and machine learning.

This technical paper proposes a framework to identify and qualify leads for a software services firm with low volume of leads data and sparse feature set. The framework proposes a 4-step approach: (a) Leads data identification and acquisition, (b) Data Pre-processing, (c) Data storage, and (d) Data analytics and prediction. The following section describes each of these steps in detail.

3   Design and Architecture of Proposed System

Based on the literature survey, and understanding of current lead qualification process in a small services company, we were able to identify the most important features and components of our proposed solution. In the training and testing phase of the model, the leads data is acquired from a variety of sources, preprocessed and fed into a regression or classification algorithm. The data is split as training and test data (70% and 30% respectively). The split percentage is decided based on the volume of initial training/testing data and general rule of thumb followed in statistical modeling. Once the model is trained, and tested, the classification results are cross-verified against historical data that is manually classified. In the prediction phase, the trained model is used to predict the class of a batch of unseen records.

As shown in Fig. 1, major building blocks of the framework are Data Acquisition and Pre-Processing Component, Data Store for pre-processed leads, Algorithmic model for training and testing of Leads Qualification, and the trained models published as a set of Web Services.

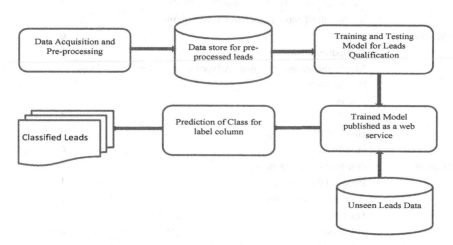

Fig. 1. Architecture of sales data analytics and prediction framework

3.1 Data Acquisition and Pre-processing

The data can be acquired through different sources like: (a) professional networking sites (LinkedIn), (b) Company profiling sites (CrunchBase), (c) Job portals, and (d) other web sources offering professional data. To this end we have used set of scripts, plugins and free online services which acquire the data in CSV format. The collected data needs to be cleansed and pre-processed to eliminate repetition, blank or invalid values. Based on historical leads data, following feature set was finalized for the proposed framework: Lead Name, Current Title, Industry, Location, Current Company, Company Type, Connect Score, Funding Score, Existing Customer, and Qualified (Label column). All the features except Lead Name and Current Company were enumerated as shown in Table 1.

3.2 Data Store for Pre-processed Leads

The output of data pre-processing component is a CSV file stored on a local machine. This is sent as input dataset to the training and testing model. Following is the sample structure of a CSV file:

Table 1. Sample enumerated values of text features

Feature	Text value	Numeric value
Current title	Default/Not applicable	0
	CEO, founder, co-founder, managing partner, principal, general manager	1
	CTO, Chief technologist, Technology head	2
	CIO, Chief information officer	3
	VP of engineering, Vice president (Product)	4
	VP of sales/Marketing/Channel management	5
Industry	Default	0
	Computer software	1
	Media and communication, Advertisement, Brand management	2
	Internet	3
	Retail	4
	Hospitality	5
	Healthcare	6
Location	Not found/Not applicable	0
	Pune, Maharashtra	1
	Any other city in India	2
	US-East	3
	US-West	4
	US-MidWest	5
	US-Central	6
	APAC	7
	Middle East	8
Company type	Product/Channel partner/Infrastructure	1
	Services	0
Connect score	First connect	1
	Second connect	2
	Third connect	3
	Not applicable	0
Funding score	Recently funded	1
	Public company/Not applicable	0
Existing customer	Yes	1
	No	0
Qualified	Yes	1
	No	0

3.3   Algorithmic Model for Training and Testing of Leads Qualification

This consists of a set of experiments for each classification and regression algorithm. Since lead qualification is a binary decision, we decided to use a number of Two-Class classification algorithms. We compared their accuracy, precision, recall and F1 score.

We designed a set of classification models by using the following classification and regression algorithms: (i) Linear Regression, (ii) Two-class Logistic Regression, (iii) Two-Class Boosted Decision Tree, (iv) Two-class Decision Forest and (v) Two-class Neural Network

   (i) Linear Regression: This is a classic curve fitting algorithm that uses one or more independent features and one dependent feature. We decided to use linear regression to get an idea about the confidence of prediction based on the dataset. The linear regression model correctly predicted the class labels very close to their actual values (1 or 0).
  (ii) Two-Class Logistic Regression: This is a supervised learning method and requires labeled dataset with numerical variables. The algorithm predicts the probability of occurrence of an event by fitting data to a logistic function. Two-Class Logistic Regression algorithm has been optimized for dichotomous or binary variables.
 (iii) Two-Class Boosted Decision Tree: A Boosted Decision Tree is an ensemble method in which second tree corrects the errors of first tree; third tree corrects the errors of first and second and so on. This method gives top performance with most of the classification tasks.
  (iv) Two-Class Decision Forest: This is Random Decision Forest algorithm based model. It is fast, supervised ensemble model. The algorithm builds multiple decision trees and then votes on the most popular output class. Voting is a form of aggregation. Each tree in the forest outputs a frequency histogram of labels. The aggregation process normalizes the histograms to get the probability score of each label. The trees with high prediction confidence get more weightage in final decision.
   (v) Two-Class Neural Network: It is a supervised learning method that expects a tagged dataset with label column as input. A neural network is a set of inter-connected layers in which the inputs lead to outputs by a series of weighted edges and nodes. The weights on the edges are learned and adjusted during training. Usually one hidden layer is sufficient if the dataset is simple.

Each model returns the scored label and scored probability for each of the test records.

Figure 2 represents the training and testing phase of the algorithmic model. In this phase, leads data is collected from online sources such as LinkedIn, Google or Crunchbase (a) company information portal). The data is pre-processed (enumerated) and split into training and testing data to feed into an algorithm. The trained model is tested using test data and the classification results are evaluated.

Figure 3 represents the prediction phase of the algorithmic model. In this phase, the trained classification model is fed with a set of previously unused (unseen) leads to

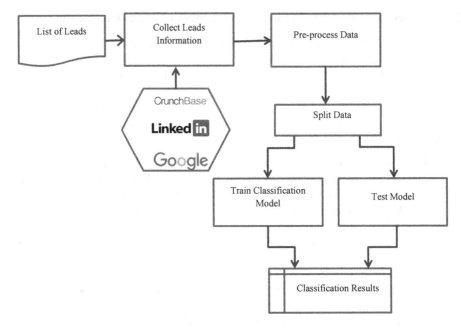

Fig. 2. Sales data analytics: training and testing

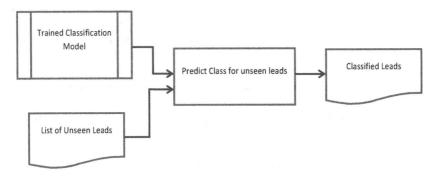

Fig. 3. Sales data analytics: prediction

predict their class (Qualified or not). The output of this phase is the list of leads, each with a class label as 1 or 0.

3.4 Published Web Services for Prediction of Class of Unseen Leads Data

For each trained model, a separate predictive model is created as a web service for prediction of class of unseen leads data. Each web service is created with an API key, default end point and a testing mechanism with request/response as single records or in batches. The batch input is a CSV file with same format as in Table 2. The label

Table 2. Sample Input Data to Training and Testing Model

Name	Current title	Industry	Location	Current company	Company type	Connect score	Funding score	Existing customer	Qualified
William Ryan	6	15	2	Curabitur Associates	1	2	0	1	1
David Cannon	4	11	3	Dictum Cursus	1	2	1	0	1
Damon Hayes	5	16	6	Egestas	0	0	1	0	0
Micah Arnold	2	3	2	Turpis	1	2	1	0	1

column ("Qualified") may or may not contain values in case of new or unseen data. Each web service predicts the value of label column for each row in the data set. The output of a web service for Two-Class classification is a csv file with two extra columns, namely, scored label and scored probabilities. The output of a web service of regression model is one extra column named "scored label".

The design decisions were mainly driven by the following factors:

(i)   Volume, variety and veracity of data: Since we worked on the leads data of small software services company (SMB), initially, the data volume was very low (just a few hundred leads). Also, leads information was gathered from professional networks (LinkedIn, CrunchBase) and job portals (Monster, Naukri). The sales team looked for companies and leads from specific domains (network, security, analytics etc.), with specific skill set requirements (fullstack, Python, Java etc.), and with specific business models (SMBs with products).

(ii) Choice of algorithms: Lead identification and qualification is a binary classification model. Hence, we decided to use the most popular Two-Class algorithms. We also decided to use Linear Regression because it is simple, fast and demonstrates the strength of relationship between dependent and independent variables.

(iii) Choice of tools and technology for solution: We have chosen all open source and free tools for the proposed solution.

4   Experimental Setup

Microsoft Azure Machine Learning Studio is a collaborative, drag-and-drop tool that can be used to build, test, and deploy predictive analytics solutions using data sources in different formats such as CSV, blob storage or tables. We decided to use Azure ML studio because of its simplicity, free offering and plug-and-play functionality. It was very easy to create input datasets using CSV files. Also, Azure ML studio has a number of Two-Class and Multiclass classification algorithms, clustering and anomaly detection algorithms implemented and ready to use (Table 3).

We used the following guidelines for selection of the algorithms:

Table 3. Selection criteria for Algorithms

Algorithm	Accuracy	Training time	Linearity	Number of parameters	Comments
Linear regression	Low to medium	Fast	Yes	5	Simplest and fastest
Two-class logistic regression	Low to medium	Fast	Yes	7	Easy to setup
Two-class boosted decision tree	Excellent	Moderate	No	7	Large memory footprint
Two-class decision forest	Excellent	Moderate	No	7	Ensemble method of classification
Two-class neural network	Excellent	Slow	No	11	Additional customization is possible

Table 4 below represents the important parameters that affect the performance of algorithms are as follows.

(i) Trainer Mode: Single Parameter or Parameter Range. We used single parameter because we had specific set of values for the features.

(ii) Regularization weights: Regularization is a method of preventing overfitting by penalizing models with extreme coefficient values. L1 regularization is applied for sparse models with high-dimensional data and L2 regularization is applied for models where data is not sparse. We used default values of these weights because the dataset was low-dimensional.

(iii) Learning Rate: This determines how fast or slow the learner converges to optimal solution. We used the learning rate of 0.1 to achieve optimal results.

Table 4. Parameter values of Algorithms

	Linear regression	Two-class logistic regression	Two-class boosted decision tree	Two-class decision forest	Two-class neural network
Param1	Solution method = Ordinary least squares	Trainer mode = Single parameter	Trainer mode = Single parameter	Resampling method = Bagging	Trainer mode = Single parameter
Param2	L2 Regularization weight = .001	Optimization tolerance = 1E-07	Maximum number of leaves per tree = 20	Trainer mode = Single parameter	Hidden layer specification = Fully connected case
Param3	Include Intercept term (Flag) = True	L1 Regularization weight = 1	Minimum number of samples per leaf node = 10	Number of decision trees = 8	Number of hidden nodes = 10
Param4	Random number seed = 1	L2 Regularization weight = 1	Learning rate = 0.1	Maximum depth of the decision trees = 32	Learning rate = 0.1

(*continued*)

Table 4. (*continued*)

	Linear regression	Two-class logistic regression	Two-class boosted decision tree	Two-class decision forest	Two-class neural network
Param5	Allow unknown categorical levels (Flag) = True	Memory size for L-BFGS = 20	Number of trees constructed = 100	Number of random splits per node = 32	Number of learning iterations = 100
Param6		Random number seed = <blank>	Random number seed = <blank>	Minimum number of samples per leaf node = 1	Initial learning weights diameter = 0.1
Param7		Allow unknown categorical levels (Flag) = True	Allow unknown categorical levels (Flag) = True	Allow unknown values for categorical features (Flag) = True	Momentum = 0
Param8					Type of normalizer = Min- max Normalizer
Param9					Shuffle Examples (Flag) = True
Param10					Random number seed = <blank>
Param11					Allow unknown categorical levels (Flag) = True

5 Results

Initially, we started with 300 records for prototyping and understanding the performances of different regression and classification algorithms. We made sure that we used the same data set across all models to compare their efficiency and effectiveness.

Table 5 presents the comparative results of all five algorithms for: (a) low volume (300 records) and (b) high volume (10,000 records) data set. We noticed that prediction accuracy of each algorithm for unseen data was 98–100% for small volumes of data (300 records). This is due to the fact that the historical data was manually generated which had close to zero false positives and false negatives. However, as the data volume grew, we were able to see the differences in performance measures of different algorithms. We trained and tested the same set of algorithms on a dataset of 10000 records. Table 5 shows 100% accuracy was obtained during training and testing phase for following algorithms: (a) Two-Class Logistic Regression, (b) Two-Class Boosted Decision Tree, and (c) Two-Class Neural Network. Whereas the prediction accuracy for unseen data stands at around 70%; this is because of the fact that the training data is generated through a tool which had uniform distribution.

The Two-Class decision forest, had accuracy and precision of 75% during training and testing with high volume data (10,000 records) whereas the algorithm predicted all the record as qualified for unseen data. This means that the algorithm is not able to recognize two unique values for label column "Qualified" as 0 and 1. This is because the algorithm builds multiple decision trees and votes on most popular output class

Table 5. Comparison of algorithm results

Number of records	Algorithm	Training and testing Phase					Prediction accuracy
		Root mean square error	Accuracy	Precision	Recall	F1 score	
300 records	Linear regression	0.026098	NA	NA	NA	NA	1
	Two-class logistic regression	NA	1	1	1	1	0.98
	Two-class boosted decision tree	NA	1	1	1	1	0.98
	Two-class decision forest	NA	1	1	1	1	0.98
	Two-class neural network	NA	1	1	1	1	0.98
10000 records	Linear regression	0.286206	NA	NA	NA	NA	0.5
	Two-class logistic regression	NA	1	1	1	1	0.7
	Two-class boosted decision tree	NA	1	1	1	1	0.7
	Two-class decision forest	NA	0.751	0.751	1	0.85	0
	Two-class neural network	NA	1	1	1	1	0.7

resulting into 30% false positives during training phase. Hence, we had to disqualify this algorithm.

For Linear Regression algorithm, the root mean square error with high volume data is 11 times the root mean square error of low volume data. This means that Linear Regression does not perform well with high volume data.

6   Conclusion

Small and medium sized businesses (SMBs), with software services as offering, are faced with the problem of identifying and qualifying leads based on their company's historical sales and marketing data. Since these businesses cannot afford expensive CRM and analytics tools, mainly because of low volume of data, they mostly rely on manual processes and human intelligence regarding lead qualification. The proposed solution in this paper tries to solve the lead identification and qualification problem for SMBs, particularly in the software services domain.

Our experiments with low and high volume data sets prove that industry standard Two-Class Classification algorithms such as Two-Class Logistic Regression, Two-Class Boosted Decision Tree, and Two-Class Neural Network are the best suitable algorithms for lead classification and prediction of class of leads. Since Two-Class Boosted Decision Tree model has the best accuracy and moderate training time required for low as well as high volume data, as compared to other algorithms, we recommend this algorithm for optimal results.

References

1. Web reference. https://docs.microsoft.com/en-us/azure/machine-learning/machine-learning-basics-infographic-with-algorithm-examples
2. Yan, J., Gong, M., Sun, C., Huang, J., Chu, S.M.: Sales Pipeline Win Propensity Prediction: a Regression Approach. IBM Research, China (2015)
3. Yan, J., et al.: On machine learning towards predictive sales pipeline analytics. In: 29th AAAI Conference on Artificial Intelligence (2015)
4. Rahmoun, A., Elberrichi, Z.: Experimenting N-grams in text categorization. Int. Arab J. Inf. Technol. 4(4), 377–385 (2007)
5. Cavnar, W.B., Trenkle, J.M: N-Gram based text categorization. Environmental Research Institute of Michigan
6. Stuntebeck, V.A.: B2B Customer Segmentation: Important Considerations when segmenting Business Customers. IBM Developer Works (2012)
7. Twigg, A.: Applying Data Science to Sales Pipelines for Fun and Profit. C9 Inc.

Bacterial Colony Optimization for Data Rate Evaluation in Cognitive Cellular Network

Sharada Ohatkar[(✉)] and Komal Tupe

Department of Electronics and Telecommunication, MKSSS's CCOEW,
Savitribai Phule Pune University, Pune, India
sharada.ok@gmail.com, tupe.komal.s@gmail.com

Abstract. The Cognitive Cellular Network (CCN) is the key to complete the requirement of the cellular user request along with the improvement in channel allocation. CCN consist of cellular user as a primary and cognitive as secondary user in which the cognitive user occupies in the cellular band without causing interference. To check and improvise the network capacity of the cellular network, the Bacterial colony optimization (BCO) algorithm is considered. The BCO algorithm is developed from the lifecycle of E-coli bacteria. The signal to interference ratio (SINR) obtained with proposed BCO is found to be better as Particle Swarm Optimization (PSO) and Artificial Bee Colony (ABC).

Keywords: Bacterial colony optimization · Cognitive cellular network
Primary user · Secondary user · Signal to interference ratio

1 Introduction

The increase in growth of cellular user population causes spectrum availability crisis.

The cellular concept plays a major role in solving spectral congestion, and in turn, increases the requirement of data rate [1]. Dynamic user behavior, bandwidth requirement specific to the application results in blocking the available wireless spectrum. The interesting solution can be access to the register band is given without disturbing the current user. In cognitive networks the secondary user (Sru) uses the register spectrum while the transmission of the registered primary user (Pru) should not disturb. If the band is already engaged by a registered user, the secondary unregister user change it path to another spectrum to avoid the interference between them, this concept is known as spectrum mobility. With reduction in interference between Pru and Sru users the spectrum can be utilized optimally [3].

The Artificial Intelligence provides optimal solution for the complex computation problem in different application like spectrum allocation, in biology and medicine, thermal power system, structural failure predication of multistoried RC buildings. The different AI techniques are Particle Swarm optimization, and Artificial Bee Colony Optimization Algorithm [6, 7].

In ABC algorithm, Computational cost can be increases with increase in population of solution, PSO algorithm has chance of getting stuck in a local optimum in multi-modal functions. In contrast, BCO has the best ability to surpass this problem. BCO could show better search ability in multimodal functions.

© Springer Nature Singapore Pte Ltd. 2018
A. V. Deshpande et al. (Eds.): SmartCom 2017, CCIS 876, pp. 292–299, 2018.
https://doi.org/10.1007/978-981-13-1423-0_31

In the proposed system, the Bacterial Colony Optimization Algorithm (BCO) is used to get optimal spectrum allocation. The concept of BCO enables to obtain better solution than only constructive moves. Therefore, BCO is applied in this work for a computationally complex problem of spectrum allocation in CCN [5].

2 Artificial Bacteria Behavior

Bacterial colony optimization (BCO) algorithm was originally proposed by Niu and Wang (2012) which is inspired by five basic behaviors of E. Coli bacteria in their whole lifecycle which are describe as follows:

1. Chemotaxis

E-coli bacteria move through the flagellum. The process of movement is chemotoxic process. The whole Process of chemotaxis is explaining into two operations like Running and Tumbling. In the process of running, all flagella rotate anticlockwise. In this way, bacteria can move straightly in one direction. In the case of tumbling, the flagella rotate clockwise, which pull the bacterium in different directions [6].

2. Elimination, Reproduction and Migration

Based on the theory of natural selection bacteria may eliminate from the area. In contrast, if bacteria succeed to find the food, they obtained the more energy to reproduce. Likewise, in the BCO algorithm, artificial bacteria with high quality have a chance to use relevant energy level. Whether a bacterium has the chance to reproduce or not that would be depending on the energy level [6].

3. Communication

Communication is important step in bacteria life cycle. The three-communication process mostly found in the bacterial life cycle i.e. Dynamic neighbor oriented, random oriented and group oriented. The bacteria share the information through the bacterial chains which is occur in dynamic neighbor oriented and random oriented process while the bacteria share the information among the group of bacteria called as group oriented process [6].

2.1 Applying BCO to Cognitive Cellular Network

There are different optimization algorithms like Genetic Algorithm (GA), Ant Colony Optimization (ACO), and Bacterial Colony Optimization (BCO) have been developed by the researchers. Most of the optimization algorithms developed today are motivated from the biological life cycles. The BCO algorithm is developed by considering the life cycle of the E-coli bacteria. It contains the five steps: chemotaxis, communication, elimination, reproduction, and migration. Steps for BCO explain as below:

Algorithm: BCO optimization algorithm

---

1. Initialize
2. for (do Each run)
3. for (do Each iteration)
4. Chemotaxis and Communication.
   Tumbling (Chemotaxis and Communication)

   $Position_i(n) = Position (T-1) + C(i) *[f_i *(G_{best} - Position_i (T-1) + (1-f_i)$

   $*(P_{besti} - Position_i(T-1) + turbulent_i]$,

5. while The maximum swimming steps are not met do
   Swimming (Chemotaxis and Communication)

   $Position_i (n) = Position (T-1) + C(i) * [f_i *(G_{best} - Position_i(-1) + (1-f_i)$

   $* (P_{besti} - Position_i (T-1)]$

6. end while
7. if Reproduction and elimination conditions are met then
8. Compute the Jhealth Reproduction and elimination
9. end if
10. if Migration conditions are met then
11. Migration
12. end if
13. end for
14. end for
15. end

2.2 Relating BCO Parameter to CCN

In Cognitive Radio Networks, the problem existing between the two users and it is formulated between the primary and secondary users. The primary user called macro while secondary called as Femto which are responsible for the making priority in spectrum access and conflict resolution. The micro cell area covers multiple macro users and base stations those are located near the center of the coverage area. The secondary Femto cells are spread equally all over the macro cell area [6]. In this process, the secondary link is formed between the Femto based station and Femto users likewise; the primary link is formed between the macro base station and macro users. The power transferred by the Macro base station and Femto base station is maximum; hence the overall power is constant over the network [6]. The bandwidth of the primary channel from LTE cellular network is considered as 20 MHz [6].

3 Problem Formulation

Signal-to-noise-plus-interference ratio (SINR) is the ratio of amount of inference power received at receiver to the power of noisy signal. SINR for secondary links is given by [6].

$$SINR = \frac{P(l)/lds(l)^{\beta}}{\sum_{m \in \Phi} P(m)/dss(m, l)^{\beta} + P(n)/dps(n, l)^{\beta}}, \quad 1 \leq l \leq Su \tag{1}$$

Where, P (l), P (m) is the power transmitted by the secondary transmitter l and m respectively while P (n) is the power transmitted by the primary transmitter n, lds (l) is the distance between transmitter and receiver referred as link distance. dss (m, l) is the distance between transmitter and receiver of secondary users. dps (n, l) is the distance between primary transmitter and secondary receiver, β is SINR threshold, Su is the number of secondary links presented in the area.

At each primary link SINR is given by:

$$SINR = \frac{P(n)/ldp(n)^{\beta}}{\sum_{k \in \Phi} P(m)/dps(m, n)^{\beta}}, \quad 1 \leq n \leq Pu \tag{2}$$

Where, P (n), P (m) is the power transmitted by the primary transmitter and secondary transmitter respectively, ldp (l) is the distance between transmitter and receiver of primary referred as link distance. dps (n, l) is the distance between primary transmitter and secondary receiver, β is SINR threshold P (u) is the number of primary links presented in the area.

The data rates of the primary and secondary link are calculated by the Eq. (3) where the data is depending on the bandwidth (B) of the channel which shared by both primary and secondary channel and it is given by the propagation environment conditions as [5, 8]:

$$Data \ rate \ (Cu) = B \log_2 (1 + SINR) \tag{3}$$

4   Simulation Result

The CCN is simulated by considering 6 primary users, 20 secondary users located in 5000 × 5000. To allocate the secondary users optimally with BCO, 100 iterations are considered. The data rate is determined from SINR by taking 20 MHz bandwidth. As we have considered LTE cellular in Fig. 1 the red dots indicate Pru, the blue astric mark indicates Sru. Base station is centrally located as shown. The final optimized locations after applying BCO is represented in Fig. 2. Table 2 shows the parameter use in BCO algorithm.

The SINR is determined with different threshold values i.e. β = 4, 6, 8 and 10. Table 1 depicts the highest data rate achieved with threshold value of 10. The computation time required is also noted. Table 3 shows the PC configuration and software which is used for this project. PC configuration used is Lenovo machine, processor is intel core i7, RAM is 8 GB, and software is MATLAB.

Particle Swarm Optimization (PSO) is SI technique inspired by bird flocking together [5]. Ant bee colony (ABC) [9] technique explores the behavior of honey bees

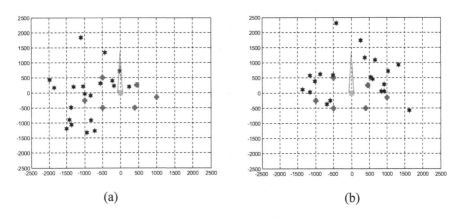

(a)   (b)

Fig. 1. (a) Initial location of primary and secondary user, (b) Final location of primary and secondary user using BCO (Color figure online)

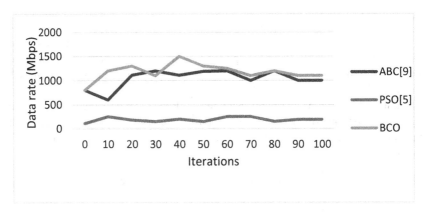

Fig. 2. Comparison of ABC [9], PSO [5], with BCO for SINR threshold $\beta = 4$

Table 1. Relation of BCO parameter to CCN

Sr. No.	BCO terms	CCN terms
1	Number of bacteria in population used for searching (S)	Number of secondary user
2	Dimension of search space (p)	Searching range of secondary user zone
3	Number of Chemo tactic steps (Nc)	Increment in searching step for secondary user
4	Number of swimming steps Ns	Searching yard
5	Number of reproduction steps Nre	Higher probability for su link
6	Number of elimination and dispersal Ned	Cluster searching elimination
7	Sr	S/2 sharing of BW between two secondary users
8	Probability of elimination and dispersal Ped	The probability that each secondary user will be eliminated

Table 2. Parameter for BCO

Sr. No.	Results for BCO	Value
1	Primary user	6
2	Secondary user	20
3	Iterations	100
4	Highest data rate in	1850 (Mbps)
5	SINR threshold value	10
6	Time required	25.032 s

Table 3. Data rate comparison between ABC, PSO, BCO

Iteration	ABC [5]				PSO [9]				BCO			
	Beta value				Beta value				Beta value			
	4	6	8	10	4	6	8	10	4	6	8	10
10	600	200	600	600	250	400	390	390	1200	1000	200	750
50	1190	1200	800	1160	150	180	150	110	1300	1100	1600	1850
100	1000	900	1160	1000	190	690	230	250	1100	1200	1250	1250

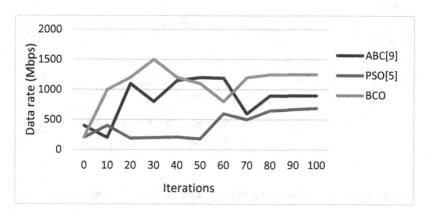

Fig. 3. Comparison of ABC [9], PSO [5], with BCO for SINR threshold $\beta = 6$

to gather food. In [5, 9] the same scenario is simulated with PSO and ABC. The results obtain with BCO is compared with PSO and ABC as reported in [5, 9].

Table 3 shows the data rate comparison between ABC, PSO, BCO for 10, 50 and 100 iteration and remaining data rate values for iteration after 10 intervals up to the 100 is shown in Figs. 2, 3, 4 and 5.

The plot of number of iterations for SINR threshold values v/s data rate (Mbps) is depicted in Figs. 3, 4, 5 and 6. It is observed that higher data rate is achieved with BCO for different SINR threshold values than with reported work with PSO [5] and ABC [9]. In [5] time require to execute the algorithm for beta = 10 is 3.0 min, and for BCO for same values of beta 25.32 s are require it shows that BCO is better as compared with PSO.

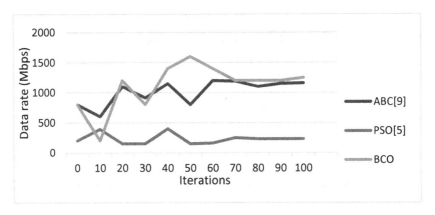

Fig. 4. Comparison of ABC [9], PSO [5], with BCO for SINR threshold β = 8

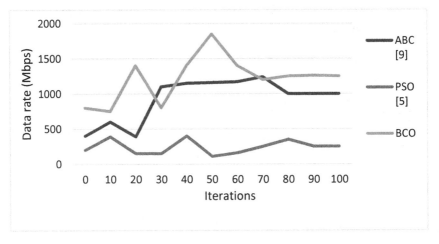

Fig. 5. Comparison of ABC [9], PSO [5], with BCO for SINR threshold β = 10

5 Conclusion

This work addresses the interference minimization in CCN. The unregister secondary user is assigned optimally. BCO technique is used to get the maximum SINR value by minimizing the interference between the primary register user and secondary unregister users. The performance of the proposed system is evaluated based on SINR and data rate. The simulation results show BCO performance is better than presented work with PSO and ABC.

References

1. Marshall, P.: Scalability, Density, and Decision Making in Cognitive Wireless Networks. Cambridge University Press, Cambridge (2013)
2. Rappaport, T.S.: Wireless Communications. Prentice-Hall, Upper Saddle River (2002)
3. Gardellin, V., Das, S.K., Lenzini, L.: Self-coexistence in cellular cognitive radio networks based on the IEEE 802.22 standard. IEEE Wirel. Commun. **20**, 52–59 (2013)
4. Ohatkar, S.N., Bormane, D.S.: Channel allocation technique with genetic algorithm for interference reduction in cellular network. In: Annual IEEE India Conference (INDICON), pp. 1–6 (2015)
5. Vargas, A.M., Andrade, A.G.: Deployment analysis and optimization of heterogeneous networks under the spectrum underlay strategy. EURASIP J. Wirel. Commun. Netw. **55**, 1–15 (2015)
6. Niu, B., Xie, T., Bi, Y., Liu, J.: Bacterial colony optimization for integrated yard truck scheduling and storage allocation problem. In: Huang, D.-S., Han, K., Gromiha, M. (eds.) ICIC 2014. LNCS, vol. 8590, pp. 431–437. Springer, Cham (2014). https://doi.org/10.1007/978-3-319-09330-7_50
7. http://en.wikipedia.org/wiki/Cellular_network
8. Cosio-León, M., Martınez-Vargas, A., Gutierrez, E.: An experimental study of parameter selection in particle swarm optimization using an automated methodology. Res. Comput. Sci., p. 920
9. Ohatkar, S., Gunjkar, Y.: ABC and TLBO technique for evaluating data rate in wireless network. In: Unal, A., Nayak, M., Mishra, D.K., Singh, D., Joshi, A. (eds.) SmartCom 2016. CCIS, vol. 628, pp. 390–399. Springer, Singapore (2016). https://doi.org/10.1007/978-981-10-3433-6_47

A Simulation Model for Concurrent Propagation of Multi-band RF Signal in Space Frequency Reuse Based MANETs

Sandhya Chilukuri$^{(\boxtimes)}$, D. Varun, Kaustubh Nabar,
and Govind R. Kadambi

Ramaiah University of Applied Sciences, Bengaluru 560058, India
reachsandhyach@gmail.com,
{Varun.ec.et,pvc.research}@msruas.ac.in,
nabarkaustubh@yahoo.com

Abstract. This paper presents a study on development of a model to analyse the concurrent multi band RF signal propagation in MANET with Space Frequency (SF) reuse. The simulation studies on the developed model clearly substantiates the realization of independent links between the source and destination nodes of MANETs with multiple hops. Drawing an analogy of repeaters in a conventional Microwave Communication Link (MCL), the model developed using AWR software simulates the basic communication operations involved in source node, multiple intermediate nodes and the destination node. Numerous simulation results are presented to illustrate the satisfactory reception of signal at the destination node of a MANET under: (a) Single path transmission with a single and Dual Frequency (DF) band of operation (b) Single path operation with combination of Omni mode and (c) Directional mode with each mode operating at a different frequency band (equal and unequal number of hops). Through satisfactory reception of signals in all the above stated scenarios, the validity of SF reuse concept as applied to a MANET system has been substantiated. This in turn implies the existence of virtually two independent RF links for concurrent data transmission. The results of MATLAB simulations reveal that SF concept delivers a throughput improvement by a factor of about 1.95 as compared to a conventional data transmission through a single path using single frequency.

Keywords: RF signal · Transmitter · Amplification · Splitter
Signal combiner · Spectrum · Mobile ad hoc networks · Antennas
Polarisation · Radiation pattern

1 Introduction

Throughput and latency are important performance metrics in MANET. Even though the concept of multiple paths for data transmission is desirable for MANET, in majority of research on MANET, the data transmission is through a single path with the other possible paths being treated as backup paths [1, 2] for use in case of disruption of the chosen initial path of data transmission [3, 4]. The data transmission through a single path does not offer greater flexible options to improve the throughput. MANET is still

© Springer Nature Singapore Pte Ltd. 2018
A. V. Deshpande et al. (Eds.): SmartCom 2017, CCIS 876, pp. 300–316, 2018.
https://doi.org/10.1007/978-981-13-1423-0_32

perceived as a single band and single polarization (vertical) operation [5, 6]. In the existing research on MANET, a single band antenna operating either in 2.45 GHz or 5.25 GHz frequency band in omni mode is widely used [7–9]. The research on the simultaneous data transmission through multiple paths using omni directional antennas is rather limited. One of the probable reasons for not taking the recourse for data transmission via multiple paths is the likely effect of interference. This interference is caused by the omni antennas on co-channels and adjacent channels, when the network operation is realized using single frequency band and polarisation. The utility of directional antennas has been extensively studied in [10–13]. Even though the likely co-channel interference caused by directional antennas is relatively less in comparison to omni directional antennas [5, 14], there appears to be a lack of significant research on data transmission in MANET along multiple paths with directional antennas. The research work conducted in [15, 16] utilise directional antenna to minimise the energy consumption and to compress the selected path length to reach the destination. The research in [14] focusses on the dual polarized directional antennas and the data transmission is along a single path. However, the research in [14] lacks the use of additional reuse technique namely the SF in addition to the SP. The primary research focus of this paper is the application of SF reuse technique associated with antennas to improve the overall system performance of the MANET with concurrent data transmission of signal at two frequencies along a single path or two paths.

Space, frequency and polarization reuse techniques are intended to be used for load sharing. In these techniques, each independent path among the available multiple paths can be assigned a particular frequency and polarization such that the transmission along the path is neither causing interference to other independent paths nor being interfered. Such a concept will lead to virtually independent communication links resulting in near ideal path for propagation or transmission of signals from source node (S) to destination node (D).

In this paper, the analysis and simulation results of the concurrent signal reception of DF at the D through the analogy of a communication system with multiple repeaters are presented. The underlying principles for the simulation of load sharing through SF reuse technique has been illustrated through a propagation of RF signal of the S through the intermediate nodes and the final reception at the D. The path for data transmission is simulated with the provision for concurrent transmission and reception of signals at two frequency bands. The reception of the dual or multiple frequency signals at the D with amplitude higher than the sensitivity of the receiver is a measure of satisfactory performance of intermediate links of the independent path.

2 Definition of Space Frequency Reuse

The term 'space reuse' implies the sharing of the available space or space between any two nodes for the multi-mode operation of the link. The multi-mode operation may involve different frequencies giving rise to SF reuse. It may also include different polarisations leading to SP reuse. To support SF reuse, two antennas operating at different frequencies with or without differing polarisation are needed. Hence, it provides two independent links between S and D with one link operating at first frequency and the second link operating at a second frequency. In space frequency reuse concept, the two antennas are assumed to be located in the very close proximity of each other as shown in Figs. 1 and 2.

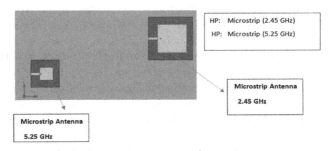

Fig. 1. Dual band antenna for space-frequency reuse concept (horizontal polarisation)

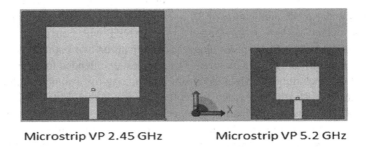

Fig. 2. Dual band antenna for space-frequency reuse concept (vertical polarisation)

Despite the close proximity, the two antennas have to retain their near original performance as if the two antennas are working in isolation. Under near ideal conditions, two independent links sharing the same path or space is realised, leading to increased capacity of the wireless channel and increase of throughput by a factor of two under ideal scenario. Ideally, it is desirable to have at least two independent paths to completely harness the potential of SF reuse concept. The present available antenna designs for wireless network in [17, 18] do not support SF reuse simultaneously in MANETs.

3   Development of RF Simulation Model of Communication Path of MANET

The simulation model for RF signal propagation along a path of MANET can be conceptualized using the repeater concept in the conventional Microwave Link. The functional role of a receiver of a repeater is to receive the signal transmitted by the transmitter and amplify the same before transmitting to the receiver of the next link.

This concept has been invoked in the development of simulation model of RF signal propagation along a path of MANET.

A single link of a path can be simulated as shown in Fig. 3. It consists of a signal source to generate a sinusoidal waveform of desired frequency of operation of link (2.45 GHz or 5.25 GHz in the present application). The other input parameter to the signal source is the transmitter power of the S. This sinusoidal signal is fed to the transmit antenna of the link. The input parameters to the transmit antenna block is the gain of antenna (usually given in dBi). The signal radiated by the transmitter will be received by the receiver block or receive antenna. The input parameters to the receive antenna block is the gain of the receiver antenna and the distance of separation between transmit and receive antennas (inter node distance of link).

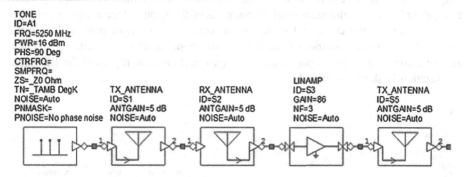

Fig. 3. Block diagram of a RF link of a repeater

With the available parameters of the source, transmit and receive blocks, the power received at the receive antenna is computed using the Friss transmission formula. The received signal is considerably weaker than the transmitted signal due to the path loss encountered between transmit and receive antennas of the link. Before the received signal is transmitted to the next receiving node, the signal is amplified with a linear amplifier by the desired level of amplification [19]. It is also common practice to compensate fully the path loss so that the signal amplitude at the next transmitter is equal to the amplitude of the signal at the source node itself. This process of transmit, receive, amplify and retransmit is continued for each successive intermediate link of a MANET till the destination node is reached. If the amplitude of the received signal is higher than the sensitivity (detection threshold), then the link is assumed to have performed satisfactorily without outage or link breakage. This procedure has been adopted to simulate the RF signal propagation along a path of MANET.

3.1 Simulation Model of RF Signal Propagation for a Link of MANET Featured with Space Frequency Reuse Technique

The simulation model developed in the previous sub-section cannot be extended to a path in which the concept of SF reuse technique for concurrent transmission of data using nearly two independent transmission links along the same path is invoked. This can be partly attributed to the fact that the model has one source of RF signal generation. For frequency reuse technique, at least two separate sources are needed. Moreover, to simulate the coexistence of two links operating at two different frequencies in space, a provision for the mixing of the two signals or equivalently the space model to combine the two signals after the two transmitters is required. A module which facilitates such combining of the two signals is called the 'signal combiner'. The number of input ports to the signal combiner depends on the number of frequencies of the signal required to be supported. The number of output ports of a signal combiner implies that it carries the combined signal of different frequencies. At the receiver side, a provision of a module to separate (split) the combined signal into the various components of frequencies is needed. Therefore, such a module is called 'splitter'. The output of the combiner is fed to the splitter and therefore the number of input ports to the splitter is one and the number of output ports of the splitter depends on the number of frequencies of the combined signal. Equivalently, each output port of the splitter represents the realized output of the link (path) operating at the specified frequency. A simulation model of the space frequency reuse technique to represent the RF signal propagation is shown in Fig. 4.

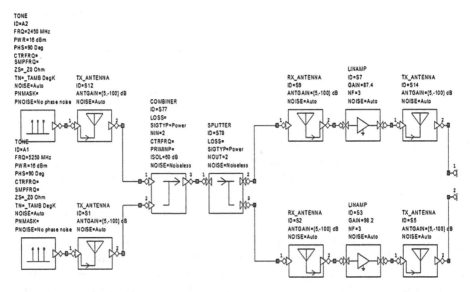

Fig. 4. Block diagram for the space frequency reuse of a RF link of a repeater in MANET

Once the separation of RF signal of each of the independent paths is realised at the output ports of the splitter, it is treated as a link of an independent path corresponding to the signal frequency of that path. The received signal of that port is amplified to compensate for the path loss before being retransmitted to the receiver of the next link (next intermediate node). This is applicable to all the output ports of a splitter. Figure 5 shows the amplification at individual output ports of a splitter.

Although the concept of SF reuse is not new to antenna or communication engineering (since they are used in diversity applications), their application to MANET is not discussed in details. The simulation models of RF signal propagation will be invoked to highlight the importance of SF reuse. The block diagram for RF signal propagation with two frequencies (2.45 GHz and 5.25 GHz) in a single channel/path using SF reuse technique is shown in Fig. 6.

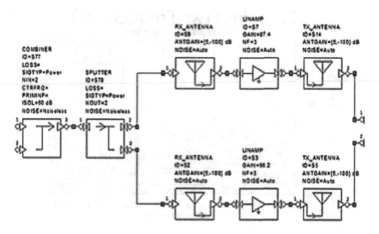

Fig. 5. Amplification at individual ports of a splitter

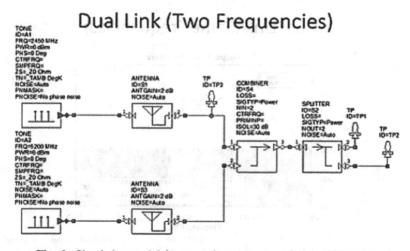

Fig. 6. Simulation model for space frequency reuse in MANET nodes

The reception of the two signals at the output port of the splitter is shown in Fig. 7. The results of Fig. 7 clearly illustrate that the two signals transmitted along the same path with two different frequencies can be received at the destination node indicating the potential of two independent links for the data transmission along the same path.

The inability of the existing MANET operating at a single frequency to invoke the concept of SF reuse technique is illustrated through Fig. 8. As seen from the results of Fig. 8, the absence of spatial separation of the two received signals implies that the receiver at the destination node is unable to differentiate the two input signals of same frequencies and hence the absence of independent links. Further, the results of Fig. 8 depict that a SF reuse cannot be realized with the two signals of same frequencies.

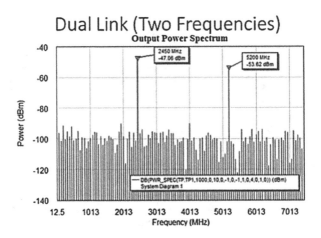

Fig. 7. Concurrent reception of signals of two frequencies at the destination node

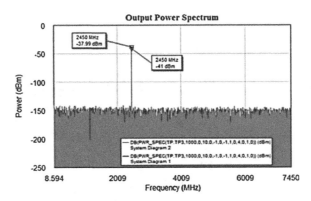

Fig. 8. Signal spectrum of space frequency reuse in MANET with two identical frequencies

4 Simulation Results

The simulation on RF signal propagation along a chosen path/route containing intermediate nodes has been carried out to illustrate the concept of SF reuse applicable in MANET to facilitate simultaneous multiple links along the same path. As stated while explaining the SF reuse concept, at least two independent paths will be ideal to completely harness the potential of SF for concurrent transmission of data. For the provision of route monitoring as well as concurrent transmission of data, the multiple paths must be independent. One of the feature of the independence of multiple paths in the above context is the absence of common intermediate nodes. For the simulation studies, a MANET scenario of 53 nodes is chosen, node 11 and 29 serves as S and D node respectively. Using a Recursive Search Independent Multipath Finding Algorithm (RSIMFA) for concurrent data transmission in DF and Dual Polarized (DP) MANETs formulated by the authors, the four independent paths obtained are shown Table 1.

Table 1. Independent paths sorted in ascending order of total path length

Sorting paths according to its sorted ranges	
Path	Paths	Range (m)
1	11 1 4 7 10 14 17 20 23 24 29	906.73
2	11 32 3 6 9 13 16 19 22 31 29	1180.46
3	11 2 5 12 15 18 25 26 27 28 29	1257.63
4	11 46 47 48 49 50 34 35 37 38 39 40 42 43 51 52 29	2042.65

In Table 1, the term 'range' stands for the total path length or total path distance required for the signal to traverse along the path from S node to D node. The independent paths shown in Table 1 are used for the simulation and illustrations presented in this section. The SF reuse has been simulated with a pair of antennas exhibiting omni directional radiation pattern as well as directional radiation pattern. The simulation has been extended to the scenario of one antenna with an omni directional pattern and the other antenna with directional radiation pattern. In the following simulation results, independent path (Path1) with 11 nodes is considered for the illustration of concurrent transmission of signals of different frequencies. Design simulations of two monopole antennas operating at 2.45 GHz and 5.2 GHz have been carried out to arrive at the parameters as an input to the developed model of RF link. Figure 9(a) illustrates the design configuration of a monopole for 2.45 GHz and Fig. 9(b) is the omnidirectional radiation pattern with VP in its azimuth plane. The peak gain of the monopole for 2.45 GHz is better than 1 dBi.

An analogous design simulation has been carried out for a monopole for 5.2 GHz with a peak gain better than 1 dBi. Its frequency response is shown in Fig. 10(a) and the associated omni directional radiation pattern of antenna is shown in Fig. 10(b).

Similarly, the microstrip antennas operating at 2.45 GHz and 5.2 GHz (Fig. 2) for radiation pattern with VP have been designed and their performance has been simulated, Fig. 11(a) shows the radiation pattern of microstrip antenna at 2.45 GHz (Gain of

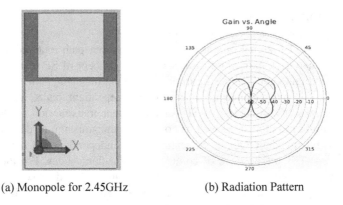

(a) Monopole for 2.45GHz   (b) Radiation Pattern

Fig. 9. Monopole antenna for 2.45 GHz and omni directional radiation pattern

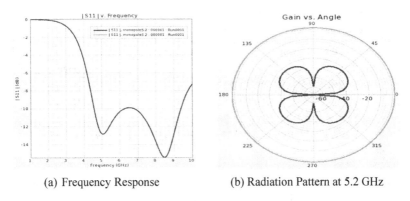

(a) Frequency Response   (b) Radiation Pattern at 5.2 GHz

Fig. 10. Frequency response and radiation pattern of monopole antenna for 5.2 GHz

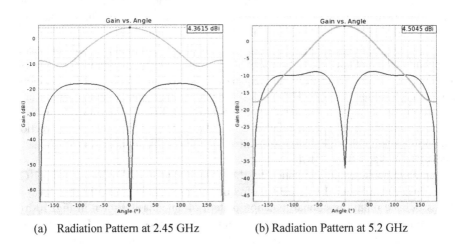

(a)   Radiation Pattern at 2.45 GHz   (b) Radiation Pattern at 5.2 GHz

Fig. 11. Radiation patterns of microstrip antennas in azimuth plane with VP

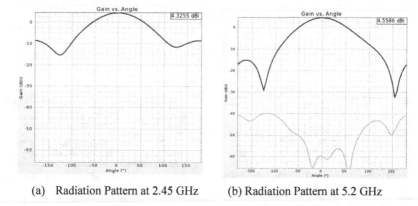

(a)   Radiation Pattern at 2.45 GHz   (b) Radiation Pattern at 5.2 GHz

Fig. 12. Radiation patterns of microstrip antennas in azimuth plane with HP

4.36 dBi with cross polarisation (HP) is less than −50 dBi along the direction of main beam) in the azimuth plane. An analogous radiation pattern at 5.25 GHz (Gain of 4.5 dBi with cross polarisation (HP) is −35 dBi is depicted in Fig. 11(b).

Similar design simulations are performed for microstrip antennas (Fig. 1) to realise radiation patterns with HP at 2.45 GHz (Gain of 4.33 dBi) and 5.2 GHz (Gain 4.56 dBi and cross polarisation (VP) of −64 dBi). The associated radiation patterns of the above antennas are shown in Fig. 12.

4.1   Signal Propagation Along a Route of a MANET Operating in a Single Frequency

To prove the efficacy of extending the developed model of a RF link between two nodes to the entire path with multiple intermediate nodes, a cascade of RF link is developed depending upon the number of nodes. The number of such cascades is (n − 1) where 'n' stands for the number of nodes in a route including the S and D nodes. The results of the simulation on RF propagation along path1 (Table 1) with all the nodes with monopole antennas (with gain of 1 dBi) operating at single frequency of 2.45 GHz is shown in Fig. 13(a). The amplitude of the signal at the destination node after multiple (10) hops is shown in Fig. 13(a). The corresponding result for directional mode (antenna gain of 5 dBi) at 2.45 GHz is shown in Fig. 13(b).

The amplitude of the received signal at the destination node of path1 after 10 hops is satisfactory. Usually, the sensitivity of the commercial receivers is better than −90 dBm. The amplitude of the received signals in Fig. 13 is much higher than the sensitivity of the receiver.

4.2   SF Reuse in Omni Mode

After establishing the validity of the developed RF signal propagation model along a route with 10 hops, the application of SF reuse concept to the same path (Path1) is analysed wherein the Path1 is subjected to simultaneous operation at 2.45 GHz and

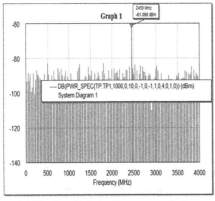 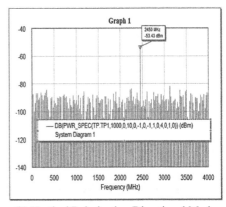

(a) Vertical Polarization Omni Mode   (b) Vertical Polarization Directional Mode

Fig. 13. Received spectrum at the destination node (Path1) after multiple (10) hops at frequency of 2.45 GHz.

5.2 GHz with all its nodes using monopole antennas with a gain of 1 dBi. The received spectra at the destination node after 10 hops after concurrent operation at 2.45 GHz and 5.2 GHz is shown in Fig. 14. From the results of spectra of Fig. 14, the amplitude of the signal at the destination after 10 hops is higher than the sensitivity of the receiver. The results of the simulation shown in Fig. 14 include the losses in the splitter of the developed model.

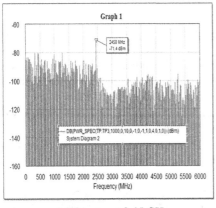 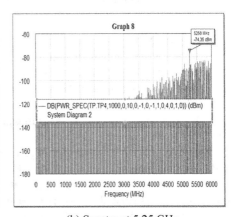

(a) Spectra at 2.45 GHz   (b) Spectra at 5.25 GHz

Fig. 14. Received spectra at the destination node operating simultaneously at 2.45 GHz and 5.25 GHz (omni mode)

The results of Fig. 14 clearly substantiate the feasibility of concurrent transmission of signals over a single path (route) of a MANET with multiple hops using the SF reuse concept. This concept can be utilized for two simultaneous operations of transmission of data using one frequency and monitoring of the route using second frequency. The SF reuse concept can also be used for the concurrent transmission of data over the same path at two different frequencies to realise improved throughput of the MANET.

4.3   SF Reuse in Directional Mode

After substantiating the feasibility of SF reuse concept along the same path of a MANET in omni mode, simulation studies are carried out with all the nodes in the path (Path1) operating simultaneously at 2.45 GHz and 5.25 GHz with directional radiation pattern (Gain 5 dBi). The received spectra at the D after 10 hops with concurrent operation at both 2.45 GHz and 5.2 GHz is shown in Fig. 15. The amplitude of the received signal at both 2.45 GHz and 5.2 GHz is above the sensitivity of the receiver thus establishing the satisfactory performance of the entire route (Path1) comprising 10 hops. A comparative analysis of the results in Figs. 14 and 15 reveals that the directional mode with higher antenna gain results in improved amplitude of the received signal.

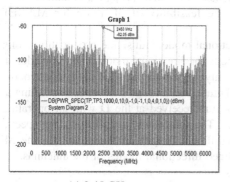

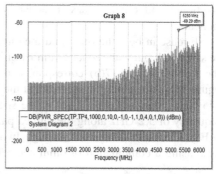

(a) 2.45 GHz   (b) 5.25 GHz

Fig. 15. Received spectra at the destination node operating simultaneously at 2.45 GHz and 5.25 GHz in vertical polarisation (directional mode)

4.4   SF Reuse with a Combination of Omni Mode and Directional Mode

In Sect. 4.2, the feasibility of SF reuse with all the nodes of Path1 in omni mode is established. The analogous directional mode for SF reuse is discussed in Sect. 4.3. The viability of SF reuse with a combination of omni mode and directional mode is presented in this section. The simulation results on the received spectra at the D using combination of omni and directional modes are shown in Fig. 16. The spectrum shown in Fig. 16(a) is for the omni mode for VP at an operating frequency of 2.45 GHz. Figure 16(b) illustrates the spectrum received by the D in directional mode with VP at an operating frequency of 5.2 GHz.

The amplitude of the signal at the D in directional mode is higher because of the higher gain of the antenna. From the results in Fig. 16, the satisfactory amplitude of the

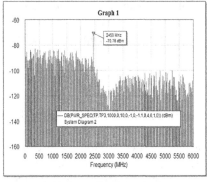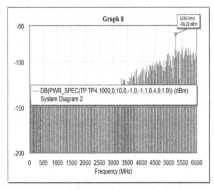

(a) 2.45 GHz (Omni Mode) VP   (b) 5.25 GHz (Directional Mode) VP

Fig. 16. Received spectra at the destination node operating simultaneously at 2.45 GHz (omni mode) and 5.25 GHz (directional mode) in VP

received signals at the two different frequencies obtained through a combination of directional and omni modes demonstrate the feasibility of SF reuse for MANET application.

SF reuse in both the omni and the directional mode with signal propagation along the same path but with reduced number of hops for directional mode is also considered. The results in Fig. 17(b) corresponds to only in 2 hops for the directional mode. Figure 17(a) illustrates the spectrum at the D received through omni mode operating at 2.45 GHz. Similarly, Fig. 17(b) is the spectrum received at the D with an operating frequency of 5.2 GHz along the refined path. The satisfactory amplitude of the spectra of Fig. 17 at the D received through two different frequencies demonstrates the SF reuse using a combination of omni and refined directional modes of the antennas.

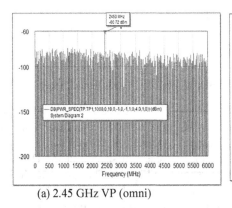

(a) 2.45 GHz VP (omni)   (b) 5.25 GHz VP (directional) with 2 hops

Fig. 17. Received spectra at the destination node operating simultaneously at 2.45 GHz (omni mode) and 5.25 GHz (directional with minimum hops)

4.5 Throughput Analysis of MANET with SF Reuse Concept

In Sects. 4.2 to 4.4 of this paper, the focus is on the utility of SF reuse concept for concurrent transmission of data as well as monitoring the route (path). The SF concept can also be used for the improvement of throughput performance of MANET. This section presents simulation studies on improvement in throughput of a MANET with the application of SF reuse concept. The combination of two microstrip antennas designed to operate at 2.45 GHz and 5.2 GHz both in VP is shown in Fig. 18(a). The two antennas are separated by a distance of 25 mm and are configured to radiate simultaneously.

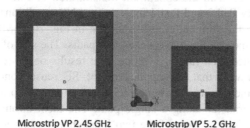

Microstrip VP 2.45 GHz   Microstrip VP 5.2 GHz

Fig. 18. Two microstrip antennas for SF reuse concept

The simulated radiation pattern of the antenna operating at 2.45 GHz shown in Fig. 19(a) indicates a co-polarization gain of 4.82 dBi with a cross polarization (HP) of −45 dBi. Figure 19(b) depicts the simulated radiation pattern of the microstrip antenna operating at 5.2 GHz. It exhibits a co-polarization (VP) gain of 5.59 dBi with a cross polarization (HP) of −22 dBi. The directional performance of the two microstrip antennas shown in Fig. 18 is satisfactory despite being in close proximity to each other. Therefore, these two antennas are used in the simulation of SF concept in MANET.

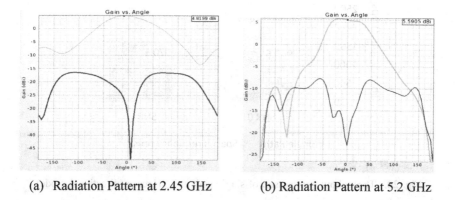

(a) Radiation Pattern at 2.45 GHz   (b) Radiation Pattern at 5.2 GHz

Fig. 19. Radiation patterns of microstrip antennas in azimuth plane with VP

To analyse the throughput performance of MANET with SF reuse, the two paths namely Path2 (with 9 intermediate nodes) and Path4 (with 15 intermediate nodes) shown in Table 1 are used in the application of SF reuse concept with node 11 as S and node 29 as D. The path2 has been assigned the frequency of 2.45 GHz with VP. For path4, the frequency of 5.2 GHz is assigned with VP. The gain parameters of the two microstrip antennas shown in Fig. 19 are taken for the throughput performance of the MANET to show the improvement in the throughput with the application of SF reuse. The proposed SF reuse concept is not amenable for implementation in commercial simulators like QUALNET and NS-2. A source code is developed in MATLAB to carry out the simulations of a MANET with SF reuse concept. The simulation results on throughput obtained with the concurrent transmission of data along the two independent paths namely Path2 and Path4 for varying SNR conditions of the channel are shown in Fig. 20. In the simulation results shown in Fig. 20, 2 MB of data has been distributed equally amongst the two independent paths. The size of each packet is 512 Bytes and the assigned data rate is 1 Mbps. The results on throughput performance shown in Fig. 20 reveal that the application of SF reuse concept results in the throughput improvement factor of about 1.95 when compared to the throughput realizable through data transfer along a single path. The ideal throughput improvement factor with SF reuse is 2 in view of the two independent paths for concurrent transmission of data. The throughput improvement factor of 1.95 realized through two independent paths (Path2 and Path4) compares favorably with the ideal throughput improvement of 2. Thus, the simulation studies presented in this section clearly substantiates the utility of SF reuse concept for the improved throughput of MANET considering the realistic radiation performance of directional antennas. Similar results are obtained with the two antennas working in omni directional mode.

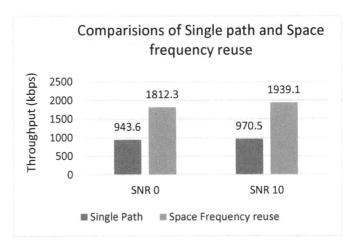

Fig. 20. Throughput comparison of single path and SF reuse (directional mode)

5 Conclusions

The concept of SF reuse technique applicable to MANET with multiple intermediate nodes has been simulated through a development of a model for propagation of RF signal from the source to destination nodes. The developed model aims to simulate the basic operations involved in source node, intermediate nodes and the destination node. Numerous simulation results are presented to represent the reception of signal at the destination node of a MANET under: (a) Single path Transmission with a single frequency operation (b) Single path Transmission with DF operation (c) Single Path operation with combination of omni mode and (d) directional mode with each mode operating at different frequencies (equal number of hops); Single Path operation with combination of omni mode and refined directional mode with each mode operating at different frequencies (unequal number of hops of nodes). Satisfactory reception of signals in all the above stated scenarios further substantiates the validity of SF reuse concepts as applied to a MANET system. The throughput analysis of a MANET with SF reuse has revealed an improvement factor of about 1.95 relative to data transmission along a single path substantiating the importance of SF reuse concept.

References

1. Prabha, R., Ramaraj, N.: An improved multipath MANET routing using link estimation and swarm intelligence. EURASIP J. Wirel. Commun. Netw. 90–173 (2015)
2. Logambal, R., Chitra, K.: Energy efficient hierarchical routing algorithm in MANETs. In: IEEE International Conference on Advances in Computer Applications (ICACA), 978-1-5090-3770-4/16 (2016)
3. Kiran, Kalra, S.: An improved energy efficient routing algorithm for MANETs. In: Innovative Systems Design and Engineering, vol. 7, no. 5 (2016). ISSN 2222-1727
4. Bojd, E.A., Moghim, N.: A new connectionless routing algorithm using cross-layer design approach in MANETs. Automatika 57(2), 514–524 (2016)
5. Li, Y., Man, H., Yu, J., Yao, Y.D.: Multipath routing in ad hoc networks using directional antennas. In: 2004 IEEE/Sarnoff Symposium on Advances in Wired and Wireless Communication, pp. 119–122. IEEE (2004)
6. Lal, C., Laxmi, V., Gaur, M.S.: A node-disjoint multipath routing method based on AODV protocol for MANETs. In: IEEE 26th International Conference on Advanced Information Networking and Applications (AINA), pp. 399–405. IEEE (2012)
7. Patel, D., Rana, A.: Power aware routing protocol to extend life-time of MANET. Int. J. Eng. Res. Technol. (IJERT), 1(10) (2012)
8. Allalili, M.A., Maaza, Z.M., Kies, A., Belbachir, R: Distributed traffic by load-balancing approach for AOMDV in ad-hoc networks. In: SAI, pp. 271–278 (2012)
9. Nagaratna, M., Narasimha Rao, V.G.: Rebroadcasting for minimization of routing based upon neighbor coverage in MANET's. Int. J. Sci. Res. 4, 616–620 (2015)
10. Ramanathan, R., Redi, J., Santivanez, C., Wiggins, D., Polit, S.: Ad hoc networking with directional antennas: a complete system solution. IEEE J. Commun. 23(3), 496–506 (2005)
11. Amith, K.S., David, B.: Routing improvement using directional antennas in MANETs. In: IEEE International Conference on Mobile Ad hoc Networks, Fort Lauderdale, Florida, 24–27 October, pp. 304–313 (2005)

12. Yamamoto, K., Yamamoto, M.: Performance improvement of ad hoc networks by deployment of directional antenna. Inf. Media Technol. **2**(3), 907–913 (2007)
13. Roy, C.R., Nitin, H.V.: Performance of ad hoc routing using directional antennas. In: Proceedings of the Fourth Annual IEEE Communications Society Conference on Sensor, University of Illinois at Urbana Champaign, vol. 22, no. 5, pp. 401–410 (2007)
14. Rinki, S.: Simulation studies on effects of dual polarisation and directivity of antennas on the performance of MANETs. Ph.D. thesis, Coventry University, UK (2014)
15. Yonghui, C., Chunfeng, Z.: A multipath routing protocol with path compression for ad hoc networks. In: 3rd International Conference on Advanced Computer Theory and Engineering (ICA CTE), vol. 20, no. 5, pp. 1–5 (2010)
16. Chilukuri, S.: Design and development of an energy efficient multipath routing protocol using directional antenna for MANETs. M.Sc. (Engg.) thesis, Coventry University, UK (2012)
17. Chuc, D.H., Duong, B.G.: Design and fabrication of rectifying antenna circuit for wireless power transmission system operating at ism band. Int. J. Electr. Comput. Eng. **6**(4), 1522 (2016)
18. Bhattacherjee, A., Roy, S., Chakraborty, S., Mukherjee, A., Bhattacharya, S.K.: Study of wireless communication through coal using dielectric constant. In: Mandal, J.K., Satapathy, S.C., Sanyal, M.K., Sarkar, P.P., Mukhopadhyay, A. (eds.) Information Systems Design and Intelligent Applications. AISC, vol. 339, pp. 831–841. Springer, New Delhi (2015). https://doi.org/10.1007/978-81-322-2250-7_83
19. Dailey, J.M., Agarwal, A., Toliver, P.: Multiband RF filter enabled through optical phase-sensitive amplification. In: Frontiers in Optics, p. FTu5I-4. Optical Society of America (2016)

Enhancement of Land Cover and Land Use Classification Accuracy Using Spectral and Textural Features of Fused Images

Parminder Kaur Birdi$^{(\boxtimes)}$ ⓘ and Karbhari Kale

Department of CS and IT, Dr. Babasaheb Ambedkar Marathwada University,
Aurangabad 431003, Maharashtra, India
dhingra.param@gmail.com, Kvkale91@gmail.com

Abstract. The main focus of this study is to measure accuracy of classification for combined spectral features and textural features of fused images obtained after applying different fusion techniques. Study area is selected with a variety of land cover features so as to understand effect of fusion on different land cover features. IHS, GS, PC, CN and Brovey fusion methods are used. A different layer stacked method has been used to create a composite image of bands 5, 4 and 3 of Landsat8, since they show maximum spectral reflectance variations in the land features present in the selected area of study. Resampling is carried out using Nearest Neighbor and Cubic Convolution, where Nearest Neighbor gave better accuracy of fused image. Classification is performed using spectral features of fused images, textural features of fused images and composite images created using spectral and textural features. Fused images are assessed for distortion using visual analysis and statistical parameters. Classification accuracy is measured using error matrix and it has observed that Neural Net classifier produced better accuracies than other classifiers like Maximum Likelihood, Minimum distance classifier and Spectral Angle Mapper. Land cover and land use (LULC) classification accuracy is enhanced using textural features of fused images.

Keywords: Accuracy · Classification · Error matrix · Image fusion
Land cover and land use · Spectral features · Textural features

1 Introduction

A large number of sensors provide different images for the same study area. Different sensor provides images with varying quality depending upon their spatial and spectral resolution. Data fusion is the method in which multiple bands from different images are combined to create a single composite image. Fusion of data results in enhancements of the image for visual interpretation and quantitative assessment. The process of fusing images can improve the interpretation of the image data visually. Fusion can be applied to images/data provided by most of the latest earth observation satellites providing high-resolution panchromatic and low-resolution multispectral data (Richards and Jia 2006). Fusion of satellite images can be carried out using methods which work on three

© Springer Nature Singapore Pte Ltd. 2018
A. V. Deshpande et al. (Eds.): SmartCom 2017, CCIS 876, pp. 317–325, 2018.
https://doi.org/10.1007/978-981-13-1423-0_33

different levels: per-pixel/data level, the features extracted from the image and the decision level (Pohl and Van Genderen 1998).

Classification technique which makes use of the spectral features is the most popular procedures for identifying LU/LC. Also, researchers combined the spectral features, the spatial features i.e. the relationship between neighboring pixels. These methods are called as object-based image analysis (OBIA). Adam et al. (2016) compared pixel-based and object- based methods in LULC classification. Authors classified LULC using nearest neighbor classifier with fuzzy logic and found that pixel-based methods have better accuracy than object-based methods. Authors concluded that better performance of object-based methods depends on the choice of correct training objects. Salas et al. (2016) used Moment Distance Index (MDI) combined with texture features for the vegetation mapping of Landsat8 image. Using random forest classifier, authors found the overall classification accuracy, 92% for the input as texture features and MDI & 84% for input as texture only.

Tassetti et al. (2010) used vegetation index (NDVI & TDVI masks) and texture measures along with edge-density features to measure its impact on LULC classification on IKONOS imagery. Authors concluded that NDVI band combined with six texture features achieved an accuracy of 80.01% compared to 63.44% of accuracy achieved by input from few spectral bands only. Wei et al. (2016) used texture images of Landsat8 imagery using a fractal dimension method. Image is classified using SVM classifier having textural and spectral features as input. Authors found that the fused SVM classifier achieved an overall classification accuracy of 83.73% for lithological applications. Zakeri et al. (2017) used texture data from SAR imagery and found that the overall accuracy is enhanced by stacking texture features and backscatter values.

Shastri et al. (2016) used LISS-IV dataset and applied Brovey Transform, Principal Component Analysis, Multiplicative Technique (MT), Intensity Hue Saturation and High Pass Filtering (HPF) methods for image fusion. Kumar et al. (2015) used dataset of Landsat-5 TM bands with spatial resolution of 30 m and World View-2 (WV-2) with spatial resolution of 2 m. Authors observed that fusing bands of 2 m spatial resolution can attain higher producer's, user's and overall accuracies as compared to the classification of medium-resolution Landsat and WV-2 data. Lazaridou and Karagianni (2016) have also attempted fusion of Landsat8 imagery and found that it enhances classification accuracies. Hebbara and Sai (2014) also found similar results on merged data of LISS-III & LISS-IV.

From all the papers studied related to this work, it has been observed that fusion has been carried out using images from high spatial resolution satellites, which is not free to access. In this paper, texture features of fused images are used from moderate/coarse spatial resolution satellite Landsat8, freely available. Landsat8 image is preprocessed i.e. raw DN values are calibrated to reflectance values. Image fusion of multispectral (MS) bands having spatial resolution of 30 m with PAN band of same sensor of spatial resolution 15 m has been carried out and results of fusion with reference images are recorded. Various fusion techniques are used to perform fusion. Spectral features and textural features of fused images are used to classify using Neural Net (NN) classifier. NN classifier is used for classifying all combined images since it outperformed all other classifiers in these experiments. It has been observed that combined spectral and textural features enhanced LULC classification accuracies for some fused images.

2 Study Area

The study site is an area in Aurangabad city of Maharashtra, India that contains both manmade and natural features. This site is selected to understand effect of fusion on different land cover features. The study area lies between 19° 10' 1.6" to 21° 16' 29.75" North Latitude and 74° 43' 44.83" to 76° 53' 42.79" East Longitude.

3 Image Dataset Details

A Level 1T (terrain corrected) scene of the OLI/TIRS sensor, of PATH & ROW: 146 & 46 Landsat-8 acquired on March 21, 2017 is downloaded from the USGS Earth Explorer database (United States Geological Survey) (http://earthexplorer.usgs.gov/). Landsat8 satellite has 11 bands with spatial resolution 30 m for 8 bands (B1 to B7 and B9) and 100 m for TIRS bands (B10 and B11, resampled to 30 m) and 15 m for PAN band (B8). Landsat8 provides imagery with 16 days repeat cycle i.e. temporal resolution.

Figure 1 shows the subset of the image used for this study.

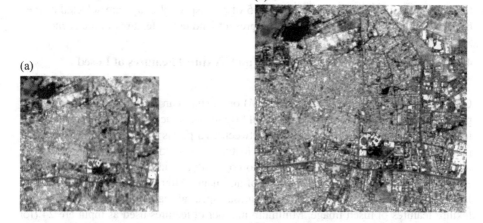

Fig. 1. (a) L8 reference image (b) L 8 PAN band of the same area

4 Methodology Used and Experimentation

After obtaining Landsat8 data, images are preprocessed and various fusion methods are applied. Fused image is taken as input and various classification algorithms are applied to check which classification techniques generates accurately classified data. Texture features of reference (L8 seven spectral band images) and fused images are obtained. Layer stacked images were created using spectral features and texture features of reflectance image and fused images.

4.1   Image Preprocess/Correction

Landsat8, L1T products are radiometrically & geometrically corrected. It uses GCPs and DEMs to perform geometric corrections. L1T image is presented in units of Digital Numbers (DNs), which can be rescaled to spectral radiance/Top-Of-Atmosphere (TOA) reflectance. Landsat8 images (MS bands and PAN band) were converted to Top-of-Atmosphere reflectance values by .applying radiometric calibration. (Information courtesy: usgs.gov/Landsat8DataUserhandbook.pdf). Accuracy of corrected image was verified with the Landsat8 surface reflectance higher level image obtained from USGS.

4.2   Fusion Methods Used

According to Pohl and Van Genderen (1998) the image fusion method can be broadly put into two types: (1) Colour related methods, and (2) Statistical methods. In this research work methods used are: Intensity Hue & Saturation (IHS) (Mather 2004), Gram-Schmidt (GS) (Laben et al. 2000), PC Spectral Sharpening (PC), Brovey Fusion (Jensen 2005), CN Spectral Sharpening (Vrabel et al. 2002) and Proposed fusion method: Layer Stack R, G NIR with PAN, resample using NN & CC: A layer stacking method has been used in which RGB composite of Band 3, 4 and 5 of Landsat8 corrected image is resampled to the 15 m spatial resolution and then it is stacked with the PAN band. Two methods of resampling are used namely Nearest Neighbor (NN) and Cubic Convolution (CC). Bands 3, 4 and 5 of multispectral image are selected as they have maximum reflectance values of the present land cover features in the scene.

4.3   Combined Images Using Spectral and Textural Features of Fused Images

Gray Level Co-occurrence Matrix (GLCM) or Texture can be defined as frequency of presence of different combinations of pixel brightness values (or digital numbers) in an image. It considers the spatial relation between two pixels at a time i.e. the reference pixel and the adjacent pixels. Textural features are computed from co-occurrence matrix as the various measures of mean, homogeneity, variance, contrast, dissimilarity, entropy, correlation and second moment of an image. After computing texture images, layer stacking is performed to combine various spectral features of fused images with texture features of fused image. Minimum number of features used as input are 24 (for IHS fused image 3 layers of I, H & S and 8 texture features of every layer) and maximum is 56 features (L8 reference image with 8 texture features for 7 bands, same for PC & CN).

4.4   Classification Methods Used in the Experiments

Supervised classification methods are based on the prior knowledge of the area to be classified. In this study methods used are Maximum Likelihood Classifier (MLC), Parallelepiped, Mahalanobis distance, Minimum distance, Spectral Angle Mapper (SAM), Spectral Information Divergence (SID) and Neural Net (NN), (Mather 2004). Five land cover classes namely water, road, vegetation, building and bare lands were found to be present in the study area. These points were selected from different locations representing identified land cover features of the study area. Two different set of training and test samples were created for classification. Training set contained 401 points as training samples. Using the training samples, the whole image area is classified into desired land cover types. Different set of 205 points were created for testing the classification accuracies.

5 Results and Observations

5.1 Accuracy Assessment of Fused Images

Accuracy assessment of fused images is done using visual analysis and quantitative analysis. Visual interpretation of fused images shows that identification of land cover features have improved due to increase in spatial resolution. The fused images are visually enhanced and have higher visual quality as compared to reference multispectral image of Landsat 8. Statistical Quality Index: Quality index i.e. amount of distortion introduced is defined to measure the similarity between images. Mean Bias is defined as:

$$\Delta\mu = \mu_{ref} - \mu_{fused} \tag{1}$$

SDD (Standard Deviation Difference) is defined as:

$$\Delta sdd = sd_{ref} - sd_{fused} \tag{2}$$

If there is no distortion or quality change between the reference and fused image then the values of mean bias and SDD should be zero. The RMS error as proposed by Thomas and Wald (2006) is calculated as the square root of the sum of the differences of the standard deviation and the mean of the reference and the fused image. The expected value is again zero. RMSE is defined as:

$$rmse = \sqrt{(\Delta sdd^2 + \Delta\mu^2)} \tag{3}$$

Among different fusion techniques, the mean and standard deviation value of all fused images in band 4 is closest to mean and standard deviation value of reference image showing similarity in spectral information. Standard deviation value of LayStkCC & LayStkNN merged images show highest variations in all three bands. Mean bias and SDD values calculated using Eqs. (1) and (2) show that spectral quality of fused images using CN fusion method is closest to reference image. CN and GS fusion methods show small mean bias and Brovey fusion method show larger bias indicating spectral distortion in all 3 bands. According to Wald et al. (1997), standard deviation difference (SDD) indicates quantity of information lost or added (noise) during fusion process. RMSE is also measured with mean bias and SDD values. CN fused image has minimum RMSE, GS has second minimum LayStkNN fused images. Table 1 shows statistical or quantitative evaluation of fused images.

5.2   Accuracy Assessment of Classification of Combined Images (Texture, Spectral and Textures Plus Spectral Features of Fused Images)

Error matrix is used to record the classification accuracy. A minimum of 35 training points per land cover class are used to prepare training set. Seven classification methods were used for classification of texture features of reference L8 image, texture features of fused images and combined spectral and texture fused images. It was found that Neural Net classifier performed best so, error matrix is shown for NN method. Table 2: Confusion matrix shows that fused images have higher classification accuracies. It is observed from values of Jeffries-Matusita (JM) and Transformed Divergence (TD) that vegetation can be misclassified as bare land as some parts of bare land has sparse trees, building as road due to similar spectral signature and vegetation as road due to trees present on roadsides. PA of water body improves for texture images constructed after fusion. PA value of vegetation class increases from 60.94% to 78.35% and built-up class from 27.27% to 73.1% texture features of PC fused image as compared to reference image. Similar is noticed for LayStkCC fused image.

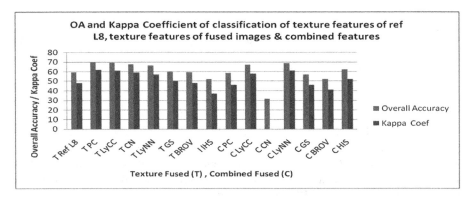

Fig. 2. Overall accuracy/kappa coefficient of classification of texture and combined features of fused images (T PC is Texture of PC fused image)

Table 1. Statistical evaluation of fused images (*Bands considered are R G and NIR)

	Ref img (L8 MS)	CN fused	PC fused	GS fused	IHS fused	Brovey fused	LayStkCC fused*	LayStkNN fused*
Mean	144.9	145.1	142.8	143.9	146.2	137.2	132.5	132.0
SD	56.66	57	54	53.66	57	56.66	56.48	55.92
Mean bias	–	−0.2	2.1	1	−1.3	7.7	1.49	1.84
SDD	–	−0.34	2.44	3.00	−0.34	0	−2.03	−1.47
RMSE	–	0.39	3.39	3.16	1.343	7.7	2.51	2.35

Table 2. Producer's and user's accuracy using neural net classification performed on texture images (Reference Image (L8 MS) and Fused Images)

Features	Ref img (L8 MS) 7 bands × 8 = 56		PC img 7 bands × 8 = 56		LayStkCC img 4 bands × 8 = 32		CN img 7 bands × 8 = 56		LayStkNN img 4 bands × 8 = 32		GS img 3 bands × 8 = 24		Brovey img 3 bands × 8 = 24		IHS img 3 bands × 8 = 24	
	PA%	UA%	PA%	UA%	PA%	UA%	PA%	UA%	PA%	UA%	PA%	UA%	PA%	UA%	PA%	UA%
WB	84.21	100	100	89.4	100	78.35	100	84.44	100	56.72	100	61.3	100	79.17	100	97.44
BLD	27.27	63.16	73.10	53.42	68.42	58.79	77.78	56.12	50.29	70.49	69.59	56.13	95.91	44.57	39.77	36.66
VEGT	60.94	76.47	78.74	90.09	78.35	87.28	60.63	90.59	75.20	73.18	43.31	85.27	67.32	85.50	78.97	56.37
RD	78.57	40.24	76.8	57.0	72.02	54.5	83.93	55.29	57.23	69.34	76.76	47.43	36.31	44.85	12.50	42.86
BL	61.11	59.60	27.14	90.0	35.00	77.78	30.00	73.68	62.14	56.86	34.29	66.67	06.43	100	39.29	39.29

Note: WB: Water Body, BLD: Buildings, VEGT: Vegetation, RD: Road, BL: Bare Land; PA: Producer's Accuracy, UA: User's Accuracy

Figure 2 shows that highest overall accuracy of classification is recorded for texture features of PC fused image with OA of 70.2% & Kappa coefficient of 0.62 as compared to texture image of reference L8 image with OA of 59.12% & .48 kappa coefficient. This is followed by LayStkCC and all texture features of fused images show better OA than the texture features from reference L8 image except IHS with 52% OA. IHS has OA of 62.21% if spectral features and texture features are combined, also LayStkNN show enhancement in OA with combined features.

6 Conclusions and Future Scope

In this study, seven image fusion methods are used to fuse Landsat8 images in which two methods of creating fused images using the concept of layer stacking is experimented. Two methods of resampling are used namely Nearest Neighbor (NN) and Cubic Convolution (CC), and NN resampling produced better quality fused image because image contains categorical data. Texture features of fused images were computed and then classification methods were performed on the reference image and texture features of fused images and combined spectral and texture features of fused images. It was observed that Neural Net classifier produced good overall accuracy of classification. Textural features of all fused images enhanced classification accuracy except IHS and combined spectral and texture features of LayStkNN and IHS fused images produced better OA as compared to only textural features of fused image.

This study can be extended on fusion of texture images from different sensors. Also classification can be further performed on fused images at sub-class level. Quality of fusion methods can be assessed for sub-class classification.

References

Tassetti, A.N., Malinverni, E.S., Hahn, M.: Texture analysis to improve supervised classification in IKONOS imagery. In: ISPRS TC VII Symposium – 100 Years ISPRS, Vienna, IAPRS, vol. XXXVIII, Part 7A (2010)

Laben, C.A., Bernard, V., Brower, W.: Process for enhancing the spatial resolution of multispectral imagery using pansharpening. US Patent 6,011,875 (2000)

Thomas, C., Wald, L.: Comparing distances for quality assessment of fused images. In: 26th EARSeL Symposium, Varsovie, Poland, May 2006, pp. 101–111. Millpress (2006)

Salas, E.A.L., Boykin, K.G., Valdez, R.: Multispectral and texture feature application in image-object analysis of summer vegetation in Eastern Tajikistan Pamirs. Remote Sens. 8, 78 (2016). https://doi.org/10.3390/rs8010078

Adam, H.E., Csaplovics, E., Elhaja, M.E.: A comparison of pixel-based and object-based approaches for land use land cover classification in semi-arid areas, Sudan. In: 8th IGRSM International Conference and Exhibition on Remote Sensing & GIS, IGRSM (2016). https://doi.org/10.1088/1755-1315/37/1/012061

Zakeri, H., Yamazaki, F., Liu, W.: Texture analysis and land cover classification of Tehran using polarimetric synthetic aperture radar imagery. Appl. Sci. 7, 452 (2017). https://doi.org/10.3390/app7050452

Jensen, J.R.: Introductory Digital Image Processing: A Remote Sensing Perspective. Prentice Hall, Upper Saddle River (2005)

Vrabel, J., Doraiswamy, P., McMurtrey, J., Stern, A.: Demonstration of the accuracy of improved resolution hyperspectral imagery. In: SPIE Symposium Proceedings, vol. 4725, pp. 556–567 (2002)

Richards, J.A., Jia, X.: Remote Sensing Digital Image Analysis - An Introduction. Springer, Heidelberg (2006). https://doi.org/10.1007/3-540-29711-1

Wei, J., Liu, X., Liu, J.: Integrating textural and spectral features to classify silicate-bearing rocks using Landsat 8 data. Appl. Sci. **6**, 283 (2016). https://doi.org/10.3390/app6100283

Wald, L., Ranchin, T., Mangolini, M.: Fusion of satellite images of different spatial resolutions: assessing the quality of resulting images. Photogramm. Eng. Remote Sens. **63**(6), 691–699 (1997). ASPRS, American Society for Photogrammetry and Remote Sensing

Mather, P.M.: Computer Processing of Remotely-Sensed Images: An Introduction. Wiley, Hoboken (2004). pp. 149–169 and 203–245

Pohl, C., Van Genderen, J.L.: Multisensor image fusion in remote sensing: concepts, methods, and applications. Int. J. Remote Sens. **19**, 823–854 (1998)

Hebbara, R., Sai, M.V.R.S.: Comparison of LISS-IV MX & LISS-III + LISS-IV merged data for classification of crops. ISPRS Ann. Photogramm. Remote Sens. Spat. Inf. Sci. **II**(8), 101 (2014)

Topaloglua, R.H., Sertel, E., Musaoglu, N.: Assessment of classification accuracies of Sentinel-2 and Landsat-8 data for land cover/use mapping. Int. Arch. Photogramm. Remote Sens. Spat. Inf. Sci. **XLI-B8** (2016)

Shastri, C.S., Kumar, T.A., Koliwad, S.P.: Advances in classification techniques for semi urban land features using high resolution satellite data. Int. J. Adv. Remote Sens. GIS **5**(3), 1639–1648 (2016)

Kumar, U., Milesi, C., Nemani, R.R., Basu, S.: Multi sensor multi resolution image fusion for improved vegetation & urban area classification. Int. Arch. Photogramm. Remote Sens. Spat. Inf. Sci. **XL**(7), W4 (2015)

http://earthexplorer.usgs.gov. Accessed 25 Apr 2017

Lazaridou, M.A., Karagianni, A.Ch.: Landsat 8 multispectral and pansharpened imagery processing on the study of civil engineering issues. In: The International Archives of the Photogrammetry, Remote Sensing and Spatial Information Sciences, XXIII ISPRS Congress, vol. XLI-B8 (2016)

A Dual Protocol Stack for Intelligent Traffic Monitoring System

S. Sasirekha[1(✉)] and S. Swamynathan[2]

[1] Department of Information Technology, SSN College of Engineering, Chennai, India
sasirekhas@ssn.edu.in
[2] Department of Information Science and Technology,
Anna University, Chennai, India
swamyns@annauniv.edu

Abstract. In recent years, there is an urge for more readily available real-time data from the Wireless Sensor Networks (WSNs) by the consumers especially in industry, healthcare, environmental observation and monitoring applications. Hence, to meet the timely requirements of these requests, there are many real-time routing protocols have been already designed. However, there exists no specific way in a programming environment, to allow the instant access to the sensor information specifically for WSN. Also, as the density of WSN grows with heterogeneity, the amount of data which is being collected from the sensors increases and using this real-time data in a flexible way results as one of the biggest challenges in WSN. But, the recent prototypes and research contribution promises the possibility of integrating Internet Protocol (IP) with the sensor to overcome these problems. Therefore, in this work, a dual protocol stack using IP and ZigBee is proposed as a solution to address this issue. To allow the instant access between consumer and wireless sensor networks, a seamless integration is enabled by allocating IP address to sensor nodes. Further, the heterogeneity and inter-networking among different sensor networks is handled by stacking the standard interfacing protocol IEEE 802.15.4, ZigBee. The performance of this dual protocol is tested and evaluated for a road traffic monitoring scenario. This evaluation is carried out for two cases; the first one is instant access to the current traffic status for a particular region and the second one is to find the optimal path to reach the destination. The results show that the road traffic management system using the proposed dual protocol seems to be simple, energy efficient and accurate. The system provides the consumer with useful data about the traffic condition in a user-friendly and easily accessible manner.

Keywords: Wireless Sensor Networks (WSNs)
Internet Protocol (IP) · ZigBee · Heterogeneity
Road traffic monitoring

© Springer Nature Singapore Pte Ltd. 2018
A. V. Deshpande et al. (Eds.): SmartCom 2017, CCIS 876, pp. 326–337, 2018.
https://doi.org/10.1007/978-981-13-1423-0_34

1   Introduction

Wireless sensor networks (WSN) often deploy a large number of smart sensor nodes to collect and propagate the environmental data. In the recent years, it is frequently used in various applications to monitor and control the physical environments from remote locations. Moreover, due to its progress in Micro-Electro-Mechanical System (MEMS), sensors are providing better accuracy than other known monitoring systems such as remote sensing, ultrasonic detectors, a camera-based system, laser based system and Infrared detectors [1,2]. Figure 1 depicts a single node/mote of a WSN. It typically consists of one or more sensors, a processing unit with processing and program memory, a wireless transceiver transmit the sensed data to sink node in the form of signals and the whole unit powered by a battery power supply.

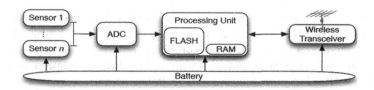

Fig. 1. Typical smart sensor node.

WSN applications started initially used by military surveillance, environmental monitoring, habitat and structural monitoring. Currently, it has broadened itself in emerging applications such as automation and supervision of buildings, surveilling underwater and follow-up patients in healthcare [18]. Due to miniaturization of the sensors, these applications deploy them in large number for efficient control, which results in several horizontal challenges. Some of them are: (i) nodes should be able to communicate wirelessly without any interference (ii) to utilize bandwidth efficiently (iii) to avoid eminent energy consumption, and (iv) nodes have to perform an efficient computation. The research contribution of this work focuses on conspicuous energy consumption and efficient computation for application with a large number of sensor nodes.

The primary goal of a sensor network based application is to provide sensing services to the user or other systems. In such a state, communication is one of the major factors which have a high impact. Survey on this factor reveals that wireless communication consumes the majority of node energy than computation. So, it is evident that there is a need for a communication system that is capable of linking these energy constraints nodes efficiently. As a result, dedicated power-efficient routing protocols have evolved to make the sensor nodes communicate with each other for the information to reach the sink node. In general, the routing protocols for WSN are classified based on its type, their main key features and Quality of Services (QoS) as data-centric protocols, hierarchical routing protocols, and location based routing protocols [13,21]. All the existing protocols restrict itself to a particular or fixed system architecture and design. Therefore, the performance of a given protocol varies for an application with a particular scenario on node deployment, data delivery modes, network dynamics, data aggregation and energy consideration [24, 25]. It is also evident from the survey that none of these identified protocols provide support for internet connectivity [6]. Elsewhere, Internet an already established means that is used to connect billions of users. It is seen as the strongest contender to extend its communication support to device-to-humans and device-to-device exchanges [14]. Therefore, with the minor fabrication of the sensor devices can enable them to join this existing network. It is easily achieved by making the devices Internet Protocol (IP) enabled [20]. Many researchers working in this area have taken similar steps to communicate with the sensor nodes and access their sensed data instantly. The results have justified that energy spent on communication is a smaller amount when compared to the traditional proxy/sink access node methods [7].

In the proposed work, to provide instant access to the data and interoperability between heterogeneous devices, a dual protocol stack using IPv4 and ZigBee is provided as a solution to this problem. That is, to allow instant access to consumer and wireless sensor networks a seamless integration is achieved by allocating IP address to sensor nodes. Further, the heterogeneity and internetworking among different sensor networks is handled by stacking the standard interfacing protocol IEEE 802.15.4, ZigBee.

The rest of this paper is organized as follows. In Sect. 2, surveys of relevant works are discussed. Section 3 illustrates the architecture of proposed system and the different components involved in it. In Sect. 4, the test environmental set up for traffic monitoring system is illustrated and in Sect. 5 experimental results and performance of the proposed solution are presented. Finally, Sect. 6 gives the conclusions.

2   Related Works

In most of the sensor network application, the sensor networks cannot operate in complete isolation. There should be a way for an entity to monitor and gain access to the sensed network. The recent survey shows, that use of IP as the addressing mechanism for WSN is being recently endorsed [19, 22]. Since, the proposed work focuses on the use of IP within WSNs and ZigBee for facilitating the integration of WSN and other networks, the some of the related works to strengthen the contribution is discussed in this section.

Dunkels [9] has introduced the first TCP/IP stack, micro IP (μIP) and lightweight IP (lwIP) for smart sensor node. Both these solutions conform to a subset of RFC 1122 and feature IP, TCP, and ICMP implementations. The μIP was primarily developed only for a very low-processing power system with 8-bit processor architectures and the lwIP seemed to occupy a larger footprint for more capable systems. Hence, these achievements clarify that for 8 bit processor architecture, TCP/IP was too complex for smart nodes.

The following studies support that many researchers have started involving IP based WSN in their applications. Dunkels et al. [10] presents an intrusion monitoring system with IP-based WSN implementation. Here, an Embedded Sensor Board (ESB) platform from FU Berlin motes which runs on the Contiki Operating System (OS) and μIP stack has been employed for building the network. The authors have used spatial IP address assignment for node address configuration, which use node position coordinates. In addition, an overlay network is used, where a set of core nodes form a backbone which receives alarm events from the smart sensor nodes. Similarly, in the health care domain a Body sensor network (BSN) with IP-enabled motes was proposed in [16]. The sensor nodes were designed to capture the human health parameters and to transmit them in an unobtrusive way. Researchers at HP Labs developed an IP-enabled BSN featuring TCP/IP for motion data capture. The nodes use TinyOS and μIP stack over IEEE 802.15.4, featuring a small amount of flash memory to store data, enabling continuous operation [12].

An IP-enabled WSN architecture named IPSense in [19] demonstrates the various issues of using IP over WSN and how it can be handled efficiently. IPSense explores node aggregation through the use of cluster heads designated as Sensor Routers that manage communication to the sink node. Sensor routers are placed as gateways between the sensor network and other networks, and benefit from more hardware resources when compared with smart sensor nodes. The features of IPSense include flexible addressing and enhanced mobility. However, the implementation of these features is not addressed in detail. Hence, the proposed work focuses on the use of IP within WSNs and ZigBee for the purpose of facilitating the integration of WSN and other networks.

In [11], an architecture for connecting WSNs to the Internet using gateways is presented. The IPv6-based communication relies on a dual-mode operation for the gateways which connect to the Internet via WiFi access point infrastructure. The idea is to exploit the widely deployed WiFi facilities which can be found easily within established areas nowadays. The issue with this architecture lies in what the authors consider its chief merit; namely the reliance on existing infrastructure. If the WSN has to be set up in areas where no infrastructure exists, which is applicable for many WSN applications, this arrangement would not be usable.

To summarize, the identified challenges of IP based WSN are: (i) size of the header is large for such a small packet wireless communication (e.g. the IEEE 802.15.4 standard [15]) (ii) need for a global addressing scheme (iii) the limited bandwidth (typically around 250 kbps or even lower) (iv) limited energy of the nodes (v) implementation challenges, and (vi) also the TCP transport protocol. So, in this research work, the aim is to concentrate specifically on providing a communication system that is capable of linking these energy constraints nodes efficiently [3].

However, to perform a real-time analysis of the proposed dual protocol, which provides dual access support such as synchronous (pull) and asynchronous (push) access types, a particular application is required to be considered for this study.

Therefore, a traffic monitoring system is chosen in this work, where this kind of system is identified to seek support for these types of access requests for availing them as a smart system.

3   Design of Hybrid Protocol Stack for WSN IP Integration

The main contribution of the proposed system is to provide instant access to the sensed information and to achieve interoperability among the heterogeneous devices. The proposed system serves as a uniform, standard and abstract development model for developing WSN applications. Figure 2 shows the layered architecture of the proposed system. The architecture includes four significant layers such as the hardware/firmware layer, the sensor network interface layer, data management and intelligence layer and the application service layer [23].

The hardware/firmware is the physical layer, built by deploying several sensor nodes which have different sensing capabilities. The sensor network interface layer provides a standard interface function to various multiple heterogeneous sensor networks. It also provides continuous monitoring and control functions for the state of various sensor networks. The data management and intelligence layer play the role of providing different query processing functions for sensor

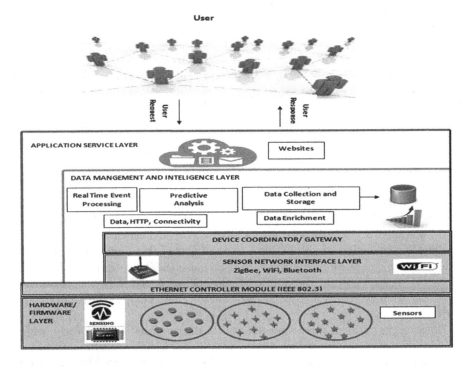

Fig. 2. Design of hybrid protocol stack for WSN IP integration.

data collected from the WSN infrastructure and real-time management functions of sensor information. Finally, the application service layer plays the role of presenting the collected and analyzed data to the user by alerting them for corrective actions.

4   Test Environment Setup for Traffic Monitoring System

The individual sensor nodes are configured as specified in Fig. 3, to enable with the dual protocol. All the nodes are connected in a star topology to establish a network environment. It comprises of end devices (sensor nodes) and a centralized coordinator as a central processing unit. Here, end devices are responsible for sensing the environment, and the role of the coordinator is to gather sensor readings from all heterogeneous end devices and to control the interconnection between them. To demonstrate the prototype of the network is set up with two Arduino UNO boards [4], one Raspberry Pi B+ board [17] and a Begalebone Board [5]. The field test is carried out by deploying the sensor nodes and the coordinator nodes for traffic monitoring and surveillance system. Next, for the purpose of monitoring the traffic, sensors need to be connected to the communication board. To provide users with accurate data about the traffic conditions and the alternate path suggestion for travelling, in the proposed system, magnetometer, accelerometer, passive infra-red sensors and an acoustic microphone are deployed respectively. Rudimental experiments were conducted to analyze

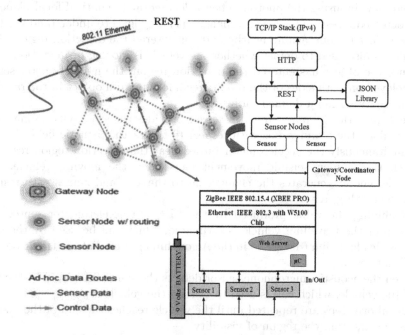

Fig. 3. Individual sensor nodes configuration.

and optimize the system performance. The sensors are attached to a pole and mounted on the two sides of the road which is 5 m apart as shown in Fig. 4 to cover the entire stretch of the road. This type of installation helps to monitor the road to a maximum coverage. The observed readings collected and analysis is carried out to estimate the traffic density.

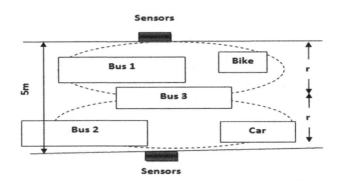

Fig. 4. Deployment of sensors on the two sides of road.

The following sequences of steps are followed to read the sensor values:

1. The PIR sensor detects for the light energy radiating from an object in the field view by using the photon detector located at the optical focal plane.
2. If detected, it estimates for any change in energy level to understand whether the object is approaching nearby and has entered the detection region. This value is also used to detect whether the vehicle is moving or in stationary.
3. Once the object has entered the detection region, the magnetometer sensor deployed on both sides of the road detects for any iron object in the range of sensitivity within a defined radius r.
4. Next, in turn, the magnetometer sensor provides the sensitivity to magnetic flux along the x and y-axis with respect to the earth magnetic field.
5. Simultaneously the accelerometer buried near the detection region responds with the sudden seismic movement caused by the moving vehicle. The accelerometer generates the changes on to the x, y and z-axes with respect to the earth gravity.
6. Combining the value produced by the PIR and accelerometer sensor, the speed of the travelling vehicle is estimated, which can be used by the data analytic algorithm (discussed in the Algorithm 1) to predict the traffic density of that region.
7. Then the acoustic microphone sensor detects the sound generated by the tyre of the vehicle, which can is used to classify the vehicle type.
8. The above steps are repeated until the vehicle reaches the end of the road or disappears from the region of visibility.

After the set up in initialized and starts to function, analysis and test were carried out to justify that the performance of the system with the proposed dual protocol is proficient in providing instant access to the sensed information and achieves interoperability among the heterogeneous devices.

5   Experimental Results

The proposed dual protocol stack provides dual access support such as synchronous and asynchronous access to the sensor data. The system provides the user with flexibility to choose the access mode based on the user requirements. The test run is carried out for the traffic monitoring system set up illustrated above. First, the analysis was done out to prove the efficiency of the system for synchronous request type, i.e., is instant access to the data (pull request). The user is provided with an option to request for the sensor value at any particular time. As the sensor nodes are IP enabled, it supports instant access to the data sensed by the sensor at any point of time to any sensor node in the network.

In case, if the user wishes to choose his/her desired route to a particular destination, an instant request to the node is made with the known IP address. The REST based web service running on this server handles the request and sends a response on the current status of traffic in that particular region [8]. Further, to emphasize that IP-based data access are proven to have high throughput and response time, an analysis is carried out. It is mainly to justify that even during peak hours in a highly traffic prone area when the number of the user is relatively more, the performance of the system is still consistent. The performance is tested and analyzed by varying the number of user requests to a single node as shown in Table 1.

Table 1. Performance analysis of instant data request

Number of request	Average response time (s)	Average throughput (RPS)
30	0.79	6
50	1.08	14
70	1.33	21
90	1.98	23
110	2.44	26
130	3.1	27
150	3.37	30
170	3.69	32
190	4.28	32
210	5.63	29
220	5.33	33
250	5.87	33

The average response time in seconds (s) and average throughput in Request Per Second (RPS) is evaluated and analyzed. The response time is defined as the amount of time sensor takes to return the results to the user as given in Eq. 1. Since, each request has its own minimal response time, to evaluate the system performance it is good to analyze on the average response time of all the requests.

$$Response\ Time = \frac{Number\ of\ Concurrent\ User}{Number\ of\ Requests\ per\ second} \tag{1}$$

After knowing the number of concurrent users at any given time and the average response time of their requests, the average throughput is calculated to identify how many numbers of requests per second can be processed by the system using Eq. 2

$$Average\ Throughput = \frac{Number\ of\ Concurrent\ User}{Average\ Response\ Time} \tag{2}$$

Table 2. Automatic pooled sensor reading at a particular time instance

Magnetometer		Accelerometer			PIR	Speed (m/s)	Microphone acoustic (dB)	Distance from pole (cm)		Detected vehicle type	Vehicle dimension (m)		Detection area occupied (sqm)
X	Y	x	y	z				Right side	Left side		Length	Width	
0	18	2	2		353	Moving 5	102	400	20	Bus 1	8	3	7
3	0	2	2		354	Moving 5	82	30	350	Car	5	2.5	5
3	3	2	1		354	Moving 5	70	20	400	Bike 1	1.97	0.07	0.8
18	0	2	2		353	Moving 5	102	20	400	Bus 2	8	3	7
12	11	2	2		354	Moving 5	102	220	220	Bus 3	8	3	7
Total area occupied													25.8

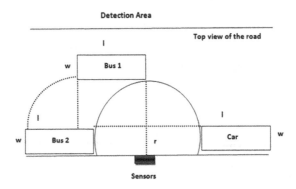

Fig. 5. Deployment of sensors on the two sides of road.

Next, the analysis has been done to prove the efficiency of the system for the asynchronous request type, i.e., periodic data collection (push request). The periodic data collected are used for analyzing and identifying the data pattern so that the major traffic problem can be mitigated in future. The time interval for data collection is set for 15 min. Therefore, it is the responsibility of the coordinator to collect the sensor reading periodically every 15 min and push the real-time data to the user. A simple data analytic algorithm is also executed to perform predictive analysis and report generation for the collected data. The collected data are also populated in the database for further analysis. The user interface is also designed to view the automatically pooled sensor reading as shown in Table 2. The coordinator automatically requests data from each sensor in a round robin scheme using a fixed IP address and displays on the webpage accordingly. From these results, it is evident that the system meets the requirement in term of its functionality.

Algorithm 1. Optimal path deterministic algorithm

Step 1: The sensitivity region detected by the magnetometer sensor is used to identify the length (l) and width (w) of the vehicle.

Step 2: Using l and w, the area of the space occupied in the detection area is estimated.

Step 3: For instance, in the above-discussed scenario for a 5m road, at the maximum, it can be occupied by 4-5 vehicles at a time.

Step 4: Here the total area occupied is calculated using the magnetometer as the sum of the area of sensitivity and area of the vehicle at all possible locations. The summation of each the detected region is defined as the detected area. One instance of the area detection calculation is illustrated with an example as shown in figure 5. Detection area is calculated as the summation of the three rectangles and the area of the sector represented as a right angle triangle. The area of one side of the sensor is given as $rl+(r+l)w+(r+l)w+\frac{r^2}{2}$. Where r is the radius of sensitivity, 'l' and 'w' are length and width of the vehicle respectively. As the sensors the deployed on two sides of the road, the total detection area is computed using equation 3

$$Detection\ Area(DA) = 2 * [rl + 2(r + l)w] + \frac{r^2}{2} \qquad (3)$$

Step 5: Based on the value returned by the detection area and speed of the vehicle the passing vehicle calculated using equation 4

$$Speed = \frac{Distance\ travelled\ in\ meters}{Time\ Taken\ in\ Seconds} \qquad (4)$$

Step 6: The traffic density is calculated using equation 5 where 'S' states the total sensitivity shown by the sensors and 'D' is the total detection area.

$$Traffic\ Density = \frac{(S * D)}{DA} \qquad (5)$$

Further, for the acquired periodic data, an analysis is also extended to suggest the optimal route to reach the destination using the optimal path deterministic algorithm. To select the optimal route, initially, the traffic density along the chosen path has to be determined. The traffic density is estimated using the Algorithm 1.

It is evident from the results obtained for both the request types that the proposed dual protocol stack performs efficiently and scaling up for a traffic monitoring scenario. In addition to providing travel guidance to the user at that particular instant or period, these data analysis can also be used to plan for a long-term solution in that locality.

6 Conclusion

In this work, a dual protocol to allow instant access to wireless sensor networks and internetworking access among heterogeneous sensor nodes is proposed. The major motivations are clearly focused on seamlessly integrating WSN with IP and adopting a standard interface to hide the heterogeneity in the most transparent way. The proposed design is evaluated on a traffic monitoring system, thereby providing an easy access and integration of data. It is evident from the results obtained for request various types that the proposed dual protocol stack performs efficiently for a heterogeneous scenario. The system provides travel guidance support for the user at that particular instant or period using the optimal path deterministic algorithm. In this work, it is also discussed that currently, IPv4 based arrangement to connect the WSN application itself manages to satisfy the vast majority of communication needs. Until there is a need to plug in a number of devices and to provide a large address space for them, there is no requirement for using IPv6. As a part of future work, these data can also push into a data analytics algorithm and can be utilized for analyzing and identifying the data pattern so that the major traffic problems can be mitigated in future.

References

1. Wang, P., Hou, H., He, X., Wang, C., Xu, T., Li, Y.: Survey on application of wireless sensor network in smart grid. Proc. Comput. Sci. **52**, 1212–1217 (2015). The 6th International Conference on Ambient Systems, Networks and Technologies (ANT-2015). The 5th International Conference on Sustainable Energy Information Technology (SEIT-2015)
2. Akyildiz, I.F., Su, W., Sankarasubramaniam, Y., Cayirci, E.: Wireless sensor networks: a survey. Comput. Netw. **38**(4), 393–422 (2002). https://doi.org/10.1016/S1389-1286(01)00302-4
3. Alliance, Z.: ZigBee specification. Technical report, June 2005
4. Banzi, M.: Arduino board and pin configuration (2005). http://arduino.cc
5. BeagleBone: Beaglebone board board/pin configuration (2011). http://beagleboard.org/bone
6. Braden, R.: RFC 1122 Requirements for Internet Hosts - Communication Layers. Internet Engineering Task Force, October 1989, http://tools.ietf.org/html/rfc1122

7. Christin, D., Reinhardt, A., Mogre, P.S., Steinmetz, R.: Wireless sensor networks and the internet of things: selected challenges (2009)
8. Colitti, W., Steenhaut, K., Caro, N.D.: Integrating wireless sensor networks with the web (2011)
9. Dunkels, A.: Full TCP/IP for 8-bit architectures (2003)
10. Dunkels, A., Voigt, T., Bergman, N., Jönsson, M.: The design and implementation of an IP-based sensor network for intrusion monitoring. In: Intrusion Monitoring, Swedish National Computer Networking Workshop (2004)
11. Gadallah, Y., Elalamy, E., elTager, M.: An IP-based arrangement to connect wireless sensor networks to the Internet of Things. In: 2014 IEEE Wireless Communications and Networking Conference, WCNC, pp. 2745–2750, April 2014
12. Kim, Y.J., Hong, S., Ha, O.K.: Design of conformance testing framework for IP-based wireless sensor networks. In: 2015 3rd International Conference on Computer, Information and Application, pp. 3–6, May 2015
13. Kumar, J., Tripathi, S., Tiwari, R.K.: A survey on routing protocols for wireless sensor networks using swarm intelligence. Int. J. Internet Technol. Secur. Syst. 6(2), 79–102 (2016). https://doi.org/10.1504/IJITST.2016.078574
14. Li, S., Xu, L.D., Zhao, S.: The Internet of Things: a survey. Inf. Syst. Front. 17(2), 243–259 (2015). https://doi.org/10.1007/s10796-014-9492-7
15. Montenegro, G., Hui, J., Culler, D., Kushalnagar, N.: Transmission of IPv6 Packets over IEEE 802.15.4 Networks. RFC 4944, September 2007. https://rfc-editor.org/rfc/rfc4944.txt
16. Neves, P., Stachyra, M., Rodrigues, J.: Application of wireless sensor networks to healthcare promotion. J. Commun. Softw. Syst. (JCOMSS) 4(3), 181–190 (2008)
17. RASPBERRY: Raspberry pi board/pin configuration (2012). http://www.raspberrypi.org/
18. Rawat, P., Singh, K.D., Chaouchi, H., Bonnin, J.M.: Wireless sensor networks: a survey on recent developments and potential synergies. J. Supercomput. 68(1), 1–48 (2014). https://doi.org/10.1007/s11227-013-1021-9
19. Rodrigues, J.J.P.C., Neves, P.A.C.S.: A survey on IP-based wireless sensor network solutions. Int. J. Commun. Syst. 23(8), 963–981 (2010). https://doi.org/10.1002/dac.1099
20. Roman, R., Lopez, J.: Integrating wireless sensor networks and the internet: a security analysis. Internet Res. 19(2), 246–259 (2009)
21. Sasirekha, S., Swamynathan, S.: A comparative study and analysis of data aggregation techniques in WSN. Indian J. Sci. Technol. 8(26), 1–10 (2015)
22. da Silva, P.A.C., Coelho, J.J.P., et al.: Internet protocol over wireless sensor networks, from myth to reality (2010)
23. Teubler, T., Hail, M.A., Hellbruck, H.: Transparent integration of non-IP WSN into IP based networks. In: 2012 IEEE 8th International Conference on Distributed Computing in Sensor Systems, pp. 353–358, May 2012
24. Thombre, S., Islam, R.U., Andersson, K., Hossain, M.S.: Performance analysis of an IP based protocol stack for WSNs. In: 2016 IEEE Conference on Computer Communications Workshops, INFOCOM WKSHPS, pp. 360–365, April 2016
25. Thombre, S., Islam, R.U., Andersson, K., Hossain, M.S.: IP based wireless sensor networks: performance analysis using simulations and experiments. JoWUA 7, 53–76 (2016)

Novel Concept of Query-Prototype and Query-Similarity for Semantic Search

Shilpa S. Laddha[1]([⊠]) [iD] and Pradip M. Jawandhiya[2]

[1] Government College of Engineering, Aurangabad, Aurangabad 431001, India
kabrageca@gmail.com
[2] PL Institute of Technology and Management, Buldana 443001, India
pmjawandhiya@rediffmail.com

Abstract. This paper is the extension of the work that explores the overall working of the proposed Smart Semantic information retrieval (IR) system. The aim of the proposed design is to improve the performance of the popular keyword based retrieval system using semantic approach. It seek the novel concept of Query prototype and Query similarity which is a promising paradigm of the proposed design for matching the user entered query with the exact prototype defined in the system and thereby identifying the service and accordingly providing the direct and relevant requested information to the user. The web is crawled and the information is classified into the various classes called services. The fetched results include the direct and relevant URL's of that service and thereby drastically improve the performance over the current information retrieval systems in terms of recall and precision.

Keywords: Information retrieval system · Semantic search engine
Semantic web · Tourism

1 Introduction

In this technical era, life without internet is beyond imagination. According to father of WWW Tim Berners-Lee the Web can be made more smart, intelligent and even spontaneous by rendering direct information to the end user. The observation were carried out for information system with the condition that if search engines index most of the content available on the web, still they have less capability to provide the pages that a user really interested in. There are different ways in which authors and developers, singly or in collaborations can uses some standard techniques so that context-understanding programs can precisely find what users demand [1]. The present keyword based IR does not consider and provide the information that suit users interest appropriately. Keyword based search is time consuming and user need knowledge of keyword search to some degree beforehand as discussed in [12, 13]. Because without stating the appropriate keywords, expected IR is not possible. Semantic search engines have gained popularity in the last decade [10]. To resolve some of these issues different approach of semantic web searching specifically for the tourism domain is proposed in this paper. The huge dynamic information is available on the Web related to tourism domain which is significantly increasing at lightning speed. In this internet world, for

A. V. Deshpande et al. (Eds.): SmartCom 2017, CCIS 876, pp. 338–345, 2018.
https://doi.org/10.1007/978-981-13-1423-0_35

better travel plan most tourists tend to search information available on the Web. Thus to boost India's position as a global tourist destination, work need to be done along these lines. In this way, India could better use its blessed natural factors and in that way increase the number of Indian and foreign visitors [2, 3]. Information needs of tourists are affected by highly dynamic parameters, like tourist spots at specific destination, information about specific tourist place, weather conditions, best time to visit, transportation information by road, by rail, by air, distance between two cities, accommodation facility etc. The design of new smart Semantic information retrieval system for tourism information may produce more effective results. The search reported in this paper explores the important concept of Query-Prototype and Query-similarity of proposed semantic IR system which is a promising paradigm of the proposed design for matching the user entered query with the exact prototype defined in the system and thereby identifying the service and accordingly providing the direct, precise and relevant requested information to the user. The remainder of this paper is structured as follows. Section 2 briefs the problem by means of challenges. Sections 3, 4 and 5 are the core of the paper presenting the system architecture, and Query-prototype and query similarity mapper implementation of Semantic search. Section 6 briefs the service finder and URL generator module of the Semantic Search. Section 7 describes the Metaprocessor module in brief. Section 8 concludes the paper and outlines future work.

2   Challenges

Semantic applications today provide benefits to numerous corporations and other kinds of organizations worldwide which explicitly or implicitly uses the semantics (i.e., the meaning) of a domain terminology in order to improve usability, correctness, and completeness [11]. The objective is to create a semantic web Information retrieval interface which is highly user friendly and provide direct, relevant result satisfying the user demand. Their experience should be as close as the one they presently have with the current web and the search engines they use oftenly. Because keyword based search is suitable specifically to the user who has knowledge of what keywords are used to index the document holding the information and accordingly can easily frame queries. This method is difficult, when the user does not have a clear idea in mind [4, 5], does not have knowledge of entity in the database [6], and the type of semantic concepts are involved in the domain [7, 8].

3   System Architecture

The System architecture is as shown in Fig. 1 and discussed in detail in [9]. Query Controller takes user entered query as input and generate the relevant output along with the time required f or execution and Meta information. The Query Controller gives the input query to the Semantic Query Mapper and Query Similarity Module which first checks the validity of Query. It checks whether the user entered the help query or empty query or non tourism domain query or tourism domain query. If Query is specific to tourism domain then it identify the specific service in the tourism domain using the novel

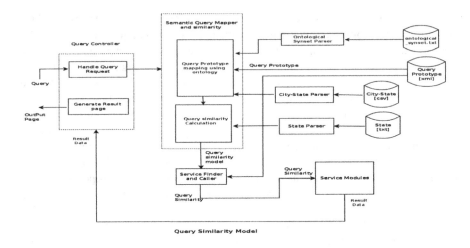

Fig. 1. System architecture

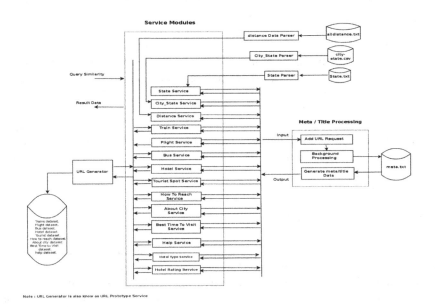

Fig. 2. Service finder and URL generator

concept of Query-Prototype and Query-similarity and accordingly display the result. The perfect match is found with the help of different parsers like state parser, city-state parser and Ontological synonym set parsers uniquely designed and implemented for the proposed system. Using the result of Query Similarity-Mapper, the system identifies the service and based on the service the results are generated. Meta-processor is also designed which will generate the Meta information of the result in the background. This result is again given to the Query Controller for the proper display of results with Meta-information and required time for query execution in the user understandable form. This is in short the overall working of the Tourism Search Engine [9].

4 Query-Prototype

The system is implemented for tourism domain. The Tourism domain is fixed. The second step is to find out the sub domain or Service based on the user query as given below and represented in Fig. 2.

   i. Weather of the particular city
  ii. State of the city
 iii. Flight from city A to city B
  iv. Bus from city A to city B
   v. Train from city A to city B
  vi. Hotels at City A
 vii. Best time to visit specific destination
viii. General information about specific destination
  ix. Distance between City A and City B
   x. About Hotel rating
  xi. About Hotel type
 xii. How to reach the destination
xiii. Cities of the state etc.

These are the sub-domains or services for the tourism information retrieval interface. The information is requested by user in the form of the query. But different user can write the same query in number of ways. Single Query can be written in thousand different ways by different users. Suppose user 'A' has enter the query "train from Pune to Mumbai". User B may enter "train from Pune to Nagpur". User C may enter "train from Pune to Delhi" and so on. Though the information being asked is different in different queries and if there are approximately 10,000 cities in India, the single query may have 10,000 crisscross combinations but the way or format of framing the queries are limited. So to provide the relevant information for the above query first following steps are designed:

a. Identify the sub-domain i.e., Train
b. Train between which two cities.
c. Identify From-City
d. Identify To-City
e. Check From-City and To-City are really the city names
f. Check whether From-City and To-City are placed at proper position.

Same is the case for other sub domains like Flight, Distance, Bus etc. Thus thousand such queries are possible with respect to each sub domain. To solve this issue the novel concept of Query-Prototype is derived. Even though queries can be represented in thousand different ways, the way to write these queries are limited i.e., the query patterns are limited represented as query-prototypes. The query prototypes with respect to all sub domains are stored in respective Service's Query-Prototype.xml. The xml file format is uniquely designed. Spring Injection Technology of the spring framework is used to parse the Query-Prototypes stored in Query-Prototype.xml and therefore the Query-Prototype.xml file format is kept as per the requirement of Spring Injection. The Query-prototypes for flight service are as follows:

(flight)from[from-city]to[to-city]
(flight)for[from-city]to[to-city]
(flight)at[from-city]to[to-city]
(flight)[from-city]to[to-city]
(flight)between[from-city]to[to-city]
(flight)between[from-city]to[to-city]
(flight)for[to-city]
(flight)[from-city]to[to-city]
(flight)[from-city]and[to-city]
(flight)[from-city]
[tocity][from-city][to-city]
(flight)[from-city]and[to-city]
(flight)[from-city] between [to-city]
(flight)[from-city]from[to-city]
(flight)[from-city]for[to-city]
(flight)[from-city]form[to-city].

In the Query-Prototype there are three types of tokens as used for flight service.

(i)   Simple Tokens (word delimits with blank space)
(ii) Template token written in Square brackets[ ]
(iii) Ontological Token written in round brackets ( ).

While defining the query prototype, The novel approach of using square bracket[ ] is used to define the Template tokens which at run time will be replaced by actual value (s) and hence handle n number of user queries using single prototype. So if the users enter the query "train from Pune to Mumbai" or "train from Pune to Delhi". Both the queries are matching with the same Query-prototype i.e., Train from [from-city] to [to-city]. The term embedded in the bracket can be the name of any valid city which the user will enter at run time. So System must scan the query properly and check for the presence of valid city names using City-State Parser. To solve this issue the databases of states and Cities are created in background and stored on the server. If the query contains the state name then system must scan the query properly and check for the presence of valid state names using state Parser. To solve this issue system maintains the database of states and territories which is created in background and stored on the server. For this special state parser, city-state parser and Ontological Synonym set parser are designed which works as follows:

State Parser: The objective of state parser is to validate the state name in the user query. State parser takes the input as total number of states and territories in India. System must know total number of states and Union territories in India. This data is fetched by background processing and stored on server. State parser reads all lines from file which is then used by state service as and when required to check for template token in []and if it is, validate state name entered at required place by the user in the query. Sample queries are as follows:

Indian state
Get states of Bharat
Find states
states
Cities of Maharashtra.

City-State Parser: The objective of the City-State parser is to determine the validity of city name used in the given query. With respect to states the list of cities are maintained and is kept in the file in a special format.

The city-state parser parse this file and as per requirement and provide state list, state-wise city list, state of particular city. Some queries contain city name only like State of Nagpur (Only city name). But when the user will enter such query, it will match with the state service (sub domain) first and then invoke the city parser which check whether Nagpur is valid city name. Also in both cases system need to check if the city/state name is valid whether they are placed at the proper place i.e. proper position in the query.

DistanceParser: When the user will enter the query related to distance between two cities, this parser will return the distance in kilometers. One more service or sub domain is Distance service which provides the distance between two cities. The distance between two cities in kilometers is calculated by processing in the background and stored in the all distance.txt file in the special format. The distance parser is designed for this which works as follows: Distance parser takes the input as state-wise distance between one city to all the cities in India. The format of the file is

#StateName
City1->City2: distance in KM for all the cities.
The unique format of the file is designed. The parser is designed to parse the data from this file. For Ex:
#Haryana
Amritsar->Mumbai: 1843.0
#StateCity1->City2: distance
City1->City2: distance
and so on, which is then used by distance service as and when required to provide the distance between two valid cities.

5 Query Similarity Mapper

The Query Controller checks the query and if it belongs to tourism domain gives it to the Query Similarity Mapper for further processing. The first step here is to divide the input query into different parts based on the token type. Basically there are three types of tokens: template token, Ontological token and simple tokens. As discussed in the Query prototype module, the template tokens are embedded in round brackets( ), Ontological tokens are embedded in square brackets[ ]. This module generates the synonyms of ontological tokens using the Ontological Synonym set parser which in turn is utilized for matching the user query with the different query-prototypes defined in the system for different services related to tourism domain. The basic objective of this module is to determine the service or sub domain based on user query. With respect to tourism domain, this module validate city name or state name or both mentioned in the user query using different parsers. It then checks whether they are placed at proper position in the query or not. Based on the validity & position check, the mapper matches the input query with the defined query-prototypes and the similarity is calculated. The similarity range is between 0 to 1. The value 1 indicated it is matching 100%. If the value is less than 1 then the prototype with which it is matching maximum, that prototype is considered for further processing. Once the prototype is identified, it gives the matching sub domain and accordingly the respective service as mentioned in Fig. 2 will be invoked. The relevant results are then provided to the end user. In some cases, the prototype may be matching100% but some extra keywords are present in the user query. The similarity mapper make use of these extra keywords to further refine the relevant results and provide most relevant results to the user. For Ex. if 10 results are retrieved based on input query, then these retrieved results were further filtered considering the keywords used for rendering more precise result set to the user. The Query similarity is calculated using the following formula.

Q_I = Input Query
Q_p = Query Prototype
$Sim = Sim_1 * Sim_2 [0...1]$
Where,
$Sim_1 = T2/(T1 + T2)$
$Sim_2 = T2/T3$
$T1$ = Number of Keywords found in Q_I.
$T2$ = Number of tokens of Q_p matched with Q_I.
$T3$ = Number of tokens of Q_p.

6 Service Finder and URL Generator

The service finder finds the respective service by considering the maximum value of similarity calculated by similarity mapper by mapping user query with each query prototype defined in the system. URL Generator will generate the actual URL's as relevant result set on the basis of identified service and provided to the user. It also provide time required for execution and meta information as shown in Fig. 2 which are generated by running the separated threads in background and would likely to be discussed in next publication.

7 Metaprocessor

Like popular search engines, the proposed Information retrieval interface also provides the meta information by using page properties of web pages. Basic information, title, status of the web pages are retrieved by spawning the separate thread in background. The actual design and implementation of the Meta processor is in progress and likely to be explained in the next publication.

8 Conclusion

In this paper, the novel and promising concept of query-prototype and query-similarity of proposed semantic IR system is proposed by simply considering the user queries for the tourism domain. These methods are implemented for Tourism Industry with the possibilities to pursue this architecture with multiple domains. The design and implementation of other two novel concepts required for giving precise result using keyword manager and the Meta information of the fetched result using Meta-processor is in progress and is likely to be published in the next extended paper.

References

1. http://searchmicroservices.techtarget.com/definition/Semantic-Web
2. Vinayek, R., Bhatia, A., Malhotra, N.: Competitiveness of Indian tourism in global scenario. Academicia 3(1), 137–138 (2013). ISSN 2249-7
3. Vinayek, R., Bhatia, A., Malhotra, N.: Comparative analysis of India and singapore on the issue of safety and security: exploring new dimensions for Indian Tourism industry. Int. J. Innov. Eng. Manage. 1(1) (2012). ISSN: 2319-3344
4. Hyvönen, E., Styrman, A., Saarela, S.: Ontology – based image retrieval, January 2003
5. Shah, D., Somaiya, J., Nair, S.: Fuzzy semantic search engine. Int. J. Comput. Appl. (0975 – 8887) 107(15) (2014)
6. Dharavath, K., Saritha, S.K.: Semantic web: a topic specific search. In: 2012 Ninth International Conference on Information Technology-New Generations, pp. 145–148 (2012)
7. Josephine, J.A., Sathiyadevi, S.: Ontology based relevance criteria for semantic web search engine. 978-1-4244-8679-3/11/$26.00 ©2011 IEEE
8. Shaikh, F., Siddiqui, U.A., Shahzadi, I., Jami, S.I., Shaikh, Z.A.: SWISE: semantic web based intelligent search engine. 978-1-4244-8003-6/10/$26.00 ©2010 IEEE
9. Laddha, S.S., Jawandhiya, P.M.: Semantic search engine. Indian J. Sci. Technol. 10(23) (2017). https://doi.org/10.17485/ijst/2017/v10i23/115568
10. Humm, B.G., Ossanloo, H.: A semantic search engine for software components. In: Isaías, P. (ed.): Proceedings of the International Conference WWW/Internet 2016, pp. 127–135. IADIS Press, Mannheim, Germany (2016). ISBN 978-989-8533-57-9
11. Bense, H., et al.: Emerging trends in corporate semantic web. Informatik Spektrum 39, 474–480 (2016)
12. Laddha, S.S., Laddha, A.R., Jawandhiya, P.M.: New paradigm to keyword search: a survey. In: 2015 International Conference on Green Computing and Internet of Things (ICGCIoT), Noida, pp. 920–923 (2015). https://doi.org/10.1109/icgciot.2015.7380594
13. Laddha, S.S., Jawandhiya, P.M.: An exploratory study of keyword based search results. Indian J. Sci. Res. 14(2), 39–45 (2017)

A Novel Feature for Recognition of Protein Family Using ANN and Machine Learning

Babasaheb S. Satpute[1(✉)], Raghav Yadav[1], and Satendra Singh[2]

[1] Department of Computer Science and Engineering, SIET, SHUATS,
Allahabad, India
satputebs@gmail.com, raghav.yadav@shiats.edu.in
[2] Department of Computational Biology, JSBB, SHUATS, Allahabad, India
satendra.singh@shiats.edu.in

Abstract. We have designed a protein surface characterizing parameter, Surface Invariant Coordinates (SIC), which is an invariant measure with respect to any orientation of the concerned protein. In our work, the possibility of SIC to be an identifier of protein family as well as its active site has been explored. The SIC can be used as a novel feature to classify proteins using ANN and Machine learning algorithms.

Keywords: Protein classification · SCOP · ANN · PDB
Back propagation algorithm · Surface Invariant Coordinate (SIC)
Machine learning

1 Introduction

Receptors are regulatory macromolecules, mostly proteins, though nucleic acid may also serve as receptors. Receptor may be the G-coupled receptors, receptor with intrinsic ion channel, enzymatic receptors or receptor regulating gene expression; they all are mostly proteinous in nature. So when we think about drug designing the first thing comes to our mind is how to get the information about the functional site of the receptor. Till now no effective method is available for detection of the functional site of receptor. We get the information about functional site from the x-ray crystallography data and another method is the evolutionary Trace method). Our method to find the surface roughness profile of a protein is a direct approach to first identify the family of a protein. We also showed how this crucial step along with the roughness feature value could be utilized in finding active site of a protein. For this purpose we have formulated and implemented the surface parameter Surface Invariant Coordinate (SIC) as a criterion for identifying family of a protein. For the purpose of cross-validation of the usability of SIC we also showed the relationship between the SIC of protein and its sequence similarity.

2 Methodology

We measure the SIC of a protein as the set of roughness values that are extracted from different indexed surface zones covered by different solid angles. We start with the existing knowledge that the functional site of protein (Receptor) is mostly the cavity or

© Springer Nature Singapore Pte Ltd. 2018
A. V. Deshpande et al. (Eds.): SmartCom 2017, CCIS 876, pp. 346–353, 2018.
https://doi.org/10.1007/978-981-13-1423-0_36

clefts that are more irregular as compare to other surface-regions [2]. So Roughness Index at the surface-region of active site of a particular protein can be expected to be of higher value as compare to other indexed surfaces of the same protein. The structures for the proteins considered in our methodology is downloaded from PDB www.rcsb. org [9]. Positional description of atoms of a protein in PDB is given by Cartesian Coordinate System (CCS) which gives no idea about the orientation of a protein. Because of this fact, we convert the CCS of PDB of a protein to an Invariant Coordinate System (ICS) designed by us. This invariant coordinate system is necessary for structural comparison of proteins having different orientations.

2.1 Steps for Formulating Invariant Coordinate System (ICS)

I. Find the CG (Center of Gravity) of the residue. For that we have taken the mean of the coordinates of the atoms. The calculated CG (say point C) was taken as the origin of the ICS.
II. Fix the mutually orthogonal axes X, Y and Z of ICS.

Fixing 'Z' Axis of ICS: We refer the three mutually orthogonal axis of the ICS as, 'X','Y' and 'Z'. From PDB we have taken the coordinate of Cα only as the representative of the concerned residue for reduction of the computational cost. For detection of a point 'Z' on the Z-axis of ICS, we measure the Euclidean distance of the Cα atoms from C. The point placed at the maximum distance from C was taken as the point 'Z' and the line CZ as Z-axis of ICS (Fig. 1).

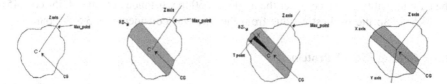

Fig. 1. Select of Z-axis   **Fig. 2.** Plane perpendicular to line CZ   **Fig. 3.** Select X-axis   **Fig. 4.** Select Y-axis

Fixing the 'X' Axis of ICS: After the Z-axis we fixed the X-axis. For that, first we draw a plane that is perpendicular to the line CZ and passing through the point C (Fig. 2). Then the perpendicular distance from the plane to the Cα atom of each residue was calculated. Then the Cα atom within a distance of 2 Å from the drawn plane was considered (shown in Fig. 2 as a lamellar strip). Among these points within the lamellar strip the point that is placed at maximum distance from the CG is taken as the point, T. The foot of the perpendicular drawn from T to the plane, *'normal to CZ and passing through C'* was referred as point, X where line CX was taken as X-axis of the invariant coordinate system for that protein (shown in the Fig. 3).

Fixing the Y-Axis of ICS: Once X and Z-axis of ICS were fixed, the Y-axis was naturally selected as the line passing through the origin and perpendicular to both Z and X-axis of ICS. Graphically it can be represented (shown in Fig. 4).

After formulating the ICS we transformed the coordinates of a protein from CCS of PDB to ICS.

2.2 Detection of Surface Residue from the Invariant Coordinates of the PDB Residue

We have developed a new simple method for the detection of the surface residue of the protein from the invariant co-ordinate system [7].

The following steps were adopted:

Step-1: Draw a line from the origin to the surface of protein making the angles β with X axis, θ with the Z axis and γ with the Y axis

Step-2: Detect the residue-points (say point-set of n number of points $\{P\beta i\}i = 1^n$) that are within 3.5 Å distance from the line CP making a cylinder of radius 3.5 Å

Step-3: Find the distances of all the n-points referred above from C. The maximally distant point among all these points was taken as the surface residue-point

Step-4: The above was repeated by fixing the angle β and by rotating the line CP about X-axis

Step-5: Step-4 and 5 were repeated by changing the angle β from 0 to 180° with discrete increase of its value covering all the residue-points.

In this method we are taking the Cα for our calculation. The bond between two Cα atom is like this Cα–C(=O)–N(–H)–Cα. So there is one C–C bond, two C–N bonds. C–C bond length is 1.54 Å and C–N bond length is 1.47 Å. So the distance between two Cα atom is nearly 4.55 Å provided the atoms remain in a straight line. But this is not the case in reality. If we consider the angle as 450 the distance becomes 4.55 (cos (45)) i.e., 3.5 Å. So the furthest residue from the line was considered as 3.5 Å apart.

2.3 Getting SIC of Protein

I. *Divide the coordinates obtained for the surface residue to eight parts for eight different octants*

Our aim is to find the SIC of different octants. So for the calculation of SIC the coordinates for different octants should be separated. So the way by which the coordinates can be divided into eight octants for different X, Y and Z value is represented in the table below (Table 1).

Table 1. Division of protein surface into octants

1	2	3	4	5	6	7	8
+x	+x	+x	−x	+x	−x	−x	−x
+y	+y	−y	+y	−y	+y	−y	−y
+z	−z	+z	+z	−z	−z	+z	−z

From the above table we can know how the total surface is divided into eight octants. Depending upon the positive and negative axis of the X, Y and Z axis eight octants are possible.

II. *Finding SIC*

We have taken the standard deviation of the distance of residue from center as the criteria for the measurement of SIC.

For 'N' number of solid angle partition, **SIC S** $= \{s_i\}_{i=1}^N$ Where,

$$s_i = \sqrt{\frac{1}{M} \sum_{j=1}^{M} (x_j - \bar{x})^2} \tag{1}$$

and $\{x_i\}$ is the set of distances between origin of ICS and the residues in j-th octant, x bar is the mean of $\{x_j\}$ and M is the total no. of residue.

2.4   Limitation of SIC and Solution by CLUSTALW

If two proteins of similar structures as shown in Fig. 5 have slight protrusion in one (Fig. 5(a)), ICS may give wrong orientation for this protein.

Fig. 5. It shows how ICS developed by us may sometimes fail to give invariant orientation to the proteins shown in (a) and (b).

In order to avoid such situation we used CLUSTALW multiple sequence alignment [3, 4]. We assumed that the residue position in a family of protein would remain constant sequence wise. So first we are calculating the 'Z' and 'X' point. The position in the CLUSTALW where maximum proteins show their 'Z' and 'X' are also considered as the 'Z' and 'X' point for all the proteins.

2.5   Protein Selected for Study

We selected some proteins of functional importance with respect to the drug designing view with the help of SCOP [10] as follows:

1. Superfamily Cysteine proteinases → Family Papain like.
   PDB IDs → 1CPJ, 1DEU, 2ACT, 1PPO, IYAL, 1AIM, 1GEC, 1PE6, 1FHO, 1CQD, 1ATK
2. Superfamily Serpins → Family Serpins
   PDB IDs → 1K90, 1QMN, 1ATT, 1E05, 1QPL, 1JTI, 1SEK, 1F0C, 1IMV, 1BY7
3. Superfamily → beta-Lactamase/D-ala carboxypeptidase → Family beta-Lactamase/D-ala carboxypeptidase
   PDB IDS → 1BZA, 1VMI, 1HTZ, 1HZO, 1G6A, 4BLM, 1BUE, 1BSG, 1MFO

4. Superfamily → Triosephosphate isomerase (TIM) → Family → Triosephosphate isomerase (TIM)
   PDB IDS → 1BTM, 1TIM, 1TRE, 1HTI, 1AMK, 1YDV, 1HG3, 1IIG, 1TCD, 1B9B, 1AW1, 1CI1
5. Superfamily → Porins → Family → Porins PDB IDS → 1GFQ, 1HXX, 2POR, 2PRN, 3PRN, 1OSM, 1E25.

We also utilized protein structure database HOMSTRAD [5] for studying SIC with respect to the structural similarity of proteins. The PDB IDS of these protein-pairs selected was shown in the Table 2 below with percentage sequence similarity.

Table 2. Structural similarity of proteins

Similarity in %	1st protein ID	2nd protein ID
87	1AQZ	1DE3
83	1DVG	1N45
67	1I74	1K20
63	1E6Y	1MRO
57	1AUN	1THW
46	1FVI	1HDM
34	1D9Y	1MRP
27	1PYS_A	1PYS_B

3   Result and Discussion

A. Result of Invariant Coordinate System

The 3D coordinates of the Cα atoms of protein-residues from PDB and that after transformation into ICS was drawn in the MATLAB [8] by the plot3 command and was shown in the Fig. 6(a) and (b) respectively.

It is clearly visible from the two structures that they are same in spite of one having transformation to ICS. It means the relative position of the residues remains constant after the coordinates have changed.

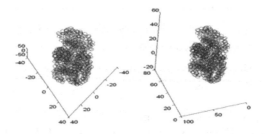

Fig. 6. Structure of 1G08 (hemoglobin) protein. Left one (a) is the initial coordinate in PDB, right one (b) is the transformed invariant coordinate with appropriate rotation to bring it to the same left orientation.

B. We have followed our method for the detection of surface residues detection. The result obtained is shown in the Fig. 7(a) and (b).

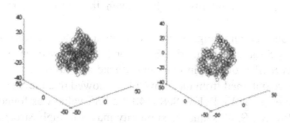

Fig. 7. It shows the protein-coordinates having PDB ID 1AFS. (a) shows all residue-points and (b) Shows only the surface residue-points

From Fig. 7 it is clearly visible that the surface of the protein was not changed after the deletion of the core residues.

C. SIC of Different Protein Families and Their Relationship

In the Fig. 8(a–d) the SIC profile of different proteins families were shown. The graph is drawn between the SIC and Octant Number in ordinate and abscissa respectively. It is clearly visible from the four plots shown in Fig. 8 that,

(1) SIC values within a family of protein had high coorelation.
(2) SIC profiles for different families of protein have significant discriminatory patterns.

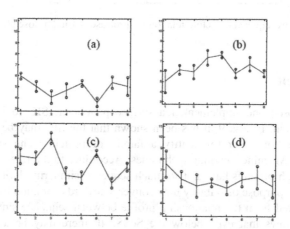

Fig. 8. (a), (b), (c) and (d) Shows the SIC profiles of protein families triose phosphate, serpin, ysteine protease and beta lactamase. The vertical bars show the standard deviations of SIC values.

D. How Far Sequence Similarity is Related with Structural Similarity – A Study by SIC

The relationship between the SIC and the sequence similarity [5, 6] is shown in Fig. 9 (a–d). For the sequence similarity we had taken the help of score obtained from CLUSTALW.

In the four plots (shown in Fig. 9) we have plotted the correlation coefficient of SIC (referred by us as Structural Similarity Score or SSS) and sequence similarity score (referred by us as SeSS) for protein-pairs in ordinate and (a) (b) abscissa respectively. The information we obtained from the above plots showed that the SSS value reached a plateau beyond the SeSS, 40. Below SeSS, 40 the SSS value was found as fluctuating. It means that below SeSS 40, sequence similarity may not imply structure similarity as well between two proteins.

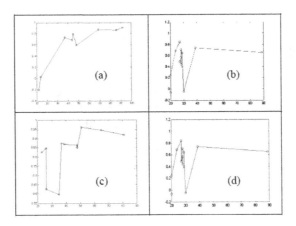

Fig. 9. (a–d) shows sequence-structure relation for protease, serpin, troiose phosphate and porin family respectively.

4 Conclusion

We have proposed and implemented a surface parameter, SIC to help identifying family of a protein. In Fig. 9, it has been shown that the SIC may be used as a very effective feature parameter to identify a family of protein using standard pattern recognition and Machine Learning techniques. According to the rule of design ability of protein, though proteins have not so much sequence similarity during the course of evolution for the purpose of stability they converge towards common fold. This finding was also validated from the relationship profile between sequence similarity and SIC where Fig. 9 shows that even below the SeSS, 40 there may be a high structural similarity. This plot also suggests that to build a good homology model the lower cut-off of sequence similarity (calculated using clustalW) should be greater than 40. Another specialty of SIC is it is independent of any orientation of protein. Thus it can be applied as a robust parameter to correlate it with many surface-active properties, e.g., functional or active site [1].

References

1. Pettit, F.K., Bowie, J.U.: Protein surface roughness and small molecular binding site. J. Mol. Biol. **285**, 1377–1382 (1999)
2. Geometry krishna's series: KRISHNA prakashan Media (P) ltd. Meerut
3. Higgins, D., Thompson, J., Gibson, T., Thompson, J.D., Higgins, D.G., Gibson, T.J.: CLUSTAL W: improving the sensitivity of progressive multiple sequence alignment through sequence weighting, position-specific gap penalties and weight matrix choice. Nucleic Acids Res. **22**, 4673–4680 (1994)
4. ClustalW: WWW Service at the European Bioinformatics Institute, Rodrigo Lopez, Services Program. http://www.ebi.ac.uk/clustalw
5. Crooks, G.E., Wolfe, J., Brenner, S.E.: Measurements of protein sequence-structure correlations. Proteins. **57**(4), 804–810 (2004)
6. Skolnick, J., Kolinski, A., Brooks 3rd, C.L., Godzik, A., Rey, A.: A method for predicting protein structure from sequence. Curr. Biol. **3**(7), 414–423 (1993)
7. Connolly, M.L.: Measurement of protein surface shape by solid angles. J. Mol. Graph. **4**, 3–6 (1986)
8. http://www.mathworks.com
9. http://www.rcsb.org/pdb/
10. http://scop.mrc-lmb.cam.ac.uk/scop/

Recognition of Protein Family Using a Novel Classification System

Babasaheb S. Satpute[✉] and Raghav Yadav

Department of Computer Science and Engineering, SIET, SHUATS,
Allahabad 211007, India
satputebs@gmail.com, raghav.yadav@shiats.edu.in

Abstract. Our aim is to identify the family of a protein from PDB co-ordinates [3] using Artificial Neural Network (ANN) classifier. For our purpose we made the use of SCOP [4] classification of protein and PDB co-ordinates of protein. SCOP classifies proteins on the basis of the surface structure of the protein. We used the parameter Surface Invariant Coordinates (SIC) obtained from the surface roughness of the protein surface [1], for the protein family recognition purpose. SIC is the standard deviation of the distances of residues of protein from the origin in an invariant coordinate system.

In our work we took into consideration the proteins from SCOP whose family is known. We took such 1208 proteins which belong to some or the other family but the known one. We took PDB co-ordinates of those proteins from PDB website. We converted those PDB co-ordinates into the SIC values and made the database of the SIC values of the proteins family wise. In all for those 1208 proteins we had 100 families. For our work we took into consideration only 32 families having 520 proteins belonging to these families. We divided the database into training and testing dataset in the proportion of approximately 70:30 i.e. if the particular family has 100 proteins then we took 70 for training purpose and 30 as testing purpose. Likewise we made the training set of 368 proteins and the testing set of 152 proteins. Then we developed the ANN classifier like feedforward backpropagation networks classifier [6–11].

Keywords: Protein classification · SCOP · ANN · PDB
Backpropagation algorithm · Surface Invariant Coordinate (SIC)

1 Introduction

It has been found that surface of the protein plays important role in determining the family of the protein [1]. We used the parameter Surface Invariant Coordinates (SIC) for identification of the family of the protein. Under this we found out the SIC values of the proteins, the SIC values can be found out from PDB co-ordinates, made the database of the SIC values of the proteins and divide the database into training dataset and testing dataset. Then we develop the ANN Classifier and trained it with the training dataset and tested it with the testing dataset.

Objective

Our objective is to develop the Artificial Neural Network Classifier for identification of the protein family from PDB co-ordinates.

© Springer Nature Singapore Pte Ltd. 2018
A. V. Deshpande et al. (Eds.): SmartCom 2017, CCIS 876, pp. 354–361, 2018.
https://doi.org/10.1007/978-981-13-1423-0_37

Why Neural Networks?

Since this is the pattern Recognition Problem, Neural can be used for this type of problems for getting better results as Artificial Neural Networks are the effective tools for pattern recognition problems.

Why to study protein surface?

Surface is the functionally most important part of the protein. For the purpose of drug designing when we think about how the drug acts, the thing comes to our mind is the cleft or cavity on the surface of protein. So in drug designing we are not dealing with the whole structure of protein. We are mostly dealing with the surface region of the protein. The functional regions of the protein are almost the cavity or the cleft on the surface of the protein. So with respect to the drug designing point of view, the whole structure of protein is not important only the cleft or the cavities on surface are needed. It may be pharmacophore drug designing or structure based drug designing the area of action of the drug is the residues and its moiety on the surface of protein [2]. Though the inner residue of protein have major role for the formation of the backbone or the protein domain, but functional aspect they have very less importance. For that we are studying the surface property.

1.1 Artificial Neural Networks (ANN)

Artificial neural networks are the networks of the computing elements called neurons. The functioning of ANN is similar to the human nervous system. The ANN learns by calculating the difference between the output it got and the expected output. The error is sent back into the network and weights on the connection are modified for improving results (Fig. 1).

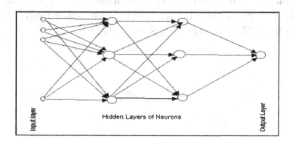

Fig. 1. Architecture of feed-forward network

Feed-Forward Back Propagation Algorithm [5]

There are three layers of neurons in the Feed-forward Back Propagation network (BPN) namely an input layer, hidden layers and output layer.

During training of the BPN, after the inputs are provided to the input layer, the network computes the difference between the output at the output layer and the actual expected output. The difference between the two is called as error. That error is propagated back and the weights of the network are adjusted in order to get the expected output.

2 Methodology

We measure the SIC of a protein as the set of roughness values that are extracted from different indexed surface zones covered by different solid angles. We start with the existing knowledge that the functional site of protein (Receptor) is mostly the cavity or clefts that are more irregular as compare to other surface-regions [2]. So Roughness Index at the surface-region of active site of a particular protein can be expected to be of higher value as compare to other indexed surfaces of the same protein. The structures for the proteins considered in our methodology is downloaded from PDB www.rcsb.org [3]. Positional description of atoms of a protein in PDB is given by Cartesian Coordinate System (CCS) which gives no idea about the orientation of a protein. Because of this fact, we convert the CCS of PDB of a protein to an Invariant Coordinate System (ICS) designed by us. This invariant coordinate system is necessary for structural comparison of proteins having different orientations.

2.1 Steps for Formulating Invariant Coordinate System (ICS) [2]

I. Find the CG (Center of Gravity) of the residue. For that we have taken the mean of the coordinates of the atoms. The calculated CG (say point C) was taken as the origin of the ICS.

II. Fix the mutually orthogonal axes X, Y and Z of ICS.

Fixing 'Z' Axis of ICS: We refer the three mutually orthogonal axis of the ICS as, 'X', 'Y' and 'Z'. From PDB we have taken the coordinate of Cα only as the representative of the concerned residue for reduction of the computational cost. For detection of a point 'Z' on the Z-axis of ICS, we measure the Euclidean distance of the Cα atoms from C. The point placed at the maximum distance from C was taken as the point 'Z' and the line CZ as Z-axis of ICS (Fig. 2).

  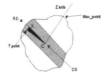

Fig. 2. Select of Z-axis   **Fig. 3.** Plane perpendicular to line CZ   **Fig. 4.** Select X-axis   **Fig. 5.** Select Y-axis

Fixing the 'X' Axis of ICS: After the Z-axis we fixed the X-axis. For that, first we draw a plane that is perpendicular to the line CZ and passing through the point C (Fig. 3). Then the perpendicular distance from the plane to the Cα atom of each residue was calculated. Then the Cα atom within a distance of 2 Å from the drawn plane was considered (shown in Fig. 3 as a lamellar strip). Among these points within the lamellar strip the point that is placed at maximum distance from the CG is taken as the point, T. The foot of the perpendicular drawn from T to the plane, *'normal to CZ and passing through C'* was referred as point, X where line CX was taken as X-axis of the invariant coordinate system for that protein (shown in the Fig. 4).

Fixing the Y-axis of ICS: Once X and Z-axis of ICS were fixed, the Y-axis was naturally selected as the line passing through the origin and perpendicular to both Z and X-axis of ICS. Graphically it can be represented (shown in Fig. 5).

After formulating the ICS we transformed the coordinates of a protein from CCS of PDB to ICS.

2.2 Detection of Surface Residue from the Invariant Coordinates of the PDB Residue

We have developed a new simple method for the detection of the surface residue of the protein from the invariant co-ordinate system [2].

The following steps were adopted:

Step-1: Draw a line from the origin to the surface of protein making the angles β with X axis, θ with the Z axis and γ with the Y axis

Step-2: Detect the residue-points (say point-set of n number of points $\{P\beta i\}i = 1^n$) that are within 3.5 Å distance from the line CP making a cylinder of radius 3.5 Å

Step-3: Find the distances of all the n-points referred above from C. The maximally distant point among all these points was taken as the surface residue-point

Step-4: The above was repeated by fixing the angle β and by rotating the line CP about X-axis

Step-5: Step-4 and 5 were repeated by changing the angle β from 0 to 180° with discrete increase of its value covering all the residue-points.

In this method we are taking the Cα for our calculation. The bond between two Cα atom is like this Cα–C (= O)–N(–H)–Cα. So there is one C–C bond, two C–N bonds. C–C bond length is 1.54 Å and C–N bond length is 1.47 Å. So the distance between two Cα atom is nearly 4.55 Å provided the atoms remain in a straight line. But this is not the case in reality. If we consider the angle as 450 the distance becomes 4.55 (cos (45)) i.e., 3.5 Å. So the furthest residue from the line was considered as 3.5 Å apart.

2.3 Getting SIC of Protein

I. *Divide the coordinates obtained for the surface residue to eight parts for eight different octants*

Our aim is to find the SIC of different octants. So for the calculation of SIC the coordinates for different octants should be separated. So the way by which the coordinates can be divided into eight octants for different X, Y and Z value is represented in the table below (Table 1).

Table 1. Division of protein surface into Octants

1	2	3	4	5	6	7	8
+x	+x	+x	−x	+x	−x	−x	−x
+y	+y	−y	+y	−y	+y	−y	−y
+z	−z	+z	+z	−z	−z	+z	−z

From the above table we can know how the total surface is divided into eight octants. Depending upon the positive and negative axis of the X, Y and Z axis eight octants are possible.

II. *Finding SIC*

We have taken the standard deviation of the distance of residue from center as the criteria for the measurement of SIC.

For 'N' number of solid angle partition, **SIC S** $= \{s_i\}_{i=1}^N$

Where,

$$s_i = \sqrt{\frac{1}{M} \sum_{j=1}^{M} (x_j - \bar{x})^2} \tag{1}$$

and $\{x_j\}$ is the set of distances between origin of ICS and the residues in j-th octant, x bar is the mean of $\{x_j\}$ and M is the total no. of residue.

3   Dataset/Materials

No. of protein Families Taken into consideration.

We have taken into consideration 32 protein families [4].
The names few of these families are as follows (Table 2).

Table 2. Sample Protein families

Family name	No. of protein in the family	Class name
A-GL-GL-G	16	00000
A-LAH-CJD-CJD	5	00001
A-GL-GL-TH	5	00010
A-FHC-FHC-LCC	4	00011
A-CC-CC-MCC	20	00100
A-GL-GL-PLPP	7	00101
A-AT-SHG-CCD	4	00110

The Sample SIC Training Data
Following is the sample training data of few proteins.

7.0854	9.2391	8.7488	10.6253	9.9041	7.6820	9.1408	7.5573
8.3177	9.0952	9.3581	10.3914	9.3855	8.3609	9.1254	7.8014
10.1822	9.7374	7.9482	9.2598	9.2741	8.0042	8.2156	6.5556
7.4712	6.7292	7.0651	7.6888	6.6028	7.9811	5.4901	6.6838
7.3966	8.6027	6.8330	7.3523	6.6331	8.1259	6.2400	6.6128

The Sample SIC Test Data

Following is the test data for class 00000

Class	00000							
3.7200	4.6256	6.6461	5.3863	6.4207	6.5149	5.2082	6.0366
6.7408	8.2145	7.0913	5.8025	7.4385	8.6800	6.0556	6.7810
6.6639	4.8488	6.7637	6.2136	8.2353	5.1398	3.6423	6.7937
6.6925	9.0295	9.6645	10.0935	8.9482	8.1583	9.2287	7.9731

4 Algorithm

Repeat step 1 to 2

1. Get the PDB co-ordinate of the protein from the site www.rcsb.org/.
2. Convert the PDB co-ordinate into SIC values using SIC conversion program.
3. Prepare the database of the protein SIC values.
4. Assign each protein family a binary class name for example if you have 32 classes then the class names would be like 00000,00001,00010...11111.
5. Assign each protein to a particular class value i.e. 00000, 00001...11111.
6. Thus determine the no. of neurons in the output layer and in the input layer for example in the above case there will be 8 input and 5 output layer neurons.
7. Now develop the neural network classifier program.
8. Divide the SIC database into training dataset and test dataset in the ratio of 70:30 i.e. 70% of the protein belonging to one particular family are taken as training and 30% as testing.
9. Train the neural network classifier with the training dataset.
10. Simulate the network.
11. Test the network performance with the test dataset.
12. Calculate the efficiency of the classifier with the following formula
    Efficiency = (no. of correct prediction/total no. of test values) * 100%.
13. End.

The Feed-Forward Backpropagation Network Classifier [7–12]

The classifier has 8 input layer neurons, 15 hidden layer neurons and 5 output layer neurons. The classifier or neural network is trained with the 168 protein SIC values dataset. The trained net is then tested with the test dataset.

The reason for having 8 input layer neurons is that, there are 8 SIC values for each protein. And reason for having 5 output layer neurons is that, we have 32 classes and we have assigned binary values to each class and $2 \wedge 5 = 32$.

5 Results

I. **Following are predicted classes for first some test proteins**

Columns 1 through 8

0.1277	0.2024	0.4055	0.0022	0.0002	0.9263	0.0669	0.0821
0.9800	0.3048	0.7191	0.3126	0.2463	0.9627	0.2158	0.3403
0.4542	0.3927	0.4525	0.2140	0.3161	0.0488	0.1265	0.1966
0.7340	0.1255	0.8296	0.0028	0.0009	0.9527	0.1402	0.1890
0.3492	0.2998	0.1442	0.3111	0.2468	0.0146	0.1490	0.2315

Columns 9 through 16

0.0559	0.3455	0.0000	0.0114	0.3483	0.2869	1.0000	1.0000
0.0472	0.2748	1.0000	0.0083	0.3479	0.8814	0.0003	1.0000
0.9524	0.5978	1.0000	0.0000	0.0002	0.2402	0.9997	1.0000
0.0600	0.3161	0.0000	0.9886	0.6517	0.1678	0.0003	0.0000
0.9487	0.3159	1.0000	0.9918	0.6521	0.0612	0.0003	0.0000

After rounding off the above values we get the exact class.

II. **Effieciency**

The efficiency is calculated as follows

Efficiency = (no. of correct family prediction of the test data/total no. of proteins in the test dataset).

We have total no. of proteins in the test dataset are 152.

And correct family prediction by ANN classifier = 66.

Therefore

$$\text{Efficiency} = (92/152) * 100$$
$$= 60.52\%$$

III. **Training Networks**

See Fig. 6.

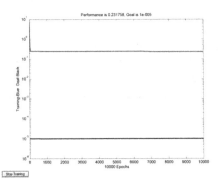

Fig. 6. Training with feed-forward backpropagation network. The black line in the graph shows the goal to achieve with training. And the blue line shows the training achieved after 10000 epochs. (Color figure online)

6 Conclusion

We developed Artificial Neural Network classifier for identification of family of the protein from PDB co-ordinates which gave the efficiency of over 60%. We used Surface Invariant Coordinates to help identifying family of a protein. SIC may be used as a very effective feature parameter to identify a family of protein using standard pattern recognition techniques.

References

1. Pettit, F.K., Bowie, J.U.: Protein surface roughness and small molecular binding site. J. Mol. Biol. **285**, 1377–1382 (1999)
2. Connolly, M.L.: Measurement of protein surface shape by solid angles. J. Mol. Graph. **4**, 3–6 (1986)
3. http://www.rcsb.org/pdb/
4. http://scop.mrc-lmb.cam.ac.uk/scop/
5. Zurada, J.M.: Introduction to Artificial Neural Systems. Jaico Publishing House, Mumbai (1994)
6. Bishop, C.M.: Neural Networks for Pattern Recognition. Oxford University Press, Oxford (1995)
7. Wang, D., Huang, G.B.: Protein sequence classification using extreme learning machine. In: Proceedings of International Joint Conference on Neural Networks (IJCNN 2005), Montreal, Canada (2005)
8. Duda, R.O., Hart, P.E., Stork, D.G.: Pattern Classification, 2nd edn. Wiley Interscience Publication, Hoboken (2001)
9. Rao, P.V.N., Devi, T.U., Sridhar, G.R., Rao, A.A.: A probabilistic neural network approach for protein superfamilt classification. J. Theor. Appl. Inf. Technol. **6**, 101–105 (2005)
10. Wu, C., Shivakumar, S., Lin, H.-P., Veldurti, S., Bhatikar, Y.: Neural networks for molecular sequence classification. Math. Comput. Simul. **40**(1–2), 23–33 (1995)
11. Wu, C., Berry, M., Shivakumar, S., McLarty, J.: Neural networks for full-scale protein sequence classification: sequence encoding with singular value decomposition. Mach. Learn. **21**(1–2), 177–193 (1995)

Author Index

Printed in the United States
By Bookmasters